W9-DIY-610

GEOFFREY CHAUCER

MEDIEVAL AUTHORS

General Editors

Roger Fowler
School of English and American Studies,
University of East Anglia

John Norton-Smith
Reader in English,
University of Reading

Already published

Geoffrey Chaucer

JOHN NORTON-SMITH

Reader in English
University of Reading

ROUTLEDGE & KEGAN PAUL

LONDON AND BOSTON

First published in 1974
by Routledge & Kegan Paul Ltd
Broadway House, 68–74 Carter Lane,
London EC4V 5EL and
9 Park Street,
Boston, Mass. 02108, USA
Printed in Great Britain by
Western Printing Services Ltd, Bristol
ISBN 0 7100 7801 3

74- 75857

FOR MARIANNE CECIL

CONTENTS

GENERAL PREFACE

The Medieval Authors Series is intended (without dilution of scholarly high standards) to fulfil two aims: first, to produce a detailed critical evaluation of the literary achievements of the most important English and Scots authors of the later Middle Ages; second, to contribute towards a generous and systematic account of the literature of the 'high' and 'late' Middle Ages—supplementing the existing and (in some cases) continuing work of the Early English Text Society, the Scottish Text Society, the Clarendon Medieval and Tudor Series, Nelson's Medieval and Renaissance Library, and the Oxford History of English Literature.

The concentration on 'authors' is a deliberate attempt to remind a rapidly growing criticism of the worth of an humane medievalism—of the continuity and originality of an individual, personal contribution to our literature, of the extent to which the individuality of renaissance authors is anticipated and largely made possible by that of Middle English and Middle Scots writers. Most of the volumes in the series will appear over the next decade. The order of appearance does not represent an historical chronology or grouping.

University of East Anglia   ROGER FOWLER
University of Reading   JOHN NORTON-SMITH

AUTHOR'S NOTE

In this book I have attempted to discuss those aspects of Chaucer's art which are concerned with the problem of specific form—what is peculiarly poematic in '*la création chez Chaucer*'. These aspects have been discussed theoretically in R. S. Crane's *The Languages of Criticism and the Structure of Poetry*, Toronto (1953), and extended analytically to medieval Latin literature by E. Auerbach in *Literary Language and Its Public*, London (1965). I have concentrated on Chaucer's major poems and some of his so-called minor poems. To eschew an encyclopedic study is not so much to confess failure as to acknowledge the persisting magnitude of the artist—not to mention the luxuriant growth of an attendant critical industry within the last twenty years. I commend the reader in need of comprehensive guidance to a number of ciceroni ancient and modern. They will be found in the Select Bibliography hereto appended.

Chapters which were originally papers for learned societies I have much revised, but chapter 3 on the *House of Fame*, delivered long ago for Freddy Bateson's 'Hypercriticals' at Magdalen College, Oxford, in Michaelmas 1958, remains almost unchanged. No recent criticism of this poem has persuaded me to change my views or alter the nature of my argument. It will be immediately obvious that I have avoided a discussion of the *Parliament of Fowls*. I have been prevented by Professor J. A. W. Bennett's penetrating account (Oxford, 1957) and Professor Clemen's convenient summary in *Chaucer's Early Poetry*, London (1963). Of course, there is more to say—especially about the vital influence of Boccaccio's early Dantean imitation, *L'Amorosa Visione*, on the structural *idée* of Chaucer's poem and how the pattern of the *Visione* explains the close thematic connection between the *Parliament* and the *House of Fame*. But this topic will have to await later treatment.

I am grateful to the Master and Fellows of Pembroke College, Oxford, for providing an opportunity for writing much of this book during 1971–2. I thank my wife for her assistance in compiling the index; Mrs J. Chennells for preparing the final typescript; Phillipa Hardman and Joan Fowler for assisting in the proofreading of it. Acknowledgment is due to Roger Fowler and Routledge & Kegan Paul for permission to include material in chapter 7 which I first published in *Essays in Style and Language* (1966). Professor Arthur Adkins supplied many useful criticisms on the Appendix. I owe special thanks to my old friends Jack Bennett and Colin Hardie for various suggestions.

The Faculty of Letters,
University of Reading

ABBREVIATIONS

Archiv   *Archiv für das Studium der neueren Sprachen*

BM   British Museum

DNB   *Dictionary of National Biography*

EETS   Early English Text Society

Index   *Index of Middle English Verse*, ed. Carleton Brown
            and Rossell H. Robbins, New York (1943)

JEGP   *Journal of English and Germanic Philology*

ME   Middle English

MED   *Middle English Dictionary*, ed. H. Kurath and S. M. Kuhn,
            Ann Arbor, Mich. (1952—)

MLN   *Modern Language Notes*

MP   *Modern Philology*

N & Q   *Notes and Queries*

OE   Old English

OED   *Oxford English Dictionary*

OF   Old French

PL   *Patrologia Latina*

PMLA   *Publications of the Modern Language Association of America*

Robinson   *The Works of Geoffrey Chaucer*, ed. F. N. Robinson, 2nd
            ed., London (1957)

SATF   Société des Anciens Textes Français

CHAPTER ONE

The Book of the Duchess

At the close of the first of the *Duino Elegies* Rilke casts in the form of a question a symbolism which unites the themes of love, death and poetry. In meditating upon some special quality perhaps bestowed on us through the realization of our transitoriness, the poet inquires:[1]

> *Ist die Sage umsonst, dass einst in der Klage um Linos/wagende erste Musik dürre Erstarrung durchdrang,/dass erst im erschrockenen Raum, dem ein beinah göttlicher Jüngling/plötzlich für immer enttrat, das Leere in jene/Schwingung geriet, die uns jetzt hinreisst und trösset und hilft.*

Is the story in vain, how once in the mourning for Linos, venturing earliest music pierced barren numbness, and how, in the horrified space an almost deified youth suddenly quitted for ever, emptiness first felt the vibration that now charms us and comforts and helps?

Recent criticism of Chaucer's perhaps earliest datable poem seems to answer this question almost as if by magic. At the touch of a Robertsonian wand (manufactured in Princeton, blessed by a long-deceased bishop) the 'dead with their nightingales and psalms' vanish—and with a reassurance as wise as a dove and innocent as a serpent a Christian apotheosis appears (in one guise or another). Blanche of Lancaster (once tenderly described by Froissart as '*jone et ioelie . . . Gaie . . . frische, esbatans, Douce simple, d'umble samblance*') sheds her celebrated mortality and appears to us in her true and final nature: the Bride of Christ, the Church, the Blessed Virgin—even Christ himself. The *démodé* French concealed references to the Honour of Richmond give way to the 'white walles' of the New Jerusalem. From this modern Hill of Contemplation how far we seem from the mental and physical torment of a protracted eight years' insomnia. If only we had known that 'eight years' was really a covert reference to the mystical number of completed

---

[1] Lines 91ff. The translation is that of J. B. Leishman (New York, 1939).

spiritual perfection we might have guessed that whatever anxiety
the poet Chaucer was passing through found rapid resolution in an
allegory resembling a Beatific Vision. As a reigning Merton Professor
once exclaimed (in another context): 'This is mighty reassuring.'

In a more recent attempt to return to an older, less sacramental account
of the poem, Dr Wimsatt,[2] lost in tracing and retracing the French
poems from which Chaucer extensively borrowed, never reached any
conclusions about the meaning and form of Chaucer's dream. The
nearly autonomous comparative method created by Kittredge proves
as unenlightening as the Exegete's Benediction. At the end of Dr
Wimsatt's vision from Chapel Hill occurs a daunting enumeration of
every conceivable Old French source for nearly three-quarters of
Chaucer's composition. One is left with the impression that Chaucer's
early art amounts to either the failed Gothic experiment beloved of
Professor Muscatine or the 'veritable mosaic of poetic quotation' dear
to another, alien, generation. No doubt the Wimsattian lists would
have interested poets brought up on Geoffrey of Vinsauf's *Poetria Nova*,
just as Virgil's borrowings from Homeric poems fascinated Macrobius.
Certainly, Froissart (who would have recognized his own words in the
opening lines of the *Book of the Duchess*) would not have been dismayed.
For Froissart the historian was to write in the preface to his own
Chronicles: 'It is said that all buildings are wrought of diverse stones.'
If we retain this architectural image in the spirit of the *Poetria Nova* (in
lines which Chaucer translated word for word in his *Troilus*):[3]

> *Si quis habet fundare domum, non currit ad actum*
> *Impetuosa manus; intrinseca linea cordis*
> *Praemetitur opus, seriemque sub ordine certo*
> *Interior praescribit homo, totamque figurat*
> *Ante manus cordis quam corporis; et status ejus*
> *Est prius archetypus quam sensilis . . .*

> The hand that seeks a proper house to raise
> Turns to the task with care; the measured line
> Of th'inmost heart lays out the work to do,
> The order is prescribed by the inner man,
> The mind sees all before one stone is laid,
> Prepares an archetype . . .

---

[2] *Chaucer and the French Love Poets*, Durham, North Carolina (1968).
[3] Cf. J. A. W. Bennett, *The Parlement of Foules*, p. 5. And cf. Vincent of Beauvais,
Speculum Doctrinale IV.93, 'De Maturitate', where this passage is quoted verbatim.

—if we keep in mind Geoffrey's analogy, then a genuine concern of literary criticism ought to lie in some statement about the *archetypus* —the unifying nature of the creative intuition which both generated and completed a specific verbal work of art.

Of the social and historical generation of the poetic impulse, little concrete remains to us at this remove. The arid fragments collected in the *Chaucer Life-Records* do not advance us further than Holzknecht's puzzled musings in the 1920s. The important rubric (which confirms Chaucer's testimony to authorship) in the Bodley MS. Fairfax 16 cannot be wholly relied on. It is not in Stow's hand (*pace* Baugh and Robinson); this anonymous sixteenth-century note reflects John Shirley's wording and Shirley's peculiar spelling of Chaucer's surname. It may well have been copied from the manuscript copy (now lost) which Thynne had access to. If so, we should make certain reservations —for Shirley's testimony no matter how reliable as regards Lydgate rests largely on hearsay as far as Chaucer is concerned. 'Made by Geffrey Chawcyer at ye request of ye duke of Lancastar: pitiously Complaynynge the deathe of ye sayd dutchesse/blanche/' in addition to correctly asserting authorship, makes two further statements, one supposititious, the other demonstrably wrong. 'At ye request of ye duke of Lancastar' has led nearly all critics (including Clemen[4] and Lawlor[5]) to image the relationship as that of client and patron—and where the poet provides some kind of ostensible 'consolation' for his putative patron. Now, if we compare the acknowledged roles of patron and poet in the instances of Gower, Hoccleve or Lydgate, we find a situation and relationship not very different from that depicted by Shakespeare in his *Timon of Athens*—or Maria Edgeworth's great novel for that matter. As for Chaucer, overt reference to living persons reveals a predilection for equal relations intimately communicated between friends who are equal in regard. With the possible exception of the envoi to the so-called *Complaint of Venus*, addresses to social 'superiors' are strictly limited to business matters. Chaucer's habitual manner (as author or poet-figure) maintains a bland indifference to, and independence from, the usage of clientship. If such relationships existed he neither advertised them nor sought profit from them. I venture that if we knew more about Chaucer's actual relationship with John of Gaunt we would be no nearer an understanding of the genesis of the

[4] *Chaucer's Early Poetry*, pp. 23ff.
[5] 'The Pattern of Consolation in the *Book of the Duchess*', *Speculum* 31 (1956), pp. 635ff.

poem—or the dream-poet's actual attitude to what may lie behind the image of a fictionalized duke of Lancaster. The second, connected, assumption, that of the presence of a 'pattern of consolation' (in Professor Lawlor's phrase), is equally remarkable. Poetic consolations are so few in the Middle Ages that to hint at a traditional treatment amounts to literary deception (it leaves Professor Curtius almost tongue-tied, if that can be imagined). Prose *consolationes*, usually of the epistolary kind, are more numerous—and nearly all seem to glance at Pliny and Seneca for their inspiration. What emerges from a reading of these no doubt well-intentioned exhortations is that every attempt (couched in whatever admixtures of art and tact) to approach nearer and ever nearer to the moment of sympathetic and articulate sharing in the personal grief opens instead a vast and uncrossable distance between the writer and the recipient. No amount of apology, modesty or intelligent indirection can conceal the embarrassing failure of the impulse—or the isolation of all concerned—recipient, writer and reader. An objective, presumptuous gulf yawns which the gestures of art are powerless to enchant—and often the gestures of love or friendship in real life only succeed if words are omitted. Quintilian wisely keeps silent on this area of human experience as a possible subject for rhetorical stratagems. If Death may be imagined as the Great Leveller, Grief soon emerges as the unapproachable despot of that revolution. In spite of the logic of Professor Lawlor, the notion of a poet-dreamer coming at last to understand the meaning of death (rather than the grieving knight) remains at best an engaging sophistry. The words and events of the poem contradict the critic at every turn of the argument. The poetic relevance of the moral concerns of the two *Jugement* poems of Guillaume de Machaut evaporates—once you have read Machaut. Further, there is no 'pattern' much less 'consolation' (in the accepted sense of that word) in the poem at all. To take this cleansing a stage further, much criticism of the poem may be said to fail because it habitually attaches to our literary experience descriptive terminology acquired elsewhere—and often quite legitimately. Thus, 'elegy', 'consolation', 'panegyric', 'Old French love-vision', 'dream-allegory', 'Christian allegory'—all have played their part in rendering Chaucer's achievement more misguidedly familiar or 'conventional' than the poem may have appeared to an audience available at the end of the 1360s or beginning of the 1370s. Dr Wimsatt is vaguely aware of this as he remorselessly ploughs on through the works of Chaucer's French contemporaries in search of some points of more than local similarity. His chief impression of French verse at the time is undeniable: that Froissart, Machaut and Granson achieved a certain concentration of charm and poetic elaboration through the expanding of certain episodes present in Guillaume de Lorris's and Jean de Meun's *Roman de la Rose*; but that these later poets achieved their effect at the expense of the economy and emphasis of narrative continuity. The fourteenth-century French longer poem thus becomes more diffuse, more episodic and more various in its allegorical or figurative mode of reference: realism, imaginative passages, set *topoi* and songs all interrupt narrative and description which have 'allegorical' and sometimes 'philosophical' implications. Dr Wimsatt, unlike Professor Muscatine, is not certain of the relevance of all this heterogeneity to Chaucer. The simple answer is, that it hasn't any. Chaucerian eclecticism has another object in view.

We need not turn to *Li Regret de Guillaume* (the only French 'elegy' cast in a dream formulation) to account for Chaucer's decision to adapt a dream-vision form for the accommodation of the subject of the death of Blanche of Lancaster. Jean de la Mote's poem bears no relation to Chaucer's poem—nor to his more fastidious and more ranging meditation. We need search no further than Warton's early account of the seminal influence of the *Somnium Scipionis* upon medieval poets generally. Macrobius, expatiating on the close analogy of dream psychology (and terminology) to the modes of reference in literature, makes the point that a verbal work of art, like an actual dream, may employ several levels of reference simultaneously. One of the most important ambiguities so shared is that a poem and a dream may be at one and the same time 'private' and 'public'. That is, the communication may possess a personal area of reference and a more public and generalized rhetorical aim. At a single stroke, in his selecting and reworking the dream-form, Chaucer, linking subjectivity and objectivity, creates a convenient area of co-consciousness whereby the audience expects the dream to include some figurative impersonation of John of Gaunt, and at the same time to retain that private, subjective dimension which allows the mourning, knightly figure to exist as a projection of the poet's imagination—that part of Chaucer who behaves and acts towards death with an intensity of emotion similar to a real husband's. In this way, a writer and a recipient are no longer separate, communicating personages—as they always were in the Latin prose *consolatio*. Further, the pre-sleep poet-figure suffers an extreme and unnatural anguish almost identical with that of the fictionalized dream-knight. There are now no distances or gulfs to bridge; no longer any

need to avoid, or at best veil, embarrassing particulars—or to indulge
in ineffectual generalizations—or appear to condescend to the application of local wisdom and a presuming charity. By the same token, the
original actuality of the relation between the poet and his subjects has
lost any value or relevance to the poem's mode of reference and artistic
means of vivid embodiment of generals and particulars. Seen in this
light, Chaucer's decision to adopt the dream device arises out of a
specific aesthetic and social problem. It is not an early experiment
(*pace* Professor Muscatine) but a carefully contrived solution.

Many years ago, before the war, Clemen in *Der junge Chaucer*[6]
stressed a point which recent criticism might well recall: 'The essential
point is that Chaucer saw new poetic and artistic possibilities in the use
of the dream.' The Chaucerian dream very distantly resembles Froissart's or Machaut's deploying of this device. The Chaucerian intention
not only creates an interplay between reality and dream (as Clemen
recognized) but provides us with a fourteenth-century novelty: the
bedtime reading *topos*—that is, the confronting of a perplexing and
amorphous 'experience' with a literary statement which only partially
satisfies some of the crucial problems posed by the as yet unexamined
experience. This confrontation re-enacts an essential process of classical
and medieval inquiry: the deliberate dialectic method of a conflict
between proof by natural experiment and proof by authority. The
common and accepted method of solution consists in a subtle concord-
izing of both experience and authority. This reconciling sequence is
seen at its most artistically satisfying in the *Parliament of Fowls*. Here,
however, in the *Book of the Duchess*, the sequence serves a psychological
need rather than a philosophical aim. The germ of the stratagem was
undoubtedly suggested to Chaucer by a very interesting encounter in
Machaut's *Liure Morpheus* (subsequently entitled *La Fontaine Amoureuse*).
Dr Hieatt manages to understand this at least in her otherwise madden-
ingly obtuse book on reality and dream in Chaucer.[7] Machaut, the
author–narrator (who has secretly overheard and written down the
tormented lover's wakeful complaint), on the morrow, by the fountain,
recites to the lover that very same account of woe and suffering:

> *Briefment tout le vrai li comptay*
> *Comment de mon lit l'escoutay,*
> *Et la päour que j'en avoie*

---

[6] W. Clemen, *Der junge Chaucer*, Bochum (1938).
[7] *The Realism of Dream Vision*, The Hague (1967).

En mon lit ou je me gisoie
Et sans celer la verité
De ce qu'ay devant recité
Dont durement s'esmervilla
Car de ce trop grant merveille a.
Son bras et son chief mist sor mi
Et moult doucement s'endormi
Droitement enmi mon giron.

(1535ff.)

The lover on hearing this account falls instantly and sweetly asleep in the poet-narrator's lap. The morbid insomniac condition is instantly ameliorated: '*sans celer la verité*'. The process we are witnessing here is that of 'objectification'. In medieval psychology the activity takes place either in sleep when reason is released in the *somnium* or fantasy in the *insomnium*, or in the waking state by recounting the experience to someone else in confidence. Chaucer is the first medieval author to apply this process of objectification to the unexpected confrontation of the anxious mind by a reading of a literary account which accidentally agrees with the melancholic's repressed experience. It has long been recognized that the dream which follows the poet's ironic prayer repeats and restates the main themes and preoccupations of Chaucer's reading of Ceyx and Alcyone—with subtle and illuminating changes. What has not been sufficiently recognized is that the main activity of the dream itself repeats and extends the scope of the process of objectification. At this juncture we are brought face to face with the much-vexed problem of the intelligence of the dreamer-poet, his obtuseness or his putative awkwardness. Clemen, who is rightly impatient with the critical debate on this point, sees the role of the dreamer as an exercise in Chaucerian intelligence:[8]

In this way the role the dreamer assumes, one of apparent misunderstanding, becomes a wise, perceptive action, a tactical move within the relationship between the two—just what we might expect of Chaucer.

Clemen sees this assumed role as largely the result of poetic skill and social tact, ironically mediated through a figure who is possibly unconscious or unaware of his methodology. But if we understand the psychological role of objectifying in the poem, a mediation between

[8] *Op. cit.*, p. 50.

waking and sleeping, grief and moderation, self-ignorance and under-standing, health and illness, the reasons for the dreamer-poet's actions and assumed *naïveté* become quite clear. Even in a confidential role involving friends, the confidant often has to overcome intentional or unintentional reticence on the part of the confiding sufferer. If the disease is in a state of crisis, the confidant is expected to use two methods: (1) a pretended state of ignorance of what he already has some know-ledge of; (2) a use of this ignorance which goes beyond the detailed objectifying technique—a deliberate use of misunderstanding which creates 'anger' in the sufferer. This last application is justified by the classical theory that 'one strong emotion drives out another'. Ovid recommends this treatment in the *Remedia Amoris* and Beatrice practises a variation on Dante in the *Divina Commedia* when the poet is deeply disturbed by the loss of his guide, Virgil. Nearer home, Pandarus employs this practical psychology in book I of *Troilus*. Mental isolation leading to madness or even death must be cured by objectification. Pandarus, by assuming a certain ignorance and maddening inability to comprehend Troilus' situation seeks to draw his friend out, to render the morbidity non-toxic:

> Yit Troilus, for al this no worde seyde
> But longe he lay, as stylle as he ded were;
> And after this with sikynge he abreyde:
> And to Pandarus vois he lente his ere
> And up his eyen caste he, that in fere
> Was Pandarus, lest that in frenesie
> He sholde falle or elles sone dye;
>
> (722–8)[9]

There follows a long dialogue in which Pandarus accomplishes his psychological stratagem. The dreamer-poet in our poem pursues exactly the same method in the face of the same symptoms. Both are engaged in 'esynge the herte'. The question of the real or assumed character of the poet, the dreamer or the poet-dreamer should not really involve us in disputes about degrees of irony or real or only apparent skilfulness of poetic technique. So misunderstood is this obvious psychological role that scholars have argued for years over Chaucer's 'misuse' of the

[9] The text of Chaucer usually quoted is that of Robinson (2nd edition), London (1957), save occasionally where better texts are available, e.g. *The Book of Troilus and Criseyde* ed. R. K. Root, Princeton (1926), and *The Knight's Tale* ed. J. A. W. Bennett, London (1954).

term 'fers' (the queen in chess) in line 741 or even the whole game of chess at line 723. It is not Chaucer who makes the misunderstanding, it is the manoeuvring poet-figure who is pretending to be contemptuous of the knight's over-literary chess-game image of his real loss. By so seeming to dismiss the knight's disguised account he makes the object of his 'game' sit down and, with a greater effort at realism, indulge in a fuller and more effective reminiscence.

The ME phrase for the process of revealing one's feelings, 'to ese the herte', seems not to have been a popular phrase but to have originated with Chaucer. Its occurrence at line 555 in this poem would appear to be the first use of the phrase in ME. By 1440 it glosses the medical term *delinio*. Its early use here, the number of times the noun 'herte' is used (thirty times in at least three connected senses), together with the extended and detailed physiological description of the knight's loss of consciousness, should perhaps warn us that it was Chaucer who first originated the linked metaphor and pun of 'heart-hunting' that Shakespeare was to put to such delicious use in *Twelfth Night*. No Old French poems show such metaphoric awareness, or the ability to concentrate and relate the whole episodes together with such verbal economy. I introduce this metaphoric activity here for it is the natural connection between 'process' and action within the dream—and the parallel between emergent health in the knight and recovered sanity in the poet. Chaucerian criticism has been slow to understand the function of the hunt in this poem. At various times it has seen the activity as an example of 'realistic description' (a sort of equivalent of Machaut's account of the plague), an impressionistic and inconsecutive atmosphere evocative of dream states, or just plain ignored (Muscatine). Efforts to find some source in Old French literature have not met with much success. Froissart's Cupidian hunting-party in *Le Paradys d'Amours* seems scarcely relevant—and Machaut's hunting conceit in the *Remède de Fortune* (ll. 1401ff.) is plainly descended from Ovid's account of Actaeon and has no real connection with Chaucer's metaphor. Source-hunting would seem to explain little in this context, for Chaucer's decision to introduce the hunting motif into the dream section returns us to his earlier interest in psychological images and processes of the mind.

If we compare the mental and physical traits of the pre-sleep poet with the dream-narrator, we notice that the projection has acquired without explanation or preparation an extroverted gaiety: a well-adjusted, active young man whose change in health becomes most obviously expressed in his impulsively joining the hunting-party. Although attended by sensitively imagined touches of dream-motion and visual plasticity, the hunt first and foremost serves as a psychological formulation, as any reader of Shakespeare's *Venus and Adonis* might have surmised. The hunt, especially deer-hunting, is the classical antidote for excessive states of inanition and mental morbidity. Ovid in a famous passage in the *Remedia Amoris* recommends it for the cure of *otium* that gives rise to love-melancholia, either of the active, erotic or of the passive, depressive kind. The knight-figure's excessive morbidity and social isolation becomes conveniently embodied in his neglect of the hunt, his complete and total lack of interest in that activity. The second purpose of the hunt is to provide a metaphoric equation for the psychological probing of the dreamer-poet. Thus, his *delinio* of the knight's uncommunicated experience becomes a hunting of the lover's psychological heart and mind. When Pandarus begins to probe Troilus in book I, the lover, suspicious of this intrusion, thinks to conceal the truth of his situation:

> Ek som tyme it is a craft to seme fle
> Fro thyng which in effect men hunte faste:
> Al this gan Troilus in his herte caste.
>
> (747–9)

The end of the dialogue and the psychological inquiry is, of course, announced by a reference which faces both internally and externally:

> And with that word ryght anoon
> They gan to strake forth; al was doon,
> For that tyme, the hert-huntyng.
>
> (1311–13)

At one level, what sleep has provided for the insomniac poet, initially 'sorwe in his ymagynacioun', the process of objectifying has accomplished for the grieving knight, 'sorwe in his herte'.

At this point we must return to Lawlor's 'pattern of consolation'. Naturally, in trying to describe something that never had any existence in the poem in the first place, the following justification is faintly plausible:

> In Chaucer's poem something unique is done: we have both consolation and a rejection of it—but not before it has done its work. Neither invalidates the other . . .

Lawlor imagines this paradox as 'present in all expressions of bereavement . . . One is the impulse to seek for consolation in the idealization of the past; the other is the rejection of all consolation in the overmastering sense of loss.' This last observation or psychological truism has applicability in so far as it applies to the genre of elegy. But it is far from certain that Chaucer meant the *Book of the Duchess* chiefly to incorporate the formal aims or content of an elegy. Further, the process of idealization has little to do with the knight's reconstruction of his life, or the figure of Blanche. The portraiture may be characterized as 'idealized', but no poetic account in the Middle Ages ever abandoned the only artistic method it possessed for the description of feminine beauty and virtue. If anything, the successive overlapping stages of the process of re-remembering show a progressive pattern of de-idealization. That is one of the aims of the *delinio*. The first part of Lawlor's theory (alas, now accepted by Clemen) is plainly sophistical. Nowhere has the dreamer-narrator considered the offer of a 'consolation'—and the knight at no point rejects what never passed between them. At the level of expectation, or unexpressed wish, it may be imagined that the knight seeks from someone who is not a friend agreement, confirmation, justification—never sympathy. In seeking this he must make the stranger understand what he himself to this moment has understood very imperfectly. Objectification itself provides the cure, as long as it attempts to depict reality. It is no accident that the description of Blanche merges into the account of two lives and ends by showing her not as an image to be admired at whatever distance, but as an activity— an activity which only has meaning in the context of mutual relations. The memory of Blanche ends where all memories faithfully recalled in the spirit of sincerity end—in inexpressibility. The knight's failure to find words shows that the present emotion and the past recollection have achieved their moment of completed identity:

> 'And thus we lyved ful many a yere
> So wel, I kan nat telle how.'

Chaucer's artistic triumph in these lines becomes the greater if we see from what sweetly embellished verse this has been developed. The passage is Machaut's in the *Jugement dou Roy de Behaigne*:

> *De nos deus cuers estoit si juste paire*
> *Qu'onques ne fu l'un a l'autre contraire;*
> *   Einsois estoient*
> *Tuit d'un acort; une pensée avoient;*

> De volente, de desir se sambloient
>   Conjointement,
> N'onques ne fu entre caus deus autrement
> Mais c'a toudis este si loiaument
> Qu'il n'ot onques un villein pensement
>   En nous amours.

Although Machaut sometimes manages to construct a fairish enjambed rhythm—so that the short four-syllable lines do not interrupt the syntactic continuity—his method is that of elaboration. A sense of climax never emerges from the enumeration. After the repetitions of *un* and *une* in emphatic positions (not to add the initial depth of feeling) the concluding statement, 'There was never a jarring thought in our love-affair', produces a sense of anti-climax. The vb. (3 indic. pret.) of *avoir* yields a weak and colourless force in this position. Turning to Chaucer, the mood seems less artistically contrived, but in fact more attention has been paid to syntax, rhythm and the placing of emphasis and climax. We should notice the accent on the ordinary trials of married life—no matter what the pain and grief—'for no woo'. You will look in vain in Machaut for this sentiment.[10] The bearing of identical joy and sorrow generates the beautifully modified *versus correlativus*, 'Yliche they were bothe gladde and wrothe', where the plural subject makes us aware that the controlling subject is 'oure hertes' in line 1289. The climax is prepared for by the reaffirmation of 'oon' and finally crests and dies away in the interjectory phrase of unexpressibility:

> Oure hertes wern so evene a payre
> That never nas that oon contrayre
> To that other—for no woo.
> For soth, yliche they suffred thoo
> Oo blisse and eke oo sorwe bothe;
> Yliche they were bothe gladde and wrothe;
> Al was us oon, withoute were.
> And thus we lyved ful many a yere
> So wel, I kan nat telle how.

This just and faithful remembrance yields the necessary truth of bearing

[10] Closer in sentiment is Petrarch, *Africa* II.226-9:
> Proh dulcis amantum
> Vita, nec alternis concordia rupta querelis
> Una quidem facies semper, mens una duobus,
> Una quies unusque labor.

both joy and sorrow. The perfect bliss of this union included pain and suffering. The narrator-dreamer has not offered this observation—but the knight has. Machaut's mediocre lines give way to more '*jolies compliments*'. Chaucer's reworking shows a sense of narrative form, of psychological tension—and moral recognition.

Does then the physician heal himself? Does the process of objectification alone produce a return to rational health and however close we come to 'consolement'? I think not. Some years ago, an Oxford don, manufacturing an examination question for a Final Honours School, concocted the following: 'Does *A Grief Observed* adequately describe Chaucer's *Book of the Duchess*? Discuss.' The borrowing of the title of the pseudonymous N. W. Clerk's account of his coming to terms with his wife's death was no mere accident. Like the knight, the author wrestled with the problem of death, memory, suffering—how to remember the beloved so that the memory is not distorted by mawkish self-pity or a de-humanizing philosophy or religion. All his positions, arguments, recollections seem to lead to no satisfying conclusion. Towards the end of his account occurs this passage:[11]

> I said, several notebooks ago, that even if I got what seemed like an assurance of H.'s presence, I wouldn't believe it. Easier said than done. Even now, though, I won't treat anything of that sort as evidence. It's the *quality* of last night's experience—not what it proves but what it was—that makes it worth putting down. It was quite incredibly unemotional. Just the impression of her *mind* momentarily facing my own. Mind, not 'soul' as we tend to think of the soul. Certainly the reverse of what we call 'soulful'. Not at all like a rapturous re-union of lovers. Much more like getting a telephone call or a wire from her about some practical arrangement. Not that there was any 'message'—just intelligence and attention. No sense of joy or sorrow. No love even, in our ordinary sense . . . I had never in any mood imagined the dead as being so— well, so business-like. Yet there was an extreme and cheerful intimacy. An intimacy that had not passed through the senses or the emotions at all.

I suggest that we should turn our attention to Blanche herself. Long ago, in the preface, Chaucer (using an amatory metaphor which has led many critics to imagine that the poet is suffering from unrequited love) states with a laconic finality never connected with that amatory image:

[11] *A Grief Observed*, London (1961), pp. 57–8.

I holde hit be a sicknesse
That I have suffred this eight yere,
And yet my boote is never the nere;
For there is phisicien but oon
That may me hele—but that is don;
Passe we over untill eft—

(36–41)

Chaucer's poetic promises are seldom unkept. The knight himself repeats the phrase when the dreamer-narrator first offers him his ear: 'Ne hele me may no phisicien/Noght Ypocras, ne Galyen' (ll. 571–2). Later, Blanche appears conventionally as his 'lyves leche' (l. 919); and her words would appear to have healing power (l. 927). These parallels should have alerted us to Blanche's role within the knight's re-creation of his life. I have talked a bit about Chaucer's early interest in psychology and states of mind. I have neglected to touch on his early philosophic interests. The poem, it is true, betrays no Italian reading, no Boethian reminiscences, no Chartrain concerns. These interests are to emerge later. In the foreground now are the French poets and Ovid. Yet, I venture, two of Chaucer's abiding philosophic concerns are here, in outline at least, represented—the concept of Nature and the doctrine of moderation. Whatever French passages Chaucer weaves into the imagining of Blanche, one striking trait—physical and mental—is repeated. The repetitions are imitated and reworked from many French poems—but here concentrated and focused on one person:

Hyt was hir owne pure lokyng
That the goddesse dame Nature,
Had made hem opene *by mesure*,
And close; for were she never so glad,
Hyr lokyng was not foly sprad,
Ne wildely, thogh that she pleyde.

(870–5)

She has to sobre ne to glad
For alle thinges more *mesure*
Had never, I trowe, creature.

(880–2)

Hyr throte, as I have now memoyre,
Semed a round tour of yvoyre
Of good gretnesse—and noght to gret

(945ff.)

> Therto she hadde the moste grace
> To have stedefast perseveraunce,
> And esy, *atempre* governaunce,
> That ever I knew or wyste yit . . .
>   (1006ff.)

These qualities of 'mesure', 'atempre governaunce', of moderation serve to connect Blanche with the soothing landscape of the poet's health-giving dream, the birdsong in lines 304–16, and the climate of lines 340–3:

> Blew, bryght, clere was the ayr
> And ful attempre for soth hyt was;
> For nother to cold nor hoot yt nas . . .

It is this moderating aspect of Blanche which perhaps provides a suggestion of the moral quality dominant in the knight's final acceptance. No startling Beatific Vision, more like Gower's 'truth in sober guise' 'for vertu is the mene, as Etik saith'—as Chaucer was later to say in the *Prologue* to the *Legend of Good Women* (in a passage grievously misattributed). By extending this ethical principle I am not advancing an instructional Chaucer—of the pious fifteenth-century imagining: 'mesure is tresor.' Chaucer's feeling for moderation is more like Horace's or Aristotle's than it is like the frigid theological adaptations and schematizations of the thirteenth, fourteenth and fifteenth centuries. For Chaucer, 'mesure' invariably concerns us in actual behaviour, in changing ratios, in relationships. The history of the influence of the concept of moderation on medieval poets is obscure (and perhaps it requires elucidation)—but surely the systematizing hand of patristic commentary and adaptation would seem to lie heavy on the subject as far as the common run of poets is concerned.[12]

If in the words of a reigning Cambridge professor, 'every book of C. S. Lewis's corrects its predecessor'—and if one may imagine that *A Grief Observed* corrects (no matter how obliquely) *The Allegory of Love* in respect to our poem, perhaps I may be permitted to observe that 'if we had only this early poem of Chaucer's, we should have the most intricately constructed and most moving poetry until we come "bi process of longe tyme" to the Renaissance and to Shakespeare'.

[12] Cf. Appendix, pp. 226ff.

CHAPTER TWO

The Complaint: Venus, Pity and Mars

> ... his thoughts are pure and simple, but wanting combination they want variety ... That of which the essence is uniformity will be soon described. His *Elegies* have therefore too much resemblance of each other.

Dr Johnson's criticism of his fellow collegian William Shenstone has special force for the critic who undertakes to estimate the artistic merits of Middle English love complaints and Chaucer's excursions into this genre. It is too *simpliste* to suppose that genres possess intrinsic aesthetic properties, yet it is true that the existence of a genre both provided much of the medieval artist's *matere* and influenced him in shaping the dominant pattern of his own creation.

Whatever the origin of the secular complaint, the Middle English complaint possessed formal characteristics which presented poets with certain structural problems. The nature of the English genre may be reasonably traced to similar poems written in French in the fourteenth century. The love complaint in France in that period admits only of loose definition. It was a poem of any length, clearly entitled '*complaincte*', having an amatory theme in which the *causa* or aim of the poem was to complain. It would appear to have been a remarkably elastic form having no fixed rules for metre, rhyme scheme, stanza length or *dispositio*. It might take the form of a *lettre*, *débate* or any variety of poetic genre. It might exhibit a simple structure based on *sermocinatio* or it might possess a more complex form: *sermocinatio* combined with narrative (as in two of Granson's complaints) or dream-allegory (in a late example by Charles d'Orléans, *Complaincte en Songe*). Yet, in comparison with other popular lyric modes, the complaint does not seem to have been a genre much favoured by courtly French poets of Chaucer's time. Froissart included longish *complainctes* in his more ambitious poems such as *Le Paradys d'Amour* (ll. 75–203) or *L'Espinette*

Amoureuse (ll. 1556-2354), but he never wrote a single, independent complaint although he composed many short poems in a variety of lyric forms. The same situation obtains for Guillaume de Machaut who included a long complaint against Fortune in *Le Remède de Fortune* (ll. 905-1480)—and the best of this has been inspired by Alan of Lille. In *La Fontaine Amoureuse* (ll. 235-1034) Machaut invented an extended lover's complaint but he wrote no separate poems of this kind. Similarly, among Deschamps's voluminous writing there are only five poems which may be considered as complaints (*Balades* 957, 1185, 1199, 1224, 1426), and in most instances these are entitled 'balades' or subtitled (for example) '*La complaincte d'un gentil homme marie en aage moien faicte par Eustache par maniere de balade*'. In Deschamps's *Art de Dictier* (c. 1392). which enunciates principles and provides examples for composing in nearly all lyric modes, there is no mention of the complaint as an independent form. The vague nature of the genre is confirmed by the evidence of our own literature: many of the minor complaints attributed to Chaucer of Lydgate appear to have been designated in manuscripts as '*balades*', occasionally subtitled 'compleynts'.

Of Chaucer's French contemporaries only Oton de Granson seems to have had a serious interest in writing complaints. Eleven of his complaints are extant. His longest and most ambitious performance, *La Complainte de Saint Valentin*, must be viewed as a failure. Here Granson tried to combine narrative, dialogue, panegyric and complaint. He succeeded only in loosely associating separate elements. The situation is monotonously developed, the sentiment appealed to blatantly naïve, and there is an unwholesome discord between plot and sentiment. On the other hand, his more successful complaints tend to be short poems, usually of eight stanzas. His modest sensibility seems to find fulfilment in these relatively simple forms.

It is significant that Chaucer, when he wrote the *Complaint of Venus* (whatever we think of this title, and it is plainly editorial), did not model his poem on any one of Granson's complaints. Instead, he adapted a series of five *balades* (entitled in the Paris MS. 'Les Cinq balades ensuivans'). Chaucer shows artistic astuteness in deciding to choose the *Cinq Balades* in that he completely avoided choosing the weak and monotonous structure of any one of the complaints. He fixed his attention on a series of related poems which contained more concentrated variety of expression, plot transitions and thematic combinations than could be obtained in any single Gransonian complaint.

Chaucer's adaptation of the five *balades* is an implicit criticism of the simple, complaining, amatory poem. None of Chaucer's changes may be described as spectacular but all of them indicate what he intended to avoid. His most obvious alteration is the omitting of sections II and III of Granson—thereby shortening the middle development by twenty-four lines. Granson's section II consisted of a catalogue description of the lady's physical beauties (*effictio*) supplemented by a similar description of her moral qualities (*notatio*). Of course, the first description was unsuitable since Chaucer had determined to change the sex of the narrator; he omitted the second description because it was a redundant amplification of lines 9–10:

> *Il a en li bounte, beaute et grace*

qualities Chaucer altered in order to strengthen the moral rather than the amatory tone of the poem:

> In him is bountee, wisdom and gouvernaunce.

Thus, section II, containing twelve lines of static, descriptive embroidery which arrested the movement of the poem, was abandoned because these enumerating qualities were unsuitable for the unified, continuously progressive plot which Chaucer wished to construct.

Section III in Granson amounts to a stock retelling of the beginning of the narrator-figure's *servise*. He is represented as having waited seven years in service without receipt of *mercy*. The climax of this section arrives in an apostrophe to the lady:

> *Helas, pite, tresdouce damoiselle,*
> *Je vous prie me soiez aidans.*
> *Contre Dangier soustenez ma quarrelle,*
> *Car il est fort et ses amis sont grans;*
> *Durete me het, et Paour m'est nuissans.*
>
> (4–16)

This conventional appeal arises out of the stock character created for the lady in section II, 'son cuer [est] plain de reffuz' (ll. 15–16). There is no place in Chaucer's poem for any of this for he treats the lovers' situation in a different way. In the *Complaint of Venus* the lovers are presented as supremely happy in themselves, their mutual affection and moral admiration threatened externally by the figure of Jealousy. In addition to introducing more grammatical figures (polysyndeton, parison, anaphora, polyptoton) into the poetic texture, Chaucer also uses personification in a more striking way. In Granson a host of

personifications, Ielousie, Dangier, Durete, Paour, are listed as enemies
—powerful psychological antagonists created by his lady's disdain.
Chaucer develops Jelosie into a more forceful, single enemy of genuine
love. Chaucer places the discordant source of the complaint in a dimension external to the lovers' characters. Compare Chaucer's (ll. 61-3):

> Now loue wel, herte, and look thou neuer stente;
> And let the jelous putte hit in assay,
> That, for no peyne wol I nat say nay;

with Granson's

> *Or aime, cuer, ainsi que tu pourras;*
> *Car ja n'arras paine si doulereuse*
> *Pour ma dame, que ne me soit joieuse.*

It may be seen from the poem as a whole, especially in this quotation,
that to imply, in Professor Robinson's phrase, that Chaucer's poem
is 'a free translation' is to misunderstand the nature of medieval poetics.
Chaucer's conservative, delicate alterations turn Granson's dull verses
into a new and aesthetically more important poem. The Chaucerian
(and entirely original) envoi composed in an added ten-line stanza is
syntactically divided into three sections (73-5: *aab*; 76-8: *aab*; 79-82:
baab). It abounds with delicate poetic echoing effects: the division of
syntax echoes the three-part grouping of '*balade-simple*' terns (three
stanzas of eight lines ending in a refrain). A new rhyme, é [ɛ:], is introduced and the dominant rhyme of the whole poem, *-aunce*, is reintro-
duced with the rhymes chiming and echoing on three rhyme-words
used earlier in lines 3, 17, 46: 'suffisaunce', 'remembraunce', 'penaunce'.
These nouns recall and restate the dominant mood of the poem: the
lovers' languishing in a painful existence ('penaunce'), made bearable
by the lady's self-sufficience ('suffisaunce') through the memory
('remembraunce') of the lover in spite of estrangement. These repeated
rhyme-words in the envoi create an effect of a personal motto or poetic
cognizance for the lady. Chaucer's unusual frankness about his 'source',
the insistence (largely ironic) on following Granson 'word by word',
and the final dominant *-aunce* rhyme on 'Fraunce' suggest perhaps that
the noble lady had some connection with that country. Could the
poem have been written for Isabella of France after her enforced
separation from Richard in 1399? Granson's 'lady' (identified in an
acrostic in the first stanza of the *Souhait de Saint Valentin*) was another
Isabel. Perhaps the 'princess' of this poem might have been expected to

remember that. The poet's disclosures about himself—his advancing years, the effect of ageing on his creative imagination, his dispiriting view of the adequacy of the English language[1]—all these remarks in the absence of any ulterior or additional artistic motive for this *ipse dixit* contribute to creating an effect of personal honesty.

The effect which Chaucer made on the form of the amatory complaint in later Middle English poetry is measurable not by a recording of direct borrowings and echoes, although many could be cited, but by the increased quality of the genre—English poems of this type are very much better structurally than Granson's short complaints. The 'Balade of Compleynt' (Add. MS. 16165) and the 'Complaint to my Mortal Foe' (Harley MS. 7578) represent very polished examples of the form and genuinely deserve to have been considered by Professor Skeat (at one time) for inclusion in the Chaucer canon.[2]

Chaucer's influence may be most clearly seen in the complaints of the MS. Fairfax 16 (folios 319b ff.). These poems were imperfectly transcribed by H. N. MacCracken and printed in *PMLA* 26. Whatever the value of attributing (on very slender evidence) these poems to the duke of Suffolk, MacCracken should not have dismembered the unified work of art to which these poems belong. This work, beginning not on folio 318b but on folio 316b, consists of a short *Oryson* addressed to the God of Love followed by a section entitled *The Epystel in Prose* which forms a feigned autobiographical introduction to the collection of *balades*, letters and complaints. The prologue is formed on an elaborately developed similitude of 'the pilgrimage of love'. The collection of short poems is represented in the conceit as the author's memorial tablets erected after the completion of his lover's pilgrimage. The work was originally composed sometime after the *Legend of Good Women* for the author in his epistle refers to the 'Legend of Cupid's Saints'. In formal terms it resembles Chaucer's poem in that it is composed of an

---

[1] Enfeeblement of the poet's creative powers is perhaps supported by the untypical Chaucerian instance of the rhyme *-oure -ure* in lines 22-3. But it is wrong to call this an 'impure' rhyme. The advanced pronunciation of sbs in stressed syllables before final *-r* showing [oː] moving to [uː] is exemplified in Chaucer by the sequence of rhymes in *Troilus* V.22-6.

[2] *A Complaint to His Lady* (Robinson, pp. 528-9) from the Shirley MS. Harley 78 (and derived Add. MS 34360) entitled by Shirley 'The Balade of Pytee. By Chaucier' seems to have been written as a continuation of the *Complaint to Pity*. It is still regarded as Chaucer's owing to its verbal polish, yet there is little literary evidence in terms of structure, argumentation and imagery to support Chaucerian authenticity.

'autobiographical' introduction which holds together a collection of self-contained pieces. In addition, many of the poems in the collection are letters. There are ten complaints in the collection, all of a fair standard. Considerable effort at a continuous plot is joined to an attempt to manage grammatical continuity which embraces whole stanzas. The poems are very short and succeed by being so limited. Six poems are in three stanzas of rhyme royal—the medieval equivalent of the sonnet for this is the form into which Chaucer had translated Petrarch's 88th in *Troilus* I. But, whereas Chaucer following Petrarch's example used an elaborate and interesting rhetorical pattern composed of *synoeciosis, erotema, exclamatio* and *allegoria*, the Fairfax complaints are practically without ornamentation. It is the author's intention that the poems should succeed by giving the impression of spontaneously uttered sentiment.

The longer the complaint, the more obvious becomes the basic weakness in the form. All meditational forms in poetry have the same structural deficiency: arbitrariness of plot transition. The longer the plot, the more numerous the transitions, the weaker the whole formal articulation of the poem. Unlike the short love complaint typified by the Fairfax collection, the longer amatory complaint never achieved a proper shapeliness outside Chaucer. For example, the *Complainte Amoreuse* (once attributed to Chaucer) and the *Compleinte Ageyne Hope* are both wandering meditations seasoned with the occasional apostrophe. Both poems suggest a 'real' situation—the former by the concluding device of 'On Saint Valentine's day I wrote this poem', the latter by the inclusion of an introductory narrative section. These additions in no way improve the unity of form. The Middle English extended amatory complaint in the fifteenth century remains untransformed in the loosely connected shape created for it by Granson a century earlier. Lydgate's attempts sometimes show near-Chaucerian intelligence in local matters, but the main problem remains unsolved.

In the *Complaint to Pity*, Chaucer (while not choosing to combine *narratio* with complaint) realized that a complexity which in some ways corresponds to plot sequence in narrative had to be invented. For *Pity* Chaucer constructed an 'allegorical episode' where any pattern which would give the simple impression of a consistent sequence of events was avoided. Instead, the episode contains a series of compressed or oblique conceits, which, although they offer no consistent *significatio*, yet correspond to an actual psychological occurrence in the lady's mind. When the poet presents himself as gazing on Pity's hearse he is, significatively, looking at her; he is in her august, forbidding presence about to utter his 'complaint'. The structure of the poem becomes impure the moment the poet-figure 'puts up' his complaint. When we are taken, unprepared, into the poet's confidence and permitted to hear the complaint, the unity of time and place in the 'episode' is broken. This false relationship is scarcely noticeable because we have been unobserved witnesses all the time. The poem's success depends on the shortness, the telescoped nature of the transition from episode to complaint. There must be no disturbance in the emotional continuity of the two sections. Thus, all we are told is:

> Then leue [we] all [þees] virtues, sauf Pite
> Kepyng the corps as ye haue herd me seyn . . .
>
> For to my foos my bille I dar not shewe;
> Theffect of which seyth thus in wordes fewe:
>
> (50–6)

Yet this transitional passage, isolated from its immediate function, seems terribly crude. Skeat and Robinson by adopting the reading of Shirley (MS. Harley 78) tried to make the transition more smooth: 'Than leve *I* alle virtues . . .' But the pleonastic phrase 'as ye have herd me seyn' in the next line effectively destroys any editorial attempt to turn the 'bille' into a proper solitary rumination. The 'bille' of complaint Chaucer gives organization by using the *allegoria* of the loyal retainer warning his lord that there is treason in the household—a theme which William Neville was to misuse by excessive amplification in his sixteenth-century *Castle of Pleasure*.

Chaucer brings the poem to an effective close by a series of outbursts which include a prayer, an emotional analysis and an affirmation of loyalty. The 'bille' proper ends at line 116, not at line 119 as in Skeat and Robinson. The 'bille', as the narrator tells us, was written when Pity was still alive. The last lines (117–19):

> Sith ye be dede—alas that hit is so!
> Thus for your deth I may well wepe and pleyn
> With herte sore and full of bisye peyn.

indirectly celebrate the narrator's own death (compare the image in line 105) and return the reader with perfect grace of form to the time structure of the episode before the 'bille'; for the last line, 'With herte sore and full of bisye peyn', repeats the second line of the poem and this echo firmly returns us to the exordium. We have this three-line narrative *conclusio* in two versions which may well represent a Chaucerian revision. Shirley's MS. Harley 78 (and Harley 7587) read: 'Now Pitee þat I haue soght so yoore agoo' for 'Sith ye be dede—alas that hit is so.' The variant line (excluding 'Now') repeats the first line of the poem. It is quite possible that Chaucer originally wrote the *conclusio* using echoes alone to achieve the poetic return from 'bille' to the sequence of the episode. If this be the case, then he must have realized that a more emphatic break in tone was necessary to point the division of the conclusion from the 'bille'. Thus, he invented the line 'Sith ye be dede—alas that hit is so' which breaks the tone of the verse by emphatically interrupting the syntax. The cunning echoic 'completion' of this aposiopetic line is the first line of stanza 4 in the narrative episode (l. 22):

> Thus am I slayn, sith that Pite is deed.

The author-figure emotionally retires to his own bier.

There is nothing quite like the *Complaint of Mars* in the Middle Ages in either Latin or the vernacular. Yet, in its own nature it displays typical Chaucerian literary characteristics: complexity of construction, amalgamization of hitherto unrelated material, humanist wit, Ovidian aetiological fabulizing, and a penetrating philosophical interest in the perplexities (and eventual heartache) of human love.

It is best to deal at once with the question of topicality raised by information preserved in a Shirley rubric and colophon:[3]

> Rubric: Þallyaunce entrayted betwene Mars and Venus . . . made by Geffrey Chaucier at þe comandement of þe renomed and excellent Prynce my lord þe duc Iohn of Lancastre.
> Colophon: Þus eodneþe here þis complainte whiche some men sayne was made by my lady of york doughter to þe kyng of Spaygne and my lord of huntyngdon sometyme duc of exestre. and filowing begynneþe a balade translated out of frenshe in to englisshe by Chaucier Geffrey þe frenshe made sir Otes de Grauntsomme knight Savosyen.

The examplar available to Shirley for his copying reflects a general, but by no means complete,[4] fifteenth-century tendency to relate the

---

[3] Trinity College, Cambridge, MS. R 3.20, *p.* 130ff.
[4] MS. Longleat 258 treats the poem as a separate entity, the title in the colophon reading 'the Complaint of Mars'. The initialling and colophoning of Bodley MS.

complaints of Mars and Venus. Given this coupling of the two poems, the colophon naturally anticipates in its wording the *Complaint of Venus* (which follows immediately in the manuscript). But the criticism (Cowling, Brusendorff and Williams) which has sought to exploit Shirley's 'evidence', arguing that Mars is a *poème à clef*, has not understood the implications of the manuscript evidence. We are under no obligation to conflate the evidence given in the rubric with that contained in the colophon. These are two separate statements. The rubric to Mars states categorically and without innuendo that it was composed at the authoritative request of John, Duke of Lancaster. Now this scribal pronouncement may be perfectly correct. On the other hand, the colophon amounts to mere additional gossip, 'some men sayne'— that there was a rumour about in Shirley's day to the effect that the poem *Mars* or the complaint section was actually composed or recited by Isabel of York and John Holland.[5] Shirley's colophon to *Venus* in the same manuscript (used to bewildering effect by Dr Braddy[6]) which asserts that there was a theory ('hit is sayde þat . . .') that Granson's *Cinq Balades* were composed with Isabel of York in mind, serves to indicate the origin of all this fifteenth-century small-talk—and how it came to be misapplied to the *Complaint of Mars*. There is no need to go further in the constructing of fantasies out of the colophon. This in no way reflects on the accuracy of the rubric. John of Lancaster may well have commissioned the poem, possibly as a treatment of a theme or for an occasion chosen patronally. Chaucer and Lancaster were closely associated in the royal household from June 1367 onwards, and it is interesting to note that one of the duke's lodges was called 'The Bird's Nest'.[7] In view of the bird-narrator and implied bird-audience of *Mars* perhaps the poem originally had some oblique connection with that place, now untraceable. The knights and ladies addressed by 'Mars' may well have been composed of the military retinue and ladies-in-

[5] In ME the phrase 'made by' never meant 'composed in respect of'. See *MED* BI (9a), and compare other uses of the phrase in Shirley's notations where it has its usual meaning.

[6] *PMLA* 14 (1939), pp. 359–68. Much of this is reworked in his *Chaucer and the French Poet Graunson*, Baton Rouge (1947). But cf. the review in *Medium Aevum* 18, p. 36, which casts serious doubt on this use of manuscript and biographical material.

[7] Cf. *John of Gaunt's Register* (ed. S. Armitage-Smith), Camden Society 20, 21: i. 85; ii. 70–1 for a number of letters written 29 July 1372 from 'þe Briddesnest'.

Tanner 346 indicates separate treatment. Of the matrix group *TLF only F (Fairfax 16) joins the poems by title.

waiting of the very large Lancastrian household. The retinue contained at one time Oton de Granson[8] who had already written a St Valentine's day poem, the *Complainte de Saint Valentine*, where narrative and complaint had been combined.

Whatever the putative social impulses or topical connections inhumed in the poem, it is doubtful if anything further can usefully be said about them. Until new and convincing evidence comes to light we should devote ourselves to trying to elucidate the poem's literary meaning. The mythological fable of Mars and Venus had been the subject of poetic treatment in the Middle Ages,[9] most notably in Jean de Meun's continuation of the *Roman*, lines 18061ff. The story as told by Nature amusingly illustrates the advantages of magnifying glasses, and Genius' rejoinder echoes common satiric observations on the persuasiveness of wifely arguments designed to conceal adultery, much in the vein of Ovid, Alisoun of Bath, and Dunbar's 'wheypat' widow. Jean's *digressio* reflects Ovid's *Ars Amatoria* II.562ff. fairly faithfully. Ovid's full narrative account occurs in the *Metamorphoses* IV.171–89, where the story forms a digressive and comic coda to one of the central and pathetic fables, that of Piramus and Thisbe. Its position in the *Metamorphoses* shows a typical Ovidian habit of juxtaposing, at virtuoso speed, several poetic textures: naturalistic, pathetic, horrific, clever and comic. The Chaucerian literary account of Mars and Venus can only come into being after the exclusively medieval creation of the concept of an idealized knighthood and chivalry. Classical and late antique poets treat the mythological Mars with a certain grim realism. The following is a fair collection of poetic epithets: *belliger, durus, cruentus, violentus, rapax, funestus*—traits not especially congenial to the view of knighthood advanced by Chaucer and elsewhere in the fourteenth century.[10] Similarly, Chaucer has bestowed on his Venus those beneficial characteristics and influences of the medieval *domina* which Boccaccio had applied to the planetary Venus in his *Genealogia* III.22—a point noticed by Dr Brewer long ago,[11] yet wholly ignored by Chauncy Wood in a more recent and entirely wayward account of the poem.[12] By the

[8] S. Armitage-Smith, *John of Gaunt*, appendix II.
[9] Boccaccio had used the myth in 1342 as an example of furtive love in *L'Amorosa Visione* XIX.1–39. It draws chiefly on the *Metamorphoses* and the *Ars Amatoria*.
[10] For a 'classical' view of the astrological and mythological Mars in Chaucer, compare *Legend of Good Women*, lines 2589–93.
[11] *N&Q*, N.S. 1 (1954), pp. 462–3.
[12] *Chaucer and the Country of the Stars*, Princeton (1970), pp. 103–60. The account of the relation of the miniature in MS. Fairfax 16, folio 14b to the poem (pp. 130,

same token, the St Valentine's day occasion is an exclusively medieval construction.

Astrological plot structures were not exactly frequent in classical, late antique or medieval poems.[13] With the exception of certain portions of the first two books of Martianus Capella's *De Nuptiis*, Ovid alone makes extensive use of astronomical material at the level of plot—and this use is reserved mainly for inclusion in his calendar poem the *Fasti*. It is here rather than in Statius' *Thebaid* that we should look for the germ of Chaucer's poem. On St Valentine's day (16 Kalends of March) we find in *Fasti* II.243–66 that in commemoration of the day Ovid has invented the aetiological fable on the origin and creation of the constellations the Raven, Snake and Bowl which were traditionally imagined as becoming visible on 14 February.[14] The story recounts how Phoebus' own bird, Corvus, in failing to perform swiftly his sacred duty was created part of a constellation as a moral lesson. Now Chaucer's possible recollection of this famous passage[15] may provide an arguable link between some of the poem's heterogeneous elements, e.g. (1) the actual day; (2) the aetiological myth; (3) myths where stellar formation signalizes moral castigation; (4) the avian interest which

[13] There is a striking use of mythologized astrology among the *tour de force* mood-setting in Petrarch's *Epistulae* VI.6ff. See especially lines 14–18:

> *Iam Venus ante alias toto pulcherrima cetu*
> *Effugit indignans contraria cuncta benignis*
> *Moribus ire suis. Stimulis non actus amoris,*
> *Ut solet, insequitur profugam Mars tristis amicam*
> *Arma suis graviora timens.*

[14] Cf. Columella, *De Re Rustica* XI.2.20.
[15] Cf. Hyginus, *Poetica Astronomica*, ll. 40.

132, 137–9) is wholly meretricious in its ignoring of the patronal intention to incorporate the composite three-panel scene with the luxurious borders and arms of William Stanley, Esquire, of Hooton(*fl.* 1440). The bookseller and illustrator gave this poem especial prominence in textual position and visual richness for William was almost exclusively a military gentleman much interested in the rules of conduct of knighthood. He has ordered a second, contemporary scribe to copy the rules of chivalry of the Knights of the Order of Rhodes on the blank leaves at the end of the manuscript (folios 329ff.). The scribe had first started to copy them on the blank leaves at the beginning (folio 3b) thereby more closely associating the rules with the miniature, but for some reason erased them. This can just be seen under ultra-violet light. The iconographic 'traditions' had nothing to do with Chaucer's original literary aims. The illuminator has now been identified as William Abell; for a bibliography cf. Pächt and Alexander, *Illuminated Manuscripts in the Bodleian Library, Oxford*, Oxford (1973), vol. III, p. 92 (item 1065).

connects a speaking bird (*Fasti* II.259–60) with a fourteenth-century St Valentine's day bird congregation and observance.[16] If this pattern of associations was in Chaucer's mind, we are entitled to ask for what poetic purpose? The controlling factor, I suggest, may be the 'aetiological' aspect of the myths which descends from the Ovidian material. Criticism to date, with the exception of Clemen and Stillwell, has generally taken the astrological element in the plot structure at face value or treated it as a kind of *jeu d'esprit*. The astrological events are of a generalized, literary nature: the actual movements of the heavens only resemble a dateable area (?1363 or ?1385) accidentally. The whole love affair is minutely realized through the observable movement of the planets and constellations in the period roughly from 12 April to 1 May;[17] the poetic language reflects a witty, self-conscious application of astronomical terms and imagery to the humanized situation.[18] The purpose of the aetiological myth in Ovid is to explain the nature of something by describing its origin (the genre ultimately descends from Callimachus). The stellification of Corvus in *Fasti* II provides a perfect example on a small scale of similar myths collected in the *Metamorphoses*—for instance, the story of Salmacis and Hermaphroditus in book IV, which both accounts for the enervating quality of the water of the pool of Salmacis in Caria, and describes the destructive and predatory nature of erotic desire. It becomes a quintessential verse essay on the effects of *otium*. In the fourteenth century, why should Chaucer have taken so much trouble over revamping and synchronizing the mythological plot structure with a scientific, astronomical sequence? The aetiological myth establishes for the reader a poetic archetype for a physical phenomenon or a moral situation. Clemen and others have

[16] See Bennett, *The Parlement of Foules*, pp. 134–9 for a discussion of the rarity of the convention of bird congregations on St Valentine's day in poetry before Chaucer.

[17] For an extended exercise of poetic wit on an elaborated image, cf. Froissart's *Amorous Clock*, where all the parts of the clock figure in detailed moral and psychological application.

[18] For example, the 'white boles grete' (l. 86) painted on the walls of Venus' bedchamber in Taurus have been remembered from Virgil's *Candidus Taurus* (*Georgics* I.218–19) as quoted by Macrobius, *Commentum* I.18 (see my review of E. Seaton, *Sir Richard Rose* in *Medium Aevum*, 34, p. 158). More recherché is the wordplay on 'valaunse' (145) where the sb. refers to Venus' headdress (cf. *Parliament* 272) and to OF *faillance*, apparently an equivalent of Med.Lat. *detrimentum* in the astronomical sense 'the condition of a planet when in the sign opposite to its house, a condition of distress' (compare sixteenth-century English 'detriment').

not been slow to notice that the *narratio* of the *Complaint of Mars* recalls *Troilus and Criseyde*. Actually, it is a miniature *Troilus*. The poem embodies a poetical application of astronomy to an aetiological myth in an attempt to establish an archetypal plot or pattern of tragic love, a complex yet compressed *exemplum* of doomed, unfortunate *fine amour*. A similar artistic purpose may be seen in Marlowe's choice of Musaeus *Hero and Leander* for the subject of his expanded epyllion. These lovers provide a definitive *ur*-text of tragic human love. Musaeus' poem was thought to be the very first love story ever written—'They were the first that euer Poet sung' in Chapman's concluding line. The Renaissance regularly confused the late Musaeus Grammaticus with the archaic mythical singer Musaeus who (from the evidence of the Orphic fragments) was imagined to be pre-Homeric.

Unlike Marlowe and Chapman's *definitio amoris*, Chaucer's myth qualifies as a poetic archetype by virtue of more than historical age. It should be remembered that the science of Chaucer's day supported generally the view of late classical astronomy that the stars 'poured down their puissant influences'. The stellar Venus, Hesperus, not only exerted her influence at nativity but post-natally influenced events and human character when she appeared at certain times of the day, and at certain positions in the sky. Chaucer's poetic intention turns on a simple peripety—that of making the 'influential' stellar goddess of love subject to the unfortunate emotional and moral implications of her own passions, and showing the effects of that 'dredful ioye' on Mars. Thus, their own enactment of an ennobling, physical love, the very paradigm of *fine amour*, is turned into a universally visible sign of impermanence, suffering and implied betrayal. In Ovid, it is only the Olympian court who are favoured with a risible view of the lovers' shaming adultery. In Chaucer, all who gaze on the heavens in the 'tempo piacente' become the witnesses of a more complex and more compassionate moral exposé. Another similarity in poetic intention may be seen in Shakespeare's epyllion of Venus and Adonis,[19] where Venus' tragic love of Adonis serves to define henceforth what all human physical love shall come to. Shakespeare makes Venus suffer her own desires, fears and anxieties—every 'rage of love'—and in the end condemn them. She says finally:

[19] His selection of this myth represents an attempt to choose a subject even older than the 'historical' fable of Hero and Leander. Boccaccio in *L'Amorosa Visione* (XIX.6) is aware of the mythological priority when he calls Mars and Venus 'antichissimi amori'.

Since thou art dead, lo here I prophecie,
Sorrow on loue hereafter shall attend:
It shall be wayted on with iealousie,
Find sweet beginning, but vnsauorie end.
Nere setled equally, but high or lo,
That all loues pleasure shall not match his wo.

It shall be cause of warre, and dire euents,
And set dissention twixt the sonne, and sire,
Subiect, and seruile to all discontents:
As drie combustious matter is to fire,
Sith in his prime, death doth my loue destroy,
They that loue best, their loues shall not enioy.
(1135-40, 1159-64)

If we compare Chaucer's poem, Shakespeare's artistic treatment shows an entirely different distribution of moral emphasis, an emphasis largely the result of employing the narrative presence of the witty, self-conscious Ovidian poet-figure, and the dramatically effective device of leaving the concluding moral commentary to the intellectually defective yet stridently capable Venus, beguiling and beguiled, outrageous and finally outraged. The Chaucerian moral attitude implied in the *Complaint of Mars* shows his usual employment of indirection and of multiple, interlocking planes of narration. Shakespeare's epyllion may be characterized as openly aetiological—that is, part of the formal pleasure of the genre consists in defining a concept by explaining the origin of that concept in the form of a myth: the destructive nature of erotic love exemplifies itself through the mythological pattern of tragic love involving Venus herself. Chaucer's moral purpose is more subtly disclosed in that his poetic method is not based on the Ovidian device of exposure. Unlike Shakespeare, the poet is not directly involved in the narrative, nor does Mars really speak for himself. The poet figure appears but parenthetically, the scandalized but faithful recorder. It is the *praefatio* (ll. 1-28) which contains the moral framework within which the narrative and complaint is set. These moral values are implied at the very beginning of the work yet never applied to the fully unfolded 'tragic' account—just as the formal end of the poem is announced by the bird-narrator (ll. 153-4) but the poem comes to no formal conclusion. Instead, it ends with Mars' appeal ringing in our ears, the narrator having evaporated. We experience a sense of surprise akin to

that created by the last bars of Debussy's *Iberia*, and realize that suspension is one of Chaucer's favourite devices.

The reader is left in some doubt as to the identity of the narrator.
That it is not a poet-spoken exordium is held back until line 13 of the
second stanza. Part of the aesthetic pleasure must have lain in the
audience's being surprised at the oblique introduction of the narrator-
figure, and in being able to recognize what to expect of aviary-authors.
Whatever the continental traditions of a poet's encounter with bird-
narrators in *chansons d'aventure*,[20] the only surviving English secular
poem featuring a bird-narrator represents a simple type of moral poem
with a refrain.[21] It may well be that an English audience might have
expected a sententious bird-narrator to offer restraining advice. Such a
reader would then have found himself offered that wisdom with a
difference. The lecturing moral aviary-pundit is reserved for a personal
tête-à-tête in the *House of Fame*. The notion of placing the poem in the
mouth of a bird amounts to much more than a way of creating an
artificial atmosphere. It introduces the reader to a brief and compressed
distinction between two amorous worlds: the Venerian inhabited by
human beings on the one hand, and an ordinary natural world inhabited
by birds and flowers on the other. The reader would have been aware
of the difference between private behaviour which has as its primary
aim erotic pleasure, and a public occasion where love and affection
openly affirm moral injunctions according to accepted and unquestioned
moral law. The birds tacitly approve a moral order; philosophical
reservations, doubts and condemnations are reserved for the mythological Mars, patron of knights and gentlemen.

The poetic structure of the very first stanza prefigures the artistic
and moral symmetry of the work as a whole. Like the overall structure
of the poem (*praefatio, narratio, planctus*), the prefatory first stanza is
tripartite: a triple adhortation. Announcing the implied moral concerns
of the poem, these repeated *adhortationes* present a clear juxtaposing of
natural affection and human-mythological eroticism. The old, popular
theme, 'nature rejoices in springtime, man alone laments', a commonplace of love lyrics such as 'Levis exsurgit Zephirus', 'Lenten with loue
is come to toun', and the charming song based on the Gregorian

---

[20] Cf. B. Fehr, *Archiv*, 109, pp. 41ff.
[21] This carol is preserved in BM MS. Sloane 2593, an early fifteenth-century
manuscript almost certainly written at Bury St Edmunds. Cf. R. L. Greene, *A
Selection of English Carols*, Oxford (1962), pp. 173–4. The fragmentary text is
printed by Greene in his *Early English Carols*, Oxford (1935), p. 322.

melody 'O praeclara Constantia', 'Foules in þe frith', provides Chaucer
with points of moral departure and return:

> 'Gladeth ye foules of the morow gray,
> Lo, Venus risen amonge yo[n] rowes rede.
> And floures fressh, honoureth ye this day,
> For when the sunne uprist then wol ye sprede.
> But ye louers that lye in eny drede
> Fleeth lest wikked tonges yow espye:
> Lo, yonde the sunne, candel of Ialousy!'

That the frank, Ovidian advice which the bird bestows on the lovers in
the second stanza, 'Time cometh eft that cese shal your sorow/The glade
night is worth an hevy morow', amounts to a disappointing consolation,
or at best a consolation inappropriate to be uttered by one of Nature's
loyal subjects on St Valentine's day, is revealed by the note of authorial
astonishment in the lines which directly follow:

> (St. Valentine! a foul thus herde I singe
> Upon thy day, er sonne gan up-springe!)

This parenthetical, ironic exclamation (which should be extended to
cover the initial four words of the next line—it is incorrectly punctuated
in all editions) makes up the only part of the poem which is *ex persona
poetae*. Any serious interpretation of the poem should account for the
presence of the author at this point only. The very next line indicates
that the advice which the bird directs to his fellow creatures who are
celebrants of love is exactly opposite to that which he has just bestowed
on the human lovers. The author-figure's final words point the contrast:
'*Yet* sang this foul:'. The bird then counsels his fellows in sober language to choose their mates, renew their service, confirm constancy of
affection, and endure hardship patiently. This calm, uncomplicated
natural love of the birds (described in language appropriate to both *fine
amour* and ordinary married love) may be seen as an implied, contrasting
setting for the kind of erotic passion, 'derne loue', which in the *narratio*
comes to be exemplified in the Mars–Venus relationship—a mutual
love which although capable of moral refinement nevertheless allows
for emotional vulnerability, despair and philosophical negativism. The
bird-narrator, in common with the human reader, has sympathy and
compassion for the humanized stellar erotic predicament, but remains
intellectually and morally detached from it—perhaps critical of some

of its basic assumptions, especially the unquestioned identification of physical beauty and moral desirability.

The rhetorical order of Mars' complaint, although it opens with a methodical pedantry suggestive of deliberation born of simple honesty and unfamiliarity with literary composition,[22] after it has concentrated on Venus and her situation, proceeds by emotional logic. The distracted mind leaps at line 217 from a variation on conventional moral and psychological observations (available in most Old French *complaincts*) to a philosophical questioning of the value of love and the object of 'God that sit so hye' in his creating of it. The psychological outcome (despair and madness) is characterized by imagery borrowed from Ovid.[23] This part of the complaint (ll. 218–44) has an imagistic force, syntactical economy and rhetorical clarity quite unlike any contemporary complaints written in Old French or Middle English. Lines 245–71 in the next *balade* grouping of three stanzas[24] ostensibly disturb the direction of the argument but amplify and concretize the related ideas of the malevolent Creator, destructive beauty, sinister power of attraction and the ultimate insanity of the possessor. The imagery shifts from the Ovidian hook and fishing metaphor (which Chaucer elaborates in terms of activity) to the visually static Theban brooch (which in the *allegoria* comes to be identified with Venus' face). This substantial, static comparison provides the intellectual centre of the poem in a manner which recalls the use of the central descriptive digression in the classical epyllion.[25] The idea of adopting Statius' description of the *monile Harmoniae* (*Thebaid*, II. 266ff.) for the purpose of providing an interpretative, philosophically-oriented conceit, is as poetically original as Chaucer's initial decision to incorporate and elaborate the astrological plot sequence. No evidence exists to suggest that Statius' conventional piece of material *ekphrasis* had become the subject of an allegorized description in the Middle Ages. Although Chaucer altered the details in the description (mainly to transform what had been a simple passage of *amplificatio* into a complex type of significative description), certain of Statius' phrases provided Chaucer

---

[22] For a deliberating exordium, cf. Froissart, *Plaidoirie de la Rose et de la Violette* lines 1–10; here the style derives from the *persona* of the '*advocat*' and forensic method prevails, '*Poins, procès, articles et ces*'.

[23] Cf. *Medium Aevum*, 34, p. 158, quoted in footnote 18, p. 27.

[24] For some strange reason two stanzas are run together in Robinson's second edition. They are correctly printed in Skeat.

[25] Cf. M. M. Crump, *The Epyllion from Theocritus to Ovid*, Oxford (1931), for a full account of the origin and development of the central digression.

with part of his creative impulse. For Chaucer, the most important single element was a particular kind of discordant power with which the necklace was endowed. Vulcan (Statius' fabricator) had anointed the metals and stones with poison and 'quae pessima ceston Vis probat', 'the wicked power which commends the girdle'. The reference to Venus' girdle and sexual desire was not lost on the Middle Ages as Lactantius' commentary (and other, later, anonymous scholia) makes clear. Another element in Statius proved attractive: the necklace's destructive beauty ('decorum possedisse nefas') provided Chaucer with the first element in his significatio. In addition to the brooch's acting as a complex unifying symbol of all the elements in the Mars–Venus relationship, it furnishes a visual link with Venus' face. Direct parallelism is established by lines 247–56 and lines 267–70. This identification is supported by Chaucer's altering of the kinds of stones set in the brooch. The Latin passage is a typical example of Statius' ornate originality. The necklace is encrusted with florid sinister designs, horrifying origins, cursed components and fatal materials. Statius'

> ibi arcano florentes igne smaragdos
> Cingit, et infaustas percussum adamantas figuras;

is softened in Chaucer to 'ful of rubies and of stones of Ynde'. The dominant colour in the work has been changed from green to red. Perhaps Chaucer's use of the impressionistic phrase 'stones of Ynde'[26] purposely reflects the difficulties in precisely rendering Statius' adamas. Although the formula of red and white complexion (lilia mixta rosis) does not figure in the Chaucerian account of the beautiful face, the notion of a beautiful countenance containing a bright red colour does so occur—for example in the description of Blanche in the Book of the Duchess (l. 905) and in the Balade on Rosemunde (l. 3) where the ruby is selected to illustrate that trait.

In order to transform Statius' necklace into a complex visual symbol capable of philosophical and psychological implications, Chaucer rejected certain elements which had been essential to his author's treatment. In the Thebaid Vulcan is the author of the necklace ('Lemnius struxerat') for the wedding gift is intended to avenge the adultery of Venus with Mars. The sin of the parents is to be visited upon the child of the illicit union. The crimes which the necklace subsequently inflicts

[26] According to the MED it may represent an equivalent of 'Indica margareta', a type of pearl, or more simply (and more likely) 'any exotic precious stone' (cf. Lydgate's uses of the phrase).

on the innocent Cadmean line is consistent with Statius' presentation
of Olympian morality. Chaucer transfers the authorship from Vulcan
to the ultimate Maker:

> *She was not cause of myn adversite*
> *But he that wroghte her . . .*
> *That putte such a beaute in her face,*

Mars' accusation poses a serious philosophic problem about the origin
of innate evil, the divine purpose in creating physical beauty and sexual
appetite—a question which Chaucer (as *auctor*) asks in another form
in the *Legend of Good Women*, lines 2228–35. In the *Complaint of Mars*,
the author's moral position (without reference to any solution) is
implied by the intricacies of the poetic form, the choice of narrator, the
selection of the St Valentine's day occasion and the advice (no matter
how conventional) to the mating fowls. The poem concludes with a
plea by Mars for human sympathy on behalf of the stellar patrons of
knights and ladies. There is nothing here to suggest that we should
withhold our compassion.

The whole poem, then, exhibits a typically undogmatic Chaucerian
interest in stellar determinism and free will (Mars and Venus are
presented as having both free will and predestined actions.) The
situation which obtains for human lovers is reflected in every aspect
by their stellar counterparts. There is a real community of interests
which this compressed pattern of 'loveres maladye of hereos' shares
with Chaucer's *Book of Troilus*.

CHAPTER THREE

The House of Fame

The tradition which connects the classical and medieval poetical device of *ekphrasis* with Chaucer's use of such description in the *House of Fame* grows out of that common experience of Roman rhetorical education which all young poets experienced. This institutionalized stability of taste and narrowness of aesthetic response maintained classical and late antique literary aims during the whole of the changeful medieval period. Chaucer's close, acknowledged reading of Virgil, Alan of Lille and Jean de Meun indicates the precise form of the common poetic impulse which he inherited.

It has been successfully demonstrated that *ekphrasis* was often employed by writers of extended narrative to provide unity of plot and theme. In Virgil, Longus, Achilles Tatius, Alan, and Jean de Hanville the description of a work of art is not mere decorative description, but constitutes a structural formula which to varying extents exploited allegory. In Alan's *Anticlaudianus* the *domus* define the conceptual inhabitant. His *House of Nature* and *House of Fortune* compose the basic pattern of the poetic impulse which Chaucer received. Through Alan's Ovidian perfection of a description of a work of art Chaucer viewed not only the pertinent literary past but his own present experience. This way of seeing and defining was available to Chaucer, as it was to all late medieval poets, in its most unified and puissant shape in *Le Roman de la Rose*.

Chaucer's creation of descriptions of works of art in the *House of Fame* illustrates the interdependence of imitation and invention within the discipline of classical and medieval poetics. Nowhere in the *House of Fame* may Chaucer's larger intention be usefully separated either from the inherited significance of his source or the smallest detail of his newly created passage of *ekphrasis*. The traditional structural use of such description is an important poetic element which lends control to the total meaning of Chaucer's poem.

But if Chaucer uses *ekphrasis* conventionally in his general design, he employs fresh narrative devices at the very outset of the poem, in the preface. The introduction is constructed in a manner unlike that of Chaucer's other *praefationes*. There are similar *exordium topoi* in the translation of the *Roman*, the *Book of the Duchess* and the *Parliament*, but all these uses show greater differences in form and content. Guillaume de Lorris in the preface to the *Roman* began with the *sententia* that:

> Maintes genz dient que en songes
> N'a se fables non e mençonges;

Guillaume, in defence of his poem's validity, maintains the opposite point of view. The author, then, appears in his poem supporting the notion that dreams are expressions of truth and quotes Macrobius to support this belief. He takes a positive position in respect of the convention in which he is composing, mentioning in lines 21ff. the occasion and purpose of the 'dream' and poem. Now this is the confident manner in which Chaucer usually opens his dream-poems. For example, in the *Parliament* we know from the preface and invocation the subject of the poet's study before dreaming and we are told the cause of the dream and the poem:[1]

> Citherea, thou blisful lady swete
> That with thy fyr-brand dauntest whom thee lest,
> And madest me this sweven for to mete,
> Be thou my help in this . . .

Chaucer employs the same technique in the *Book of the Duchess* and in the *Legend of Good Women*. The formula of the bedtime reading *topos* (a literary device unique to Chaucer) does not occur in the *House of Fame*. In spite of the absence of such an 'autobiographical' linking element, some critics have suggested that events from Chaucer's private life form part of the poem's subject. Nothing in the sense they intend is further from the truth. In another sense, no poem of Chaucer's is so much concerned with Chaucer—Chaucer the poet. But if the theme usually presented in the bedtime reading device is missing from the poem, whatever remains in the preface must be regarded as equally important to the main preoccupation of the poem. It cannot be (as

---

[1] *Parliament*, lines 113ff. In these lines Chaucer refers to two functions of Venus: (a) the goddess of sexual desire, as symbolized by the firebrand (cf. *Roman* 15778; Isidore, *Etymologiae* VII. 9–10); (b) an aspect of the planetary Venus which aids poets in the composing of verses (cf. Boccaccio, *Genealogia* III. 22).

Professor Manly once suggested) simply an extended piece of *amplificatio*. Briefly, the significance of the preface turns on the sense of the word 'dream'. In Macrobius' *Commentum* to Cicero's *Somnium Scipionis* the fiction of the dream is shown to be the form of a 'fabulous narrative' in which philosophical truths are concealed. When, centuries later, Guillaume de Lorris, Nicole de Margival or Chaucer write of the dream they 'dreamt', they intend figuratively the poem they have composed. When Chaucer in his preface questions the causes and truthfulness of dreams, he intends not only the 'raw material' out of which the poem is imagined to have been shaped, but the literary vehicle, the poem itself. There is no difficulty in Chaucer's referring to kinds of poetry by terms appropriate to an analysis of dreams for Macrobius had already introduced dream terminology into the language of literary criticism in the *Commentum*. There he had analysed Cicero's work according to the genres of dream—by an appropriate confusion of form and content. Thus, in the introduction to a dream-poem the conventional themes of ordinary genres might be adapted to the *visio* form. The old *exordium topos* 'I bring songs as yet unsung' appears in the dream-poem as 'I dream dreams never dreamt before'.[2]

Unlike Guillaume de Lorris, Chaucer ends his discussion of dreams[3] by deferring to the great scholars who have provided authority for possible opinions on the topic. This tentative, sceptical suspension is simply a method for introducing an idea which may be taken up and developed later in the poem. The theme of authority and personal belief is taken up in book II in the conversation between the poet and Jove's eagle. Another instance of the poet pondering this theme occurs in the F version of the *Legend of Good Women*:

> But wherfor that I spak to give credence
> To olde stories and doon hem reverence,
> And that men mosten more thing beleve
> Then men may seen at eye or elles preve,
> That shal I seyn when that I see my tyme:
> I may not al at ones speke in ryme.
>
> (97ff.)

In the *House of Fame* all the usual Chaucerian *topoi* of the preface

[2] Cf. E. R. Curtius, *European Literature and the Latin Middle Ages*, pp. 85–6, for a discussion of the *topos*; and *Book of the Duchess* 276ff. and the *House of Fame* 59ff. for Chaucer's adaptation.

[3] *House of Fame* 53ff.

are fused and telescoped. The main theme of the poem is not introduced in a bedtime reading formula nor is any cause of the dream indicated. Instead, the dream or poem itself takes the centre of the stage, thereby implying that the office of the poet and the validity of his art are to have some not unimportant place in the total meaning of the poem.

Just as the books of Spenser's *Faerie Queene* find their rhythmical and intellectual unity in 'allegorical houses', *domus* presented by means of static, descriptive allegory, so the *House of Fame* contains three *domus*: the temple of Venus in book I and the castle of Fame and house of Aventure in book III. Much has been said about the ostensible direction of the plot structure which links the three *domus* together: the reward which the poet is to receive at the patronage of Jupiter—the opportunity of hearing new 'glad tydings' of lovers. Many critics have accepted this version of the plot as the undoubted truth. But there is no reason to suppose that the eagle wrote the *House of Fame*. Actually, the plot of the poem is leading in another direction.[4] The plot plainly digresses away from the eagle's promised version of the *conclusio* towards a new, or rather different end: a complete exposé of Fame. The *House of Fame* may share with the *Parliament* the concluding theme of the poet's desire to learn of 'tidinges of Loves folke If they ben glade', but in the *Parliament* this is only a small part of the poet's object in poring over his books. It is what the poet eventually hears in the birds' concluding rondel, but the complex experience of the poem cannot be represented by this simple mood of affirmation. In the *House of Fame* the words of the 'man of gret auctoritee' would have to set forth more, presumably, than 'tales' which illustrate a joyful solution of human love, if book III as well as book I is to be considered as an organic part of the poem.

What might have been Chaucer's purpose in changing the focal point of the poem from an examination of love to an exposé of fame? Gardner Stillwell[5] suggested some time ago that his moral aim was to convince a special audience that the verity '*vanitas vanitatem*' had yet to be understood or applied. If Chaucer had meant to turn legal eyes from gewgaws he would have composed a shorter, more pointed poem. Fame, not vanity, is Chaucer's text, and he is not preaching to an ostensible audience exhorting them to abandon their crooked ways. The *House of Fame* is Chaucer's dream and the poet-dreamer is con-

[4] Cf. H. S. Bennett, *Chaucer and the Fifteenth Century*, Oxford (1948), p. 46.
[5] 'Chaucer's "O Sentence" in the *Hous of Fame*', *English Studies* 37 (1956).

cerned primarily with his own conscience. It has been suggested here
that in the preface Chaucer is concerned with the validity of his own
art of poetry. This combined moral and aesthetic interest manifests
itself in a sustained treatment throughout the whole poem—this
double interest stimulates and causes reflection on the 'allegorical'
events of the *narratio*. The poet's attitude to his material (as in the
Parliament) reveals itself in a reflective mood in which the humorous,
the scientific, and the philosophic are delicately blended by poetical
art. As a poet of Venus, Chaucer is obliged to examine at least two
important powers as motivation—Venus and Fame. Through elaborate
allegory Chaucer in this poem delineates (after the manner of the
philosophical epic[6]) the hidden sources which urge him, as a poet, to
both write and think about certain problems. Unlike the *Parliament*
which is concerned with a single problem (the paradox of human
love), the *House of Fame* represents an attempt to clarify two related
problems:[7] (1) to define the kind of love traditionally considered part
of the subject of a great poem, exemplified in the *House of Fame* by
Virgil's *Aeneid*; and (2) to define the impulse which caused the writing
of celebrated philosophical poetry, exemplified by the poets Virgil,
Homer, Claudian—those poets who in their art had travelled to the
remote and absolute regions—the Underworld where so many moral
and metaphysical secrets were offered authoritative solutions. Chaucer's
already created love poetry affords the poet an occasion for examining
his own attitude to literature and life. In the *Prologue* to the *Legend of
Good Women* (F text) Chaucer indicated the extent and seriousness of
his literary service to Venus and declared his interest in the authority
of 'olde stories'. These same preoccupations are in the foreground of
the *House of Fame*. The scope of Chaucer's interest in these questions
differs in no way from that of Boccaccio. If *Il Filostrato* embodies
something of Boccaccio's notion of human love, books XIV and XV
of the *Genealogia* analyse and defend his views on poetry and Fame.
Yet Chaucer's view of love and poetry is distinct from Boccaccio's—if
we compare his *Troilus* and the *House of Fame*. Boccaccio's *Gloria*
(like Petrarch's) is the embodiment of the assumption that a genuine

---

[6] Alan of Lille's *Anticlaudianus* is the best of this form and the most familiar to
Chaucer. Spenser's *Mutabilitie Cantos* owes much of its formal structure to Alan's
poem.
[7] The close connection of Amor and Fama as motivating forces in the poetic
mentality is demonstrated in Boccaccio's *Amorosa Visione* which provided the
structural *idée* for Chaucer's *Parliament*, p. xi above.

public recognition is never accorded to the unworthy. Chaucer, whose philosophic taste is suggested by his translating of Boethius, inclines in the *House of Fame* to Boethius' more sceptical characterization of Fame when he imagined the great goddess as 'a grete sweller of ears'.

If Nature is the goddess central to our understanding of the *Parliament*, Fame occupies a similar central area in the *House of Fame*. Venus represents the opposing deity in the *Parliament* yet the keynote of that poem proves to be order and harmony. The keynote of the *House of Fame* emerges as disharmony and a jumbling disorder—yet Chaucer has created no easily identifiable opposing force. Fame is linked with her sister Fortune in book III and aided by Venus in book I. But it may be argued that no 'celestial' conflict is necessary to produce disorder. Fame is as much the goddess of discord as Nature is the goddess of concord in Chaucer's view. The whole façade of the castle of Fame in book III provides just such a definition of Fame. It is her discordant aspect that Chaucer emphasizes in his description of the three principal pipers there enshrined. A sense of damning praise is insinuated:

> Ther saugh I than Atiteris
> And of Athenes dan Pseustis
> And Marcia that lost her skin,
> Bothe in face, body and chin,
> For that she wolde envyen, lo,
> To pipen bet than Apollo.
>   (1227ff.)

Pseustis is the lying pagan poet of the *Ecloga Theoduli*, a text used in medieval schools. He is an Athenian,[8] and plays upon Rumour's pipes.[9] His name (*pseûstis*—'falsehood') is noticed by many of the commentaries to the poem.[10] He is a stock exemplary figure who represents a type of poet whose art is skilled but whose morality is false. The figure of Truth in the *Ecloga* unmasks him at line 187:

> . . . *tu sine fine,*
> *Tu sine principio nos vincere falsa iubeto.*

Atiteris is more difficult to identify. If we accept Holthausen's emend-

[8] Cf. *Theoduli Ecloga* 4: 'Natus ab Athenis . . .'
[9] *Ibid.*, 6–7: '. . . rigidas perflavit fistula buccas Emittens sonitum per mille foramina vocum.' Cf. Ovid's phrase in the description of the roof of Rumour's house, *Metamorphoses* XII.44: '. . . ac mille foramina tectis . . .'
[10] Cf. Bodley MS. Auct. F 2.14, folio 53b, or MS. Digby 100, folio 75b: '*Pseustis interpretatur falsitas . . . et dicitur a pseudon quod est falsitas Latine.*'

ing[11] of the line so as to read 'dan Titeris' it is difficult to see what significance the figure of Tityrus would have in this passage. Marcia (Marsyas) is obviously a type of foolish poet who hybristically dared to out-sing a god and has been severely punished. Tityrus in the company of Pseustis and Marsyas could scarcely refer to Virgil's Tityrus. Possibly the passage is not corrupt and Atiteris is a name concocted for the occasion. I suggest that Atiteris is a compound composed of *a* and *Titeris*. In classical literature Tityrus had been identified with Virgil by Propertius (II.34.72). Servius in the commentary to Virgil's *Eclogue* I encouraged the identification. Virgil came to represent the Poet for the Middle Ages. For example, he is used as a personification of the poetic activity in Alan's *Anticlaudianus* I.142. In the *Bucolics* of Marcus Valerius,[12] Tityrus represents both Virgil and the muse of good verse. Chaucer possibly combines this conventionally extended sense of Tityrus with *ab* (with the force in compounds of 'unlike') to create an exemplary figure who stands as the practitioner of bad verse. Fame would then be the impartial muse of poetasters as well as poets.

When Milton describes Pandaemonium he conveys his value judgment by insinuation, a satiric undercurrent which crests in the throw-away bathos of: 'The roof was fretted gold.'[13] The demonic bad taste, or absence of spiritual imagination (gold groining traditionally had been an image of it[14]) is represented by phonetic symbolism. The flat half-line mirrors the bad decor. Chaucer's treatment of the castle of Fame is in an elaborate style more suited to fourteenth-century taste: a style which has a certain affinity with Lucan's description of Cleopatra's palace.[15] Lucan opens his description with 'the roof was all of fretted gold', but seventeen lines later when the poet has finished with marbles and woodwork we experience a detailed revulsion at the encrustations of bad taste which symbolize Egyptian moral degeneracy. Chaucer produces in his verses the effect of the overcrowdedness of the ornamental style—an excessive elaboration which embodies wrongness of motive and purpose.

The catalogue of musical instruments (ll. 1214–26) described here in the hands of the musicians (possibly to be imagined in postures similar to the figures in the minstrel gallery at Exeter Cathedral or the Maison de Tambour at Rheims) is a commonplace of medieval

---

[11] Cf. 'Chaucer und Theodulus', *Anglia* 16 (1893), pp. 264–7.
[12] *Marci Valerii Bucolica*, ed. F. Munari, Florence (1955), *prologus* 7.
[13] *Paradise Lost* I.717.   [14] Cf. Horace, *Odes* II.18.2.   [15] *Pharsalia* X.111ff.

poetics. Skeat and Robinson cite the *Roman* and Machaut's *Le Remède de Fortune*. But Chaucer need not have had these authors in mind. Other catalogues of musical instruments might be evidenced from the *Roman de Troie* (ll. 14775ff.), Beaumanoir's *La Manekine* (l. 2295), Nicole de Margival's *La Panthere d'Amours* (ll. 155ff.) and the B and C manuscripts (late fourteenth and fifteenth centuries respectively) of the *Roman de Thebes*. But Chaucer has enriched the rhetorical device by adding an allegorical dimension (this catalogue was conventionally used for decorative amplification) at the same time adding a touch of contemporary realism in the mentioning of Dutch and Spanish pipers.

The court and figure of Fame may have been suggested to Chaucer by the so-called French Courts of Love, but Glory's antics are Chaucer's own invention. It is a tribute to the lucidity of Chaucer's art that book III as we have it possesses a strong, demonstrable unity. From the invocation imitated from Dante's *Paradiso* I (with its important change from 'O buono Apollo' to 'O God of science and of light'—so suggestive of a clarification and receiving of superior knowledge) to the transition from the castle of Fame to the house of Aventure, Chaucer with 'minute inquisitive sagacity' exposes the activities of Fame in all her roles.

It is a commonplace of philology that ME *fame* conveyed more senses than its modern use now does. ME *fame* (as in classical and medieval Latin) conveyed three related meanings: (1) renown, (2) rumour, (3) ill-repute. This complex of meanings is essential to the treatment which Chaucer accords to Lady Fame—a treatment identical with that which Philosophy gave Fame and Fortune in book II of the *De Consolatione*. If the ostensible unity of book III may be characterized as an exposé of Fame, that literary unity to a great extent will depend on Chaucer's concept of Fame.

In book II, prose vii, of the *De Consolatione*, Philosophy conducts a lengthy argument against the concept of Fame as a motive for human conduct. Philosophy is not concerned to present a new argument but contents herself with polishing the traditional attack on Fame as it had been delivered by Seneca[16] and Pliny.[17] Philosophy conducts her arguments through the device of *meiosis* and *ironeia*:[18]

[16] *Epistulae* 43.   [17] *Epistulae* II.8.
[18] Cf. Isidore, *Etymologiae* V: '*Famae autem nomen certi locum non habet. Quia plurimum mendax est, adjiciens multa, vel demutans de veritate: quae tamdiu uiuit quamdiu non probatur. At ubi probaueris esse cessat, exinde res nominatur: non fama.*'

Vos autem nisi ad populares auras inanesque rumores recte facere nescitis et relicta conscientiae virtutisque praestantia de alienis praemia sermunculis postulatis.

Fame here, renown which pretends to rest on good works, is really founded on popular blasts ('*populares auras*'), vain rumours ('*inanesque rumores*') and others' tittle-tattle ('*alienis sermunculis*'). The climax of Philosophy's proof culminates in the reduction of Fame to Rumour because the Latin noun contains both senses. Philosophy is naturally taking a linguistic advantage to prove her point. Chaucer's notion of Fame is not very different from that of Boethius, but it is constructed in greater detail and with characteristic subtlety. The most important satiric point to note is, that for the personification of Fame ('renown') Chaucer has impudently used the figure of Virgil's Fama ('rumour'). Chaucer's portrait of Fame derives, with minor decorations, entirely from Virgil's famous description in *Aeneid* IV.173ff. The general impression of a '*monstrum horrendum*' (*Aeneid* IV.181) had to be made less grotesque, more refined. Thus, Chaucer provided the conventional touch:

> Hir heer that oundy was and crips
> As burned gold hit schoon to see.
>
> (1386–7)

But Virgil's portrait remains central to Chaucer's allegory: (1) Fame's indefinite size; (2) her innumerable eyes, ears and tongues; (3) her family relation to Fortune (Chaucer calls her Fortune's sister)—a relation which Chaucer took from Boethius and Virgil (see *Aeneid* IV.175, '*Mobilitate viget*'). The partridge wings which grace Fame's feet (l. 1392) present some difficulty for the reader who would like to think that Chaucer was not misreading his Virgil. Servius has a long note on this passage which makes Virgil's meaning quite clear. It is tempting to think that Chaucer had some artistic purpose in making Fame's ankles partridge-feathered and that Isidore's article on *perdix* (*Etymologiae* XII. 7) influenced the poet in his choice of plumage from one of the most fraudulent of birds:

> *Nam masculus in masculum consurgit et obliuiscitur sexum libido ipsa praeceps. Adeo autem fraudulenta, ut alteri oua diripiens foueat: fraus fructum non habet . . .*

Chaucer's additions to Virgil's portrait are both delicate and pointed. Our attention at line 1383 is directed at Revelation and we are expected

to compare Fame's throne (ll. 1393ff.) with God's; to see the parallel
in the heavenly voices; to remember the manner of God's rewarding
of good and evil. In all of her ambitious activities Fame is more than
faintly blasphemous. Mr Henkin years ago wished us to see Chaucer's
Fame as a blend of Virgil and St John—a mixture of sacred and
profane.[19] But Fame does not purposely reward the good, nor do the
angels sing her praises. It is the Muses who create the 'hevenish melodye'
—and one eye should be kept on Philosophy's words in the *De
Consolatione* I prose i, when she calls the muses 'sirens'. This figure, then,
is Renown—Rumour in royal trappings. Just as Fame is declared by
Chaucer to be Fortune's sister:

> For this folk, ful wel I wiste,
> They hadde good fame ech deserved
> Although they were diversly served;
> Right as hir suster, dame Fortune,
> Is wont to serven in comune.
>
> (1544ff.)

so the presiding deity of the house of Rumour which concludes book
III is not Rumour but Aventure or Chance:

> Yet hit is founded to endure
> Whyl that hit list to Aventure
> That is the moder of tydinges,
> As the see, of welles and springes.
>
> (1981ff.)

Chaucer is scarcely original in arguing that Fame, Rumour and
Fortune are to be linked together philosophically. Such a connection
did not come about, as Dr Sypherd once suggested, through the verbal
formula 'fame and fortune'—the connection is stressed throughout the
De Consolatione by Philosophy. The mountain of ice upon which the
castle of Fame is founded is taken (as critics have noticed) from Nicole's
house of Fortune in the *Panthere d'Amours* (ll. 961ff.), a *locus* which
derives entirely from Alan's house of Fortune in the *Anticlaudianus*
VIII. 107ff.:

> *Venismes droit a la maison*
> *De Fortune l'aventureuse.*
> *Moult est la maison perilleuse,*
> *Car elle siet toute sous glace,*

[19] 'The Aprocrypha and Chaucer's *Hous of Fame*', *MLN* 56 (1941), pp. 583ff.

Qui dure quel temps que il face.
(La Panthere d'Amours 961ff.)

The conceit of a house built upon ice which continually thaws and freezes is Nicole's own happy invention. But the *significatio* was suggested by Alan's description of the setting of the house of Fortune in the *Anticlaudianus* VII.416–17:

> ... *dum flos incipit esse*
> *Explicit et florum momento fallitur etas.*

Even while the flower begins to spring, it ceases, and the lifetime of the blossoms is checked in a moment.

This is translated by Jean in the *Roman*, lines 6684ff.:

> *Si que la flor i perte son estre*
> *Sitot cum el commence a nestre.*

Naturally, Chaucer for his allegory of Fame's mountain invented new and more extensive imagery, but the substance and the durability of Fame's foundation is the same as that of Fortune's. The connecting links between the castle of Fame and the house of Aventure become clearer if it may be understood that the house of Fortune in the *Anticlaudianus* is generally implied in Chaucer's sources and the resulting Chaucerian invention. At line 1918 Chaucer places the house of Aventure in geographical relation to the palace of Fame:

> Tho saugh I stonde in a valeye
> Under the castel, faste by,
> An hous ...

In Alan, Nicole and Jean the mountain and the valley upon which the house of Fortune rests convey the notion of good and bad Fortune—prosperity and adversity. Both the *sedes Fortunae* and the *domus Fortunae* allegorize the double, contradictory nature of the goddess. The same contradictory nature is to be observed as present in the Lady Fame, renown and ill-repute. But Chaucer had already delineated that double aspect of Fame in his description of the goddess's conduct in the awarding of good and bad reputation—where her arbitrary actions implied her character. Chaucer's poetic point at this stage of the allegorization is to present that aspect of Fame which is rumour. This he does by blending Ovid's house of Rumour (*Metamorphoses* XII.39ff.) with

certain details taken from Alan's house of Fortune *via* Jean's amplification of Alan in the *Roman*. In the *Anticlaudianus* VIII.7ff., the palace
of Fortune subsides into ruin into the valley over which that prosperous
part of the dwelling has been constructed:

> Pars in monte tumet, pars altera vallis imo
> Subsidet, et casum tanquam lapsura minatur
> Fulgurat argento, gemmis scintillet, et auro
> Resplendet pars, una domus, pars altera vili
> Materie dejecta jacet; pars ipsa superbit
> Culmine sublimi, pars illa fatiscit hiatu.

One part of the house swells up onto a mountain, the other
subsides into the depths of a valley; one part of the house gleams in
silver, sparkles with gems; the other part lies sunk down in its
base substance; this part is magnificent on its towering summit,
that falls to pieces in its depth.

Alan's description of the *domus Fortunae*, as re-imagined by Jean de
Meun, is sensitively illustrated in the fifteenth-century MS. Douce 371
of the *Roman*.[20] The ruined, 'adversity' half of the palace is not the
ruin of a grand building but that of a rude, primitive dwelling made
of thatch. This is Alan's *vilis materies*.

> D'autre part sunt li mur de boe
> Qui n'ont pas espes pleine paume
> S'est toute couverte de chaume; . . .
> [il] . . . tremble toute esfraée
> Tant se sent foible et esbaée,
> Et porfundue de crevaces
> En plus de cinc cent mile places.

Alan's abstract expression 'base substance' Jean concretized into a thin
mud dwelling, weak and gaping, covered over by thatch, pierced by
innumerable holes. Alan's fundamental notion of base substance was
germane to Chaucer's allegory of Rumour, and some details of Jean's
amplification attracted his attention. The unusable details in Alan
and Jean were rejected. For example, the idea of a ruin was appropriate
to an allegorization of the physical state of adversity, but it would not
suit an allegorical treatment of Rumour. The notion of a primitive

[20] Compare Lydgate's rendering of these lines in *A Mumming at London*, lines
38-51.

dwelling was germane to Chaucer's subject, for Rumour is a low, primitive type of Fame, just as the rude, rustic dwelling is the primitive original of the palace. In the opening passage of Chaucer's *descriptio* this relationship of Rumour to Fame is partially expressed by the parallel contrast of 'mountain' to 'valley', 'castle' to 'house'. The image of a primitive dwelling which Chaucer sought, by necessity of the allegorical concept, had to be less ruinous, more substantial. The most basic, universal model of primitiveness to which Chaucer could have referred was Isidore, *Etymologiae* XV.12, in his article '*De Aedificiis Rusticis*':

> *Casa est agreste habitaculum palis atque virgultis arundinisque contextus . . . rotunda in modum furnorum.*

The suppliants at the knee of Fame beg notice of their lives and deeds (real or fictitious) in the form of Renown. The crowds of shipmen, pilgrims, pardoners and messengers who cram the house of Aventure have no such exalted ambition. They are absorbed in, and indistinguishable from, the rumours themselves. They are interested in the lowest activity of Fame, rumour. The *rumigeruli* themselves belong to the class of the common people and the meanness of the house of Aventure is suited to their 'estat' in medieval social life.

As editors have noticed, many of the features of the house of Aventure derive from Ovid's *Metamorphoses* XII. In both the castle of Fame and the house of Aventure the allegory invites us to compare the activities which characterize the suppliants for Fame and the gossip-spreading of the rumour-mongers. Although a multitude supplicates before Fame, the action is measured and orderly, as polite as the presenting of petitions to Venus in the Courts of Love. In the house of Aventure there is only confused, barbarous grasping after news of any kind, true or false. The nightmarish jumble of rumour-mongers which finally ends in a mounting, disordered heap was suggested to Chaucer by Ovid, *Metamorphoses* XII.53–5:

> *. . . Veniunt, leve vulgus, euntque*
> *Mixtaque cum veris passim commenta vagantur*
> *Milia rumorum confusaque verba volutant.*

Crowds fill the hall, shifting throngs come and go, and everywhere wander thousands of rumours, falsehoods mingled with the truth, and confused reports flit about.

Ovid's lines (44–6) earlier in the passage are the source for the final touches in Chaucer's house of Aventure (ll. 1945–50):

Innumerosque aditus ac mille foramina tectis
Addidit et nullis inclusit limina portis
Nocte dieque patet.

And eek this hous hath of entrees
As fele as leves been on trees
In somer whan they grene been.
And on the roof men may yit seen
A thosand holes and wel mo,
To leten wel the soun outgo.

Jean's description of the house of Fortune in the *Roman* probably
suggested the original notion of conflation to Chaucer:

Et profendue de crevaces
En plus de cinc cent mile places.

Jean's lines:

[il] ... tremble toute esfraée,
Tant se sent foible et esbaée.

clearly suggested the *significatio* in lines 1979–80:

For hit was sixty myle of lengthe,
Al was the timber of no strengthe ...

   In spite of the unfinished state of book III, the allegory is unified by
subject, and the narrative coherent in movement. The whole intellectual and visual progress is untroubled by unsympathetic transitions.
The entrance of the 'man of grete auctoritee' amounts to the major
transition—the most arresting turn in the *narratio* of book III—and
here the poem breaks off. Chaucer dreams himself alone in book I,
and the eagle of books II and III represents the only major character
other than the figure of the poet Chaucer. It would be reasonable to
assume that this seeming 'authority' would have proved as important
as the eagle as a guiding figure.
   The major problem for the critic is to find a unity for books I and II
in a coherent relation to book III. The plot of Guillaume de Lorris's
part of the *Roman* is basically feigned event: an *éducation amoureuse*
embellished by sententious observation through all its stages of
development of a young man and woman. The *House of Fame*, like the
Parliament, has a plot that is not a series of imitated events, but is the
equivalent of a guided tour. The plot itself is the gradual increasing

of the poet's awareness in the presence of a half-submerged philosophical
and personal problem which controls the contours of the dream-world.
In this sense the unity of the plot is strong and continuous from book I
to book III: a continuous moral journey. But why should the plot
take this precise form?

The beginning of Chaucer's moral journey is the temple of Venus
and the desert in which it stands. The general notion of such a temple
(as has been noticed) came to Chaucer from the citadel of Juno in book
I of the *Aeneid*. Virgil's passage did not provide Chaucer with any
further details. A certain narrative quality is present in both passages
but the arrangement and significance of the descriptions are totally
different. Symmetry is the key to Virgil's pattern: the presentation of
pairs of scenes. Chaucer divides his description into convenient
narrative blocks, each introduced by a variation of the formula 'tho
saugh I'—a mannerism which he had acquired in the process of translating Guillaume's description of the figures on the wall of the garden
in the *Roman* ('*Ens ou milieu je vis Haine*')—a stylistic mannerism more
pronounced in Chaucer than it had been in Guillaume.

For reasons of narrative economy, Chaucer has condensed his
Virgil after the manner common to the Middle Ages—as Simon
Chevre d'Or had done in his *Ilias*.[21] But in the narrative, as in the source
of his description, Chaucer pursues a completely original method.
Three points are important: (1) the increased emphasis on Venus;
(2) the essential quality of the action depicted differs radically from the
scenes invented by Virgil for the temple of Juno. The 'anonymous'
artist in *Aeneid* I is presented by Virgil as having painted scenes inspired
entirely from life, the real fall of Troy. Thus, the paintings on the
walls of Juno's temple contain more incidents than Homer had
described.[22] The inside of Chaucer's temple of Venus is adorned with
descriptions not so much of the destruction and refounding of Troy as
it is with Virgil's poetic version of that history. The close translation
of the opening four lines of the *Aeneid* identifies its author[23] and indicates that artifice, the poet's craft, has had an essential, inseparable part
in the evolving of the themes themselves. The figure of Virgil is one

---

[21] A. C. Friend, 'Chaucer's Version of the *Aeneid*', *Speculum* 28 (1953), pp. 317–33.
[22] Penthesilea is not part of the Homeric account as given in the *Iliad*. She is the
thematic counterpart and foreshadowing of Camilla, cf. Norton-Smith, 'Auerbach
on Literary Language', *Medium Aevum*, 36 (1967), pp. 159ff.
[23] In MS. Fairfax 16 and Bodley 638, Virgil's lines have been written by the scribe
of the text in the margins opposite lines 143ff.

of the important secondary links between books I and III, for he is to
appear with other famous pagan poets who hold up the heavy roof of
fame; (3) condensation is not the only alteration in narrative pattern
which Chaucer has made. On the contrary, he has amplified that part
of the episode in book IV in which Dido's tragic love is shown affecting
Dido herself—a part of the story which Virgil purposely avoided
treating in detail but which Ovid characteristically chose to exploit
in *Heroides* VII. In fact, the whole character of Dido has been altered
by Chaucer, as well as the interpretation of Aeneas' treatment of her.
Both views of Aeneas, the Virgilian and the Ovidian, are present in
Chaucer's legend of Dido in the *Legend of Good Women*. Of the sixty
lines which compose Dido's lament in the *House of Fame*, only a half
dozen lines, if that many, have any parallel in Virgil. For example,

> For through yow is my name lorn,
> And alle myn actes red and songe
> Over al this lond on euery tonge.
>
> (346ff.)

derive from Virgil's:

> . . . *te propter eundem*
> *Extinctus pudor, et, qua sola sidera adibam,*
> *Fama prior.*
>
> (*Aeneid* IV.321ff.)

but the Virgilian passage is only a point of departure for Chaucer's
lines. 'Name', 'reputation', represent Virgil's *pudor* but Chaucer has
added and subtracted. He has added what is important for this poem—
that henceforth all of Dido's acts (public and private) will become the
themes of ballad-mongers; and, perhaps more important, taken away
the phrase 'I have lost . . . that former Fame, by which alone I was
winning a title to the stars'. Chaucer exonerates Dido from the motive
of seeking after Fame in order to make her entirely sympathetic and
to create an antithesis between Love and Fame which is not in Virgil.[24]

Chaucer's treatment of Dido's character and situation, then, contrasts sharply with that of Virgil or Ovid. Virgil's Dido is a sombre,
restrained figure who faces her misfortune and the moral and political
consequences. Ovid's queen possesses no *magnanimitas* but instead

---

[24] In Virgil the antithesis is between Aeneas' proper concern for 'Renown' and
Dido's loss of 'Fame' through 'Sensuality', cf. Mercury's rebuke in book IV.272ff.
Boccaccio, too, was aware of this interpretation.

retains a cruel illusion of hope based on persisting sexual fantasies. Yet both such dissimilar women resemble each other in that neither possess introspective, analytic temperaments. They are not interested in the kind of love which has been offered them and which they have accepted.[25] On the other hand, Chaucer's Dido shows such an interest in the kind of love from which she is suffering. In lines 300–10 she analyses the causes of infidelity in men. Here the theme of Fame is introduced into book I—Fame which destroys human love:

> ... of oon he wold have fame
> In magnifying of his name,
> Another for 'frendship', seith he,
> And yet ther shal the thridde be,
> That shal be taken for delyt,
> Lo, or for singular profyt.

The connection between the three motives, Renown, Friendship and Pleasure is contained in the seeming afterthought 'singular profyt', a concept implicated in the notion of erotic love which Chaucer had criticized in the *Parliament* and contrasted there with the *profyt comune* of Nature. 'Seith he' is as satiric as the famous *dicit* of Horace, 'that's what he says'. The relation between Fame and *profyt singular* is a traditional one and Chaucer need not have looked further than the *De Consolatione* to have seen that Fame, Love and Fortune are there represented by Philosophy as related forms of 'private advantage'. But Chaucer means to emphasize not only the relation of Love to Fame in human life, he wishes to stress the moral relation of the poet to his theme. Chaucer, Jove's eagle tells us in book II, has been in the service of Venus, not as a lover, but as her poet:

> ... thou so longe trewely
> Hast served so ententifly
> His blinde nevew Cupido
> And fair Venus, goddesse, also.
> To make bokes, songes, dytees
> ... in reverence

[25] A later, French, Dido begins to show an analytic turn of mind, cf. *Roman d'Eneas* 1823ff.:

> *Nos senton molt diversement:*
> *Je muir d'amour, il ne s'en sent,*
> *Il est en pais, jo ai les mals;*
> *Quant ne senton comunalment.*

> Of Loue and of his seruants eke,
> That have his servise soght and seke,
> And peynest thee to preyse his art,
> Although thou haddest never part.
>
> (615ff.)

Whatever comes to Chaucer's eye in his allegory, the relation of Chaucer to his material is at once moral and artistic. The bond between Love and Fame or Love in the service of Fame, explicit in Dido's soliloquy and implicit in Chaucer's recasting of *Aeneid* IV, is developed in book III in the petition of the sixth company before the goddess in lines 1731ff. These petitioners have been idle in the service of Love during their lifetimes yet now they wish to appear active and successful. At Fame's command they are:

> Yit lat us to the peple seme
> Swiche as the world may of us deme
> That wimmen loven us for wood.

The strongest unity which embraces books I and III is, in the nature of the allegorical mode chosen, bodied forth in the passages of *ekphrasis*, in the descriptions of the palace of Fame and the temple of Venus. Just as a contrast is intended in the *Parliament* between the exotic, metallic artifice of Venus' temple and the 'hille of floures' upon which Nature sits:

> Of braunches were hir halles and hir boures
> Ywrought after hir craft and hir mesure;
>
> (*Parliament*, 304–5)

Chaucer in the *House of Fame* implies certain parallels between Venus and Fame in the descriptions of their dwellings. The underlying connection in the *significatio* is deception and distortion. Chaucer begins book I inside the temple of Venus where the poet notices first the substance of the temple. It is made entirely of glass. There is no doubt that Lydgate took this detail for his *Temple of Glass*, but for the less complex purpose of his own poem did not take Chaucer's *significatio*.[26] The significance which Chaucer intended for glass is that it is a substance which is brittle, easily broken. Lydgate employs just this quality for glass in the *Fall of Princes* V.588ff.:

[26] For Lydgate's meaning, cf. J. Norton-Smith, *Lydgate: Poems*, Oxford (1968), pp. 176–9.

> Fortunis favours be maad—who loke wel,
> Of brotel glas rather than of stel.

The substance of the temple of Venus allegorizes the brittle, insubstantial kind of love which Aeneas offers Dido, a love easily made and easily broken, which appears solid, yet is false and breakable.[27] This theme of the deceptive stability of sexual love is continued by *exclamatio* and *sententia* at lines 265-6:

> Allas! what harm doth apparence
> Whan hit is fals in existence!

to which Chaucer adds in line 272 the famous proverb of Alan of Lille: *Non teneas aurum totum quod splendet ut aurum*. The allegorical qualities reinforce Chaucer's interpretation of *Aeneid* IV: a story of tragic, erotic love. The temple of Venus gives the appearance of being solid, rich and ornamented. In reality it is an unsound, fragile structure. Parallels with the temple of Venus and the palace of Fame are similarly treated poetically in terms of substance and decoration. Just as Venus' temple is made of glass, so the palace of Fame is fashioned entirely of beryl 'that shoon ful lighter than a glas'. The *significatio* is developed in lines 1288ff.:

> These walles of beryle
> That shoon ful lighter than a glas
> And made wel more than hit was
> To semen, euery thing, y-wis,
> As kynde of thing of Fames is.

That is, appropriate to the nature of Fame, the beryl magnifies, makes everything look larger. Chaucer probably took this significance from a common tradition as reflected in Marbodus' *De Gemmis*[28] where we find under '*De Beryllo*' that '. . . et se portantem perhibetur magnificare'. Chaucer is here playing on the sense of *magnificare*, 'to glorify'. The linking theme of deceptive appearance and reality, common to the natures of Love and Fame, is continued in Chaucer's account of

---

[27] Cf. Henryson, *The Testament of Cresseid*, lines 568ff., in a series of short similes which characterize unsteadfast love:

> Because I knaw the greit unstabilnes,
> Brukkill as glas, vnto my self I say,
> Traisting in uther als greit unfaithfulnes;

For the other kind of love, constant true affection, 'ay love of stiel', cf. *Troilus* IV.323ff.

[28] Migne, *PL* 171, col. 1747.

the decoration of the castle of Fame. We need only glance at the
gold-plating half a foot thick (ll. 1341ff.) which parallels the seeming
richness of the temple of Venus. This is gold, presumably patronal
gold, which is to prove to Chaucer as thin as a Venetian ducat.[29]
Similarly, the gate to Fame's castle appears well carved, but in reality
artistry has not contributed much to its design:

> And yit hit was by aventure
> Ywrought, as often, as by cure.
> (1297–8)

The façade of Fame's castle, ornamented excessively with musicians,
poets and magicians, culminates at lines 1280ff., with the figure of
'Colle tregetour', Colle the sleight-of-hand artist, who, as an exemplary
figure of deception, carries a windmill under a walnut shell.

The rewards of Love and Fame are comparably empty. The poets
of the pagan world who sought Fame by glorifying certain cities,
peoples or gods, stand upon appropriate pillars, holding up upon their
shoulders the very Fame which they have created in their poems. The
poets are, of course, imitating their sovereign mistress who bears upon
her shoulders the huge ensigns and renowns of Alexander and Hercules.
This imagery of appropriate activity Chaucer possibly developed from
Dante, *Purgatorio* X. In this canto, the group who are expiating the sin
of Vainglory appear, bent low under stones. In lines 130ff., Dante
compares them to corbels which hold up a roof:

> *Come per sostentar solaio o tetto*
> *Per mensola talvolta una figura*
> *Si vede giunger le ginocchia al petto,*

As to support ceiling or roof is sometimes seen for corbel, a
figure joining knees to breast.

In Chaucer the architectural detail is changed, and the force of the
significatio shifted. In Dante the cold, inhuman stone symbolized the
sin of Pride (the mother sin of Vainglory). Chaucer, treating Fame in
particular rather than Pride in general, shifts the emphasis from Pride
to the actual created Fame itself. The weight of expiating a fault has
given way to a more exalting aspect of literary glory. These are Fame's
poets.

The desert into which Chaucer steps from the temple of Venus in

---

[29] Lines 1347ff.

book I allegorizes the reward of sexual love. Just as the garden in the Middle Ages became a formula, the *locus amoenus*, a universal image for fecund, pleasing nature, the desert became the symbol of sterile, unusable nature. Isidore, *Etymologiae* XIV.8 has an account of the *deserta* as well as the *locus amoenus* because they both have become conventional *loci*. Chaucer, in fact, need not have had Dante's use of the desert *topos* (*Inferno* XIV) directly in mind, although the *significatio* (sand: sterility) is shared by both passages. The main source of the *significatio* is Lucan's *Pharsalia* IX.431ff.—the literary place to which Dante refers in canto XIV in the phrase 'the sands which Cato trod'. Lucan describes in a typical geographical excursus the *deserta Libyae*.[30] His description ends:

> . . . *Natura deside torpet,*
> *Orbis et inmotis annum non sentit harenis.*

Nature is inactive, the lifeless expanse, with sands that are never ploughed, is unconscious of the seasons.

The same contrast, between the fullness of Nature and the sterility, the total absence of Nature, is made in Genius' long speech in the *Roman* ll.19640ff.:

> *Cil que si leur pechiez enfume*
> *Par leur orgueil qui les desreie*
> *Qu'ils dispisent la dreite reie*
> *D'ou champ bel e plantereus,*
> *E vont com malereuses*
> *Arer en la terre deserte*
> *Ou leur semence vait a perte.*

A similar contrast is made by Deschamps in a poem which Chaucer almost certainly never read, *Le Lay du Désert d'Amours*.[31] In this poem a contrast is made between the days of glory and satisfaction in love (ll. 99–120) and middle age when favour is lost, when Venus does not celebrate a second May or April. The desert here does not symbolize middle age, but what life has become when it is unrelieved by a single impulse of constant, mutual love. This desert allegorizes loneliness

[30] For Chaucer's overt reference to the Libyan desert see *House of Fame*, lines 486ff.:

> For all the feld nas but of sond
> As small as man may see yet lye
> In the desert of Libye;

[31] Eustache Deschamps, *Oeuvres*, SATF, vol. 2, pp. 182ff.

which has been the result of a misspent youth, of indulging in erotic
love for its own circumscribed end. It is conveniently the opposite
of the fertile garden of delight in the *Roman*. At line 236, the woman
once worthy to have been called the daughter of Venus, punning on the
sb. *dessert*, 'reward', and *desert*, warns the reader:

> *Ne venez pas en ce desert*
> *Ou il n'a fueille, ne boys verts,*
> *Herbe, fleur, fruit, n'autre verdure,*
> *Tout chant d'oisel y ert desert;*
> *Noif, gresil, et toute foidure*
> *Esté fault la, l'yvers y dure*
> *En tout temps; Celle le dessert*
> *Qui Amour en jeunesse sert*
> *Loyaument; ce desert procure*
> *Ou je me treuve d'aventure.*
> *Ma folie en ce leiu m'appert:*
> *Li liens est ses de sa Nature*
> *Ou venir ne voy creature*
> *Fors ceuls que fol amour aert.*

This, then, is the reward of erotic love: in no way distinct from that
which Venus had offered in the *Parliament*—*profyt singular*, sterility. In
the *House of Fame* this 'desert of Libye' allegorizes the kind of love
which Aeneas offers to Dido, a love which results in Dido's suicide,
in death not life. The environment and its implied significance strikes
terror in the soul of Chaucer. Book I ends with a serious prayer for
immediate deliverance.

Book II, the most humorous, scientific, lively book, contains the
antidote to both Fame and Love. The position of book II is pivotal,
referring back to book I and forward to book III. It foreshadows the
missing resolution of the poem (presumably contained in the words
of the 'man of grete auctoritee'), just as the summary of what Scipio
sees in his celestial journey in the preface of the *Parliament*, lines 51ff.,
foreshadows the effect of the judgment of Nature in her decree of
common advantage and natural personal and social harmony. The
ebullient *ordo naturalis*, the more natural, freer style of the *House of
Fame* does not eliminate the topics of the 'artificial style', it merely
allows the poet to rearrange the order in which they may appear.
Thus, the summary of Scipio's vision of an harmonious universe is
placed in the *praefatio* in the *Parliament*. In the *House of Fame* a similar

account of a vision of a well-ordered universe occupies the central portion of the *narratio* in book II.

The narrative of book II is an expansion of a favourite medieval literary theme: the journey beyond. Its pagan dimension unfolds in book VI of the *Aeneid*, and the origin of the Christian dimension is to be seen in Cicero's *Somnium Scipionis*. The *topos* was old before Dante used it in the *Divina Commedia*, having been developed by Martianus Capella as a framework fable in the first book of his *De Nuptiis Philologiae et Mercurii*, by Bernardus Silvestris in book II of the *De Mundi Universitate*, and by Alan in the fourth, fifth and sixth books of his *Anticlaudianus*. Chaucer need not have imitated any one of these poets, and, in fact, he borrows from more than one of them. Chaucer pursues his own aims and provides his own inventions. What Chaucer sees on his journey and what he learns differs from what either Martianus Capella, Dante, Bernardus Silvestris or Alan wished to teach. That such a journey was a powerful moral lesson may be seen from Lydgate's use of the theme in *Reson and Sensualytee* (a partial translation of *Les Echeques Amoureux*), lines 941ff. The spirit and phraseology of the Lydgatian passage often recalls the *House of Fame*. In the interview between the poet and Nature (in which Lydgate is roused up from sleep and idleness), Nature commands the poet:

> ... goo for to visite
> Rounde this worlde in lengthe and brede,
> And consider, and take good hede
> If ther fayle in my wirkynge
> Of fairnes any thinge.
> Or of beaute ther wanteth ought
> And of wyssdom that may be sought—
> To fyn, that thou maist comprehende
> The mater, and thy self amende,
> To preyse the Lord eternal
> The which made and caused al ...
>
> (519ff.)

Thus, the poet sees in his tour of the world the fullness and usefulness of God's creation:

> And some [rivers] also men myghte see
> Flowying fro the salte see,
> Some so myghty and so large
> To bere a gret ship or barge,

> The which, in many sondry wise
> Serveden for marchaundyse,
> And wern also ful profitable,
> And unto manne right vayllable.

Lydgate after his fashion goes on for another twenty lines to list the plains, woods, meadows and beasts—all the fecund, useful nature which Chaucer had seen so clearly from the eagle's claws:

> And I adoun gan loken tho
> And beheld feldes and plaines,
> And now hilles and now mountaines,
> Now valeys and now forestes,
> And now, unethes, grete bestes;
> Now riveres, now citees,
> Now tounes, and now grete trees,
> Now shippes sailinge in the see.
>   (*House of Fame* 896ff.)

The spirit and rhythm of Chaucer's catalogue of plenitude, so different from the 'little speck of earth' which Scipio and Dante had seen, derives from Bernardus Silvestris's *De Mundi Universitate* II prose i. 51ff.:

> *Terra vides quo modo ex elementis fecunditate concepta nunc fluviis, nunc graminibus, nunc silvis comantibus hilarescit. Amphitritae limitibus circumplexa victum animantibus de medio subministrat. Pars frugibus, pars virescit arboribus, pars odoramentis aspirat . . . Quodque illud et Oceanum in plurimas distraxerim sectiones, regionibus, provisum est, ut ad eas navali evectione necessaria commearent.*

Poetic catalogues of various objects in nature were made fashionable by Ovid's catalogue of terrestial life in *Metamorphoses* II.15ff. included in the description of the orbs engraved on the door of the palace of the Sun:

> *Terra viros, urbesque gerit, silvasque, ferasque*
> *Fluminaque, et nymphas, et caetera numina ruris.*

The most important transitions in the narrative of book II, occurring at lines 888 and 925, have been imitated from Dante, *Paradiso* XXII.19 and 128—in Chaucer's words 'Now see . . . yond adoun', and 'Now turn upward thy face'. Dante is being prepared by Beatrice for his meeting with the triumphal hosts in the eighth sphere. To this purpose

she bids him strengthen his heart by recollecting his experiences in
the course of his heavenly journey up to this point; and by gazing back
to the very beginning of the journey she bids him realize how far he
has left the earthly world behind:

> Col viso ritornai per tutte e quande
> Le sette spere, e vidi questo globo
> Tal ch'io sorrisi del suo vil sembiante
> E quel consiglio per migliore approbo
> Che l'ha per meno . . .

With my sight I turned back through all and each of the seven
spheres, and saw this globe, such that I smile at its sorry semblance;
and that counsel I approve best which holdeth it for least.

The lesson which Dante learns—to despise earthly things—is much
the same lesson as that which Scipio had received from his famous
ancestor. Philosophy had so instructed Boethius. But Chaucer's earth
is not quite the same 'littel erthe'. Nor does Chaucer's upward glance
at the heavenly universe agree with Dante's. Instead of gazing up at
the figure of St Benedict, advocate of the contemplative life, Chaucer
gazes up at a heavenly order and fullness such as Nature and Phronesis
had seen in the *Anticlaudianus*, and such as Urania had shown Nature
in the *De Mundi Universitate*. Chaucer's wonder at the vision causes
him to exclaim:

> O god, quod I, that made Adam,
> Moche is thy myght and thy noblesse!
> (970-1)

Chaucer's admiration at the works of God is primarily caused by the
dual aspect of Nature, which is both full and ordered according to the
laws of God and Nature his *vicaire:*

> Tho gan I loken under me
> And beheld the eyrish bestes,
> Cloudes, mistes and tempestes,
> Snowes, hailes, reines, windes,
> And th' engendring in hir kindes . . .
> (964-8)

If Venus and Fame are the goddesses of distortion and magnification,
Nature is the goddess of things as they really are. Book II emphasizes

the world of things in their proper order and size, as devised by God
and executed by Nature. As the eagle diligently, in plain, unadorned
language, teaches Chaucer:[32]

> That every river to the see
> Enclyned is to go, by kinde.
> And by these skilles, as I finde,
> Hath fish dwellinge in flood and see,
> And trees eek in erthe be.
> Thus, euery thing, by this resoun
> Hath his propre mansioun,
> To which hit seketh to repaire
> As ther hit shulde not apaire.
>
> (*House of Fame* 1240ff.)

The full, ordered world of Nature is meant to contrast with the sterile
deceptive world of Venus in book I. Chaucer contrasts the same features
of Venus and Nature in the *Parliament*. In this way, books I and II are
related through the contrast of sexual love with the undistorted world
of Nature. If Chaucer made Fame agree with Venus, it is because both
'goddesses' offer appearance not reality. It is this relation between
Nature and Fame which connects books II and III. That this is the way
Chaucer intends to direct us is made unambiguously clear by the seventh
metre of book II of the *De Consolatione*. This metre sums up Philosophy's case against Fame:

> *Quicumque solam mente praecipiti petit,*
> *Sumumque credit gloriam,*
> *Late patentes aetheris cernat plagas,*
> *Arctumque terrarum situm:*
> *Brevem replere non valentis ambitum*
> *Pudebit aucti nominis.*

In Chaucer's translation:

Who-so that with over-throwing thought only seketh glorie of
fame, and weneth it be soveregn good: lat him loken upon the
brod shewing contrees of hevene, and upon the streite site of this
erthe, and he shal ben ashamed of the encrees of his name.

[32] Chaucer here echoes Jean in the *Roman* 17940ff.:
> *Li peisson, qui leur fleuve sivent,*
> *Si come il est dreitz e raisons,*
> *Car ce sont leur propres maisons . .*

Philosophy wished to impress Boethius with the smallness of the earth compared with heaven: an argument of ever-diminishing distance, in which Fame finally appears as small and weak as human breath itself. Chaucer who had been shown this comparison in book II.906ff., 'all the world . . . no more semed than a prikke . . .' wished also to show that a positive doctrine of natural, worldly good essential to the doctrine of plenitude must satisfactorily answer not only the selfish, sterile arguments of Venus, but must answer the uncertain, deceiving self-interest of Fame. The *Parliament* answers Venus by explaining to us Nature. The *House of Fame* was mainly intended to answer the blandishments of Fame. But the poem in its unfinished form does no more than provide the evidence for Chaucer's reply to Fame. In book II Chaucer has gone beyond any of the recognized 'authorities' on the subject. He could not make his man of 'auctoritee' any historically verifiable personage. Boethius, 'that blessed soul which exposes the deceptive world to any one who gives ear to him', had not really solved the problem of Fame. He had turned his back on Renown as he had done on Love and Fortune—as he had done on all worldly things. Alan, in *Anticlaudianus* VII, could not make his mind up about Fame. As Professor Lewis pointed out long ago, Alan was a poet who assumed rather than created a state of philosophical peace.[33] Unlike the scribe of MS. Fairfax 16 who left three blank leaves after line 2158, I think we have all of Chaucer's most puzzling poem. We must try to establish Chaucer's meaning in so far as we can. In the words of Plato which Philosophy quotes to Boethius, words which surely lie behind the eagle's discourse:

Nedes the wordes mosten be cosines to the thinges to which they speken.

[33] C. S. Lewis, *The Allegory of Love*, p. 105.

CHAPTER FOUR

The Legend of Good Women

The formal disposition of the *Legend of Good Women* insists upon the absolute centrality of the narrator as actual and potential author-figure, this manifest and 'autobiographical' emphasis in turn presenting the 'self-conscious reader' with a certain polarization of the author's interests and poetic technique. A set of deliberate contrasts emerges as the narration develops: a kind of highly-conscious reflection of related yet contrasting attitudes, namely: (1) the rival claims of 'assay' ('preve' *per experientiam*) and literary authority ('olde storie'); (2) the author's instinctive sympathy with certain areas of his original literary material (in the main Ovidian), modified by the poet's 'subversion' of his material, using *suppressio veri* and new 'inventions' to create a recognizable mode of poetic irony; (3) the author's acknowledged intense personal involvement with the Alceste-figure as muse, contrasted with the author's amusing and ironical portrait of Amors as a literary critic; (4) the simple, quasi-religious origin of the author's creative impulse (and devotional behaviour) interacting with the poet's literary sophistication in openly and ironically manipulating the 'religious' structure of the *Legenda Aurea* type of collection. All these 'polarities' are generated by two 'true' relationships connected with the influential figure of Alceste—that of the poet Chaucer and the queen as muse, and Amors' marriage with his queen—one relationship literary and cliental, the other natural and marital. Whatever ironies are created by the poem, the author's total dependence on the queenly muse[1] and Amors' entire love for his royal wife, these two parallel and independent relationships are never touched or changed by the exchanges in the *Prologue* or the subsequent literary or moral concerns

[1] Lines 84–96 (F version only) are a remarkable account of the poet's relation with a royal figure. The imagery, figuring the lady as muse (Boccaccio, *Il Filostrato* I.2,4,5) and the poet as musical instrument (Cicero, *De Oratore* 3.57.216) has been almost entirely ignored. This will be discussed later in the chapter.

of the *vitae*. The poem's true origin lies in that elusive royal figure, a figure which is partially a transfiguration of real experience based on Anne of Bohemia[2] in her intercessorial role of *advocatus clementiae* in the dispute between the king and the city of London on 29 August 1392,[3] and partially a mythopoeic[4] creation pre-dating the historical present of the late fourteenth-century literary cults and fashions:

> Ne I not who serveth leef, ne who the flour.
> Wel browken they her service or labour;
> For this thing is al of another tonne,
> Of olde storye, er swich stryf was begonne.
>
> (193–6)

This is why the so-called G version of the *Prologue* is so profoundly unsatisfactory. As a version necessarily dependent on the queen's sudden death in June 1394, Chaucer's revamping removes a whole set of these closely-related polarities, and in so removing the reality-based portion of the queen-figure, the poet's personal devotion to his 'muse', all the quasi-religious terminology and emotions,[5] it effectively excises the positive poles in the initiating artistic tension, leaving the negative and 'ironic' responses intact and unrelated.[6]

If this disturbing of the delicate balance of artistic pressures and attitudes were not enough, the G version robs the poem of any effective formal means for bringing the work to an imaginable satisfactory conclusion. For in the F version there are two important prefigurings of a possible shape of the formal means for ending the work: (1)

[2] She came of a literary family with long traditions of patronage. Her poet uncle, Wenzel of Luxemburg, was a patron of Eustache Deschamps; Anne's father, the emperor, had been a patron of Petrarch. Her grandfather was a patron of Guillaume de Machaut. The family's literary interests, then, were very close to Chaucer's. It we accept the latest identification of the author of the *Cuckoo and the Nightingale* or as we now must call it, the *Boke of Cupide*, then this poem contains a reference to Anne in residence at her royal manor at Woodstock between the years 1384 and 1391.

[3] Cf. Richard de Maidstone's poem in Latin elegiacs on the occasion (ed. T. Wright, *Political Songs and Poems*, vol. I, pp. 282–300). There is a translation of passages from the *Concordia* in E. Rickert, *Chaucer's World*, pp. 35ff.

[4] This is perhaps preferable to 'mythological' in that Chaucer's aetiological myth of Alceste as daisy is unique, in spite of the attribution to Agathon.

[5] The key words are 'honouren' (27), 'feyth', 'ful credence' (31), 'deuotion' (39), 'service' (81–2).

[6] Burrow's observations (*Ricardian Poetry*, p. 105) would seem to be based on a reading of the G version alone.

ironically, the queen's penance would be a hard one for a literary man, that is, to spend the greater part of a lifetime composing interminable *legendae*. This unlimited and unreasonable imposition (ll. 481–90) is modified and supplanted by Amors' final charge[7] in lines 554–62. His penance allows for the penitent's alteration of persons and numbers of worthy women ('as the lest'), and directs the poet's attention towards the ladies named in his own *balade*, indicating an acceptable limitation of nineteen *vitae* at the outside;[8] (2) in the F version the author's engagement on actually writing the *legendae* takes place within the dream (ll. 578–9).[9] Thus, the conclusion of the poem may be imagined to take the form of some variation on 'the awakening device', so essential to the conclusions of all types of dream-poem[10]—and the reader knows that a dream cannot last the rest of one's life. Now, in the G version there is no modification of the queen's extravagant demand ('I charge the no more', line 541), and the author's penitential period of composition, his submission, begins after he has woken up (ll. 544–5). Thus, the reader no longer has any rhetorical expectation of how the poem may end or what it might include.[11] The only end which can be imagined for the G version is fictional or real boredom, exhaustion or death[12] or merely a state of being 'unfinished'. Real boredom was what Lydgate was to postulate some thirty-five years later when he wrote the *Prologue* to the *Fall of Princes* I.333ff. The G version gains for the reader nothing more than a certain increase in ironical material—the inclusion of further information and gossip

---

[7] Amors' modifications partially derive from the queen's pleasure, cf. line 437 'as ye wol avyse'.

[8] According to Chaucer's reckoning (F 283, G 186).

[9] Burrow, *op. cit.*, p. 153, *n*.51 says: 'In the F version there is no dream.' Yet he says (p. 38), 'In pseudo-dream poems, there is the pseudo-dreamer—in *Confessio Amantis* and the F version of Chaucer's *Legend*.' The F version, fictionally, is set within a type of dream convention, cf. F 209–10.

[10] Cf. J. Norton-Smith, *James I of Scotland: The Kingis Quair*, Oxford (1971), pp. 79–80.

[11] Further, in the G version Amors cannot direct the poet's attention to his own *balade* for that inset lyric has been taken away from the author-figure and given to the ladies of Alceste's entourage.

[12] Cf. R. W. Frank, 'The Legend in the *Legend of Good Women*', *Chaucer Review* I (1966), pp. 110ff. This article notes the presence of typical genuine Chaucerian interests and styles but fails to appreciate the formal difficulties created by the G version's revising. Lydgate's remark (and similar later conjectures) may well prove 'myths', but this does not *prove* that Chaucer actually did not weary of his poetic task. The G version removes any fictional means for ending the poem, short of merely stopping and leaving the work unfinished.

about the poet Geoffrey and more of Amors' literary *nugae*. While the poem's public artistic origin (perhaps even pre-origin) in the famous passage in *Troilus* V.1772–8 is preserved, its precise personal origin in the medieval system of patronage disappears without a trace.[13]

Had we lost the knowledge of this single relationship we would have been no poorer in our understanding of the complex nature of the relation of client to patron in England in the fourteenth century. The documentation for an informed view of this artistic situation simply does not exist, nor does it seem that the period troubled itself

---

[13] Another important element which disappears in the G version is the obliquely insinuated philosophical and normative background to the extremes of amatory behaviour to be subjected to self-conscious literary manipulation in the writing of the legends of Cupid's martyrs. This underlying area of the poet's even-tempered common sense is indicated in the description of the temperate pre-sleep landscape. The relation of pre-sleep ambiance to the significance of the dream-poem is vitally important, even in a dream-poem which is more 'impure' allegorically or more Froissartian and social in emphasis than the more 'philosophically' oriented dream modes of the *Parliament*, the *House of Fame* or aspects of the *Book of the Duchess*. Lines 153–74 in the F text describing the natural yet at the same time morally-guided conduct of the bird celebrants as they participate in the poet's annual ritual of daisy-observance give us some idea of the sophisticated moderation which reigns at the heart of the poet's various, often ironic, literary concerns. The importance of moderation and 'the mean' to 'ruled Curteyse' ('the code of civilized behaviour which rules and is ruled'—the phrase is only paralleled in ME by Hoccleve in *La Male Regle*, line 70, 'reuled reform') is made clear by the linguistic discussion of the sb. 'innocence' in lines 163–5. Skeat offered the following explanation of the passage: '. . . the poet does not approve of immodesty or weakness, because in all things the chief virtue is moderation or the "golden mean". Beauty should be neither too yielding nor too pitiless.' I cannot see that 'beauty' is the subject of this passage. Chaucer's emphasis falls on moral conduct in general, 'their' ('hir') mutual conduct. Specifically, the discussion dwells on the meaning of 'innocence'. It seems to me that Chaucer is saying that he does not think of *innocence* as 'want of good sense', 'foolishness' (*folie*, v. ME *innocence*=*imprudentia*, *Legend of Good Women* 1254) or as a conscious application of 'misplaced compassion' (*fals pitee*, v. ME *innocence*='forbearance')—that is, where either self-forgiveness or forgiveness of others' faults is based on an unjustified use of uncritical compassion to excuse misconduct. The phrase 'as Etyk seith' has been misconstrued. Chaucer merely notes 'as moral philosophy instructs'. The singular noun is regularly used in this sense in Latin and ME (cf. Gower, *Confessio Amantis* VII.1651). Robinson's note is misleading. A medieval reader would have thought of Aristotle in this context (as Skeat did) rather than of a minute (and mistranslated) phrase in the *Polycraticus*. Cf. Lydgate, *Pilgrimage of the Life of Man*, line 11868: 'Go red Ethikes, where thou shalt se . . . Vertu set ay in myd place.' See Appendix, pp. 252–6 for a discussion of 'the mean' and 'moderation' in Chaucer's verse.

to provide any useful record of it. If extensive vernacular correspondence took place (apart from certain exceptional instances, e.g. the Paston letters or the letters of Margaret of Anjou) they were not preserved. Even in the surviving collections or individual items the forms are rigidly formulaic and the insights and sentiments expressed therein of a severely practical, limited nature. There is little which may be described as 'introspective' or resembling an extensive confiding of thoughts or feelings. In this respect the second half of the twentieth century closely mirrors the fourteenth. In the light of John Shirley's unfailing interest in Chaucer in his social context, we will look in vain for his comments on the court origin of the *Legend*. It is difficult to believe that he would have been wholly ignorant of its existence.[14] Part of this lack of information is artistically deliberate rather than socially inevitable or historically accidental. Chaucer conceals from the reader what has no place in the poem: the 'actuality' behind the work of art. What is important for the formal structure he reveals: the positive creative impulse for the poet's endeavour, tempered no doubt by the natural scepticism of his imaginative response to the patronal suggestion. Perhaps more important, he emphasizes the author's genuine dependence on Anne as more than a mere patroness, or as a patroness of a single work. She is imaged forth as a mortal divinity 'in this werk and in my sorowes alle'. The sb. 'sorowes' has a double emphasis. In one sense it reaches out into the semantic area of personal disturbance, connecting with the unspecified melancholy of line 50, where the sight of the natural daisy performs for the poet a parallel symbolic comforting:[15] 'softneth al my sorwe.' In the immediate context of Chaucer's apostrophe to Alceste, 'sorowes' refers to his other literary ventures,[16] the pl. sb. here acting as a calque on the Latin usage *curae* signifying 'literary labours', 'writings'.[17]

[14] Cf. Bodley MS. Ashmole 59, folio 38b. Shirley, in an introductory rubric to his own poem, includes a bare note of Chaucer's authorship of the *Legend*.

[15] See the use of 'comfort' in *Legend of Good Women*, lines 278–9 (F): 'For nadde comfort ben of hire presence, I hadde ben ded, withouten any defence.' A popular name for the daisy in OF was *petit comfort*, cf. Lydgate, *Temple of Glass* (*GS version), line 406. Cf. Sir John Clanvowe, the *Boke of Cupide*, lines 241–5 for the 'healing', 'comforting' aspect of the daisy, extended from its medicinal use in the Middle Ages.

[16] In view of what we know about the chronology of later Chaucerian works, and in spite of our very inexact knowledge of dates, this almost certainly would refer to the *Canterbury Tales*.

[17] This unique application of the sb. in Chaucer and in ME is not recorded by *OED*. The use (imitating Greek *meléte*) is reasonably common in classical Latin

Mr Burrow has recently reminded us of the prevailing lightness of style in the *Legend*, its 'chamber-music', 'sophistication', 'the manner of the *dit amoreux* with its superficial use of allegories'.[18] This may appear to be the prevailing mode of composition (I should have thought more like Froissart or Deschamps in grace and flexibility than the deliberate and predictable Machaut), but this new Chaucerian-Gallic sophistication accommodates a variety of alterations of style and textures. At least three crucial passages show a seriousness of tone, strength of continuous syntactical nervousness, and density of imagery and allusion, which, if taken in isolation, would suggest a Chaucerian preoccupation with 'neo-classical' diction. I refer, of course to the Alceste-apostrophe (ll. 84–96), the apostrophe to Virgil (ll. 924–7) merging into the narrative as far as line 953, and the apostrophe to the Creator, '*Deus dator formarum*' (ll. 2228–43). These passages are authorial interventions not addressed to the reader, conveying to the audience deep concern, personal, literary and philosophical—in that order of presentation.

In the Alceste-apostrophe (ll. 84–96) the change in style from the light, graceful *narratio* which precedes it is immediately obvious. This special quality is accentuated by the dramatic and abrupt change in pronoun in line 96 (unaccompanied by vocative positioning, interjections or appositional epithets), and the deliberate method of a return to the narrative sequence by digressing retrospectively to the exordium discussion of authority and experience, thereby isolating lines 84–96 from the main narrative continuity by means of a separating verse paragraph (ll. 97–102). The accompanying rhythmical alteration in these lines is unmistakable too. The accenting becomes weightier, pace and stress grow slower, shedding the lighter movement of the lines before. The decorative elaborating of the 'harvesting metaphor' of lines 70–6 gives way to an Italian invocatory concern with poetic inspiration. This concern is introduced through imagery which recalls addresses to the Blessed Virgin.[19] The Boccaccio-inspired assimilation of the lady to the function of muse (this is unclassical, although Propertius once is impudent enough to say so: '*non haec mihi cantat Apollo*/

---

[18] *Op. cit.* pp. 49–50.
[19] See *Il Filostrato*, l. 2 *passim*; for the phrase 'verray light' compare Chaucer's *ABC*, line 105.

---

verse, and occurs in the Latin verse of Chaucer's day, cf. de Maidstone's *Concordia*, line 17: '*Parce precor curae, parcere debet amor.*'

ingenium nobis ipsa puella facit'[20]) has been reworked from the invocatory stanzas to *Il Filostrato* I, stanzas which Chaucer had discarded as
unsuitable for his *Troilus.*[21] Boccaccio's amatory emphasis has been
displaced by an increased sense of dominating, august, feminine
abstraction—'Maystresse' recalls Boethius' address to Philosophy (*De
Consolatione* I prose iii), 'O Maystresse of alle vertues', rather than any
converse with 'wommanly creature'. As the syntactical period enlarges, the Italian literary concerns are modified by a long, complex
simile in which the poet's soul ('hert') becomes a mere instrument
obedient to the musician-muse's masterly fingering. Now, while this
passivity and human subordination reflect classical ideas of inspiration,[22] the comparison of the poet or the innermost being of the poet
to a musical instrument is alien to classical Latin literature. References
to skilful performance on a stringed instrument (with concrete application, or metaphoric of poetic composition) usually employ the general
sb. *digitus*, 'playing', where the emphasis seems to fall on the 'touch',
the percussive, plectrum activity of the musician.[23] Chaucer's use of
the musical image shows an interesting technical development.
'Fyngerynge' probably refers to the action of playing a stringed
instrument where a finger-board plays an essential part in altering the
tone and pitch.[24] The technical complexity of Chaucer's simile
possibly reflects his memory of a passage near the end of Cicero's *De
Oratore* 3.57.216:

> *Omnis enim notus animi suum quemdam a natura habet vultum, et
> sonum et gestam; totumque corpus hominis, et eius omnis vultus,
> omnesque voces, ut nervi in fidibus, ita sonant, ut a motu animi quoque
> sunt pulsae. Nam voces ut chordae sunt intentae, quae ad quemque
> tactum respondeant: acuta, gravis, cita, tarda, magna, parva.*

For all motion of the soul corresponds naturally in some way
with facial expression, sound and gesture; and the whole human

---

[20] *Odes* II.1.3–4.
[21] Three separate passages have been conflated: (1) sta. 2: '*Tu donna, se' la luce
chiara e bella/Per cui nel tenebroso mondo accorto/Vivo . . . tu se' mia musa . . .*'; (2) sta. 4:
'*Guida la nostra man, reggi l'ingegno,/Nell' opera la quale a scriver vegno.*'; (3) sta. 5:
'*Tu se' nel tristo petto effigiata/Con forza tal, che tu vi puoi più ch'io.*'
[22] Cf. Horace, *Odes* IV.iii.24: '*Quod spiro et placeo, si placeo, tuom est*' [Melpomene].
[23] Ovid, *Metamorphoses* X.205 is fairly typical.
[24] 'Harpe' in ME seems to cover a variety of kinds of stringed instruments, some
of them provided with finger-boards. See the examples cited by *MED*.

body, all the physiognomy, tones of voice, vibrate together, just as the strings of a lyre, obedient to the movement of the soul which sets them in sounding. Indeed, tones of voice are like taut strings, emitting under the hand which touches tones—acute, grave, rapid, slow, strong, soft.

The intermingling and developing of images taken from Boccaccio and Cicero in this unique Chaucerian celebration of royal inspiration generates linguistic usage peculiar to this poem: 'the voice of the soul' (ll. 92–3)[25] and 'earthly god' which may be a memory of a phrase in Deschamps's *Lay de Franchise*, line 52, '*déesse mondaine*'.[26] We have already commented on the peculiarity of 'fyngerynge' and 'sorowes'.

As we have seen from this apostrophe, what at first view seems a tissue of the conventional becomes on closer inspection a rich and subtle nursery of original and quite personal expression. It is as easy to refer uncritically to traditions as it is to ignore them. The symbolic[27] court of Amors and Alceste is habitually referred by modern critics to French literary conventions and contemporary court fashions, thereby lending Chaucer's poetic invention a general and undeserved conventionality. From the evidence we possess, e.g. the famous passage in Gower, *Confessio Amantis* VIII.2462–93,[28] the detailed and florid poetic descriptions of Richard, Anne, the court and ceremonial inventions in Richard de Maidstone's *Concordia*, the *objets de luxe*,[29] and the famous frontispiece illumination of a court poet reading to an appropriate audience (now associated with Chaucer reading his

[25] The conventional phrase 'myn herte seyth' (*Troilus* IV.1118,1603) has nothing to do with communication or 'creations'. It is shorthand for unspoken beliefs or intuitions.

[26] Two Chaucerian passages, *Anelida* 252, *Troilus* V.321, show that the commonly used amatory phrase 'soverein lady' might in certain contexts have an exclusively religious application. Phrases used of the lady in this passage point to an indeterminacy of application if we were to think in purely secular or religious terms. The royal personage as the inspiration for, and object of literary creation is a mixture of the subjective and objective: a literary symbol.

[27] 'Symbolic' in that, although compounded mainly of already existing public rhetorical elements, its poetic methodology is personal and individual, and within the court context of the day would probably have been recognized as a highly personal invention.

[28] Professor Bennett's note on this passage (*Gower Selections*, Oxford (1968) p. 168) should be consulted.

[29] Cf. G. Mathew, *The Court of Richard II*, pp. 38–9, 47–9.

Troilus at court),[30] the 'newe guise of Beawme'[31] consists of a sophisticated proliferation of rich and sumptuous effects, visual and aural.
Lavishness of elaborate artifice is its keynote: delicate gold fretwork,
'cercles' bearing crowns or intricate garlands, a dazzling *mélange* of
costly fabrics and complex colours,[32] a superfluity of gems and precious
stones of all kinds.[33] Chaucer's personal devotion to the daisy seems to
grow out of French poetry, mainly Froissart and Machaut. But compared with Froissart's polite and evanescent effusions to the 'mar-
guerite' (and Machaut's older, more pedantic offerings), Chaucer's
angle of vision seems more natural, less mannered. Of the court of
Amors, the vocal music (there is no mention of complex instrumenta-
tion[34]), the dress, colours and ornaments evoke a deliberate simplicity
—'real habit grene', royal though the vestment may be, it is not a royal
colour much less a complex combination of colours. The Bohemian
touches are few, one for Amors, one for Alceste. In the F version King
Amors is crowned with a radiant sun (ll. 230–1) and this image as a
personal emblem occurs in Richard's funeral effigy.[35] Alceste's fret
carries a single, fantastic pearl which composes the major part of the
crown:

> For of o perle fyn, oriental,
> Hire white coroune was ymaked al.
>
> (221–2)

This is a fitting concession to the Bohemian style.[36] Chaucer has here

---

[30] Corpus Christi College, Cambridge, MS. 61, 1b. The illumination was
executed well after the lifetimes of Richard and Chaucer.

[31] Perhaps a more appropriate terminology than the more recent 'Ricardian'
borrowed from the historians (with an unrecognized change of meaning). 'The
Bohemian style' is scarcely noticed by Mr Burrow in his *Ricardian Poetry*, and
treated dismissively by some art historians.

[32] Cf. Gower, *Confessio Amantis* VIII.2467: 'Garlandes noght of o colour.' This
point is supported by Richard de Maidstone.

[33] Cf. Maidstone's comment on Anne: '*Ad caput a planta nil nisi gemma patet.*'

[34] Cf. Gower, *Confessio Amantis* VIII.2476–82.

[35] See G. Mathew, *op. cit.*, p. 28; and cf. Gower's use of a long sun similitude as
applied to Richard, *Confessio Amantis* VIII.*3005–3013. The image may have been
drawn from *Troilus* II.862ff. and Boethius, *De Consolatione* I.m.3, but the application gains in poetic power through the emblematic association.

[36] See Gower's (disapproving) description of headdresses in *Mirour de l'Omme*,
lines 9280ff.:

> *Vestont les cercles et les frettes,*
> *Crimile, esclaires et burettes*
> *E bende avoec la perle entoure.*

created a poetic image of court culture quite unlike the prevailing royal mode of dress and entertainment. If the radiant sun-crown of Amors deliberately recalls one of Richard's personal emblems,[37] the complementary daisy-crown of Alceste is a more personal literary invention. No symbolism publicly connected with Anne may be related to the daisy[38] (unlike Margaret of Anjou). Anne's peculiarly arranged 'Hours of the Virgin'[39] was perhaps produced too early (just before her marriage when she was living in the Low Countries) to reflect such emblematic connections.[40] One bare note of a collar suggests that rosemary may have been associated with her.[41] Thus, when the *Prologue* of the *Legend* had to be recast following the untimely death of Anne in June 1394, it was unnecessary to alter any of the details of the Alceste-figure's poetic costume since the image was non-public in origin and form of reference. But Amors' sun-crown had to be removed since the object had a recognizable public meaning. The revision of the *Prologue* had nothing to do with the advent of Henry IV (as has sometimes been suggested), for Richard's intense devotion to Anne was such that the poem could not have tactfully remained in its finished form. I say

[37] And compare Amors' 'gilte heer' with Maidstone's *Concordia: 'Vernula quam facies fulvis redemita capillis/Comptaque sub serto praeradiante coma!'* ('How youthful his face crowned with yellow hair in combed locks glittering forth under his headdress.') Gower also mentions Bohemian use of comb, *Confessio Amantis* VIII.2466: 'Here hevedes kempt.'

[38] Sir John Clanvowe's *Boke of Cupide*, written before 1391, contains references to daisy-observance and to a green and white colour emphasis (61–5, 241–5). If we allow that the *Legend* was written after the queen had played her clementious role in the *Concordia* of 1392, then Sir John's poem pre-dates it, and Chaucer's use of the daisy-imagery in connection with Anne probably draws on the literary imagery of this poem. In the *Boke of Cupide* the parliament of creatures is to take place 'Before the chambre-window of the quene/At Wodestok . . .' This would refer to Anne's royal manor there (deeded after 1384).

[39] Bodley MS. Lat. liturg. f.3. Cf. O. Pächt, *Illuminated Manuscripts in the Bodleian Library, Oxford*, Oxford (1966), vol. I, p. 23, item, 299.

[40] The usual public images occur, e.g. the arms of England (folio 5b), the spread eagle of Bohemia (70a), lion rampant of the Emperor of the Romans (15a, 71a), arms of France (68a), the mystical arms of St Edmund (40a), a frontispiece St George.

[41] Cf. J. H. Wylie, *History of England under Henry the Fourth*, London (1896), vol. 4, p. 196 in the Wardrobe Accounts of 1400, notes 'collar of livery of Queen Anne of branches of rosemary'.

Macaulay's dating of the *Mirour* (no later than 1379, pp. xlii–xliii) would support the view that Bohemianism was well-established in England before Anne's arrival.

'finished' for the fictive terms of the royal penance (in both texts) allow for the serial appearance of new *vitae*, and permit the work to remain 'in progress'. Richard's overmastering grief at the death of Anne at Shene took one form in his ordering the destruction of the royal apartments there. Chaucer's personal and literary disappointment occasioned by her death may be seen in his dismembering of the delicate unity of the *Legend*, and the destruction of those personal, quasi-devotional passages connected with her in the F version of the *Prologue*.

The differences between the F and G versions end with the *Prologue*. Aside from minor variations, the bulk of the extant manuscripts agrees on the shape and scope of the ten *vitae* (IV contains *Hypsipyle* and *Medea*). In narrative emphasis they resemble Gower's stories in the *Confessio Amantis* in that they are composed in a style which makes frequent use of the *via brevitatis* and many times openly resorts to *abbreviatio*. To imply that the literary interest in these fictions is mainly 'narrative' is to mistake Chaucer's intention.[42] For the 'stories' have an overall intellectual interest in 'ironic' treatment—an interest in the methods by which Chaucer changes his 'auctor's' material, often recommending the 'original' as testimony to Chaucerian accuracy, or as supplementary research.[43] At a less oblique level, each 'life' contains an 'area of special interest' (sometimes identified, as in *Dido*, lines 1160–1, sometimes unidentified) which cannot be associated with moralization or any general aspect of narrative pleasure. These areas or 'cores' usually reflect an habitual Ovidian emphasis as found in the *Heroides*: the delineation of passion as cause and effect in psychological states and the interplay of morality and sentiment, either presented directly (as in Ovid) or reflected in the author's analysis (as so often in Gower).[44] The interaction between the levels of the 'ironic' and the psychological interest helps to sustain a continuous interplay between

---

[42] Cf. Burrow, *op. cit.*, pp. 74ff.

[43] After all, in *Troilus* V.1854–5 Chaucer openly rejected the authority of 'olde speche In poetrie'. His next poem, the *Legend*, reintroduces in a new and sophisticated way the 'forme' and material of the rejected pagan verse, sometimes by altering the import of the author, sometimes by showing us how freely classical authors (as Virgil and Ovid in *Dido*) treated their material. Chaucer always makes us aware of the free spirit of a classical education whether he appears to be agreeing, disagreeing or suspending judgment.

[44] Cf. C. Schaar, *Some Types of Narrative in Chaucer's Poetry*, Lund (1954), pp. 37ff.; see especially pp. 54–5, where the combining of three types of narrative style is described as 'narrated with a great deal of psychological detail'. This observation is unfortunately taken no further.

wit and pathos, yet another Ovidian quality found in the *Heroides* and the *Metamorphoses*.[45]

Although these 'cores' or 'areas of special interest' show a brief reflection here and there in the narrative (as one would imagine from a text which presents us with the occasional short description of developing emotions), yet each individual legend may be said to contain a specific area or areas where this recurring emphasis is more pronounced and has an identifiable position in relation to the narrative pattern. The favoured position would seem to occur just before the short, perfunctory (often parody) moral *conclusio* in the form of a set speech (*sermocinatio*) or an emotionally intensified presentation of a scene including speech (*demonstratio*). In other words, in legends I, II, IV, VI and VIII the general narration leads up by *ordo naturalis* to a passage of rhetorically elegant, pathetic utterance, thus showing an overall formulation similar to that of the narrative-amatory complaints such as *Mars*, *Anelida* and *Pity*. This group of legends shows the following distribution of special areas:

I CLEOPATRA

> *sermocinatio* (ll. 681–95): a 'testament' of love, showing a concentration on simply composed pathos. There is no 'source' for this utterance, and the story has an uncomplicated climactic structure.

II PIRAMUS and THISBE

> (a) *sermocinatio* (ll. 756–66): mutual complaint by both lovers.
> (b) *sermocinatio* (ll. 833–49): Piramus' complaint.
> (c) *sermocinatio* (ll. 890–912): Thisbe's complaint.
> The pattern consists of a series of three climaxes producing an increasing pathetic emphasis by accumulation within a simple narrative pattern. The pathetic material has been enlarged from passages in Ovid's *Metamorphoses*.

IV HYPSIPYLE and MEDEA

> Epistle (as written utterance) (ll. 1672–7): Medea's *accusatio*. The style imitates Ovid's mixture of indignant

---

[45] Frank, *op. cit.*, p. 129, notices 'the fluctuation of sober and light' in the *Legend* but merely sees this as characteristically 'Chaucerian'.

emotion and rhetorical elegance in *Heroides* XII.[46] The double tale is narratively very simple and matter-of-fact, providing a deliberate contrast to the complexity of structure and style in III, DIDO.

VI ARIADNE

demonstratio and *sermocinatio* (ll. 2185–217): the awakening of the abandoned Ariadne on Naxos. This shows an Ovidian blend of natural observation, pathos and eloquence, rendering a mind in the grip of delusive hope and desire. The whole of this scene is closely imitated from Ovid, *Heroides* X.12ff.

VIII PHYLLIS

epistle of Phyllis (ll. 2496–554). The letter is divided into two parts: (a) the exordium, lines 2496–512, a parody exercise in reproducing in ME the worst stylistic excesses of the *Heroides*: the tendency to enumerate a series of elegant *expolitiones* interlarded with periphrastic expressions and allusions. The style is criticized and rejected by Chaucer in lines 2513–15; (b) the body of the epistle, exemplifying good Ovidian writing (Chaucer commends this excellence in line 2517). This is closely worked from *Heroides* II.

The other legends show interesting variations of this basic structure, showing different structural positions for the Ovidian areas of special interest, i.e.

---

[46] Chaucer sometimes remembers a turn of phrase from the fourteenth-century Italian prose translation of Filippo (cf. S. B. Meech, *PMLA* 45 (1930), pp. 117ff.). Usually the phrase amounts to an explanatory addition, but in the case of *Medea* Chaucer's line 'And of thy tongue the infinit graciousnesse' (*linguae gratia ficta tuae*) has been suggested by '*la infinita grazia della tua lingua*'. It will be noticed that Chaucer has kept Ovid's poetic inversion of the word-order. *Pace* Meech, this is not Chaucer blindly following Filippo's 'mistranslation', but Chaucer appreciating Filippo's invention of an ironic, disdainfully polite Medean turn of phrase. He was so pleased by the Italian that he made her remark more sardonically polite by coining the abstr. sb. 'graciousnesse', a unique occurrence in ME. The sb. does not appear until much later in French.

III DIDO

(a) Virgilian *apostrophe* and *epitome* (ll. 924–57): periodic and Virgilian in style and moral emphasis: the heroic Augustan view as created by Virgil for Aeneas and the escape from Troy.

(b) personal 'English' *apostrophe* and *epitome* (ll. 1254–89): Chaucer's address to innocent women of his own day.

(c) Ovidian *demonstratio* (ll. 1332–65): a detailed representation of pathos in action, description and speech: the neoteric Augustan view of book IV as exemplified by Ovid.

The triple distribution of areas imitates the structure of II, and the location of the final climax resembles the structure of the main group. But the juxtaposition of Virgilian and Ovidian styles gives the narrative an oblique and complex texture.

V LUCRECE

praesentatio and *similitudo* (ll. 1757–69): a direct recording of the effects of erotic passion on a disturbed mind, closely worked from *Fasti* II.761ff. The ostensible moral emphasis in the story (repeatedly mentioned by Chaucer) is on Lucrece's regard for her chastity. The actual developed interest is in Tarquin's mind and emotional dislocation. The simile constitutes one of the finest examples of Ovidian delineation of emotion in medieval literature.[47]

VII PHILOMELA

author's *apostrophe* to the Creator (ll. 2225–43): this is a simple 'reversed' structure; the *narratio* has no genuine structural climax since the injured Philomela has been rendered mute, and Chaucer is obliged to remove Ovid's horrific climax, the sister's cruel, inhuman revenge on Tereus. The opening *apostrophe* is, in a sense, made on behalf of the silenced Philomela.

[47] Cf. C. Schaar, *The Golden Mirror: Studies in Chaucer's Descriptive Technique*, Lund (1955); he says sensibly '. . . Chaucer takes a particular interest in the desperate nature of Tarquin's love . . .' (p. 52) but merely notes the Ovidian source for the account of that state of mind. This in a chapter headed 'Description of Emotions'!

IX HYPERMNESTRA

> *demonstratio* (ll. 2678–708): showing the intellectual and
> emotional dilemma of Hypermnestra in the form of a
> poetic *suasoria*. This is closely imitated from Ovid,
> *Heroides* XIV.

We cannot pronounce definitely on the position of this last 'special
area' in relation to the narrative pattern, for the story is unfinished.
Robinson and Skeat are probably right in taking the final line (2723) as
an introductory statement, where 'conclusioun' should be taken to
mean 'intention', 'purpose' (cf. *Troilus* II.259, *Legend of Good Women*,
l. 2646). Brusendorff appears to have understood the line as an editor's
attempt to finish the narrative in a single couplet, taking 'conclusioun'
in the sense 'the end of an account' (cf. *Knight's Tale*, l. 1869).

After the long and doubtless extremely exhausting period spent
composing his *Troilus* (a triumphant example of a complex, integrated
narrative structure), Chaucer seems to have turned his attention to
narrative forms allowing for serial composition—forms in which
'parts' or 'episodes' may be appreciated in themselves without immediate reference to a larger aesthetic unity.[48] The *Legend* seems to
have been his first venture in this direction. We have seen how delicate
the overall unity was for the *Legend* as based on the structure of the F
version, and how inconclusive and 'ironic' the total form became after
the G version had been conceived. But even allowing for the F version's
'delicate possibilities', the *archetypus* for the whole poem contains several
weaknesses. I leave on one side the more general weakness (if that is the
word) inherent in the literary criticism of the Middle Ages: the lack
of any theoretic or practical discussion of the artistic problems created
by the scope and complexity of long narrative fictions. Classical
criticism, too, was rather short on this sort of advice, but at least writers
had the example of practising epicists with all their faults and virtues.
The best the Middle Ages could manage was an occasional 'epic'
based on a *vita* structure.[49] Though founded on a biological image of

---

[48] Possibly it was more important for Chaucer to be able to compose in separate
units. From the state of the *Canterbury Tales* this is surely how he worked; but
we have little hard evidence to prove that he published parts separately—although
the confusion of the order and linking of tales in all manuscript groups has led
scholars to imagine this. The long-held view that he fell to 'cannibalizing' earlier
material for certain tales, although attractive, is equally difficult to prove.

[49] I suppose it began with Statius' *Achilleis* which was, ominously, unfinished.
The *Waltharius* (?late ninth century) although not entirely annalistic in approach is

unity, it is an area of unity where the controlling factors are remote from the possibility of artistic alteration—as if the ink and not the author were responsible for the written word.

The first weakness in the *Legend's* structure lies in its lack of developmental capability. The *legenda* type of collection allows for no genesis of a 'middle' in an Aristotelian narrative sequence. Every episode can achieve only the status of a repetition or a variation. Second, all the actual and potential unifying factors tend to be collected into the *Prologue*, leaving the work seriously unbalanced in terms of the relation of parts to whole. Third, the fiction of an author selecting *legendae* from a wide, necessarily disconnected classical past allows for little development of crossing and connecting interests, personages or places. How well Virgil manages this in creating a community of interests within the *Eclogues*, and how poor Spenser is in understanding what is required for the *Shepheardes Calendar*. Chaucer attempts a few connections in the persons of Jason and Theseus[50] but the result is not distinguishable from any of the other *vitae* in terms of sustained development. The main benefit which Chaucer derived from attempting serial composition in the *Legend* was to learn what sort of problems arise for the writer in this kind of additive, episodic patterning. The *Legend* was an excellent training-ground for the poet of the *Canterbury Tales*— a work which shows a clear and comprehensive appreciation of the potential uses of unity of place (as suggested by a title such as *Gesta Romanorum*)[51] and unity of activity. The germ of this *idée* probably came from another English Geoffrey, from Geoffrey of Vinsauf's tale *De Clericis et Rustico* (and compare the versions in the *Disciplina Clericalis* and the *Gesta Romanorum* itself) where we find the motifs of the pilgrimage to a shrine, the story-telling competition between pilgrims, and the gustatory reward for the best-told tale.[52] As Dr

[50] Chaucer also seems to be moving in the direction of involving himself in the question of inherited evil and the gradual debasement of 'form' or 'essence' by successive generation. But the interest remains undeveloped in terms of thematic continuity.

[51] Mentioned thrice by Chaucer *only* in the *Canterbury Tales* (*Merchant's Tale* 2284–5, *Man of Law's Tale* 1126, *Wife of Bath's Prologue* 642).

[52] Chaucer's possible knowledge of Sercambi's *Novelle* is not necessary for his conceiving of the basic narrative plan. The Latin material was nearer to hand and

pretty poor stuff. In the twelfth century Walter of Chatillon's *Alexandreis* is much better constructed, but still suffers from episodicism, historical fragmentation and set excursus. In the same century Joseph of Exeter is worse structurally, and no criticism has been able to explain away the structural inadequacies of *Beowulf*.

Raby remarked long ago, although the form may be French in origin, the aptitude in the twelfth century for *iocosa materia* and *comoediae* is English. It was to be so again in the fourteenth.

---

far better known. Boccaccio's *Decameron* is another issue and will be discussed later.

CHAPTER FIVE

The Canterbury Tales

I Narrative structure

Undoubtedly the compositional periods of the *Legend* and the *Canterbury Tales* at some point coincided. I have given some weight to the notion that the *Legend*, in the F version at least, makes oblique reference to the roles of Anne and Richard in the *Concordia* of August 1392. But we have no firm idea of how the poem was composed and what kind of revising was involved. It may well have been that the 'later' G version, with its removal of the quasi-religious and 'inspirational' relationship with the Anne-Alceste figure, marked a return to an earlier structure—that the later revision falls back on a version of the *Prologue* which existed before the role of Anne came into the poem. This might help to explain why criticism has been so divided over the question of 'priority' in the relating of the two drafts. For, as I have argued, 'priority' is not essential to the generating of the two distinct forms.

The *Canterbury Tales* has learnt from the structural problems encountered in the evolving of the serial-episodic plot of the *Legend*.[1] For one thing, in the *Tales* we are presented with an additive sequence which in its journey and competition structure is able to generate a beginning, middle and end movement. The sequence also has a fixed time structure, measurable in terms of external references to geography, and a fictional 'duration of time' as established inside the 'reality' of the work by means of *chronographiae* and the dramatic development of the interplay of personages. The *Tales* has all the means fictionally of coming to a controlled, complete conclusion without the obligation of reproducing or fulfilling the exact terms of the 'compact' made in the *General Prologue*. It has a kind of guided-tour plot structure (as we

[1] *Pace* J. A. Burrow, *Ricardian Poetry*, p. 67. His preference for 'circular forms' in 'the period' is quite arbitrary.

find in the *Parliament* and the *House of Fame*) without an authoritative
guide. We expect no special wisdom from that figure other than that
of worldly tolerance. In other words, it possesses a deceptive, not
wholly predictable, sometimes erratic movement which resembles
those two dream-poems, yet it remains within the logic of the waking,
active world. Once the first half of the journey (from Southwark to
Canterbury) is completed and a representative number of tales told,
the implicit 'pilgrimage of life' metaphor itself is completed. It is
further brought to completion by including in the work the pseudo-
personal epilogue 'the author taketh leve of his boke': a statement
which seems to manoeuvre us even closer to reality. We seem to be
reading something which has strayed into the work by accident—a
final statement or testimony of a poet whose authorial career is drawing to a close. He appears to be saying 'farewell' not only to the *Tales*,
but to all other acts of composition.[2] In the closing sentence the author's
own mode of existence is brought within the terms and purposes of
the Parson's exposition of the penitential way of life. This intellectual
mood has been developed from (1) the *'farewell* to pagan literature'
epilogue of *Troilus* and (2) the fictional life of literary penance for the
poet's *legendae* in the *Legend of Good Women*. In *Troilus* and the *Legend*
the moods of 'farewell' and 'penance' are partial and complexly qualified. In the *Tales* it gives the impression of being absolute. The *Tales*
also derives another very important structural element from the
Legend as it stands in both versions. This is the invention of a serial
plot structure in a suspended form.

In the *Legend* Chaucer has conceived a form dependent for all its
intrinsic unity on a single complicating link between the *Prologue* and
x-number of *vitae*. Whatever the resulting structural imbalance, the
initiating terms of the *Prologue* (a finished referential framework)
allow for an 'unfinished' state not to interfere with the 'completed'

---

[2] The *licentia authoris* is in no way a 'retraction'. Caxton was the first reader of
the *Tales* to fall into this assumption. Cf. O. Sayce, *Medium Aevum* 40 (1971),
pp. 230–46. She notices the 'allusion to St. Augustine's *Retractiones*' but she does
not see that the pl. sb. cannot function as an equivalent of the singular. It should
be capitalized and italicized. Chaucer invents his own late work, 'my *Revisions*',
citing items as an index. Unlike St Augustine, the order is not chronological but
dramatically random, as if he were spontaneously calling them to mind. This
section almost certainly pervades Gascoigne's fifteenth-century account of
Chaucer's death-bed abjuration of his literary works and rejection of worldly
vanities. Cf. J. W. Hales, 'Geoffrey and Thomas Chaucer', *Athenaeum* (31 March
1888), pp. 404–5 and M. M. Crow and C. C. Olson, *Chaucer Life-Records*, p. 547.

THE CANTERBURY TALES 81

meaning of the work. The formal *conclusio*, presumably, would have amounted in the F version to a merely conventional use of the 'waking device' to bring the work to an end. In the G version there is no possible concluding device. The work merely rests 'unfinished' yet in meaning, *sentence*, complete. Chaucer is fond of 'undogmatic' endings as we can see from the suspensive conclusions of the *Parliament* and the *Book of the Duchess*. In the *Parliament* he succeeds in convincing us that the work is only a progress report by referring to other possible poems as not yet written and further reading and study which lies ahead. In the *Book of the Duchess* we are assured that the 'poem' which we have just read has not yet been written. The 'dream' is finished but the work of art lies in the future. In the G version of the *Legend* where the dream structure has been removed the work lies unfinished, and in terms of the 'penaunce' uncompletable save with the ending of the poet's life. This penchant for a suspensive type of serial structure anticipates yet another feature of the *Canterbury Tales*—its quality of *imperfection*.

All Chaucerian criticism holds *a priori* that the *Tales* now exists in an unfinished state; that its proper completion was forestalled by Chaucer's death. This is no doubt true. But in spite of the seeming chaotic state of the work, the unfinished *Cook's Tale*, the later account of the Cook's inability to tell his tale, the lack of head and tail links, the muddled order of the tales in the manuscripts, yet the whole poem is in an important sense 'finished'. In 1420 Lydgate in prologue 18–19 of his *Thebes* refers to the *Canterbury Tales* as 'complet' ('completed'). In an Aristotelian narrative structure the beginning section (the *General Prologue*, group A, and group B in the Skeatian terminology) and the ending section (linked groups H and I) are perfectly complete. The middle section, although imperfect in realization, is basically complete—in the way in which the community of interests, ideas and fictional relationships generate and mediate on a continuous sequence of related moral preoccupations. The late entrance of the Canon's Yeoman near 'Boghtoun under Blee' (G 556) shows us how far we have travelled in our mental journey from the jovialities of the South Bank—from the trivial though bitter personal animosities of the Miller and the Reeve. The *Yeoman's Tale* leads nowhere in terms of the pilgrim's interests. For their collective interests and dissonances have developed out of a shared fellowship in which ideas are becoming more important than personal animosities. Debate has wholly replaced competition.

Although no single more-or-less 'complete' manuscript gives us the final, definitive order of the tales, yet the work provides us with the means of coming to at least a reasonable or arguable version of that order. By combining what knowledge we have, i.e. (1) the deliberate references to journey topography, (2) the links and internal references, (3) taking some versions of the links to be what Chaucer finally intended (e.g. the link between E/F as represented in the Ellesmere arrangement), then we have a fair idea of the basic order. That is, Skeat and the Chaucer Society's 'rationalization' is fairly close to the truth in so far as we can reconstruct it. By 1450 persons unknown who may well have been alive during Chaucer's lifetime undertook by means of 'spurious' links to complete the work. This does not mean that Chaucer had a less exact idea of an 'authoritative text' than we have. St Augustine's account of a perfect text given in his late *Retractationes* (475) agrees with Chaucer's views as embodied in his words addressed to his personal scribe. But St Augustine's awareness of the dangers involved in scribal transmission and multiplication of a text shows us that medieval authors were conscious of the very imperfect nature of commercial and monastic copying. It was less accurate than the classical system of consultation between public libraries. I wonder if, in spite of the interruption of the 'perfect' nature of the *Canterbury Tales* by his death, this suspended, 'imperfect' form may not have been part of Chaucer's original artistic conception—that the *archetypus* itself allowed for planned imperfection in the same way that the *Legend*'s *idée* in the G version anticipates a state of being unfinished.

If so, then the notion of an 'imperfect work' arose out of three main factors: (1) the structural use of a suspended, 'unfinished' narrative form in the *Legend*; (2) the notion of man's life being in a sense *in opere imperfecto*.[3] We have several references to perfection/imperfection in the *Tales* themselves, most significantly in the *Parson's Tale*. The Parson himself in his verse prologue overtly refers to the metaphor of the pilgrimage of life and its connection with the process of this very Canterbury pilgrimage when he says:

> I wol yow telle a myrie tale in prose
> To knytte up al this feeste, and make an ende.
> And Ihesu, for his grace, wit me sende

---

[3] Cf. Psalm 138 (Vulgate), 16: '*Imperfectum meum viderunt oculi tui, et in libro tuo omnes scribentur.*' It is interesting that Lydgate in his *Thebes* calls Chaucer the 'Chief Registrer' of the pilgrimage. The phrase 'perfect works' occurs in Deut. 32.4: '*Dei perfecta sunt opera . . .*' (Cf. The closing prayer in Skelton's *Colin Clout* 1260–8.)

> To shew you the wey, in this viage,
> Of thilke parfit glorious pilgrimage
> That highte Ierusalem celestial.
>
> (46–51)

Two pilgrimages are here contrasted, and the spiritual journey only is capable of perfection. Later, in commenting on the possibility of human life in terms of the need for complete and honest confession he says: 'For certes Ihesu Christ is entierly al good; in hym nys noon imperfeccioun; and therfore outher he foryeveth al parfitly or never a deel.' (l. 1006). After Chaucer's own tale (*Sir Thopas*) is interrupted and left unfinished, the author himself subscribes to the notion of disagreement and incompleteness as a state of literary being not incompatible with the whole truth of the work's meaning and purpose. Such a state of incompletion is exemplified in the Gospels themselves:

> As thus, ye woot that euery Evangelist,
> That telleth us the peyne of Ihesu Crist
> Ne seith nat alle thyng as his felawe dooth;
> But natheles hir sentence is al sooth,
> And alle acorden as in hire sentence,
> Al be ther in hir tellyng difference.
> For somme of hem seyn more, and somme seyn lesse
> Whan they his pitous passioun expresse;
>
> (*2133ff.)

(3) The third factor is the way in which the *Canterbury Tales* acts as literature on the reader. It is a work (as I understand it) which in Proust's phrase 'takes us back into life', returns us to experience itself with more capacity to observe and analyse. Thus, in the prefatory chapter to *Jean Santeuil* the novelist-figure explains to the I-author of the work the peculiar power of Balzac's fiction. The best 'critics' of Balzac, he holds, are country gentry, ageing aunts and retired colonels. These readers naïvely confuse the fictional world of Balzac with their own experience of the world. By becoming confused with life by the reader prepared to experience it as reality, the work of art performs its artistic intention: to powerfully transform our own life into a more discrete and penetrating understanding of its moral and 'poetic' nuances. In this way the generations are never isolated, past and present life becomes capable of being re-experienced and re-possessed. Later, Proust explains that this is not a special gift of the artist—it is possessed in some degree by all men and women in the exercise of memory.

The *Canterbury Tales* as a type of the sophisticated-naïve worked in this way on the minds of the fifteenth century. 'This is your life', it seemed to be saying—from the numbers of manuscripts and hosts of allusions and works inspired by it.[4] It still has this power (a power shared in by both 'lered and lewed') from the multitude of scholarly disagreements and 'subtle' discussions to the crudity of the current demotic forms transmitted through the mass medium and the sexualized voyeurism of the theatre. To the mind which objects that planned confusion of life and literature is not part of the medieval critical heritage, it must be answered that this is not so. When the eagle in book II of the *House of Fame* endeavours to turn Chaucer's attention from the stupefying world of books to the excitement of life his whole emphasis is on the multiplicity, contradictoriness, incompleteness of the terrestrial scene. The last environment of that poem, the house of Aventure, teems with abundant, confused life, life generated out of sheer curiosity.

> And, Lord, this hous, in alle tymes,
> Was ful of shipmen and pilgrimes,
> With scrippes bret-ful of lesinges,
> Entremedled with tydynges.
>
> (2121)

With little prompting when Chaucer gazes on the order of the heavens and on their fullness, he perceives its stability and perfection in contrast with the relative impermanence of earthly life and its frail reflection in the 'congeled matere' of the foundations of human literature. The astonished poet swears 'By seynt Thomas of Kent' (*H of F* 1131) when he realizes the inscribed ice is a 'feble fundament'. This is the only reference to St Thomas Becket outside the *Tales*. Nevertheless, it is this 'reality' towards which the eagle urges Chaucer to turn his literary attention.

---

[4] A very early reference is a quotation from the *Knight's Tale*, ll. 1785–6, which begins Sir John Clanvowe's poem the *Boke of Cupide* (written before 1391). This verbatim quotation begins the poetic questioning which generates the dream-debate. It shows the close connection with the tale as generating new literature and the close social identification of the writer with the 'estate' of the tale's fictional author. In a sense James of Scotland's courtship and marriage has been experienced through Palamon and Emily. Another early use of the *Tales* occurs in Lydgate's *Thebes* (1420) where close social identification passes into overt impersonation. The continuator of the *Tales* ('Lydgate') places himself within the compact of the *Prologue* and joins the party on the way back.

Among the many arguments conducted during the Middle Ages about the relation of Art and Nature, one of the most interesting discussions which Chaucer certainly read[5] was that of Jean de Meun in the *Roman*, lines 16005–248. In this excursus (derived from what Alan's Nature had said in the *De Planctu Naturae*) Art is seen as wholly dependent on the power, design and completeness of Nature:

> *Mais par moult ententive cure*
> *A genouz est devant Nature,*
> *Si prie e requiert e demande,*
> *Comme mendiant e truande,*
> *Povre de science e de force,*
> *Qui d'ensivre la moult s'esforce,*
> *Que Nature li vueille apprendre*
> *Coment ele puisse comprendre,*
> *Par son engin, en ses figures,*
> *Proprement toutes creatures . . .*
>
> *Mais tant est ses nuz e linges*
> *Qu'el ne peut faire choses vivres,*
> *Ja si ne sembleront naives.*
>   (*Roman* 16019ff.)

Not only is 'poor' Art reduced to 'aping' Nature but it fails in its attempt to imitate Nature's manifest 'perfection' of work:

> *Zeusis neis par son bel peindre*
> *Ne pourrait a tel forme ataindre,*
> *Qui, pour faire l'image ou temple,*
> *De cinc puceles fist exsemple,*
> *Les plus belles que l'en pot querre*
> *E trouver en toute la terre, . . .*
>
> *Si con Tulles le nous remembre,*
> *Au livre de sa Retorique,*
> *Qui mout est science autentique.*
> *Mais ci ne peust il riens faire,*
> *Zeusis! tant seust bien pourtraire,*
> *Ne colourer sa poutraiture,*

[5] There is extensive reminiscence and quotation of this section of the *Roman* in the *Physician's Tale*, lines 11–28.

Tant est de grant beaute Nature.
Zeusis! non pas trestuit li maistre
Que Nature fist onques meistre;
                    (*Roman* 16185ff.)

The argument about the relative imperfectness of Art is concluded by Jean by exposing the relative imperfection of Nature in the face of the work of God, the perfect artist and *opifex*.[6]

In all the reality of the pilgrimage situation, the scientific nature of the author's descriptions, in the total model for the overall narrative sequence, its waywardness, its *ordo naturalis*, Chaucer is inviting us to experience what seems to be a direct, often subjective record of actual contemporary life in a recognizable total environment. It is significant that within this reality of the tales we only experience the *perfection* of Nature in man's rational idea of that design—most significantly at the beginning of the journey and at the end. The Knight presents his fellows with a version of Boethius' neo-Platonism (recalling *De Consolatione* III prose x). The Parson presents the company with an answering ecclesiastical view—not a model which the Christian intellect can comprehend, but an imperfection which the form of active penance brings to relative completion, 'verray penitence, confessioun and satisfaccioun to doon in this present lyf'. Beyond this lies the image of the absolute perfection of the Heavenly Life.

If we understand the *Tales* as modelled, then, on a biological metaphor partaking of the '*pèlerinage de la vie de l'homme*', and that of the *opus imperfectum*, realized through a 'natural' mode of construction which possesses all the power and inventive capacity of Nature rather than the limiting perfection of medieval artifice, we can also see how narrowing it would be to apply to the *Tales* any imposed scheme of moral or religious analysis—such as the Seven Deadly Sins or a doctrinaire contrasting of religious and secular moralities in one form or another. A major part of the 'Canterbury contentment' lies in its suspension, its deliberate creation of an expanding ironical dimension, of the many and conflicting interpretations which the poem mischievously provokes. Yet the biologically based metaphor of the pilgrimage of life and the final spiritual resignation of the author suggests a powerful tendency towards an acceptance of the orthodox 'other-worldly' religious view of human activity. After all, these matters

---

[6] The neo-Aristotelian view is taken up by John of Salisbury in the *Metalogicon* II.xi.

'up-groweth with [our] age'.[7] As Pandarus notes in another context (when he identifies 'conclusioun', 'purpose', with the 'ende' of a narrative work):

> How so it be that som men hem delite
> With subtyl art hire tales for to endite,
> Yet for al that, in hire entencioun,
> Hire tale is al for some conclusioun.
>
> And sithen the ende is every tales strengthe . . .
> (*Troilus* II.256ff.)

It is typical of Chaucer (not so much Pandarus) that this comparison soon loses its way syntactically and ends in a question—where Pandarus' meaning lies unexpressed. Criseyde has to guess at his 'entencioun'. How often that word 'entente' occurs in the *Tales* compared with its use elsewhere in Chaucer—from its first use in a compositional context in the *Knight's Tale* to its last uttering by Chaucer *ipse* in the *licentia authoris* when he quotes St Paul, Romans 15.4 (already cited by the Nun's Priest (ll. 4631-2)): '"Al that is writen is writen for oure doctrine" and that is myn entente.'

[7] Although Chaucer does not refer directly to his age, the hints are plain to see (prologue to the *Man of Law's Tale*, lines 49-50, 55). The contemporary audience would have known that he was well advanced in years. The G version of the *Prologue* to the *Legend* inserts the following uncalled-for observation:

> Whil he as yong, he kepte youre estat;
> I not wher he be now a renegat.
> (400-1)

The dramatic accelerated ageing of the author-lover in order to provide the grounds for Venus' release of Gower from her contract at the end of the *Confessio Amantis* (VIII.2440ff.) provides a certain parallel. Gower, too, takes a lingering farewell of literature and human love: '. . . it is to me for the beste/For this day furth to take rest/That I no more of love make.' In the version intended for King Richard personally, Venus bids Gower to urge the aged Chaucer, now 'upon his latere age', to take care to wind up his literary affairs and 'make his testament of love'. In view of the similarities between the *Legend* and book VIII of the *Confessio*, in the collections of lovers (and specific lovers) and the interviews between poet-figure and Amors and Venus, the Chaucerian 'testament' here suggested may have been a hint for the penitent Chaucer of that work to write a conclusion to his *legendae* in which the poet would include his farewell to human love. Chaucer did not oblige directly but added his 'last will' to the completed biological image of life at the end of the *Tales*.

II   The disposition of the narrative

We have been told that Gower was too judicious a narrator to oblige his readers to spend their time 'continuously' working their way through the *Confessio Amantis*'s ambitious and sometimes subtle *granarium* of moral and fabulous material.[8] Elsewhere we are assured that certain poets of the last two decades of the fourteenth century began to indulge in 'learned' divisions of narrative poems into 'books'.[9] Both these observations, though welcome, remain at too primitive a level for literary criticism. Gower's *distinctiones* are quite different from Chaucer's art of disposing a narrative into parts. The structural mode of the *Confessio* is the encyclopedic: it is a work which achieves its formal effect by a certain deliberate accumulation and classification of exemplary information. The intellectual and emotional points of climax are reserved for the final one thousand lines of book VIII where the Amans-Confessor relationship emerges brilliantly into the foreground; elde creeps into the main of light together with Amans' relation with Venus. Here the psychological connection between moral education and the sometimes denied but always yielded to desire for elucidation and understanding (both of the world and the self) utterly transforms the history and historicized mythology which heretofore has been presented as providing a basis for our 'doctrine'—our reasoned moral conduct. The royal reader's experience (in the 'Ricardian' version) becomes at this point distinct from that of the author-Amans—and so does that of the ordinary reader—although every reader is made to understand that he will one day face a similar searching confession and absolution. The final, reserved, moral and psychological triumph of the work owes very little to its encyclopedic structure. For Gower's book divisions are schematic and rely on formulaic repetition for their effect, especially the closing rhythm of the intimate exchange between the Confessor and Amans which usually announces another 'sin' or imperfection to follow. The encapsulating exordia and *conclusiones* in their repeated emphatic position help to give the exemplifying variety

---

[8] J. A. W. Bennett, *Gower Selections*, Oxford (1968), p. xvii.
[9] Burrow, *op. cit.*, p. 59. It is implied that this would have been considered a novelty. It would only have been so considered for a reader without Latin, that is, without any formal education.

of the work a solid, referential sense of shape—an 'envelope', in a currently fashionable expression. Yet in essence the book divisions are in the pedantic, compendious nature of the *oeuvre* as a carefully, deliberately, structured *thesaurus rerum antiquarum*.

It is significant that Gower's overall encyclopedic architectonic finds little space in Professor Bennett's sympathetic, penetrating appreciation of the *Confessio*.[10] In spite of Gower's occasionally successful linking of books by anticipating the main thematic emphasis of the following book (as in the Aristotle–Alexander link between books VI and VII[11]), the dimensions of the individual books seem to look to no narrative 'norm' of length or structure. The longest line length of book is nearly seven times that of the smallest unit (comparing book V to book I). In a short unit of hundreds of lines the dispositional imbalance is not so immediately felt; but in units of thousands of lines the reader eventually loses consciousness of any regularity or relatable pattern of abbreviation or extension. As in the *Mirour de l'Omme*,[12] the regulatory principle resides in the deployment of an extrinsic *summa*-type organization. The 'family tree of sins' takes root and grows, spreading and exfoliating and branching according to the author's ethical interests and supply of exemplary material. Like a *summa* or encyclopedia, the developing internal sectional relationships and book divisions provide a schematic, guiding index. Seven sins and their orderly subdivisions or the seven liberal arts in their proper order and the appropriate subsections, always tell the medieval reader (without benefit of an extensive Renaissance index) where he is. But no matter how inventively adapted to the fictional structure (as in Martianus Capella or Alan of Lille) this paradigmatic organization never becomes a fully-integrated poetic form.

Chaucerian arrangement into narrative parts according to 'books' takes a form utterly distinct from that of Gower's schematical and referential patterning. Although the *Vox Clamantis* may be argued to show Gower trying to divide his material into more easily manageable

[10] The editor (p. xvi) refers once to 'his discrete architectonic', but the matter is allowed to rest there.

[11] This educational relationship is exactly parallel with that of Gower and Richard II.

[12] The surviving index divides the work into ten parts ('X parties') in a hand different from that of the text. The text is not so divided. After the first two 'parties' there is a recapitulation in summary 18373–420. The rubric at this point suggests a new section. The effect in reading the *Mirour* is of following a continuous, ramified, diverging and converging compilation.

units with more equally proportional material (the ratio of shortest to longest books is 3:1; most books average between 1,000 and 1,500 lines), the arrangement of material and literary expression emerges as 'conceptual' rather than 'poetic'. After book III the author abandons his literary prologues and shows less concern with the atmosphere of dream or reality, certainly less invention of poetic detail.

If we turn to *Troilus*, we find a disposition of the narrative into a five-book structure[13] where the conclusion-sequences are invented out of the actual poetic material, using dramatic context, metaphor and formal rhetorical devices to establish intrinsic modes of pause, rest and anticipation. The author is no longer dependent on extrinsic, already created patterns. The Boccaccio-inspired *matere* as well as the nine parts of the *Il Filostrato* formulation has been inventively transformed. The line lengths of each book show a scrupulous care for a standard 'norm' of reading time: all books fall within the length 1,000–2,000 lines, the ratio of smallest to longest is 1:2 and the mean average is 1,650. Carefully read aloud such a unit length occupies nearly two hours.[14] Criseyde and her women pause and stop their reading of Statius' *Thebaid* at the exact end of book VI where the rubric to book VII announces the approaching death of Amphioraus.[15] Pandarus interrupts the tragic Theban story exactly mid-way. When we hear of the epic again it is near the end of book V. Cassandra completes the whole tragic story, relating the Theban material to Troilus' dream both

[13] The five-unit disposition represents a 'tragic' arrangement suggested by Horace's Aristotelian analysis in the *Ars Poetica*, and Nicolas Trivet's *Commentary* to the plays of Seneca. It shows Chaucer's awareness of the relation of the tragic form to psychology, emotional empathy and the properly 'dramatic'. These properties are discussed by Trivet. It also shows his understanding of the triadic, climactic structure of five-act drama.

[14] This corresponds to Shakespeare's representation of the ideal time duration of a stage presentation. The unit is probably based on some medieval educational or ecclesiastic conditioning process. These mental work-patterns of attention and relaxation usually have a long and persisting history. For example, Oxford undergraduates who read their essays aloud are advised to write eight foolscap sides (twenty minutes' reading time) for this is about the length one can write spontaneously in an hour and so provides exact training for writing a paper in Final Honours School (three questions in three hours). University lecturers who still take the trouble to write formal lectures usually find that draft chapters of books tend to occupy about twenty quarto pages of typescript. In some provincial universities the long ten-week term is generally 'weakened' in terms of the teaching done in the first and last weeks so that the ancient Oxford–Cambridge eight-week term is unofficially preserved.

[15] *Troilus* II.102–4.

personally and generally. The historical nemesis quickens and closes, the recapitulation of Statius gathering together the destructive pagan past and its literary record, synchronizing its inevitability and its epical status with the declining Trojan present. This complex literary use suggests that Chaucer may be remembering *Aeneid* I where Aeneas sees on the temple of Juno represented the tragic past of Troy.[16] In Virgil's use as a 'beginning-motif' the scenes prefigure the future epical events of books VII–XII, an eventually triumphal sequence. We will look in vain for this degree of complex, literary use of pause-rest, completion-anticipation images in Gower or any other of Chaucer's contemporaries.

Criseyde's casual account of her pause in reading aloud provides us with Chaucer's basic concluding pattern for each book—the simultaneous presentation of two contradictory rhythms, of conclusion and continuousness. Unlike a rubric, 'lettres rede' (Gower is fond of them), Chaucer's anticipating, continuous rhythm is not a summary of an approaching event or episode. It usually consists of a poetic image or 'fiction' which in an elusive and allusive manner symbolizes 'continuousness' itself in the recognizable imaginative terms of the individual creative context.

The end of book I establishes Chaucer's artistic use of the two rhythms: (1) the concluding fiction which is signalled by an initial and ultimate formal statement in the concluding stanza: 'Now lat us stynte of Troilus a stounde . . . And thus he dryveth forth his aventure.' This firmly establishes the rhetorical-verbal basis of this rhythm; (2) the invention of a continuative image out of the fictional 'reality' of the work. The moping, inert life of Troilus changes through the wise attentions of Pandarus, and Troilus 'lay tho no lenger doun'. He has become active and robust at the end of book I. Yet Chaucer in the last stanza revives the image of an unwell man, transferring its reference from the level of the actual to the metaphoric. Troilus becomes in a double *similitudo* 'as an esy pacient', waxing well of his mental wound, paying due attention to his regimen, bearing his doctor's prescriptions in mind. This 'image' provides the continuousness at a level of reality, establishing this anticipatory pattern in the reader's awareness. After the formal invocation to book II, this image knits with the continuing fictional reality but now amusingly transferred to Pandarus, the metaphorical doctor, whom we find abed quite unable to heal himself

[16] This Virgilian passage provided Chaucer with material for book I of the *House of Fame*.

(II.57–63). The end of book II shows the same close attention to an intelligent deploying of the two conclusive rhythmic devices. Formally, the section ends with a rhetorical *demande d'amour*. Thus the first, concluding 'fiction' is contained in a rhetorical and verbal structure. The second, continuous, rhythm, expressed at the end of book I in the form of the patient-metaphor, has now passed from the figurative to the full level of 'reality' (II.1750: 'Com of therfore, and bryngeth hym to hele') for Troilus is pretending to be seriously ill. This image of continuousness connects directly with the plot-line of book III.

The climax of the dramatic structure in book III shows Chaucer complicating and lending a certain irony to his concluding formulae. In a passage which recalls the summarizing approach to book I's ending, we are given the author's quiet epitome-history of Troilus' happy, morally beneficial way of life. It is formally concluded by a rhetorical apostrophe to the celestial muses. The reader expects this precise manner of concluding for it is manifestly rhetorical and verbal in structure. But we find that the book here ends for the author is fatigued and the heavenly muses are leaving (III.1812). In terms of the emotional turning-point of the plot and the whole unfolding of the rest of the work of art *they never return*. In the *proemium* to book IV Chaucer is now forced to call upon the Furies to provide his poetic inspiration. They become the infernal muses who 'this ilke ferthe book me helpeth fyne'. The poetic emphasis has suddenly changed, chiastically. The concluding 'fiction' becomes the vehicle for the continuative image. The departure of the celestial muses is more than the formal 'end' of a single book. On the other hand, the usual continuative image in the fictional reality of the work ceases to perform its accustomed function. Here, Chaucer's depicted 'reality' returns us unrealistically to the dominant note of book III, the liaison of the joyful lovers:

> My thridde book now ende ich in this wyse,
> And Troilus in lust and in quiete
> Is with Criseyde, his owen herte swete.

This manner of life is doomed not to continue. What will persist is the tragic nemesis under the inspiration of the Dirae. The reader expects the rhythm of the fictional reality to transmit the continuing image. It does so only in a deceptive form.

The conclusion of book IV is skilfully managed by reference to the time structure ending of the lovers' last night together. It connects directly with the deceptive physical and emotional state depicted at the end of book III, the liaison of the lovers. In the concluding rhythm, the rhetorical-verbal structure laconically synchronizes the time of day with the action of Troilus: 'day gan rise and Troilus hym cladde' (IV.1690).[17] Time moves ruthlessly on and the author repeats the same synchronized expression and action to end with a dramatic exit-image[18] which incorporates Troilus' whole loss of emotional life:

> Which that his soule out of his herte rente.
> Withouten more, out of the chaumbre he wente.

The second, continuative image is conveyed by the lovers' pathetic vow to meet again: 'Or nyghtes ten, to meten in this place' (IV.1685). This deceiving, unsatisfiable time-pattern provides a major part of the plot-line of book V as far as line 1204, contributing all its ironic, depressing logic. Hope is fitfully prolonged (ll. 1205–9) for six days. As the extra week is completed the narrative rhythm breaks into a deliberately discontinuous series of final cadences, each reflecting some concluding aspect of the poem—of Criseyde's constancy, of the life of Troy itself, of the life of Troilus, of the pagan world of values, finally of all human temporal aims and purposes. Between books IV and V there is no pronounced formal pause, no rhetorical invocation, only a brief, laconic apostrophe to the Fates and a controlled and beautiful *chronographia* (V.8–14) describing the dawning of the day of Criseyde's departure and at the same time summarizing the whole epical time-scale of the work: 'three years' since Troilus began to love Criseyde. The reader is made to feel that it is three years to the day from love at first sight to this final parting.

With the exception of the concluding invocation to the departing muses of book IV.1807–13 (transposed from *Il Filostrato* I.3 with a complete change of application and tone) all the concluding passages just discussed are Chaucer's own invention and owe nothing to

---

[17] Cf. the *Knight's Tale*, line 2273: 'Up roos the sonne and up roos Emilye.'

[18] The 'dramatic' potentiality of an exiting image can scarcely have come to Chaucer's attention from Seneca's tragedies. There are only three possible instances in his works (*Medea* 300; *Oedipus* 708, 880; *Troades* 815–16). Seneca's act and scene divisions are nearly all anticipatory, continuous and *abstract*. Chaucer would have understood the 'dramatic' function of exiting from classical comedy. Exiting through doors is a standard scenic device in Plautus (a curriculum author); see, for example, *Amphitryon* I.3, 1.4/11; II/111; III.3/4; III/IV; IV/V; V. This comes about from the taking over of the domestic, Menandrian use of houses and doors. After all, Roman comedies had an actual history of stage production. Roman tragedy did not, as Seneca the elder reminds us.

Boccaccio or anyone else. Their creative positioning shows Chaucer's desire for a large, ambitious, independent narrative structure: in its formal properties moving away from the manner of the *roman courtois* towards the more intensely integrated form of the epic proper. What are we to say, then, of the *Canterbury Tales* in respect of its formal divisions? Like Gower's intention in constructing his *Confessio Amantis*, Chaucer cannot have expected his readers to wander 'continuously' 'to Canterburyward', no matter how 'ful devout' their 'corage'. Is the medieval reader merely presented with a superficial and mechanically random choice of closing his copy at the end of a tale or a series of tales? In view of the complex linkage in some groups, the very varying lengths of individual tales, the accumulated length of some groups of tales, the emerging of cross-referenced animosities and debates past and developing—it is surely naïve to imagine such an uncontrolled, arbitrary sense of formal development, as providing Chaucer's considered answer to what is a serious structural problem, given his transformation of the old, very static, framework-story collection. In the whole of Professor Ruggiers's discussion of the 'form' of the *Tales* (to cite but one modern instance) there is much mention of 'framework' and 'tales'—as if the poem were a static, topically arranged, compilation with but two moving parts—but there is no discussion whatever of the formal disposition and development of the *narratio*.[19] Perhaps the unfinished nature of the poem has excessively obscured this question.

The complex aesthetic pleasure arising out of the 'doctrine' and 'art' of the *Tales* begins and grows more intense with the degree of the reader's identification with the reality delineated. The more fully he enters into the confusion of art with nature the more interesting, instructive and genuinely affective the form of the *comoedia*. I think it is possible to see that the formal narrative structure is similarly affected by one's degree of sympathy with the fictional 'reality' and memory of the detailed relations one is invited to imagine. That is, degree of familiarity with the Canterbury fellowship brings into being the poem's proper creative rests and pauses, its alternations of completion and anticipation, attention and relaxation. At the superficial level, the novitiate reader mechanically follows the physical arrangement of the manuscript, its visual shape. One is invited to pause (for however long) at 'explicits' and begin at 'incipits'. Often the physical way in which a manuscript has been put together predisposes the reader to

[19] P. G. Ruggiers, *The Art of the Canterbury Tales*, pp. 1–50.

close his book; for example, when a tale ends in a quire where the last verso side is left blank. There is a great temptation not to read on. As the reader becomes more familiar with the material and becomes more absorbed creatively by the reality presented, Chaucer provides his audience with more intelligently placed divisions within the narrative where the eye and mind may pause for creative recollection. The modern reader has already been given larger, more intelligent units, namely the numerical sections or the alphabetically designated groups. The medieval reader had no such unit because the terminology and concept was developed during the nineteenth century.[20] No doubt, the medieval reader individually arrived at a consciousness of 'groups' (often the narrative divisions coincide) but these possibilities for pausing were not ready made: they had to be formed out of the individual medieval reader's familiarization with his text. Although the ordering of the tales in Robinson's second edition arguably represents (in its following of the richly produced Ellesmere MS.) the best reading experience a medieval reader may have had at his disposal by the second decade of the fifteenth century, we are perhaps denying ourselves the best and final order which Chaucer himself would have wished for his public.[21] I have stated previously my reasons for preferring the Chaucer Society's reconstructed arrangement and I shall use this pattern as the basis for trying to locate the original and natural divisions in the narrative structure.

For the purpose of the long verse narrative it may be argued from the size chosen for the books of *Troilus* that Chaucer regarded 1,000 to *c.* 2,000 lines as a reasonable unit of length for continuous reading silently or aloud. All the legends in the *Legend* taken together total no more than a little over 2,000 lines, with a 580-line prologue.[22] If we

[20] Some manuscripts show the use of arabic numerals, but these notations indicate a view of the order of tales. They refer only to single tales (and, where appropriate, introductory or epilogic material).

[21] From the state of the manuscripts (most of them with extensive contamination) it is certain that none of them represents Chaucer's final order. If we postulate from the quotation in the *Boke of Cupide* and Chaucer's reference in the *Envoi a Bukton* that the poet circulated separate tales either privately or publicly, it is nevertheless unlikely that a 'whole' version of the *Tales* would have been published with the author's knowledge. The statement in the *licentia authoris* referring to the collection as a 'whole' by title cannot bear the interpretation that the author had so consented. The *licentia* is not an afterthought or addition but formed an integral part of the poem in whatever state of composition it had ultimately reached.

[22] The units of the book structure of the *House of Fame* are designed on a different

apply a similar unit of length to the *narratio* of the *Tales*, a pattern of
natural 'rests' emerges with a certain consistency of supporting types
of rhetorical pointing, usually purely verbal in arrangement, sometimes
coinciding with a total break in continuity and 'end' of the modern
type of grouping, sometimes supported by a pronounced fictional
'image' of conclusion. What Chaucer never gives us is an episode or
standard pattern of concluding *topoi*. Boccaccio in the *Decameron* gives
us just such a repeated, schematic pattern: the division into days with
ten tales assigned to each of the ten days, making up a perfect number
of 100. Each day is divided from the next by a formal rhetorical
chronographia. After the Canterbury-reader has spent the night before
the journey at the 'Tabard' he is never offered another 'inn' or 'night-
draws-on' metaphor or image of 'herbergage'. At the level of the fictional reality we are never out of the saddle. In this way Chaucer
strengthens the unity of action in a purely intellectual and abstract
dimension; the argument is kept continuous, even the references to
actual topography are kept very brief. But the rhythm of the distance
between places is important. The first reference (Deptford) is a short
one (five miles); then the distances to Sittingbourne lengthen out
regularly to ten miles or more. As we reach the end of the journey the
distances again shorten (Boghtoun under Blee in Group G; Bobbe-up-
and-down, Under the Blee in H group). The pattern is intelligible not
in terms of an actually realized route (trees, houses, objects) or the
exact number of days spent on the road (it is incalculable), but in terms
of the felt duration of the unity of argumentative action.[23] Any elaborate method of dividing the narrative which would distract the reader's
attention from the continuous dimension of the pilgrims' contending
voices is eschewed.

   In addition to the benefit gained from the principle of alternating
periods of attention and relaxation, the rests allow for the internalizing,
psychological linking devices to become another important element

---

[23] An accurate sense of distances in miles is attested to in the *Tales*, especially near
the end, cf. G 172 (in the tale, the distance to via Appia) G 555, 561 (Canterbury
miles). *Miliarii* (milestones) seem not to have been a regular feature of English
roads in the fourteenth century.

---

model: that of a progressive, constant ratio of increase, giving the reader a sense of
accumulation. Book I: *c.* 500 lines; book II: *c.* 1,100 lines; book III: *c.* 2,200 lines.
Each book almost exactly doubles in size. The sense of accumulation is supported
by the mounting sense of rapid confusion we encounter in III.1950ff. The final
movement we are offered (2145ff.) is of a mounting, disordered heap.

THE CANTERBURY TALES 97

in the continuousness of the narrative pattern, chiefly by providing units of continuousness which span more than one or two tales. We can now experience moments of tension outside the duration of a tale which occur firmly within an integrated narrative sequence. The links have ceased to be just mechanical extensions of the portraiture of the *General Prologue*. These links often provide the reader with the grounds for retracing his steps, for turning back in the narrative progression, of comparing one 'version' of reality with another. In the 'imperfect' middle section of the work the disposition of the links helps to draw the reader's attention to a basic Chaucerian method of construction: the recurring pairing arrangements indicating that some of the tales have been deliberately written in contrasting 'twins' with a single link section between them.[24] That is, through the 'device' of imperfection (failure to link these pairs into larger, continuous sequences) the reader is given a glimpse into a vital compositional feature: the use of the philosophical method of defining things by opposites, the evaluating of reality by comparison, 'By his contrarie is every thyng declared'.[25] The subjectivization of 'authority' is obvious from the initial satiric technique of the *General Prologue*. Every man becomes his own authority, 'experience' appears to have become the queen of the proofs of truth. The idea of a wholly relativistic construction built out of oppositions of views of reality offered in the form of tales probably came to Chaucer from Boccaccio's *Decameron*—for Boccaccio's work is constructed on just this principle.[26] But whereas the structure of contraries in the *Decameron* is given a certain supporting emphasis by the schematic and symmetrical divisions of the narrative, Chaucer never calls too much attention to this emphasis. Instead, consonant with the avoidance of providing a recurring 'image' of rest, the poet always gives the reader the impression of a free plasticity of movement, of additional elements of surprise and natural evolution within the journeying fiction.

In the completed opening section of the narrative, the first division [I] naturally falls within the *Knight's Tale*. If we take the *General*

[24] The C group: Physician–link–Pardoner; the E group: Clerk–link–Merchant; F group: Squire–link–Franklin.
[25] For an account of this *topos*, cf. Norton-Smith, *Lydgate: Poems*, Oxford (1968), pp. 178–9. For Chaucer's use, see *Troilus* I.637ff. We should add the famous passage in Seneca, *Epistulae Morales* 107.8 which ends in the apothegm: '*Contrariis rerum aeternitas constat*', 'Eternity consists of opposites.'
[26] Cf. A. D. Scaligione, *Love and Nature in the Late Middle Ages*, University of California Press (1963), pp. 83ff.

Prologue and the *Knight's Tale* together, the originally marked section ending *Explicit prima pars* at line 1354 yields a total unit of 2,209 lines. The concluding rhythm used here is reminiscent of the verbal arrangement which occurs at the end of *Troilus* II, a short epitome-history followed by a *demande d'amour*. The second division [II] begins with *Sequitur pars secunda* and extends as far as the conclusion of the Knight's narrative. This unit makes up 1,754 lines. This is a natural resting-place, for unexpected events occur immediately. The quiet order of the tales undergoes complete alteration as the Host proves unable to dictate the sequence of tellers. The Monk is satirically supplanted not only by a churl but by a very drunk one. The author-figure intervenes to warn the reader with a weak stomach that he should not only 'turne over the leef' but that he should skip the Reeve's tale as well in order to arrive at a more suitable tale—one containing 'gentillesse', 'moralitee' and 'holinesse'. This ironic warning (anticipating many of Sterne's moral warnings) conveniently marks out the section to which the Miller's prologue belongs. If we exclude the Cook's prologue and scarcely started tale, the Miller and Reeve begin to make up a unit of 1,215 lines. The Cook's prologue marks a dangerous direction in the psychological composition of the *Tales* for it establishes an extensive personal rivalry between the teller and the Host. In the general un-folding of the work this relation should be avoided for it destroys the comic impartiality and wonder of the Host. It ruins his brand of simplicity. Later, in the host's heated altercation with the Pardoner it is the Knight who characteristically separates them and quickly forces a reconciliation. For this reason Chaucer very early must have had second thoughts about including the Cook at all. By the end of the work we are told that he has been excused his tale. The warning to turn over the Miller and the Reeve implicitly anticipates some more moral tale which properly belongs to this group. In spite of the seem-ing break in continuity,[27] in terms of a natural length the Man of Law's prologue and tale properly belong to this division. It is a tale redolent of 'gentillesse', 'moralitee' and 'holinesse'. If so, this division [III] as far

[27] The abrupt juxtaposition may be deliberate in order to indicate to the reader that he is not expected to mechanically compute a time-scheme on the basis of how many days occupy the pilgrimage. I think he is also signalled that the length of the tale and the fictional time imagined for the speaker to tell the tale are of no importance. The Host refers to the fourth part of the artificial day as being over and that it is nigh on ten o'clock in the morning (B 1–15). The arithmetic unit which immediately springs to the reader's mind is three hours. Three tales have been told (if we exclude the Cook's fragmentary remains).

as the conclusion of the *Man of Law's Tale* makes up 2,377 lines. If we accept the genuineness of the epilogue to the *Lawyer's Tale* (as I think we must) then the next unit—epilogue, *Shipman's Tale*,[28] link, *Prioress's Tale*—makes up a division [IV] of 1,910 lines, ending properly in absolute and prolonged silence. This horrid little 'miracle' reduces the Canterbury company (as well as the modern reader) to blank amazement. This is one of the rare moments of medieval embarrassment shown by a heterogeneous social group. The moment is thus especially marked before the inclusion of the *fabulae Chauceri*.

The fifth section [V] seems entirely composed of Chaucerian material, containing the prologue, the interrupted *Tale of Sir Thopas*, the link and the *Tale of Melibeus*. The prose length of the *Tale of Melibeus* is visually difficult to equate with lines of verse. Carefully read aloud it occupies the best part of an hour and twenty-five minutes. Thus, the prose plus the verse material would make up a verse-line unit of about 1,800 lines. The sixth section [VI]—beginning with the prologue and tale of the Monk (interrupted and unfinished), link, followed by the *Nun's Priest's Tale*—makes up a natural unit of 1,557 lines.[29] The following section [VII] begins with the unrelated *Physician's Tale* and takes in the whole of the C group and the D group as far as the end of the *Wife of Bath's Tale*, making a natural break and rest after such a brilliant, major narrative moment. Every manuscript I have seen bears witness in the form of rubbing, discoloration and marginalia that this prologue and tale were considered as a major sequence in the narrative. This unit contains 2,199 lines. The eighth section [VIII] extends from the prologue to the *Friar's Tale*, link and the *Summoner's Tale*. This comprises a short unit of 1,029 lines but it seems to be marked for a conclusion in one of the few effective uses of an image taken from the journeying fiction. It breaks abruptly and conclusively into the narrative in its finishing moment: 'My tale is doon, we ben almoost at

[28] The arguments about the sex of the narrator based upon lines *1202–*1209 ignore the strong possibility that these lines should be enclosed in inverted commas as a quotation. It is an impersonating speech, mocking a shrewish wife. There is more mocking impersonation of the wife by the narrator in lines *1258–9, where these lines, too, should be printed in inverted commas. The simpering greeting is immediately echoed in line *1288.
[29] The epilogue to the priest, although probably genuine, cannot be described as a 'link' with anything, for it merely anticipates another, unspecified tale. This potential link would seem to have survived in an unfinished and contaminated state. It survives in five secondary manuscripts and in a more contaminated version in four additional manuscripts.

toune.' This is a natural image of rest and it is significant that no
linking material follows. The next section [IX] is long and completely
unified, bringing together the Clerk's prologue, tale and the skilfully
related Merchant's prologue, tale and epilogue. This unit occupies
2,440 lines and ends with a repetition of the phrase which concluded
the preceding section: 'my tale is do.' This section is disconnected.
The tenth section [X] begins with the unconnected introduction to the
Squire's Tale (imperfect), link and the Franklin's prologue and tale.
This section, too, is concluded with the phrase 'my tale is at an ende'.
In its imperfect state it makes up 1,624 lines. The divisions in this
analysis are beginning to coincide with the alphabetical groupings, for
example, E and F coincide. The penultimate section [XI] begins with
the Second Nun's prologue (unconnected), her tale, link and the
Canon's Yeoman's prologue and tale. The concluding phrase of this
section is 'for ended is my tale'. The unit occupies 1,481 lines and
corresponds exactly with group G. The last section [XII] begins with
the Manciple's prologue, his tale, link and the *Parson's Tale* with the
licentia authoris. Chaucer has kept the Manciple's material extremely
brief (altogether only 361 lines), but even so, the prose of the Parson,
although lighter in rhythm and syntactically smoother than Melibeus'
still takes a little over two hours to read aloud. Although the treatise
is divided into parts, pausing at any one of them seems to serve no
literary purpose.

This 'reading version' of the structure and divisions of the *narratio*
as a single, continuous movement, can (given the nature of the evidence)
merely achieve the status of another conjecture. But it is an attempt to
replace the present arrangement, which is a hybrid model made up
from an attempt to produce mechanically the order of one manuscript,
and to divide the poem into 'groups' which satisfy the principle of
intelligent editing as far as the internal continuity of single parts is
concerned. It is the child of editorial caution and unlimited conjecture.
Whatever it is, it is not a good 'reading version' for it automatically
confines us to think in 'tales' or 'groups' by visually and mentally
involving us in the complexity and paraphernalia of unsolved editorial
problems: starred lines, alphabetical groups, numerical groups,
alphabetical groups subdivided and subnumbered, numerical and
alphabetical groups which do not correspond. There is something to
be said for reading the poem even in a contaminated medieval manuscript version.

This order and dividing of the poem has arisen out of an attempt to familiarize myself with the text, and my natural sense of elation and fatigue as an ordinary reader. It has meant a more numerous division of the *Tales* into parts than the purely editorial sorting into groups. I now wish to consider in detail the prologue to the *Parson's Tale*[30] which contains nearly all the fictional elements for bringing the work to a final close. It contains all the concluding images and *topoi* just as the *Prologue* to the *Legend* contains the essentials for the conclusion of that work.

The Parson's prologue is constructed round a common rhetorical device for concluding a work, the 'end-of-day' *topos*. Chaucer had used it earlier to conclude his *Prologue* to the *Legend of Good Women*. The last words of the Host to the Parson make this obvious:

> 'Telleth', quod he, 'youre meditacioun
> But hasteth you, the sonne wole adoun;'
>
> (I.71–2)

The method for measuring this penultimate literary moment is exactly that which had been used in the introduction to the *Lawyer's Tale*: an exact scientific observation using the length of a shadow cast by an object. But in the earlier use it had been just another object in the landscape, a tree. Now it has become the physical body of the author of the *Tales*. Although the principle of measurement remains objective, one unit of measure has been transferred to the personal and subjective. The geometric system is also accompanied by certain astronomical observations, the degrees in the sun's arc remaining above the horizon and the complementary ascending of the moon's 'face', Libra. The last detail is erroneously noted by Chaucer, who has used the sb. 'exaltacioun' for 'face'—or has written 'Libra' instead of the correct 'Saturn'. This is not an easily explained slip of the pen, and I suspect the mistake is deliberate: in order to call attention to the non-astrological application of some of the scientific observations in the long *chronographia*. This is literary astronomy. The numbers employed in this calculation have a non-astronomical field of reference in addition to their obvious import. The number twenty-nine in the calculation 'Degrees nyne and twenty' is conveniently one degree short of the

---

[30] The concluding position of the *Parson's Tale* as a penitential sequence in the narrative (determined by internal structural factors) is paralleled by a similar emphasis in the pseudo-Vincentian *Speculum Morale* (dating from the first half of the fourteenth century). The encyclopedia is concluded by a 'De Poenitentia' (III.ii.x) which follows a very extensive description of the sins.

complete, round number of thirty (there are thirty degrees in each two-hour unit, cf. *Astrolabe* II. 10). There is one more tale to be told. Twenty-nine is an obvious penultimate number. It is also the exact number of tales which the original compact specified to be told, as based on the number of pilgrims in the company (A *General Prologue* 24). This cannot be accidental.

Although the reader may expect the shadow cast by Chaucer at the end of the day to look towards a common religious application of the diminishing life of man, the shadow of his physical existence (cf. Job 17.7, etc.) or the shadow of transitory things (Boethius, *De Consolatione* III prose iv), the shadow of Chaucer the poet lengthens.[31] This image of measurement, I suspect, is intended to refer to his literary existence, the size of the author as exemplified in this work growing as the work itself lengthens. The image turns on ME 'shadow' and Latin '*umbra*' containing the sense of 'an image, somewhat imperfect'. The figurative use of the sb. is common in classical authors and occurs in the Vulgate in St Paul, Hebrews 10.1. Significantly, the author's shadow measures 'ellevene foot', another penultimate number. The unit lacks one integer to make up twelve, the complete number of hours of daylight in the artificial day. Twelve is also the complete number of divisions or 'rests' which have emerged from my analysis of the structure of the narrative. Eleven divisions are over, one remains. Further, 'my lengthe' is 'parted/In six feet equal of proporcioun'. I think this division of the author's shadow refers to Chaucer's intention (not completed) to arrange his *Tales* in two major divisions, each ending with a prose tale. It is no accident that in my analysis Chaucer's *Tale of Melibeus* ends the fifth section, occurring nearly in the middle of the narrative progression.[32] Further, the closing prayer of Melibee (3070ff.) forgiving his opponents' sins, his dwelling on the *contemptus mundi*, the reference to the final repentance of all men and God's perfect for-

[31] This image of lengthening shadows to signify the end of the literary work would seem to have been suggested by Virgil's *Eclogue* I and II. The end-of-day *topos* in each case uses this progressive image. Cf. I.83: '*maioresque cadunt altis de montibus umbrae*' ('and lengthening shadows fall from the mountain heights'), and II.67: '*et sol crescentis decedens duplicat umbras*' ('and the retiring sun doubles the lengthening shadows'). For the Virgilian mood of pensiveness and serenity evoked by this image in *Eclogue* I, cf. V. Pöschl, *Die Hirtendictung Virgils*, Heidelberg (1964), pp. 62–3; and cf. *Georgics* I.342.

[32] In terms of distance along the road to Canterbury the *Tale of Melibeus* ends almost exactly on the half-way line, as the reference to approaching Rochester (Monk's prologue, line 1926) makes plain.

giveness, all this looks forward to the ideas and emotions of the Parson's 'meditacioun', as well as the *licentia authoris*.

However naturally these rests and divisions arose out of Chaucer's gradual putting together of the *Tales*, consciously the whole structure harkens back to a type of total poetic long narrative shape with which Chaucer was very familiar: that is, the epic, and especially Virgil's *Aeneid*. It is possible to see in Chaucer's arrangement a reflection of the twelve-book structure of the epic, and Virgil's particular division of the *Aeneid* into two six-book units (the Iliadic and the Odysseyian narrative patterns)[33] with the closing Roman prophecy of Anchises in book VI looking forward to the triumph of Aeneas in book XII. There is nothing mysterious or arcane in this possible Chaucerian use of numerological symbolism. It is based on (1) broad and general patterns arising out of our traditional way of measuring time and our response to round numbers; (2) the traditional and well-known method of constructing epical narratives.

III   The narrator

There is a tendency in modern criticism of medieval poetry to imagine that a full description and elaborate definition of the various roles of an author-figure in an extended narrative will give us a reliable method for increasing the amount of 'epistemological relativism among the characters'[34] and at the same time will provide us with a unifying image of an 'entire conception of man'—a human intelligence who may be imagined as capable of understanding the work as an 'audience' yet not necessarily capable of appreciating the work as his own creation. Thus, it has become fashionable to separate the figure of the 'author' from that of the 'narrator'. No doubt this is a wise distinction. But the very act of isolating or 'identifying' roles and figures involves us in a certain concentration upon a projected personage whose continuous and total presence as author is omnipresent in the work in any case. Professor Durling is well aware of this problem as a footnote citing Professor Booth's *Rhetoric of Fiction*[35] serves to indicate. Yet his

33 Cf. Macrobius, *Saturnalia* V.6.
34 Cf. R. M. Durling, *The Figure of the Poet in Renaissance Epic*, pp. 8–9. He rightly objects to this.
35 W. C. Booth, *The Rhetoric of Fiction*, Chicago (1962).

subsequent use of an identifying technique sometimes obscures 'the author as revealed in the totality of his work'.[36] Authorial presence is best established, I think, by examining the dominant characteristics of the authorial style and form in its pervasive linguistic existence. By this method one may avoid some of the distortions which can result from concentrating too exclusively on 'voices' and 'presences'. This is the strength methodologically of the late Professor Auerbach's approach to the problem of authorship, individuality, formal meaning and tradition of expression. A fictional version of the author or narrator is a self-consciously contrived projection and so may not represent a totality at all. Such a figure may be invented for limited or localized purposes in a narrative structure. We must be made aware of how the author seeks to influence our sensibilities, to engage our emotions, to inform our intelligence. The sum of these techniques yields a truer image of the poet in all his creative stratagems.

Chaucer was aware of this tension between an intrusive version of the artistic mind and the total poetic intelligence implied in every word of the poem. A convenient paradigm for this awareness may be seen in the *balade* against Fortune where the *visage* which emerges is not only Fortune's but the author's. The whole structure of the poem is modelled on ironic impersonation. In his *Troilus* we are presented with a dual intrusive image of author and narrator, but over and above this a demonstrable astuteness of stylistic procedure makes us aware of Chaucer's version of Virgil's 'subjective style'[37]—the classical counterpart of Flaubert's 'indirect free style'. In this mode of narrative the author (as is well known in nineteenth-century fiction) passes almost imperceptibly in and out of a character's speech or mind, using the character's 'thought' or 'words', always qualifying the *donnée* by means of impersonation or withdrawal of empathy by minute or extensive reversions to authorial knowledge. All of this is conducted at the stylistic level. Virgil's evolution of a subjective, editorial style was plainly dictated by the necessity of avoiding the introduction of an author-figure into a pseudo-Homeric impersonal epic style. Chaucer's reliance on authorial figures, authorities and guides has evolved from a long medieval tendency to locate literary *auctoritas* in a non-contemporary, antique time-scheme. His use of humility formulae and willingness to submit to 'correction' supports the view that Chaucer shares to

---

[36] Durling, *op. cit.*, p. 3.
[37] This technique is discussed by Brooks Otis in his *Virgil: a Study in Civilized Poetry*, Oxford (1963), pp. 41–96.

a certain extent the medieval poet's lack of confidence in his own potential authority. In Gower and Lydgate the lack of neo-classical individual confidence seems to me genuine. In Chaucer it is only genuine 'up to a point'. The apologetic or dependent mode is more an artistic convenience. The verse epistles to Scogan and Bukton, perhaps not intended for a public audience, show a confident, allusive Horatian style and projection of the poet's personality. Boccaccio already thinks of Dante as an 'authority' by 1342. Chaucer shows no such inclination. Chaucer has literary confidence in his near-contemporaries and so draws on their creative guidance, Boccaccio in *Troilus*, Dante in the *House of Fame*. But his identified 'auctor' turns out to be a Latin author 'Lollius' (fictional) and his Dante finds no occupiable pillar in the palace of Fame.

For an illustration of the flexibility and introspectiveness of Chaucer's style, the reader should turn his attention to the original episode which passes between Criseyde and Diomede in book V.92–189. The main technique is that of the omniscient author but Chaucer is also to be observed entering into the character of Diomedes. The 'thought' of the character is rendered directly (ll. 100–5), but his speech is sometimes expressed indirectly when the author is narrating (ll. 108–16). There is continuous and intense immediacy in the mode of representation. The circumambience and feigned inexperience of Diomede's heartless stratagem is reflected in the involved and repetitious sentence structure of the narrator. Thus:[38]

> For trewliche he swor hire, as a knyght,
> That ther nas thyng with which he myghte hire plese,
> That he nolde don his herte and al his myght
> To don it, for to don hire herte an ese;

shows un-Chaucerian repetitiousness of words and phrase in awkward positions. This is plainly an example of an impersonating style. As the Diomedian strategy develops, the ingratiating style appears to gain in confidence and stylistic fluency: little rhetorical graces are introduced, e.g. the parallelism in 'thynges grete' and 'gret delyt' (ll. 136, 138), the climactic *antimetabole* of lines 143–4, the clinching ambiguity in 'But

---

[38] Lines 113–16. In line 115 Robinson, following the so-called γ-group of manuscripts, reads 'peyne' for 'herte'. I prefer Root's retention of 'herte'. Certainly the phrase 'to don [ones] herte' is unique in ME but the phrase may be intended as a Diomedian nervous error, a nonce-usage.

this enseled til another day' (l. 151) which exploits the primary figurative sense 'to seal up', 'to keep secret until later' and the underlying (and
more common) sense 'to ratify'. Instantly, Diomede commands her
to take his hand (the action symbolic of entering into a contract) and
swears himself in as her knight. As she offers no physical resistance, the
impression of a binding agreement is insinuated. The omniscient
narrator tells us that she has heard only 'a word or two' of all this. At
the end of the interview (ll. 186–9), Chaucer shifts the narrating tense
from the past to the present: 'she accepteth it in good manere',

> But natheles she thonked Diomede
> Of al his travaile and his goode cheere,
> And that hym list his frendshipe hire to bede;
> And she accepteth it in good manere,
> And wol do fayn that is hym lief and dere,
> And trusten hym she wolde, and wel she myghte,
> As seyde she; and from hire hors sh'alighte.
>
> (183–9)

This shift indicates that this statement and what follows makes extensive
use of submerged quotation. The narrative after three present indica-
tives passes back through a past tense, 'wolde trusten', then slips back
into a beautifully modulated 'narrative present' which includes (a) the
past presented as present, (b) historical present and (c) immediate
narrative present in terms of what is to come. This phrase, 'and wel she
myghte' is finally qualified by 'As seyde she', indicating that some
expression equivalent to 'and wel she myghte' belongs to what she
actually said. The phrase is ominously ambiguous and shows that, for all
her distraction, Criseyde is aware of the erotic implications in the relationship. The 'good manere' which is not really part of the author's
view (since it was Criseyde's expression) is severely qualified by the
phrases 'and wel she myghte', 'as seyde she'. Here the author and
the character are mutually aware of the deception practised and the
obliquely expressed intention.

The effect of this stylistic attention, of passing subtly in and out of
the present and past between narrator and characters is to make the
crystallization of the moment of awareness almost simultaneous for
character, author and reader. The moment occurs in a passage of formal
politeness. The author truncates the shared moment by passing in an
abrupt, laconic half-line into an ultimately positioned preterite which
suddenly completes a physical progression: Criseyde sitting in the

saddle, nearly sliding off her saddle (l. 182, in ultimate position), finally dismounted. The *raison d'être* for the authorial style deployed here (and elsewhere) in the poem is not simply to create an illusion of immediacy but also to distribute appropriate moral concern. The result of the author's choosing to bring us closer to the actual scene is to make Diomede not merely a 'parody' of Troilus but to establish concretely his moral odiousness—without that judgment escaping from a firmly subordinate context.[39] In the case of Criseyde, the episode does not compromise any possible view of her 'simplicity', 'passivity' or degree of moral culpability; but we now realize that henceforth in her new setting she will require a certain interpreting and understanding given this presented (and now experienced) reality. Beyond the moral implications resulting from the characterization, this method of authorial presentation increases our admiration for the artistic resources, poetic intelligence and perfection of form. In spite of the pathos created by the affectiveness of the construction, the poem never becomes a type of the harrowing. It causes elation and satisfies our yearning for completed artistic excellence through its heightened use of formal expressive inventions.

The reader who has suddenly turned from the authorial mode of *Troilus* to that of the *General Prologue* to the *Tales* will scarcely 'recognize' the author of this work by his style or method of proceeding. It is not enough to account for this difference in terms of literary ambiance, a reconstructed pagan past as contrasted with a known and everyday reality. Nor is a different audience intended, as if we could begin to identify a single audience much less a number of them. The first impressions of this Chaucerian style are: (1) narrative impetus and velocity; (2) procedural directness; (3) syntactical simplicity; (4) epigrammatical nervousness; (5) strength and regularity of stress in identifying the rhythmic units with sense and grammatical completeness. The disposition of ictus and pause alone seems to dictate to the ear the expectation of a crisp, couplet-like unit to be completed. The combined effect of these elements is to give the verse a pronounced isomorphic appearance. Although, initially, conservative in diction, unadventurous in syntax, unremarkable in choice of metaphor, the methods used to create isomorphism also create an easily identifiable

[39] Chaucer, unlike Gower, has a well-developed sense of narrative perspective. Arrangement is not based on a model or pre-existing pattern but shows close Horatian attention to neo-classical notions of internal unity and coherent development of episode, character and symbolism.

literary style, an individualized 'presence'. While one were reading through a medieval collection of anonymous or unidentified verse, even a short extract of this Canterbury trotting style[40] would instantly distinguish itself. In my reading experience there is no other style like it in the period 1350–1400. Later, in the fifteenth century, there appear no obvious imitators of Canterburyese. Lydgate in his impersonating of a Canterbury pilgrim in *Thebes* deliberately avoids the decasyllabic measure, choosing instead the octosyllabic. That Lydgate understood the elements of this crisp, economic manner may be gathered from his not wholly unsuccessful imitation in *The Mumming at Hertford* which I have tentatively dated before 1430. Compare the following passage describing the wifely care of Beatrice Bittersweet[41] (ll. 37ff.):

> Than sitteth Beautryce bolling at the nale,
> As she that gyveth of him no maner tale;
> For she al day, with her jousy nolle,
> Hath for the collyk pouped in the bolle,
> And for hed-ache, with pepir and gynger
> Dronk dolled ale to make hir throte cleer.
> And cometh hir hoom whan hit draweth to eve
> And then Robyn, the sely, pore, Reeve
> Fynde non amends of harme ne damage,
> But leen growell and soppeth cold potage.
> And of his wyf hath noon other cheer
> But cokkrowortes[42] vnto his souper.

[40] The summonour (*Canterbury Tales* D 838) uses the gaits of riding (amble, trot, pace) comically to apply to styles of narrating or speaking: 'What! amble, or trot, or pees, or go sit doun!' The item 'pees' is usually taken to mean 'peace' used as an exclamatory imperative. The items here function as sbs or vbs where the last, climactic phrase of command could also be considered comically as a mode of speaking, substantively referred to. For 'pees' as a term of riding, cf. *Canterbury Tales* G 575.

[41] The only extant text is in the hand of Shirley; therefore, I have regularized the spelling (MacCracken, *Minor Poems*, EETS, vol. 2, pp. 675ff.). The possible existence of a folk type with this engaging spousal name may lie behind Shakespeare's character of Beatrice in *Much Ado about Nothing*. For her 'bitter disposition' cf. II.i.215; by Act IV she has become 'sweet Beatrice'.

[42] This unique ME compound would seem to represent a loan-word from the Low Countries signifying 'greens cooked the day before and kept overnight' (*MED*). Its otherwise unrecorded existence indicates the sharpness of particularized reality associated with this Chaucerian style. The *General Prologue* of the *Tales* abounds in localizing nomenclature. Lydgate's 'pouped in the bolle' is a very amusing reworking of *Canterbury Tales* H 90. There are other reminiscences.

In the *General Prologue*, the first two aspects of the initial impression of a Canterburian style are closely related: the brisk, rapid velocity of the verse and the general procedural directness. As has been noticed, the opening *chronographia* is entirely 'scientific'. It is concerned with the physical operation of the natural world. So much so that the intellectual connection between season and the present desire for pilgrimaging is expressed in one condensed, parenthetical observation ('so prikketh hem nature in hir corages'). This observation on creaturely natural desire reflects the just-mentioned reawakening of vegetable nature. Scientifically, we move upward through the three 'faculties' of the soul: the vegetable to the sensitive to the rational. In each the season itself calls into being that faculty's nature, its power to revitalize in its own special way.[43] In the lowest function of soul, the vegetable, the power is for growth; in the sensitive, the impulse to love and reproduce; in the rational, a religious desire to give thanks for aid received during a recent illness. Human nature is assimilated to all other natural activity in the briefest and most compressed way. We are not intended to examine these relationships. It is part of the *donnée*. These are all acts of 'poetic worship' as the *Complaint of Mars*, lines 1–4, makes clear.

The syntactical arrangement, although allowing us rhythmical pause sufficient to admire the rapid opening and closing of the couplet units, rushes us forward in the narrative development. Lines 1–18 compose one verse paragraph where the larger structure is built of two adverbial clauses introduced by *anaphora* ('Whan . . . Whan . . .') and completed by one adverbial temporal clause ('Thanne longen . . .') in line 12. The overall structure is thus made up of two parts balanced on the fulcrum of 'When . . . then', and so mirrors the pivoted, pairing pattern of the smaller rhythmical couplet units. The opening adverbial 'when' clause is made up of two couplets of enclosed rhythmical vitality joined by a single co-ordinating conjunction where all verbs are governed by the initial 'Aprill'. This clear, precise rhythmical unit immediately establishes for the ear the underlying, normal rhythmical and syntactical expectation. The body of the verse paragraph (ll. 5–14) prepares the ear for the variations on the basic pattern: (1) enjambment arising out of enlargement of units beyond couplet length, and (2) the opposite technique of interrupting the couplet unit, separating

---

[43] The effect of the time of year on the functions of the soul in the macrocosm and the microcosm is a philosophical commonplace, cf. Lydgate's translation of the *Secreta Secretorum*.

rhyming couplets in sense completion: lines 11–12 though they rhyme together belong to two distinct units of sentence-sense. The verse paragraph deliberately returns to a final unit of four lines in two enclosed couplets, where the link seems to be simple appositional arrangement: actually, the strict grammatical completion of 'they wonde . . . for to seke', a purpose clause, is obscured by moving the direct object, 'the holy blisful martir', ahead of the infinitive. This inversion of subject-object exactly parallels the inversion of the couplet 15–16 where the governing subject and verb is held back to the ultimate position.

The couplet unit established in the period 1–18 reminds one of the rapid terseness of Dryden's couplets, the 'hand-gallop' as Dr Johnson characterized it. But Chaucer's couplets are not constructed on Ovidian or Tibullian lines. The opening-closing rhythm is scarcely assisted by any chiastic arrangements of syntax, of antithesis, balance or parallelism. Thus, the grammatical formulation of couplets and series of couplets appears natural and hardly contrived. The reader's whole consciousness of the economic justness of the couplet is conveyed by the author's establishing an alert expectation of metrical regularity and precise distribution of pauses. The pulse of the lines is strongly iambic and the *volta* or pause at the end of the line (emphasizing the rhyme-words) equally pronounced. The pause at the caesura tends to a marked regularity. It shows no great movableness or multiplicity within a single line. The line regularly divides in terms of feet 2/3, 3/2 without much use of qualifying phrases or emphatic, pointed stress of lexical items to play against the iambic, regular impetus of the line, couplets or larger verse units. Syllabic smoothness and the conscious distribution of poetically determined syllables, too, seem to play very little part in the creation of the impression of regularity within the single line or couplet.

The earliest example of couplet-rhymed decasyllabics in Chaucer (incidentally, probably the earliest use of this measure in ME), in the *Legend*, shows an entirely different, asymmetrical employment of rhythm, rhyme and syntax. The initial poetic period of the *Prologue* makes up a modest unit of nine lines ending emphatically on a split couplet: the paired rhymes are separated:

> A thousand tymes have I herd men telle
> That ther ys joy in hevene and peyne in helle,
> And I acorde wel that it ys so;

> But, natheles, yet wot I wel also
> That ther nis noon dwellyng in this contree,
> That eyther hath in hevene or helle ybe,
> Ne may of hit noon other weyes witen,
> But as he hath herd seyd, or founde it writen;
> For by assay ther may no man it preve.

In syntactical structure it is divided into two uneven units (1–3; 4–9) where the overall syntactical movement is based on *gradio* (climax). Each unit culminates in an emphatic, reasoned assertion (3,9). All the lines in each unit are enjambed and the syntactical organization is continuous (in spite of Robinson's tendency to over-point). No opportunity is afforded for a *volta* after the rhyme-words and no pause is offered at the metrical caesura. Although the distribution of the ictus is iambic, there is no strong stress insistence in a regular accentual pattern. Syllabic smoothness prevails with single, repeated lexical items placed for special, argumentative stressing—words indicating negation. In line 5 one can imagine considerable displacement of stress. It gives the effect of good, civilized discourse without calling the slightest attention to rhymes or couplet symmetry. The first couplet shape we are allowed arrives in lines 17–18, lines which compose the opening of a new thematic paragraph, calling attention to the importance of literature. The same rhythmic organization is repeated in lines 25–6, in a couplet which sums up the author's reverence for ancient letters:

> And yf that olde bokes were aweye,
> Yloren were of remembraunce the key.

lines cited and paraphrased by Edward of York in his *Prologue* to the *Mayster of the Game*, written scarcely a decade after Chaucer's death: 'Be wryteng haue men of ymages passed for writyng is the keye of alle good remembraunce.'[44] Even when Chaucer seems ostensibly to be translating Ovidian distichs (ll. 1355–65) the enclosed couplet rhythm appears only occasionally (cf. ll. 1364–5), and with some rhetorical parallelism but little chiastic verbal arrangement. A fine couplet such as lines 1338–9 with enclosed rhythm and a certain Ovidian charm of verbal arrangement turns out to have Virgilian origins. Thus,

[44] The collocation 'good remembraunce' occurs in the later *Assembly of Gods* 998, in a list which includes 'Reason' and 'Discresion'. It probably signifies the faculty of accurate memory, not merely 'remembering'.

And seyde, 'O swete cloth whil Juppiter it leste,
Tak now my soule, unbynd me of this unreste.'

has been invented from *Aeneid* IV.652–3:

'*Dulces exuuiae, dum fata deusque sinebat,
Accipite hanc animam meque exsoluite curis.*'

The verbal economy of making the epithet 'swete' connect with the phrase 'whil Juppiter it leste' comes directly from Virgil, but the second half of the couplet shows an elegance which is not in Virgil. The co-ordinating conjunction is suppressed, the two imperative verbs are placed in parallel positions in the hemistich, and the last verb and its object are given equal syllabization and identical first phonetic elements as prefixial compounds: $un+bynd/un+reste$. The addressee in the apostrophe, a cloth, lends to the abstract verb ('deliver') a concrete quality.[45] This kind of elegant, effective rhythmical shape Ovid would have approved of. But these rhythms are not the normal mode of narrative procedure. On the whole, the rhythmic and syntactical shape of the *Prologue*, lines 1–9, is a fairly accurate indication of the general narrative style.

The rapid movement of the Canterbury couplets takes us in under 900 lines through a simplified prologic plan with only three major parts and two minor transitions. The *dispositio* is extremely clear:

[small]   (1) *chronographia* and *praepositio* (1–42)
[large]   (2) *ethopoeiae* (portraits) (43–714)
[minor] { (3) transitional epitome looking forward to *narratio* (715–23)
           (4) *excusatio:* an authorial statement on style, content and procedure (724–46)
[small]   (5) *narratio* (containing *ethopoeia* of the host) (747–858).

The effect in general narrative rhythm is of a tripartite arrangement: one small unit (42 lines) + one large unit (671 lines) + one small unit (143 lines). Thus, the economy of the smaller verbal arrangements is successfully matched by the larger formal conciseness. Whatever the general origin of this pattern, the effect on the reader is immediate.[46]

[45] Nearly all Chaucerian uses of the verb 'unbind' have implied concrete association. The *Parliament of Fowls*, line 523, would seem one of the notable exceptions.

[46] Many theories have been advanced. J. V. Cunningham (*MP* 49 (1952), pp. 172ff.) advanced the notion that the *Tale's Prologue* relates to the 'dream vision prologue in the tradition of the Romance of the Rose'. His archetypal story-pattern is too simplified from the beginning to prove his case. The series of portraits of pilgrims as introductory to a narrative episode probably reflects Chaucer's

His attention is mainly trained on the portraits (as foreground) and around this main focus he easily disposes the secondary material. After the experience of the *ethopoeiae* the reader will naturally feel that the connecting *narratio* (ll. 747ff.) is of the next order of importance. For the reader interested in the author as poet, the statement of lines 724–46 is of great value, especially in qualifying and extenuating the impression which we have already received of the narrator as pilgrim and recent member of the 'Tabard' fellowship.

As the 'portraits' or 'acquaintances'[47] unfold, the character of the pilgrim narrator in terms of his verbal 'style' similarly enlarges. It is a 'muse of easy access', reminding the modern reader of the plain, healthy vigour of Crabbe's couplets. The poetic atmosphere seems composed of country weather: tweeds, walking sticks, the voice of Boythorne in the land. The narrator reaches after no 'charm' of thought or especial literary or court gracefulness. The actual compositional pattern of the *ethopoeiae* is of prime importance in extending the style of the narrator. We should remember that in rhetorical construction the *ethopoeia* had an 'aim' attached to it: either to 'praise' or 'blame'. Examples of physical or moral description of persons (*effictio* and *notatio*) were not morally or poetically neutral. In the *Tales*,

[47] The sb. 'introduction' in the sense of a 'formal social act of introducing' seems to have originated in eighteenth-century usage. The medieval verb is 'acquaint' (*House of Fame*, l. 250) and the sb. 'acquaintance(s)' refers to the process, and persons so introduced (cf. Gower, *Confessio Amantis* VII*3236–7). There is a long comic version of the form of social acquainting in the prologue to the *Canon's Yeoman's Tale*, lines 593–662. It seems to consist in a series of precise questions: (1) what social position does the person hold ('conditioun'); (2) what are his clothes like ('array'); (3) where does he live. In *Gawain and the Green Knight* persons meeting formally for the first time ask a series of searching questions. Gawain is so greeted at Haut Desert. Thus, in the *Prologue* to Lydgate's *Thebes* when the author meets the host, after the short formal phrase of 'welcome', the poet is greeted with a series of questions (86–91): (1) name; (2) address; (3) why are you so dressed. From his general appearance the host already knows Lydgate's 'condition' (a monk) and so hails him. An exactly parallel method for introducing one's self is reflected in the protocol of Charters, a series of functional definitions ending with '*salutem*'. It would appear that in the Middle Ages one was entitled to be more openly inquisitive than is now permitted. By the same token one was allowed to be more self-descriptive and forthcoming. The result is a fuller descriptive ceremony and rather closer to Chaucer's *ethopoeiae* than the formal phrase or two of the modern introduction. These *ethopoeiae* function, then, as social introductions.

memory of the *Roman* 12015ff. where a similar series introduces the journey and gulling of Male Bouche and his confession and murder.

by constructing an unschematic, 'informal', individualized method Chaucer has removed the simple rhetorical polarization of the portrait into the vituperative and the laudatory. The Canterbury portraits achieve a kind of negligently planned neutrality—not the objectivity of a claimed or pretended 'realism', but a modified or 'extenuated' account.[48] The narrator's satiric sharpness is modified by the inclusion of an endearing quality and vice versa. It is essentially an excusatory style, extenuating by adding simply and directly adjunct after adjunct. There is nothing feline in the technique; it is thoroughly manly and 'bonhomous' yet has some resemblance to Mrs Gaskell's method of establishing a character through extensive modification.[49] Chaucer's method is basically notational: using *synoeciosis* as the underlying rhetorical and logical method. It amounts to a kind of 'behaviourism': an 'ymage' or 'peynture' emerges as a bundle of qualities or adjuncts with the whole moral character and coherent temperament cunningly left out or only obliquely indicated. The *Tales* are meant, often in an obtuse way, to provide the psychological continuity, not in a static, descriptive way but through activity, conversation and debate. Alan of Lille's initial whole vision of Nature consisted of a static, intricate description of a person and her garments. In Chaucer it is seen in the activity of a parliament, emerging through a pattern of disagreement.

While the 'ymage' in the *Tales* has been extended beyond the twin emphases of *effictio* and *notatio* to include mannerisms and manners, the old dichotomy dependent on social status in the rhetorical tradition remains. That is, persons of high social status tend to receive a more 'idealized' treatment in character description. For them, abstractions

[48] The arguments about the basic nature of the aesthetic system employed, 'realism', 'type', 'conventional', 'individual', are based on a peculiar assumption. It is assumed that all aesthetic systems in societies with historical consciousness, command of various modern languages, the working knowledge of one ancient language, a complex legal system with views of responsibility and validity of evidence, will be total. The argument is complicated by the fact that the medieval physiological and psychological theory of the complexions ('temperaments') results in an identification by 'type'. If the type is thought to be an adequate explanation of reality, then it is not automatically opposed to 'individual'. The 'extended' or 'extenuated' style of portrait was well known in classical literature, cf. Sallust's brilliant character of Cornelius Sulla in *Bellum Jugurthinum* XCV.3–4.
[49] Significantly, the best accounts of Chaucer's portrait technique are by women, Rosemary Woolf (*Critical Quarterly* 1, 1959) and Pamela Gradon (*Form and Style in Early English Literature*, pp. 315ff.). Miss Woolf notices the 'Horatian' mixture of the seemingly unpoetic pilgrim as author with the satiric sharpness of some observations, a form of beguiling exposure.

(moral and physical) are not only more appropriate socially but convey a more realistic emphasis in spite of any lack of 'particularization'. Persons of less exalted rank tend to be more realistically particularized—often very cruelly. This stylistic division of descriptive method in Chaucer is partly inherited mechanically from the rhetorical system, and partly from the fact that socially influential persons are able to perform activities and effect achievements. They create history and influence events. Various forms of metonymy (abstract for concrete, quality for substance, role for shape, title for identity) suit the higher 'estates'. The functionalization of social role in the less influential estates lends the individual a passive, static quality. These persons merely reflect happenings. They do not belong to the 'routine of great ideas' and so are not recognizable in terms of action, theories or ideas. They are most recognizable in terms of the physical facts of existence or status.[50] But however 'abstract' or 'typical' the description of the Knight may appear, for example, the effect is one of 'particularization' —the verse is rifted with the ore of localizing nomenclature: Lettow, Garnade, Belmarye, Algezir, Lyeys, Satalye.[51] These are actual places which figured in at least two separate military campaigns. That modern scholars should have been tempted to identify Chaucer's fictional Knight with a recognizable historical person (e.g. Henry IV when he was Earl of Derby) indicates the success of the author's intended realism. Chaucer's method here seems close to that sometimes used by John Betjeman, who (in Philip Larkin's phrase) 'gives us the brand-names of things'.

One trait of the author's style I have not mentioned. It is sometimes referred to as 'the unexpected detail' introduced rapidly, often disconcertingly at random, into the description. It is a peculiar turn of style and does not always seem to isolate or qualify any significant

[50] The particularized fact of an elevated person's 'existence' in the Middle Ages also tends to abstraction in that identity takes an heraldic form. Palamon and Arcite, for the purposes of capture and ransom, are identified by their coat-armour. Their features are quite immaterial at the public level. On the other hand, a sovereign is identifiable by the minute particularization of his features—in a death-mask. His individuality is legal, the evidence for declaring him dead. While alive, the seals and symbols of power are of far more 'real' value.

[51] For a similar effect of realism in describing military campaigns, cf. Machaut, *Le Dit dou Lyon* 1443–57; see especially:

> En Pruce, en Pouleinne, en Cracoe,
> En Tartarie ou en Letoe,
> En Lifflant ou en Lombardie,
> En Atenes ou en Rommenie . . .

aspect of the *ethopoeia*. These particularizing 'surprises' tend initially to appear at the very end of the portrait. For example, at the end of the Yeoman's portrait we are presented with an isolated line (117) which ends the *ethopoeia* in mid-couplet: 'A forster was he soothly, as I gesse.' The line seems oddly detached, weakened by the pleonasm, rhythmically inconclusive. The Monk's description, too, ends with an isolated, split couplet (207): 'His palfry was as broun as is a berye.' The Friar's portrait ends in a split couplet line providing the wholly unexpected: 'This worthy lymytour was cleped Huberd' (269). In the Cook's description the couplet 385–6 (calling our attention to an open sore) clearly is intrusive, in fact, a stray thought which has interrupted the process of describing the Cook's skill in preparing dishes in the lineal sequence 383, 384, 387. In the portrait of the Shipman, the description comes to a momentary pause with the isolated detail of complexion of line 394. Line 395 connects vaguely by association with what follows but shows another hesitation in the rapid impetus of the narrative direction. The last line (668) describing the Summoner again has a kind of disconnected, detached quality. In many places the connection of the transition from one aspect to another is not always clear or especially unabrupt. Given the economy, rapidity, business-like movement of the narrative as a whole, these 'falterings' and sudden shifts of attention are oddly effective. They are not so much 'unexpected details' as *non sequiturs*, syntactically isolated additive units without logical relationship. Often, as digressive pauses, they seem to allow the narrator time to gather his thoughts for another burst of headlong 'remembraunce'. It is, I think, a deliberate stylistic method for establishing the age of the pilgrim-narrator.[52] These are the stylistic indications of the wanderings, sudden dartings of intelligence, mental falterings of a mentally active man now in old age who has possibly just recovered from a recent illness: *senecis sermo nervosus et abruptus*.[53] In the *Tales* Chaucer is extremely conscious of styles and tries to reproduce the appropriate attributes, e.g. the wandering, digressive transitions of the hard-of-hearing Alisoun of Bath; the paratactical, serial, loose style of the Franklin with his awkward double endings to verse paragraphs; the beautifully nostalgic moment when the Clerk retraces an itinerary through Italy, the first-hand reminiscence of Petrarch and humanist

[52] For the importance of the reader's awareness of the advanced age of the poet, cf. pp. 87, 158–9ff.
[53] Cf. *General Prologue* 17–18. Lydgate in the *Prologue* to *Thebes* admits to a recent illness being his reason for visiting Canterbury.

eloquence—a moment when the Clerk's utilitarian fable-style suddenly and unconsciously develops into a Latinate sophistication as splendid as any of Petrarch's devising. It is a beautifully concrete evocation of Renaissance Italy, an exact embodiment of an aesthetic landscape fused with a miraculous southerly movement of geography and syntax:

> I seye that first with heigh stile he enditeth
> Er he the body of his tale writeth,
> A prohemye in the which discryveth he
> Pemond and of Saluces the contree
> And speketh of Apennyn the hilles hye
> That been the boundes of West Lumbardye,
> And of Mount Vesulus in special
> Where-as the Poo out of a welle smal
> Taketh his firste spryngyng and his sours,
> That estward ay encresseth in his cours
> To Emele-ward, to Ferrare and Venyse;
>
> (41–51)

This magnificent anticipation of Surrey's English neo-classical style (continuousness, chiasmus, periodic suspension, hyperbaton, movable caesura) is the more exciting in that it has emerged suddenly out of another narrating style and gleams through the rhyming form with instant authority. The continuous falling movement of the syntax, mimetic of the motion of the River Po in its geographical course has been suggested to Chaucer from a simile of Dante's in *Inferno* XVI.94–102:[54]

> *Come quel fiume, che ha proprio cammino*
> *prima da Monte Veso in ver levante*
> *dalla sinistra costa d'Apennino,*
>
> *che si chiama Acquacheta suso, avante*
> *che si divalli giù nel basso letto,*
> *ed a Forlì di quel nome è vacante,*

[54] Chaucer's material has been derived from Petrarch's Latin prose *proemium* to his translation of Boccaccio's story of Griselda (*Epistolae Seniles* XVII.3). But Petrarch's prose cursus and syntax alone would not have suggested Chaucer's poetic arrangement, although the last prose period shows a well-modulated conclusive movement. But it lacks the condensed tension between 'encresseth' and the falling finality of the tricolon.

rimbomba là sovra San Benedetto
dell' alpe, per cadere ad una scesa,
ove dovea per mille esser ricetto:

The Wife of Bath cites 'reality' as her sole authority yet quotes her
Dante from a mere text. The Clerk (in opposing her) gives us a deliberate, unabashed moral fable as his authority but his acquaintance with
his author is through experience. Like Chaucer, he has been to Italy
and knows of things first-hand. Until the relevant Italian documents
come to light we shall never be certain that Chaucer had met Petrarch.
The quality of reminiscence here devised for the Clerk suggests that
he had.

Finally, at lines 725–46 the poet deliberately puts aside the pilgrim's
hat and allows the reader to see him in his poetic turban, after the old
fashion. The method of the intervening poet-figure bears some
resemblance to the extenuating, modifying portrait technique of the
pilgrim-narrator. Further, Chaucer places his authorial statement in
close proximity to the *sermocinatio* of the Host (ll. 761ff.), thereby
providing the reader with the grounds for making an unforced
comparison. The 'styles' are not dissimilar. Harry Bailey's utterance
contains two un-Chaucerian elements which henceforth always
characterize him: (1) a governing cast of mind (the landlord makes the
rules); (2) a fondness for oaths, common and recherché. Otherwise,
the Host and the poet share a broad area of 'plain speaking'. This
common ground establishes the narrator's style as the *koine* of the pilgrim troop. On the other hand, the 'thought' of the poet-figure in its
complex qualifying movement and shrewdness of manoeuvring reveals
that old cunning perspicacity of the courtly poet of the *Legend* and the
Parliament. It is not identifiable with the simplified extenuating style
of the pilgrim-narrator:

> But first I pray yow, of youre curteisye,
> That ye n'arette it nat my vileynye,
> Thogh that I pleynly speke in this mateere,
> To telle yow hir wordes and hir cheere,
> Ne thogh I speke hir wordes proprely.
> For this ye knowen al so wel as I,
> Whoso shal telle a tale after a man,
> He moot reherce as ny as evere he kan
> Everich a word, if it be in his charge,
> Al speke he never so rudeliche and large,

Or ellis he moot telle his tale untrewe,
Or feyne thyng, or fynde wordes newe.
He may nat spare, althogh he were his brother;
He moot as wel seye o word as another.
Crist spak hymself ful brode in hooly writ,
And wel ye woot no vileynye is it.
Eek Plato seith, whoso that kan hym rede,
The wordes moote be cosyn to the dede.
Also I prey yow to foryeve it me,
Al have I nat set folk in hir degree
Heere in this tale, as that they sholde stonde.
My wit is short, ye may wel understonde.

(725-46)

The keynote of this passage would seem to lie in the persistent repetition
of concessive clauses: 'Thogh' (727), 'thogh' (729), 'Al speke he' (734),
'althogh' (737), 'al have I nat' (744). One must pay close attention to the
alternatives offered in this cat's cradle of *apologiae*. The first two concessive uses bring into mutual extenuation two main notions: (a)
Chaucer is not automatically to be assumed to be uncourtly or ill-
bred on account of his neglect of the airs and graces of the king's
English;[55] (b) he nevertheless has attempted a plain, open style, although he cannot imitate that style with absolute fidelity. The next
and plainer statement moves emphatically towards endorsing the
poet's future attempt to capture faithfully the difficult, impersonating
manner (730-8). Thus, the impersonating raconteur must get *every*
word correct, otherwise he is bound to falsify the material and style,
substituting new inventions for the original reality. The summatory
couplet (737-8) makes this plain. But we already know that the author
is quite incapable of such a perfect imitation. The passage closes by
offering to us the authority for (a) plainness and openness of style
(Christ) and (b) truth to the reality which is to be represented (Plato).
The effect of all this qualifying and final ironic modesty ('My wit is
short, as ye may wel understonde') is to make us aware of the complex
interplay between the poet's 'real' intelligence, the extent of his ability
to impersonate certain styles, and the kind of reality he has set himself
to imitate. We are also made aware that the author reserves, out of his

55 Cf. the *Astrolabe*, proem 50-60, for an early and unmistakable reference to the
superiority and universality of the king's English—whatever the social standing
of the user. 'Polycentricity' in the matter of regional variation in literary language
appears to have been unacceptable to Chaucer.

inadequacy, the right to invent new words and hence deviate from strict reality. However deviously or modestly offered, the poet here makes us aware of the limitations of his materials and the range of his ability to present and transform them (*per contra*)—not least by conveying an honest appraisal of all the difficulties, objective and subjective, which the fictional 'viage' and creative task imposes on his talents as pilgrim-narrator and as courtly poet. However mutually qualifying the images of narrator and poet, they are presented (with all the attendant ironies) as one and the same man. The sense of something which has happened and something which is about to begin enter the same dimension of imaginative time. We are now properly prepared to depart into the Canterbury region.

IV   Some *Canterbury Tales*

The 'reading text' and compositional arrangement which I have argued for earlier in this chapter presuppose that the meaning of the separate tales arises out of a mode of narration which is commensurate with a reasonable immediacy of comprehension,[56] no matter how extensive the ironies, qualifications and complex interpretative modifications which subsequent re-reading and cross-referring will necessarily produce. The action of 'comparing' and following the process of debate and controversy (oblique and direct) requires as a basis a mutually intelligible world for the characters (who know their own minds though they may not wholly appreciate other points of view) and the reader who wishes to know more yet must remain satisfied with the evidence at hand. These colliding aspects, these personal worlds of experience, must co-exist in multeity (to use Coleridge's terminology); they must be taken to exist at the same fictional dimension of 'reality' internally and one and the same critical dimension externally. It is no use arguing for a 'numerological', 'astrological' or 'allegorical' interpretation of a single tale. The critical method advanced must be extensible to all tales. It is equally vain to argue, for example, that the Knight's mentality allows him complex 'astrological' computations while the Miller cannot be imagined as so doing, for the author is constantly present

[56] The *Tales* are probably meant when Lydgate (*Fall of Princes* I.246) refers to Chaucer's 'fresh comedies'.

in his tale as narrator and poet. The character and his tale in the process of being created cannot stray far from the expectations which the poet-narrator has aroused for us or from that narrator's declared abilities. We know from the *General Prologue*, lines 726ff., that we should be aware of these shifts in narrative intelligences and attempts by the author to achieve certain impersonating effects. It is fallacious also to argue that since interpretative complexity may be freely attributed to the author's 'mind', then any special kind of complexity may be introduced at any given moment. We feel instinctively that whatever complexity or system of interpretation may be imagined as arising, the pilgrims themselves would have to have had some chance of under-standing it. That is, as a system for interpreting experience (not just literature) it must have common intelligibility and fourteenth-century relevance. This must be so, for the author is subjectively, as a character, present in the pilgrim fellowship in a way which is distinct from his presence as author-dreamer in the *Parliament*, the *House of Fame* or the *Book of the Duchess*. In these poems the literary tradition of interpreting *significationes*, of locating the *sensus acutus* is deliberately evoked and exploited. But the Canterbury world is 'out there', connected indis-solubly with fourteenth-century reality. It asks another kind of involve-ment, lying beyond the poet's study windows, as the eagle insists in the *House of Fame*. The Chaucerian dream-poem in its very construc-tion juxtaposes literature (as an authoritative version of experience) and experience itself. The dream emerges as an analysing and con-cordizing conflating of these two poles through the personal intelli-gence of the poet. The poetic form in each case invites this construc-tion. In a sense, the form enacts it for us, whether we understand the 'dream' or not. The *Canterbury Tales* has no such mimetic basis. Its underlying image is one of movement, change and development—away from one place towards another. The distance covered is not in the least 'visionary' or indirect, it is 'real'. The poem has a public, creative setting, beginning in an actual, identifiable hostelry in South-wark, not in any part of the poet's private dwelling. In the fragment of the Cook's prologue and tale (A 4358) the Host is identified with an actual innkeeper of Southwark. It is quite possible that other pilgrim-figures were based to some extent on well-known London citizens of the time. When the poem first circulated this kind of recognition probably formed part of the aesthetic pleasure. Another form of comparison (involving ironic possibilities) was thus invented within the terms of actual life.

By contrast, Langland's Will wakes frequently wherever he last laid his head, and once in the bosom of his almost Blakean family. The intersecting curves of the plot-spiral always cross in the 'feld of folk'. The dreamer-narrator enters the poem most subjectively in the *vita* where the purposeful wandering includes psychology. But that side of the dreaming character most forcefully exists as an abstraction: as the functions or faculties of a mind totally unrelated to a discernible man with exterior features. Chaucer and Langland's England (as Professor Bennett once argued) agree, and agree in detail, but the literary presentations are wholly distinct. There is a solid, humanist basis for the Chaucerian inward journey to develop from. Langland's literary form *ab initio* is part abstraction, 'fantasies' and reality. It is not quite dream and never wholly reality. When the dream progress turns inwards in the *vita* it becomes more difficult to identify as an individually controlled imagining or even as a collection of subjective points of view. External particulars remain obstinately minute and exact while the psychological areas remain unattached and finally abstract. Often and for long stretches, the poem breaks down into summaries or mere quotations at length of other texts—as if the poet's imagination no longer held the shaping power to assimilate and represent the objects of his own investigation. Langland certainly intends this, for the only point of connection arrives in the person of Christ in Passus 18. This is the only figure, *vita* or whole activity which draws together the accumulating material of more than one episode. Langland's Christ has no artistically created element of personality in his own figure. The Passion flowers in pure activity, in 'doing'. The harrowing of Hell, too, is all dramatically coherent movement, a performance. This section, the unifying sequence for the whole poem, must have gripped the reader's imagination with all the impact of a staged performance such as we find in the mystery plays. It is this 'pleye' of the so-called cycles which corresponds most nearly to the dramatic complexity, historical pregnancy and *modus theatrali* of the significance-charged space of classical drama. Langland's poem, in common with the medieval 'pleyes', has only a single, late occurring, unified and complex sequence in which has been packed material which corresponds to catastrophe, peripety, recognition and denouement. But in ordinary historical reality, a knowledge of human imperfection bites deep into Langland's sense of experience; its power to disorganize extends beyond society and time far into the poet's imagination. His poem's peculiar shape expresses this sense of disintegration.

These introductory remarks may serve to indicate that Chaucer has been assiduous in creating a possible formal context for a unified level of response to the separate tales. By so guiding us he implicitly limits the range of the qualifications and ironies which we are entitled to see in the poem. If we do not understand the overriding claims of a certain naturalism, if we ignore the method and purpose of the *General Prologue* in awakening those just limits of common experience which provide the grammar of the *koine* of the experiential Canterburian milieu, then the *Tales* may be treated as Donatus treated Virgil, Augustine the Scriptures, and more recently, Professor Fowler Spenser (*si licet parvas conjungere magnis*).

THE KNIGHT'S TALE

Pre-eminently the *Knight's Tale* is one of those stories where the 'conclusion' contains the whole meaning or message of the narrative process, that kind of moral tale which Pandarus had referred to in *Troilus* II. The 'end' of the tale provides us with several connected concluding rhythms. In the complex denouement the physical action, a *conflictus*, is brought to an end; the suspended relationship between Palamon and Emily concludes (after the seemly lapse of some years) in marriage; Theseus takes magisterial control of the role of narrator and concludes the narrative pattern by giving the characters (and the reader) a peroration. It performs the satisfying function of a formal espousal speech with Theseus not only acting paternally as the protector of the bride and groom but actually causing them to become engaged and afterwards married. The conclusion of Boccaccio's *Teseida* is differently managed. In book XII there is no concluding formal occasion and oration. It is at the very beginning, as an exordium motif, that Teseo advises Palemone and Emilia to marry. The long-held view that here Boccaccio makes no reference to a formal political gathering (such as a parliament) is difficult to maintain in the face of the text. Teseo calls together his supporters (unspecified as to rank), Palemone and other 'kings'. They are then addressed in solemn convocation by Teseo in a formal oration. The crucial phrases are: (XII.3) *'con lui essendo li Greci adunati'* ('having with him [Teseo] the Greeks who had been called together'), and (XII.4) *'con molti di quei re accompagnato, /Non sappiendo esso pero la cagione'* ('with may of those kings accompanying [Palemone], being kept in ignorance of the nature of the case').

If a similar convocation in book VII is anything to go by, the venue may be the *'teatro'*, that is, the amphitheatre built for exhibiting martial games. The sense of the Italian noun has been affected by Virgil's use of *theatrum* in *Aeneid* V.288. This is the sense which Chaucer understands from his description of the theatre in *Knight's Tale* 1027 (1885). Although Boccaccio does not specify the exact nature of the gathering, it is plainly political even if it lacks the exact name and political *raison d'être* given it by Chaucer. At this point in Boccaccio there is no searching philosophical explanation of the universe of the romance epic. The metaphysical view occurs not as a verbal account but as an 'action' in book XI and is vouchsafed the dead Arcita in the famous apotheosis of his soul. It amounts to a philosophical consolation—that classical view of the universe where his achievement is rewarded after the old Roman manner; *virtus*, martial courage, is acknowledged as a passport to celestial reward and Fame. Earthly love, affection between men and women (even affection between the living and the dead) has no place in this stern scheme of public, civic morality. This is the universe of Cicero's *Somnium Scipionis*, that account which Chaucer had found so profoundly unsatisfying before he went on to dream in the *Parliament of Fowls* of the new Chartrain synthesis which had superseded the Roman vision of Cicero's dream. It is the same Ciceronian universe in which Troilus' spirit eventually finds its antique *quietus*. The concluding rhythm of the *Teseida* is serial and begins in book XI. It consists of a series of visits to temples. Egeo places Arcita's ashes in the temple of Mars. Palemone builds a commemorative temple to Juno which contains an artistically rendered history of the deeds of Palemone and Arcita. Finally, in XII, all the participants go to the temple of Venus for the wedding. The various wedding festivities are then described in a similar serial fashion. Chaucer's idea for ending the *Knight's Tale* with a philosophical oration delivered before a parliament probably derives from Nature's speech to the council of the Virtues which ends the *Anticlaudianus* I. Statius' *Thebaid* ends with a miniature epic, 'the Theseid', in imitation of *Aeneid* XII. The action of *Thebaid* XII begins in the temple of Clementia where Theseus and Hippolyta hear a petition in formal audience. This temple audience has perhaps suggested to Boccaccio the beginning scene of *Teseida* VII, stanzas 1–13, where Teseo with the other *regi labdacii* holds a formal audience in the amphitheatre addressing the assembled *baroni* on the Theban dispute (*'li Theban quistione'*). His address is pragmatic in tone and wholly concerned with the means to reach a rapid settlement.

In Chaucer, Theseus' formal oration, delivered at a state occasion, provides a ceremonious climax parallel with the elaborate funeral preparations for Arcite. But the content of Theseus' speech is not concerned with immediate realities or conventional moral advice.[57] Like Nature in the *Anticlaudianus* or Spenser's Nature in the *Mutabilitie Cantos*, the prince assumes an aspect of gravity, enacts the physical gesture of responsible power ('His eyen sette he ther as was his lest') and after a sober pause symbolic of deliberation, embarks on a philosophical justification for the betrothal of Palamon and Emily.[58] The last, satisfying, rhythm resides in the emerging recognition for the reader that this justification also acts as an explanation of the whole action of the tale. Theseus expresses his concern that our universe should be whole, perfect and intelligible. His formal address embodies that intelligibility and invites us to apply this wisdom to the process of the total poem. But we must accept this wisdom as having sovereignty over our understanding just as Theseus has ultimate rule over Palamon and Emily and his barons—indeed the same authority as that possessed by the king of France in *All's Well that Ends Well*. Subject these figures to literary irony or interpretative relativism and the formal and intellectual coherence of the works disappears. It is this 'meaning' which the

[57] Teseo's words are only 'philosophic' in a conventional and general sense. He talks about the aims, purposes, means of human life, but there is no coherent philosophical system proposed. He argues the universality of Necessity, '*anzi più tosto necessarie in tutto*', and has previously asserted '*E però far della necessitate virtu* . . .' But in his practical context this is worlds away from Theseus' similar expression. Theseus places these ethical directives within a metaphysical pattern. Human obedience is not wholly dependent on the fact that we cannot avoid our common destinies. Our obedience and patience follow from the perfect nature of the First Principle in whom there is no intended harm.

[58] The rhetorical gestures of Theseus derive from the presence of Teseo. Cf. *Teseida* XII.5:

> *E quivi, poi ch'ogni uom tacitamente*
> *si fu posto a seder, Teseo stette*
> *per lungo spazio sanza dir niente;*
> *ma già vedendo di tututti erette*
> *l'orecchie pure a lui umilemente,*
> *dentro tenendo le lagrime strette*
> *ch'agli occhi per pietà volean venire*
> *così parlando incominciò a dire:*

But cf. Alan's Nature:

> *Concilii stetit in medio Natura, parumper*
> *In terram demissa caput, concepta severis*
> *Vultibus exponens, dextraque silentia dictans.*

reader is asked to understand and apply in a responsible manner to the whole action of the poem. This philosophy arises directly out of the actual language of the poem. It is not a system derived from another context.

Now, the most recent studies of the *Knight's Tale*, although obsessed with the question of 'meaning', strive to locate that meaning outside the area of Theseus' peroration—a meaning which exists in some absolute schematic form far beneath the surface of the *narratio*, in addition to being wholly unrelated to Theseus' wisdom. In the Fowler–Brooks astrological excursus[59] this paradigm (delivered, as it were, from a Regius Chair rather than a 'roial chaar') is reached by trying to explain 'scientifically' the distinguishing features of two very minor figures[60] who have been given an 'exact' astrological-biological basis as character, and, Arcite and Palamon identified with their 'rule', the rest of the *narratio* is then 'fitted' in. The final summary of the tale's 'meaning' is not as astounding as the actual argument of 'fitting in' might suggest. It focuses tamely on the concept of order (though not in a Muscatinian sense), an order seen as a 'growth to wise maturity through a succession of ages and attitudes; of the soul's formation and ascent through a series of planetary stages'.

Whatever value we place on the astrological explanations adduced, a concern with order (as we know from Theseus' own words on the subject in lines 2145ff.) would seem to be of some importance. The deliberate position of the tale within the journey sequence suggests that Chaucer wished the first pilgrim to provide a representation of experience in a unified, coherent account—where this account would bring together the three branches of philosophy, metaphysical, natural and moral, in order to explain the composition of our universe, especially commenting on action, choice, will and appetite. Thereafter

---

[59] Cf. *Medium Aevum* 39 (1970), pp. 123ff.

[60] The reason for the descriptive presence of these two figures is provided by the extended catalogue series of *ethopoeiae* which occupies nearly the whole of *Teseida* VI. It is an epical *topos* deriving from the serial, accumulating portraits of Virgil which form the end of *Aeneid* VII (the list of the confederation ranged against Aeneas). Boccaccio's use shows little appreciation of Virgil's aesthetic sense of the urgent and dramatic placing of the *topos* at this point in the narrative. Gavin Douglas, by inventing the satiric-dream prologue to book VIII, shows that he understands Virgil's intention perfectly. Chaucer's economic selection of two antagonists supporting the hero's claims creates a sense of equality of means in achieving victory. It suspends the balance of power on the realistic level. The stellar-parliament opens our eyes to the greater reality.

the reader should have the sensation of unity of represented experience breaking down into a less coherent, sometimes trivial, multiplicity. At the same time, the Host's authority for arranging the order of the telling of the tales gives way to the anarchic pressure of contending personal wills. When we have finished reading the tales we may see the Knight's contribution as occupying this position of initiating unity in the narrative and so providing a certain parallel with the *Parson's Tale* in its exegetical and ultimate position. In Professor Muscatine's older view,[61] the tale presents us with a simple collision between order and disorder. The disorder of reality, experience, is resolved through the application of an ordering art, as reflected in the poetical art of the tale and the various ceremonies and civilizing customs of the society depicted. This kind of philosophical resolution seems to belong to the symbolist and post-symbolist period. Medieval philosophy resembled classical thought in that both saw external phenomena and internal phenomena as sharing the same problems and the same solutions. They did not conceive of a universe where an infinitely chaotic and meaningless physical world could be inhabited or interpreted by a finite, logical and coherent perceiver of that unintelligible reality.

Both Muscatinian and Fowlerian views resolve the problem of order and what is not order by abolishing it: Muscatine, by establishing an infinitely unintelligible world where there is an unresolved flux of 'unorderableness' since no philosophy or mental activity can ever give more than an 'account', interpretation or representation of it (a view which much resembles that of Bergson). Fowler unfolds a static universe where will and appetite have no real or substantial existence, for all is resolved by the individual's acquiescence in an affective pattern which will produce some kind of appropriate order and wisdom whatever we contemplate, decide or perform (this view seems Spinozan). You are what you are. Free will is the correct operation of the entity designed to operate in that way. This view next relates the complex pattern of personages, times of rising, prayers, descriptions of temples and divinities to the scene of the astrological-mythological parliament (ll. 1580ff.)—with one disastrous miscalculation, that of identifying Theseus with the Jupiter of line 1584. This, in the context, is the beneficent planetary Jupiter and should not be confused with the philosophical 'Juppiter the king', the prince indistinguishable from the Prime Mover (l. 2177). This identification encourages the authors to

[61] I have never agreed with this presentation. Cf. my review of *Chaucer and the French Tradition*, *French Studies* 13 (1957), pp. 57ff.

assume that the planetary deities in the parliamentary scene have
unlimited power to act, and uncircumscribed intellects for understanding the ultimate purpose of their decisions. The intellectual system
which Theseus expounds in his peroration makes no such error of
determinism. In his view the chain of command passes out from the
ultimate perfection of the *Primum Mobile* ('Juppiter the king') through
a gradation of successive perfection. This perfection grows less and
less as it moves further and further away from the *Primum Mobile* in
physical distance (ll. 2149–52). Thus, there is, philosophically, no
genuine imperfection or 'evil' in the universe, only 'lesser good' or
lesser perfection. This is the neo-Platonic resolution which Philosophy
arrives at in Boethius' *De Consolatione*—a text which Theseus would
seem to be remembering. The planetary deities thus 'decide' at a level
more 'influential' in the scale of power and knowledge than mankind,
but at a level inferior to that of their lord and master (the other Jupiter)
who resides beyond their planetary spheres, far beyond the sphere of
the fixed stars, far out in the *Primum Mobile*. These planetary barons
show no recognition of a higher power and are as ignorant of the
supreme power's intentions as man is of their planetary resolves. If
the reader does not understand Theseus' recapitulation of this philosophical explanation of our universe, then the poem's cosmology,
metaphysical and moral, will remain forever obscure.

The other main Boethius-derived problem, one emphasized and
resolved by Theseus in proposing the marriage of Palamon and Emily,
is the correspondence, in certain cases, of external physical phenomena
with rational, moral behaviour. In a neo-Platonic universe the macrocosm and the microcosm share some important features and arrangements: mind and matter may guarantee each other's legitimate functions and definable existence. Thus, the principle of love, love which
combines opposite substances into a whole cohering form on the basis
of a ratio which is to be identified with moderation, this love in the
physical universe operates in the 'feyre cheine of love', the chain of the
elements. Man, who is composed of the same elements as 'humours',
is joined together and insures his perpetuation through a moral and
physical bond known as matrimony (as Theseus stressed in his direct
citing of Boethius II.m.8 in lines 2236–7). Hence, in this view, some
natural laws may be identical with some positive or formal laws, for
they share the same principles and were constructed for the same
purpose. It is here, in the sphere of the possible identity of laws, natural
and formal, where we find the *essential* difference between Arcite and

Palamon. Arcite, after his seeing of Emily, in a chop-logic fashion outwits Palamon on this exact point (ll. 304–28), using a single Boethian quotation quite accurately to prove his case. But in his eagerness to dissociate himself from the positive law of 'sworn brotherhood' to Palamon (who legally has the prior claim to his help for the affections of Emily, whatever Arcite's *voluntas*),[62] Arcite has constructed a sophistry where he has necessarily denied the possible identity of *lex naturalis* and *lex positiva*. He has constructed a natural law ('a gretter law') which not only breaks positive laws, but reduces human relationships to appetitive monisms ('Ech man for himself, ther is noon oother'). The reader will perceive that Arcite's natural law of love is no 'law' at all. Within this formulation of natural desire, legitimate order may be revoked automatically by merely citing this principle. The sworn friendship of the two men, a mutually binding social contract in formal law, is declared illegitimate by this excuse. Thus, all positive laws may be dispensed with.[63] The logical extension of Arcite's argument would take in marriage as well as friendship. He says so in line 313: 'or elles wife.' This is one reason why it never occurs to Arcite to address himself later to the goddess of love. He is a pragmatist who subscribes to the notion of a divine order but subscribes to no ascertainable philosophical method for identifying how that order might operate in terms of human desire and choice. It is Arcite who quotes Juvenal to this effect (l. 402). As one reviewer (Professor Strang) once said, 'He cannot see further than the end of his nose.'[64]

The medieval or Renaissance reader, I submit, faced with either of the above-mentioned modern *scholia* would have been genuinely perplexed: by the dissociation absolutely of natural and mental phenomena of the one, and by the absolute psychological and moral determinism of the astrological-biological scientology of the other. The medieval or Renaissance reader would have had no insuperable difficulty in understanding Theseus' moderate blend of Aristotle and Boethius. For example, Edmund Spenser, as a Renaissance reader with medieval interests, seems to have understood clearly the *Knight's Tale*'s conflict and its philosophical implications. In the *Faerie Queene*

---

[62] The Fowler–Brooks interpretation understands this morally, but seems to draw no other philosophical conclusions from the observation.

[63] There is no limiting principle in Arcite's proposition. The word 'any' in line 308 makes this clear.

[64] A. V. C. Schmidt's article in *Essays in Criticism* 19 (1969), pp. 107–17 would seem peculiarly misguided.

IV.ii, Spenser sets out to narrate the episode of Cambel and Triamond. This choice of subject has been universally accepted as Spenser's attempt to finish the incomplete *Squire's Tale*, where Chaucer had raised the possibility of treating Cambalus (ll. 667–8). But the Spenserian episode begins in stanza 32 with the line: 'Whylome as antique stories tellen us.' This near quotation of the first line of the *Knight's Tale* should alert us to the possibility that the Chaucerian subject may have been suggested by its mention in the *Squire's Tale*, but that in providing more literary substance the *Knight's Tale* may prove of greater relevance. Spenser's declared intention in the *laudatio* on Chaucer (stanzas 32–4) ends with the confident assertion:

> I follow here the footing of thy feete
> That with thy meaning so I may the rather meete.

Such confidence owes more to the path[65] of the *Knight's Tale* than it does to the non-existent part of the *Squire's Tale*. The actual episode of Cambel does not tell us much more about Spenser's reading of the *Knight's Tale*, but the *ekphrasis* of the house of Ate (Discord) in canto I. xxi tells us a great deal:

> And all within, the riven walls were hung
> With ragged monuments of times forepast,
> All which the sad effects of discord sung:
> There were rent robes and broken sceptors plast;
> Altars defyld, and holy things defast;
> Disshiuered speares and shields ytorne in twaine,
> Great cities ransackt and strong castles rast,
> Nations captiued and huge armies slaine:
> Of all which ruines there some relicks did remaine.

The list of those affected by discord includes (stanza xix) 'Some of sworne friends, that did their faith forego', and this is meant to remind us of Palamon and Arcite. But more important is the source which Spenser has chosen for the *domus* of the goddess of supreme disorder and chaos. Stanza xxi has been reworked from the *Thebaid* VII.40ff.— the house of Mars—the common source for Chaucer's temple of Mars in the *Knight's Tale*.[66] It is not just the shared destructive power of Mars and Ate which has dictated Spenser's choice to conflate the two, but the persisting memory of Chaucer's association of Arcite and

---

[65] The metaphor 'footing' in Spenser has been suggested by *Troilus* V.1791.
[66] Upton noticed this in the eighteenth century.

Arcite's mentality with his chosen temple of Mars. In view of Spenser's association of Ate with Mars, and the tale of Cambel and Triamond with Chaucer and the *Knight's Tale*, it is instructive to look at Chaucer's temple of Mars again.

The treatment of temples in Chaucer differs radically from Boccaccio's more or less even-handed arrangement. In the *Teseida* the praying of Palemone and Arcita, the journey of the personified prayer and the temple's description give the impression of equality of treatment, in the order of Mars then Venus.[67] Emilia's visit to Diana is managed differently. In Chaucer, the order is changed: Venus, Mars, Diana, and the length and emphasis rearranged. The temples of Venus and Diana are given equality of treatment in length (thereby pairing Palamon and Emily),[68] and these temples allowed to retain their conventional, mythographic neutrality (as Robinson's citations of 'Albricus Philosophicus' suggest). The centrally placed temple, Mars, has been vastly lengthened in descriptive emphasis and incorporates newly invented material imported from sources other than Statius or Boccaccio. Stylistically, the Chaucerian temples of Venus and Diana reflect the descriptive style of Boccaccio: flexible, flowing and not schematic in the use of rhetorical *figurae*. Boccaccio's temple of Mars has this same flexibility and variety of types of clauses and word-order (the style has been closely modelled on Statius' description of the temple of Mars in *Thebaid* VII). Stylistically, Chaucer's temple of Mars indulges schematic employment of rhetorical devices in a very pronounced fashion. The long, catalogue use of parison, anaphora, *partitio* and various forms of metonymy (ll. 1139-50, 1155-64) has the effect of arresting the reader's attention and distinguishing this material in the reader's imagination from the other descriptive passages. While much has been said about Chaucer's attention to 'symmetry' in the design of the tale, little has been written about his interest in asymmetrical emphasis—and here is an example of such emphasis.

In general, Boccaccio follows Statius fairly closely, changing a detail here and adding something there. The verbal style and the mixture of realistic and mythographic details are very similar. All critics have noticed Chaucer's increase in the realistic violence of the physical detail, but few have commented on the alteration of the pattern

[67] This is the effect Chaucer achieves by balancing the descriptions of Lycurgus and Emetreus.
[68] The Knight himself in the closing lines of his tale calls his story 'Palamon and Emilye', (A 3607).

and the significant additions. Having dispensed with Arcita's apotheosis (*Teseida* XI) and the consequent necessity of stressing his military valour, Chaucer has changed the central figure in the Martian design. In Statius (51–2) we find '*tristissima Virtus/stat in medio*' ('in the centre of the temple stood harshest Valour'), and Boccaccio follows: '*e'n mezzo il loco la Vertu tristissima sedea . . .*' There is no such central figure in Chaucer. He breaks the parallel rhetorical schemes and gives us:

> Amiddes of the temple sat Meschaunce,
> With disconfort and sory contenaunce.

This is a new figure, 'Calamity', 'Disaster'.[69] This personification of universal catastrophe has been suggested by Boccaccio's (and Statius') Discordia:

> *lì Discordia sedea e sanguinenti*
> *ferri avea in mano, e ogni Differenza.*

Discord's attributes have been given by Chaucer to 'Contek' ('Differenza'). The figure of Discord has been subverted from its place in the introductory catalogue and been transferred to the central position in the design. Parallel in emphasis to the middle personification is the new invention, the figure of 'Conquest' or Victory sitting above the whole scene:[70]

> And al above, depeynted in a tour,
> Saw I Conquest sittinge in greet honour,
> With the sharpe swerd over his heed
> Hanginge by a soutil twynes threed.

Above Conquest hangs another new invention, the Damoclean sword, probably suggested to Chaucer by Statius' original figure of Discordia who held a '*geminum . . . ferrum*', 'a two-edged blade'.[71] The temples of

[69] ME 'meschaunce' should not be translated 'ill-luck'; 'disconfort' is a past part. adj. not a noun. In line 2205 (1150) 'cold deeth' is a proper personification and should be capitalized (cf. '*e oltre a ciò volto sanguinoso/La Morte . . .*'). It is parallel to 'The crueel Ire' (1997) ('*L'Ire rosse come foco*').

[70] The position of Conquest has perhaps been remembered from Ovid's famous passage in *Metamorphoses* VIII.13ff. where a doubtful Victory hovers over the battle: '*volat dubiis Victoria pennis*'.

[71] The sword of Damocles did not come to Chaucer's notice from the general reference in Boethius, *De Consolatione* III prose V (as Robinson suggests) but from another of his favourite books, Macrobius' *Commentum* to the *Somnium Scipionis* where there is a concrete image of both the deceiving luxury and the perilous sword: '. . . *gladium uagina raptum et a capulo de filo tenui pendentem* . . .' This *exemplum* occurs in a series of illustrations of types of Hell.

Venus and Diana in Chaucer are mythographically and morally neutral. These walls depict indifferently good and bad aspects of the
inhabiting deity. With the departure of 'sternest Valour' there is
nothing good in Arcite's temple of Mars. In the midst sits discordant
Calamity while above the scene sits a deceived and terrified Victory.
By this time it must have occurred to the reader in general (as it had
to Spenser) that this temple of Mars, Arcite's oratory, has now become
identifiable with those attributes commonly assigned to Saturn in the
late antique and medieval periods.

The *maestrevol arte*, the masterful cunning, shown *en passant* by
Boccaccio's unrepresented and unidentified gods (VII.68) gives way
in Chaucer to the stellar domestic scene. This epical *topos*, the divine
council, has a loose narrative shape: there is no symmetrical emphasis.
Diana (being non-astrological) has no place in the scene. Instead,
grandfather Saturn, whose seniority in the household gives him
precedence in wisdom, decides the whole business (so he arrogantly
thinks). He alone is described:

> Min is the drenching in the see so wan;
> Min is the prison in the derke cote;
> Min is the strangling and hanging by the throte;
> The murmure, and the cherles rebelling,
> The groyninge, and the privee empoisoning . . .
>
> (1598–602)

It can plainly be seen by the schematic rhetorical organization of these
lines, that Saturn's portrait of himself is meant to recall the content
and the stylistic features of the description of Mars. Thus, throughout
the poem a continuous series of identifications has been made: Arcite
chooses a philosophy which commits him to a single act of anarchic
appetitiveness; in so doing he denies the validity of 'formal law' and
'natural law'; when brought within the compass of formal law by
Theseus he prays to a Mars who is totally destructive and overtly
identified with universal disorder; Saturn, the god of disorder (who
shares the destructive features of Mars), settles his fate.

It remains to say that the closing funeral of Arcite is intended to
balance the opening denial of funeral rites by Creon. Thus, the opening
causus belli turns on the same Theban denial of the observation of
formal law, there the rites of burial. Theseus shows a steady concern
with the sanctity of formal laws and at one place in the text (ll. 806–15)

is associated with that 'Juppiter the king', the Prime Mover, whose
wisdom he commends to us at the end of the tale:

> The destinee, ministre general,
> That executeth in the world overal
> The purveiaunce, that God hath seyn biforn,
> So strong it is, that though the world had sworn
> The contrarye of a thing, by ye or nay,
> Yet somtime it shal fallen on a day
> That falleth nat eft withinne a thousand yeere.
> For certeinly oure appetites heere,
> Be it of werre, or pees, or hate, or love,
> Al is this reuled by the sighte above.
> This mene I now by mighty Theseus . . .

The qualifying formula is important: the philosophical dimension has
both universal and particular application. In this view there is no
astrological scheme at the heart of the *Knight's Tale*. The astronomy is
used quite conventionally to support the physical working out of the
philosophical pattern, lending to this Boethian or neo-Platonic pattern
of a whole, perfect and connected universe, the satisfying, minor details
of its physical operation in terms of natural science. As Coleridge once
observed (commenting on Hartley's idea of the laws of mental association), it is the player holding the billiard cue who hits the ball, not the
billiard cue.

As in *Troilus*, the hero and heroine of whom we approve are basically
passive, endowed with a kind of religious dignity. Noble as these two
kinsman are in nearly every respect, a philosophical gulf lies between
Arcite and Palamon. But however strictly we judge Arcite philosophically, his habitual ethical fairness and dying magnanimity commend him to us, as these qualities distinguish him in the eyes of his
associates. The world of the old 'complications of honour' is no longer
ours in any form.[72] In its ceremonious, intricately legalistic, formally
organized atmosphere, every simple action generates many qualifying
effects. Gilbert de la Hay's manual on knighthood (edited in its
Scottish translation by Stevenson, Scottish Text Society, 1905, 2 pts)
is a good guide to the complications of chivalry for a gentleman on

[72] In Dryden's *Marriage à-la-Mode* the dramatist stands divided in himself between the old world of honour (which draws on rich associations from *The
Winter's Tale*) and the new of 'honesty'. The new world in the subplot surfaces
and torpedoes the main plot.

active service. The section on escape from confinement is a revelation for the modern mind. An equally elaborate etiquette (the ME sb. is 'ceremonye') underlies the 'luf-talking' and 'daliaunce' between Sir Gawain and Bertilak's lady—as the complex and intricate 'ceremonyes' of the intercalated hunting episodes serve to indicate. Further, the poem's whole formal shape has been derived from an amalgam of the patterns of several formal games, all of which were originally games of forfeits or exchange. The reason why the Gawain-poet chooses the metaphoric structure of a 'game' as an image for ordinary, secular social or ethical relationships is partially explained by John Stevens in his chapter 'The Game of Love' in *Music and Poetry in the Early Tudor Court*.[73] In his exposition of the habitual use of such an image of 'an intricate plan or scheme' as the basis for examining social relationships, he comes close to defining ME 'game' as 'a riddle concerning some love problem', and compares the literary use of the maze-game in the *Assembly of Ladies*. Of that poem, Stevens says: 'and the losers, too, had their reward.' The early reference in Gawain to Christmastide 'handy-dandy', a game of forfeits and exchanges (ll. 66–70):

> Ladies laȝed ful loude, þoȝ þay lost haden,
> And he þat wan watȝ nat wrothe . . .

sets the pattern or 'game' for the poem.[74] The Gawain-poet uses the conventions of the literary world of romance, the supernatural elements and enchantments, 'in game', in a riddling fashion. He uses these 'vncouth', 'marvelous' conventions as Jane Austen was to use the literary Gothic horrific world in *Northanger Abbey*. As the heroine soon comes to learn, it is the actual contemporary world of social relationships which contains the genuine and deeply humiliating horrors. After Gawain's final test, Morgan le Fay, the well-known enchantress, may be the 'romaunce' reason given by Bertilak for the cause of the 'game' but she also turns out to be Gawain's aunt and in Bertilak's words would be terribly hurt if Gawain did not come back to Haut Desert and spend

---

[73] London (1961), pp. 154ff.

[74] Christmas and the New Year used to be the traditional time for the playing of such games. Benedict Burgh (*obiit* 1481) wrote a poem called 'A Christemasse game' where the twelve apostles are called by Christ on their deaths to the celestial throne to receive their everlasting rewards, or rather to exchange their worldly gifts or palms of martyrdom for their true reward of eternal bliss. Shirley says in his rubric: 'echeone off them were baptiste . . .' That is, they are given their names as saints and rebaptized in 'this bathe of blisse'. The exchange of 'medes' constitutes the game.

Christmas with the family. It is a measure of the unseen wound done to Gawain's *amour propre* that he declines the invitation. Romance literary conventions and the ceremonies of ordinary aristocratic fourteenth-century life are continuously and deliciously interwoven. One of the great aesthetic pleasures of that poem is the recognition of that 'interlocking' quality.[75] But the reader must understand that this complicated world of honour was once a living, breathing hour, not simply a romance literary concoction or an astrological chart or medicinal scheme of temperaments and humours.

THE MILLER'S TALE

Between the intricate social usage in the patterned, intelligible philosophical world of the Knight and that Oxford of the Miller who 'illegitimately' follows him in the telling order, there is but one mental similarity. These two worlds of experience share but one quality. The Knight, in describing Arcite's entirely private lovelorn, inconsistent mental condition makes the following conventional observation on the nature of love-melancholy:

> Whan that Arcite hadde romed al his fille,
> And songen al the roundel lustily,
> Into a studie he fil sodeynly,
> As doon thise loveres in hir queynte geres,
> Now in the crope, now doun in the breres,
> Now up, now doun, as boket in a welle.
> Right as the Friday, soothly for to telle,
> Now it shyneth, now it reyneth faste,
> Right so kan geery Venus overcaste
> The hertes of hir folk; right as hir day
> Is gereful, right so chaungeth she array.
> Selde is the Friday al the wowke ylike.
>
> (1670ff.)

The folk proverb 'Friday is seldom like any other day in the week' does not so much call attention to the special quality of Venus' day, as it provides a compact way of saying no one day of the week is much like

---

[75] Edward Albee's play, *Who's Afraid of Virginia Woolf*, is constructed on a 'games' pattern (albeit a private game) where there is a continuous interplay of fantasy and reality.

any other. Monday,[76] the fatal evening given over to the bestial harmonizing of Alisoun and Nicholas, the gulling of Carpenter John and the humiliation of Absolon, is no exception. The underlying philosophical point in the folk proverb stresses the continuous, unpredictable mutability of reality as we experience it from day to day. It is measured by the working week and looks no further. Years, reigns and 'ages' lie outside its concern. In the Knight's application, this common wisdom is directed at one aspect of the lover's imagination when it alternates between two extreme states: 'Now up, now down.' This verbal formulation is itself part of folk-proverbial wisdom and belongs to a very large ME collection of such sayings.[77] It is precisely this folk wisdom about the unexpected mutability of all moments of reality which the two tales share. In the case of the *Knight's Tale* it is an isolated observation applied to a single quality of the lover's mentality. The Knight's whole metaphysical view takes in more than this. In the *Miller's Tale*, this folk world-picture is extended to include every aspect of human experience, in true keeping with that type of folk wisdom's original application. It is no accident that the Miller's churl's eye-view of the world shares one feature of Arcite's imagination for the Miller's 'Oxford week and a bit'[78] derives root and branch from the doctrine of 'ech man for himselve', a continuous striving of wills and appetites.

Most critics have tried to see the *Miller's Tale* as an intentional burlesque or parody of the *Knight's Tale*, imagining that it is the Miller's professed object to 'quit' the Knight by telling 'a noble storye for the nones'. This view, alas, fails to read further in the prologue. To quit the Knight is, indeed, his initial 'for-dronken' intention, but it is not his last. The Miller has elbowed his way past the Monk (whose turn is properly next) and who has been asked to say 'sumwhat to quyte with the Knight's tale'. The Miller picks up the other man's challenge. The Host, opposing this most impolite intrusion, then reminds Robin that 'som bettre man' has the right to speak. After

---

[76] The day is specified thrice (3516, 3633, 3659).

[77] Cf. B. J. Whiting, *Proverbs, Sentences and Proverbial phrases*, Oxford (1968), N479. The collection is huge and widespread. The formulation is also the subject of three ME poems, cf. *Index*, items 356, 2341, 2376.

[78] Nicholas and Alisoun's *amour* begins on the first Saturday when the carpenter had gone to Osney (3274); Nicholas's 'game' begins the next Saturday (3399–400); the fatal night is next Monday (3659, 3665). The duration of the passion and courtship is in keeping with the Miller's philosophical calendar and Reason's observations on erotic love in the *Roman* 3283ff.

threatening to leave the fellowship, the Miller gets his own way and announces his subject:

> 'For I woll telle a legend and a lyf,
> Bothe of a carpenter and of his wyf,
> How that a clerk hath set the Wrightes cappe.'

I submit that all notions of quitting the Knight by telling however perverse a 'noble story' have fled from the Miller's tipsy mind. The choice of his 'genre', 'a legend and a lyf', is a malicious hit at the Monk (his 'bettre'),[79] for in ME a 'legend' normally refers to the life of a saint. Later, when the Monk is given his turn, he thinks about offering the Life of St Edward before he decides to deliver himself of his tiresome collection of tragedies. If the Miller is to be imagined as about to parody any form, a better candidate might be the Saint's Life. But this, too, is not to be. For just as he is announcing his instant subject, his eye rests on the next object of his ranging, malicious wit—Oswald the Reeve, who is by trade a carpenter. Instantly, the Reeve is drawn into the tale, emerging in the Miller's satiric consciousness by arguing with him. In the bitter exchange which follows it would appear that Oswald and Robin may have had some knowledge of each other. But however interesting it is to speculate on the possible degree of prior acquaintanceship, two main points are being made: (1) we are actually seeing 'reality' in the process of being transformed into fiction; (2) the quickly established sequence of changed Robinian intentions creates a variable, unpredictable movement of alteration where the active, irrational, malicious imagination maintains a constant satiric course. The Miller's *inventio* passes through the pilgrim's world like a baleful planet, shedding personal misfortunes as it goes. Like Saturn, his imagination encompasses nothing but 'pleyn correccioun'. This depiction of the Miller's protean and malevolent *courage* establishes another connection with experience seen as a harsh alternation of contending, variable moments.

Before we examine the creative results of the Miller's malicious imagination, a poetic faculty as impartially unjust as that of the author of *Such Darling Dodos* and *The Wrong Set*, it is best to return to a more comprehensive exposition of the tale's underlying pattern of proverbial folk wisdom. In the tale itself Chaucer employs two complementary

---

[79] Thereby confirming the truth of the folk proverb 'But who is a churl wold eche man were the same' (Lydgate, *The Churl and Bird* 474), and cf. Whiting, *op. cit.*, C262, F409.

comic rhythms: (1) a swift, alternating, mutable succession of momentary reality, 'now this, now that'; (2) a deliberating, cunning accumulative pattern of comic retention which awaits a final and sudden relief. In a sense these two rhythms or forces are seen in simple opposition to each other in the persons of husband John and lodger Nicholas: the one simple, volatile and accepting, the other clever, circumspect and constructing. In another way, all the male persons share in the first rhythm in that their cherished hopes meet with sudden, sharp reverses—not merely a check, but an extreme, opposite fulfilment. All the male characters share in the second, accumulating, swelling, comic rhythm in that their 'affectiounes', their fantasies, rise and swell out of all proportion to the very mundane, simple end in view. Their complicated activities tower grotesquely over a tiny purpose. Alisoun is exempted from this scheme. She is merely the mechanical carnal object of masculine 'frenesie'. At the end of the tale she is excused any share in the physical moment of comic disillusionment and authorial exposure. One feels it will be no particular inconvenience for her to be deprived of 'hende Nicholas' during his convalescence: she is a 'toun girle' and she knows that there are more 'hende clerkes' where he came from.

The first rhythm, that of short alternations of mutable extremes, may be illustrated in the mentality of the simple carpenter. When he has learned that Nicholas has locked himself in his room, he comes instantly to the conclusion that tragedy is just around the corner. He reflects on his own experience and says:

> 'This world is now ful tikel, sikerly,
> I saugh today a cors yborn to chirche
> That now on Monday last, I saugh him wirche.'
>
> (3428-30)

This observation on the swift mutability of experience has been contrived at the level of reminiscence from the common proverbial type 'here today, gone tomorrow'.[80] This proverb is closely related to the type 'now this, now that' as Whiting's examples show. Compare, for instance, Gower's *Praise of Peace*, line 292, 'That now is up, tomorwe is under grave.' The carpenter's 'tikel world' is full of such extreme alternations. Just before he is about to be outwitted by Nicholas's stratagem, John again reflects from the store of his own experiences on the dangers which beset clever people in view of 'A man wote

[80] Cf. Whiting, *op. cit.*, T351 and N479.

litel what him shal abide' (l. 3450). He observes in cadences reminiscent
of present-day Oxfordshire:

> 'So ferde another clerk with astromye;
> He walked in the feldes, for to prye
> Upon the sterres what ther sholde bifalle,
> Til he was in a marle-pit yfalle;
> He saugh nat that.'
>
> (3457ff.)

This sobering episode, too, has been derived from a common proverb[81]
stressing the formula 'now up, now down'. It is exactly the comic
alternation of up/down which is going to befall the roof-launched
carpenter through that same ignorance ('vanitye') he has just blessed:

> 'Ye, blessed be alwey a lewed man
> That noght but oonly his bileve kan!'
>
> (3455-6)

At the comic denouement, all the male persons of the Miller's invention
undergo simple, painful reverses of fortune: an unexpected mutation
from one extreme to another. This concluding pattern has been suggested by the proverbial collections of the 'now this, now that' type:[82]

> Now myrth, now sorrowe, now dolour, then gladnesse.
> Now better, now worsse, now plesure, then payne.
> Now to want, then to have, now love, then disdayne.
> Now ebbe, now flode, now corupte, now pure; now hote
> now colde, now drought, now rayne.

Thus, Absolon is converted from physically pure to impure through
the *baiser de fesse* ('now pure, now corupte'); at the same time he undergoes a total revulsion from sexual passion ('now hot, now cold').[83]
The simple John falls from his fearful fantasy on the roof-top to
instant and painful contact with the real ground ('now up, now down').
In his mind he goes from a fearful fantasy of 'Nowell's floode' to the
reality of dry ground ('now flode, now ebbe, now rayne, now drought').
Nicholas, at the height of his carnal joy, goes from pleasure to intense
pain ('now pleasure, then peyne'); his comic exuberance and delight

[81] Cf. Whiting, *op. cit.*, S684.
[82] *Ibid.*, N479, This example is dated *c.* 1400.
[83] The pattern for the episode is referred to in line 3754: 'His hoote love was
coold and al yqueynt.'

at the discomfiture of Absolon passes to instant misery ('now myrth, now sorrowe').

The second comic rhythm, that of the enlarging, irrationally-centred construction which develops into a building up of comic retention awaiting sudden relief, is based on a commonplace of classical psychology and closely related to the main physical image of 'flood' which lies at the heart of Nicholas's needlessly complicated plot to dispose of the carpenter to gain one night with Alisoun. In honest John the fantasy develops out of his excessive doting on Alisoun which in turn engenders a sudden and overwhelming fear. The rhythm of swelling and inundation is explicitly linked with the 'passiouns' in the Miller's analytical account of the husband's mental process:

> Lo, which a greet thyng is affeccioun,
> Men may dyen of ymaginacioun.
> So depe may impressioun be take.
> This sely carpenter bigynneth quake;
> Hym thynketh verraily that he may see
> Nooes flood come walwynge as the see
> To drenchen Alisoun, his hony deere.
>
> (3611ff.)

The flood is both the object of the carpenter's fearful imagining and quasi-metaphoric of that projection, unlimited and overwhelming. The source of this image is not proverbial but literary. The whole of Boethius' *De Consolatione* I.m.7 is devoted to just such an image of the passions, and two other passages are relevant. Compare IV.m.2:

> *Hinc enim libido versat*
> *Avidis corda venenis,*
> *Hinc flagellat ira mentem*
> *Fluctus turbida tollens . . .*

The connection of *fluctus* with a wide range of emotions is well illustrated by many passages in Lucretius, book VI. Chaucer translates:

> For lecherye tormenteth hem on that o side with gredy venymes; and troubable ire that areyseth in hem the flodes of trowblinges . . .

The process is described in greater detail in I, prose v:

> *Itaque lenioribus paullisper utemur, ut quae in tumorem perturbationibus*

influentibus induruerunt, ad acrioris vim medicaminis recipiendam, tactu blandiore mollescant.

Chaucer translates:

> For which we wol usen somdel lyghtere medicynes, so that thilke passiouns that ben waxen hard in swellynge by perturbaciouns flowynge into thy thought, mowen waxen esy and softe to reseyven the strengthe of a more myghty and more egre medicyne, by an esyere touchynge.

Philosophy prescribes a 'light' medicine, 'an esyere touchynge', to relieve this condition. The Miller's malicious comic invention proposes a hard and painful remedy—physical humiliation of some kind: impure and distressing contact, a broken arm, first degree burns of a tender part of the anatomy. As Boethius had said:

> *cur aegri etiam quibus lenibus, quidam vero acribus adjuvantur.*
>
> (IV prose vi)

> and also why that some syke folke ben holpen with lyghte medicynes, and some folk ben holpen with sharpe medicynes.

In the Miller's universe there are no 'light' medicines, the remedies are all reversals to the other extreme, and extremes are always sharp. Thus, the Miller sets in motion a complex opposition of the two comic rhythms with yet another turn of the screw, so that the more cunning and constructing of the characters are themselves outwitted by the world which they seek to dominate. The carpenter's fantasy-dominated state is suddenly punctured and he passes rapidly through physical injury to total psychological humiliation. Absolon's ludicrously musical and fastidiously clean courtship of Alisoun ends in a disgusting and unexpected physical contact; 'nice' Nicholas's absurdly elaborate programme for husband-eliminating ends in lodger-crippling. So much for his advice given to the carpenter (l. 3530): 'Werk al by conseil, and thou shalt nat rewe!' The final comic irony is that the Miller's imagination has an answer to human intelligence, too. The world of violent fluxation, the alternations of extremes, defeats even the 'conseil', the deliberating mind of Nicholas. It is the 'clerkes', the scholars of Oxford who pronounce the merely gullible carpenter mad. They, too, are wrong. In the Miller's view, all physical and mental states are destined to achieve only momentary satisfaction. In the human will's contentious search for satisfaction which ends in a determination by extremes (and therefore opposites) it resembles Heraclitus' account of physical reality and the soul.[84]

The complex climax and release of the knot of comic tensions is brought about by a related series of sharp physical blows, contacts or sudden movements. 'Speke' commands Absolon in order to sight his target. He is answered by a 'blinding' fart, a 'thonder-dent'. This explosion is answered by the physical blow ('smoot') with the red-hot iron. In turn, this is answered by an instant cry for water. The answer to 'water' is the carpenter's axe-blow which sends him pell-mell to the ground. The comic chain of irrational cause and effect gives way to a momentary state of calm, a temporary suspension of conflict, summed up in a general clownish gaping ('kiken and they cape'). This, too, is destined to be momentary, for the comic tranquillity gives way to 'stryf', debate and argument. The Miller's 'experience' thus carries on with its ruthless dialectic.[85]

The sudden relief of comic retention[86] which forms the climax of the *narratio* has the sequential movement of a parody version of a romantic courtship: passing from the lover's question ('Speke'), to the *domina*'s answer (a fart), to a kiss (branding), to the *domina*'s granting of 'mercy' ('Water!'), to the physical resolution (axe-blow leading to fall and broken arm). All of this passes irrationally between the three

[84] Chaucer seems to have known nothing of this philosopher. He might have gathered something of his metaphysical system from Cicero's summarizings or from Aristotle's observations in the *Metaphysics*. But there is no evidence of Chaucer's having seen the relevant passages. Part of the Heraclitan view of the physical universe passed into later Stoic usage. Chaucer would have met this in Boethius, especially Philosophy's early descriptions of the quality of human life when it is guided by purely material or hedonistic motives. Chaucer could have read an account of Heraclitus in Walter Burley's *Liber de Vita et Moribus Philosophorum*, chapter 47, which was written c. 1340 and was very popular. But apart from commenting on the obscurity of his thought (*Hic propter ipsius nimis obscuras sentencias dictus est a philosophis 'Eraclitus tenebrosus'*) and quoting disconnectedly some of his axioms (collected from Seneca, St Augustine and Diogenes Laertius by Vincent of Beauvais) Burley's brief life would have given Chaucer little idea of a Heraclitan philosophy.

[85] It is not quite as ruthless as the Reeve's avenging universe which has been based on the proverb: 'For all your boost and your orguyl,/Man shal threste in your cuyl.' Cf. Whiting, *op. cit.*, C607. This example is cited from *Richard Coer de Lyon* 1831–2; the poem is dated c. 1300.

[86] It is perhaps significant that one of the 'causes' in the final comic resolution is the necessity for Nicholas to get up and relieve himself (3799). This same action is a major cause in the revenge in the *Reeve's Tale*.

men in the amorous situation. Alisoun is again exempted, although
she is, properly speaking, the *causa causans*.

We are aware in our co-consciousness that the Miller could never
have managed this degree of comic intelligence and invention. This
impersonating virtuosity belongs to Chaucer, not his *persona*. The
tale is not a 'fableau' or even the parody of a *fabliau*.[87]

It combines plot-lines found singly in some analogues but never
found in complex combination in any one anecdote. There is the
Chaucerian addition of philosophical and moral consistency, psychological observation, impersonation of speech rhythms, the creation of
the Miller's vocabulary.[88] Sometimes Chaucer's genius stoops to invent
characters who are even more ignorant and idiotic than the Miller or
the carpenter. Compare the exquisite boobyism of the Augustinian
canon of Osney when asked about the whereabouts of carpenter
John:

> ... 'I noot, I saugh hym here nat wirche
> Syn Saterday; I trowe that he be went
> For tymber, ther oure abbot hath hym sent;
> For he is wont for tymber for to go,
> And dwellen at the grange a day or two;
> Or elles he is at his hous, certeyn.
> Where that he be, I kan nat soothly seyn.'
>
> (3664–70)

We are also made aware by that same co-consciousness of those
limitations in the Miller's churlish imagination which may prevent him
from carrying out his own literary intentions (he asks us to blame it on
the drink, we know better). For example, the Miller presents us with

---

[87] Professor Schlauch years ago (*PMLA* 61, pp. 416ff.) demonstrated the absurdity
of assigning any of Chaucer's tales to naïve sub-literary types, *fabliaux* or Breton
lays or romances.

[88] The Miller's language is mainly established by the inclusion of single non-
literary lexical items. There may be grammatical vulgarisms, but they are not
obvious. The items are mainly sbs, e.g. *gnof* ('lout'), *bragot* ('a type of honey and
ale fermented together'), *meeth* ('mead', the beta-form ending in -*th*), *lendes*
('loins'), *thakked* ('love-tapped'), *brokking* ('singing of the nightingale'), *viritote*
(? a vulgar form of *viritrate*, unexplained in *Friar's Tale* 1582). There are some
vulgar word-plays we shall never understand; for example, the swearing by 'St.
Note'. This may contain some reference to singing 'bi note', by written notation
and hence conceal a play on 'prikk-song' (not recorded until *c.* 1463). Cf. *Romeo
and Juliet*, II.iv.21. The Kentishism 'celle' (sill, ground) may be some indication of
the dialect-area for the Miller's origin.

that ever-increasing medieval object, the student drop-out. Yet we are assured that Nicholas is an experienced seducer who knows how to go about these things with subtle tact. When he comes to make his declaration to Alisoun there is nothing in the least subtle about it. The Miller may pun on 'prively' and 'queynt' but his inability to imagine anything but near-rape creates a more subtle, 'unconscious' area of literary pleasure for the reader. The famous *ethopoeia* of Absolon, the textbook figure of such a description of masculine beauty in Peter de Riga's *Aurora*, is spoilt by the infamous 'hiccupped couplet' in lines 3337–8. The enjambment and awkwardness of this final unit is comically positioned:

> In al the toun nas brewhous ne taverne
> That he ne visited with his solas,
> Ther any gaylard tappestere was.
> But sooth to seyn, he was somdeel squaymous
> Of fartyng, and of speche daungerous.
>
> (3334ff.)

From the above analysis it can be seen that I do not think that the *Miller's Tale* is a piece of unconscious self-exposure after the manner of Jean de Meun's creations in the *Roman* (the Pardoner, on the other hand, is a good example of this type). The *Miller's Tale* is a subtle blend of Chaucer and the *persona* which yields a rich comic philosophy and comic narrative. The Reeve seems to me very much the self-exposure of a mood, a mood of intense anger, an imbalance in the 'complexion' which creates a universe of hate and revenge. There is nothing comic in his tale, no comic rhythms arising from fantasies or desires. The rhythms are insistent, mechanical, repetitiously destructive. It is summed up in the sexual image which enacts revenge: 'He priketh hard and depe as he were mad' (l. 4231).[89] Our attention to psychological origins is aroused in the prologue, lines 3863–98, a passage pathetic, angry, self-examining and utterly depressing. The last thing to die in an old man is anger: 'I pray to God his nekke mote to-breke.' The comic universe of the Miller belongs to the delusions of Monsieur Jourdain, the Reeve seems closer to the isolated misanthropy of Alceste.

[89] The physical action of spurring a horse is also suggested, cf. the *Tale of Sir Thopas* 1964, 'And pryked as he were wood.' The Ellesmere MS. reading (supported by Univ. Lib. Camb. 11.8.27) 'sore' for 'depe' may be preferred. Pleasure and hate are combined in this activity.

FABULAE CHAUCERI

The Aristotelian 'middle' of the *narratio* contains the fables of Chaucer, as one Bodley MS. entitles this group. To say the least, they are a peculiar contribution. Since all the tales are of Chaucerian invention in any case, what does the poet gain by having an identifiable authorial contribution? Obviously, he gains an ironic dimension in that none of the pilgrims (including the Man of Law) has the faintest idea that this is Geoffrey Chaucer, the poet. The creation of a pseudo-objective image of the poet reduced to the level of one of his own creations, and to a certain extent answerable to them, allows Chaucer under the comic sleight of anonymity obliquely to comment on some aspects of Canterbury poetics and possible audience response. In allowing the Host to give a short *ethopoeia* we not only get a seemingly objective glimpse of the poet,[90] but we are instructed that any mechanical matching of prologue-portrait to a given tale had better be revised. The predetermined physiognomy may not always tell the truth or fulfil the suggested 'scientific' type. The Host imagines 'some deynte thyng . . . by his cheere'. He is sadly disappointed. By this example we are invited to entertain other ironic possibilities.

What the poet gives the Host is two literary monstrosities. He supplies first a tale in 'rime'[91] which, in obedience to the Host's request for 'a tale of myrthe', is 'o solas'—a poem constructed exclusively to delight ('of myrthe and of solas'). It is so delightful that it 'never deviates into sense'. Everything, including the passion of Sir Thopas, is fantastical. Romance motifs are indeed burlesqued, but the main attribute of the

[90] The phrase 'elvyssh by his contenaunce' seems to bring several possibilities together, including 'shy', 'mysterious', 'strange' and 'devious'. It also has a physical connection with the phrase 'smal and fair of face'. A passage in *The Wars of Alexander*, 5258ff. suggests that an abnormally fair complexion was a sign of fay beauty: 'Scho was faire and so fresche, as faucon hire seemed/An elfe out of anothire erde, or ellis an Aungell.' This whole description indicates that Chaucer was compact and dainty of build, inclined to fat, of regular unpronounced features, fair of complexion and very blond. The Harvard portrait very distantly resembles this Chaucer.

[91] This is the only tale to be told manifestly within the fictional terms in *rhyme*. None of the other tales are to be so imagined. There is one general reference in the *Knight's Tale* A 1459 where it does not refer to the mode of the tale. There is one use of the vb. in the *Canon's Yeoman's Tale* 1093 where it represents the ME vb. 'rimen', 'to reckon up', 'recount' (v.OE riman). This vb. is not distinguished by Skeat, Robinson or Baugh.

tale is its monomaniacal concentration on entertainment: mad min-
strelsy. The Host is right, this sort of thing could go on for ever. What
enchants and amuses is its aesthetic extremity, a theory out of control.
When the Host has silenced Chaucer, he suggests 'prose' and perhaps
'som doctryne'. The authorial voice gives him exactly that: a 'moral
tale vertuous'. Thus is born the other literary monstrosity: a tale entirely compounded of 'sentence'. Every element in the *Tale of Melibeus*
is sententious, made up of lists upon lists of maxims and authoritative
pronouncements, a *tour de force* of unrelenting didacticism. The plot
of the *Tale of Melibeus* may be fairly represented by one modest
sentence, the rest is proverbial. As we lose ourselves in the multiplying
briar patch of contending 'sentences', 'figures', 'proverbes', 'morali-
tees', 'counseils' and 'sawes', we gradually come to realize that behind
this elaborate jest, a tale of 'o sentence', lies the Proverb Absolute:
'There's a saying for everything,'[92] The reaction of the Host to this
ridiculous formulation is utter delight. He applies the treatise literally
to his own situation. With touching ignorance he yearns for the forbearance of Prudence in place of the oppugnancy of his own wife.
Like Nurse Angelica in *Romeo and Juliet*, Dame Goodelief (l. 1894)
hardly lives up to her name. But the conceptual Dame Prudence
would hardly make a wife.

By providing us with these two absurd theoretical excursions, we
are obliquely presented with Chaucer's criticism of the Horatian (and
medieval) formulation that poetry or literature in general should both
delight and instruct.[93] Whatever literature is, it is not simply to be
identified with these two aims or any mode of expression which may
be defined as 'delighting' or 'instructing'. Chaucer is again guiding us
by 'contraries'. What has Chaucer omitted from the tales of both
Thopas and Melibeus? Exactly what all the other tales in varying degrees
possess: a large sense of reality, abundant psychological observation,
literary complexity, stylistic interest—a sophisticated literary awareness
of formal ends and means linked to a genuine philosophical acuity—
not just learning for its own sake or pretty gems of patterns.

Part of the Chaucerian literary 'game' resides in taking in not only
the fictional pilgrim fellowship but the reader as well[94]—as he vainly

---

[92] Cf. Seneca, *Epistulae Morales*, 94.35: '*Infinita praecepta sunt.*'

[93] Cf. *Ars Poetica* 333–44.

[94] The Chaucerian intention is evident from his use of the vb. 'write' in his
closing address to the pilgrims, 'lordinges alle' in the head-link 953–66 where the
inappropriateness of the vb. in the fictional context signals the momentary

tries to find something worthy of the poet's genius in these two blagues. Chaucerian criticism has on many occasions taken the bait. The figure of Sir Thopas initially amounts to a collection of verbal conventions, and after his dream of a wholly abstract elf-queen, nothing more or less than disembodied natural impulse—Sir Courage (in the beastly sense). The frequent use of the vb. 'priken' (eight times in less than eighty-five lines) suggests more than a mere romance parody. Lines 778–81 go a long way towards suggesting an improper sense. Our 'gem of a knight' (in Skeat's phrase) is Flemish and is lord of the manor of Poppering. I am not persuaded that there is some political reference here. This place was the origin of a type of pear.[95] It would seem to have been long and thin and may have resembled a 'popper', a type of small dagger.[96] This type of pear is the subject of a notoriously improper remark of Mercutio's in *Romeo and Juliet* II.i.33–8. The romance conventions embodied in this tale are of several kinds; they range from syntactical imitations, descriptive *topoi*, rhymes, words and phrases, to the use of the supernatural to explain morality and social behaviour.[97] In a thoroughly delightful and sometimes unexpectedly original way the tale provides a serious critique of the shortcomings of ME romance as an account of reality. Thopas's attitude to women is preposterous (none are worthy of his interest), his conversion from chastity to rampant 'love-longinge' unaccountable. The condition of his horse is both comic (so blown with sweating that it can be wrung out) and horrible (the horse's sides run with blood). So portrayed, the romance world is one of stylistic exaggerations which mask simple and primitive actions (riding, dressing, fighting and eating): the poetic equivalent of a fantastically ornamented cod-piece. Bishop Hurd long ago called our Knight a 'Don Quixote in little', but he is a wee Quixote without a Sancho Panza, a quest-motif without a touch of human nature.

It is impossible to write anything further on the *Tale of Melibeus* since it has no Chaucerian characteristics: it is a very close rendering of the OF. The last paragraph on penance (itself a prose paraphrase of

[95] The earliest recorded example of the place-name in this connection appears to be Skelton, *Speke Parrot* 72.
[96] Cf. *Reeve's Tale* 3931.
[97] The many parallels and verbal similarities are listed in Bryan and Dempster, *Sources and Analogues of Chaucer's Canterbury Tales*, pp. 496–559.

conflation of these two audiences. Chaucer occasionally allows himself a momentary drop of the fictional guise. Cf. *Knight's Tale* 1201 and elsewhere.

I John 1.9) is the only significant Chaucerian addition. This has been added to give the *Tale of Melibeus* an anticipatory and parallel thematic concluding interest with the *Parson's Tale*. It is a structural invention which relates to the total design of the *Tales*. This has been explained in the section on the disposition of the tales on pp. 102–3.

JOURNEY'S END:[98] THE MANCIPLE AND THE PARSON

Chaucerian criticism has been unhappy with the Manciple's prologue and tale. It has best defended the 'unity' of the prologue and tale by making the Manciple the object of his own moral advice,[99] a self-administered rapping on the knuckles for openly chastising the Cook. It has given the tale literary interest by delivering it over into the hands of multiple parody: a collection of stylistic ironies.[100] Both these accounts seem wide of the mark. There is indeed a unifying element between the prologue and tale but the connection arises out of social comedy and a particular comic process.

The essence of the prologue lies in its unrestrained 'horse-play' and the comic reconciliation through the gift of good wine leading to helpless drunkenness: the human transformed into mime or mumming. In connection with the Parson's prologue and tale, the Manciple's contribution represents a final, festive, carnival moment before the lenten fable of the Parson. As an example of a 'paired opposite', it represents a juxtaposing of the spirit of free indulgence of animal appetite (cf. the digression on the unnaturalness of caging birds—or locking up wives) and the doctrine of salvation through the penitential disciplines. Out of this a further opposition develops: permitting a free rein to natural feelings gives way to chastisement (cf. Phoebus' remorse and the punishment of the crow), what Byron meant when he said 'there's no sterner moralist than pleasure'; and out of following the narrow way of penance the human spirit is liberated through seeking self-satisfaction. These are the larger structural rhythms which unify the final section XII (groups H and I).

[98] For the use of this phrase as an organizing critical concept, cf. S. C. Chew, *The Pilgrimage of Life*, New Haven (1962), pp. 226–52.
[99] Cf. M. Donner, 'The Unity of Chaucer's Manciple's Fragment', *MLN* 70 (1955), pp. 245–9.
[100] R. Hazelton, '*The Manciple's Tale*: Parody and Critique', *JEGP* 62 (1963), pp. 1–31.

The comic bridge which joins the Manciple's prologue to the tale
is more subtle. The literary festival atmosphere arises out of the unforced mixture of rivalry, 'bourding' (l. 81)—turning something into
an amusing joke—and the comic reconcilement through the offering
of a peace-token in the form of yet more wine. As Chaucer says, 'What
neded hym? he drank ynough biforn!' (l. 89). At the end of this
reconciliation through the very excess criticized, the Host exclaims in a
good-natured pagan prayer:

> O thou Bacus, yblessed be thy name,
> That so kanst turnen ernest into game!
> Worshipe and thank be to thy deitee!
> Of that mateere ye get namoore of me.
>
> (99–102)

Line 102 hints at a lewd, pagan ribaldry which the Host suppresses,
turning instead, very quickly, to the tale at hand. Is this merely an
abbreviatory asseveration or is the intelligent reader expected to
remember something? I suspect that the physical image of the very
drunk Cook, scarcely able to sit his cart-horse, at one time falling off
and having to be lifted back into the saddle, there to sit precariously
nodding and snuffling, drinking still more wine from the Manciple's
'gourd' (a huge measure of about a half-gallon), grinning ('wonder
fayn'), beaming in speechless thanks ('thanked hym in swich wise as
he koude')—this vivid image of mindless inebriety has arisen out of
Chaucer's memory of the famous Bacchanalian scene on Naxos in
Ovid's *Ars Amatoria* I. 543ff. where the besozzled Silenus riding in the
religious procession can barely sit his ass. As the procession makes its
way, Silenus falls off and has to be urged by his satyrs to get back on.
After this entourage, Bacchus himself rides in his chariot.[101] The Cook's

[101]   *Ebrius ecce senex pando Silenus asello*
              Vix sedet; et pressas continet arte jubas.
         Dum sequitur Bacchas, Bacchae fugiuntque petuntque;
              Quadrupedem ferula dum malus urget eques;
         In caput aurito cecidit delapsus asello.
              Clamarunt Satyri: Surge age, surge, pater!
         Jam Deus e curru . . .

Behold, drunken old Silenus scarce sits his ass, and leaning clings tight to
the mane under his nose. Whilst he pursues the Bacchanals and whilst they
slip away and return to the attack and whilst the maladroit rider urges on
his mount with his crop, he falls off the long-eared ass and topples head-

physical condition and position in the riding order recall that of the Miller. The Miller, leading, pipes the company out of Southwark; as the company reaches Harbledown village the Cook has fallen far to the rear. The drunken Miller insists on telling his tale; the Cook nearly speechless with drink merely submits to being passed over. The Miller almost falls out of the saddle; the Cook actually takes a purler. The beginning and ending sections repeat (with variations) rhythms which are suggestive of each other. The Ovidian image of the Cook as a kind of fourteenth-century Silenus provides an underlying literary link between prologue and tale. As has been long recognized, the almost exclusive source of the *Manciple's Tale* is Ovid, *Metamorphoses* II.531–632; and a couplet in *Ars Amatoria* II.239–40 may have provided the immediate link. Thus, Ovidian reminiscence provides the partially hidden connection between prologue and tale. But the comic method of the prologue provides the main, ostensible connection. The Manciple's comic process is that of the 'bourde' (l. 81). I think the semantic force here is not simply 'a little joke' but refers to the larger process of turning something through ridicule into a frivolous amusement. This sense is common in ME, and even 'mummings' are sometimes referred to as 'bourdes' in ME (cf. *MED bourde* 2 (b)). In the prologue the physical appearance of the Cook himself becomes the object in the 'bourde'. He is openly made fun of[102] and turned into two comic images: (1) the gaping, stinking mouth, according to the folk proverb, has admitted the devil. In its fatal, pestilential, devouring aspect (ll. 35–9) it recalls hell-mouth;[103] (2) the Cook is transformed by drink

---

[102] The 'bourde' here has a certain resemblance to 'bobbing', the cruel mocking of someone who is helpless to resist (cf. *MED bobben* vb.). A reminiscence of this vbl. sb. may be connected with the comic onomatopoeic nonce-formation 'Bobbe-up-and-doun' for Harbledown at the beginning of the *Prologue*. The nick-name presumably arises out of the slightly undulating movement of the landscape. It may also in this context be taken to refer to the Cook's nodding, drunken movements.

[103] Cf. *Legend of Good Women* 1104: 'the swolowe of helle.'

---

foremost. The Satyrs cry: 'Come, father, get up!' Now in his chariot came the god [Bacchus] . . .

Lines 97–8 of the Manciple's prologue translate *Ars Amatoria* I. 238: '*Cura fugit multo diluiturque mero*'. Silenus' braying ass figures in the discovery of Priapus (Ovid, *Fasti* VI.319ff.), remembered by Boccaccio in the *Teseida* and translated by Chaucer with more Ovidian detail in *Parliament* 253–6. Another Silenian scene (Ovid, *Metamorphoses* XI.85–147) is described by Gower in *Confessio Amantis* V.141ff.

into the animal characteristics appropriate to the sanguine temperament, 'ape-drunk'. This last metamorphosis contains a further satiric point in that the Cook is not in the least ape-like in his drink but dull and stupid—'sow-drunk'. The Manciple has already called him a 'stynking swyne'.

The Host agrees with the Manciple's strictures, yet considers his open reproof too strict ('to nyce'). He warns:

'Another day he wole, peraventure,
Reclayme thee and brynge thee to lure;
I meene, he speke wole of smale thynges,
As for to pynchen at thy rekenynges,
That were nat honest, if it cam to preef.'

(71–5)

To meet this contingency, the Manciple indulges in yet another 'good jape' (l. 84) by becoming comically reconciled with the Cook through making him more and more drunk—thus, depriving him of the ability to say anything intelligible or to remember anything of the episode when he will awake from this terrible indulgence. The 'bourde' and the Bacchanalian interlude provide the basis for the main connection with the tale. In the tale we are presented with a reworked version of Ovid's aetiological fable on the origin of the crow's colour, extended to include a concluding, sharp sermon on the wisdom of holding one's tongue and keeping one's own 'counseil'. The moralizing element is obliquely present in Ovid, and more directly present in Gower's use of the tale in *Confessio Amantis* III.768ff. But the Manciple's rehearsal of 'the words my mother taught to me' which provides the sermonizing climax of the tale, are not meant to refer to the Manciple, but constitute yet another 'bourde'. The comic addressee of 'mi sone' is not the Manciple, but the Cook. The words 'mi sone' introducing an admonishing injunction, are repeated over and over again with the insistence of a comic physical cudgelling—a 'bourde' turning into a 'bobbing'.[104] In the prologue, the only direct admonishment delivered by the Manciple to the Cook is 'Hoold cloos thy mouth, man . . .' (l. 37). Anger engenders in the Cook a state of absolute speechless rage (ll. 46–8). The possible threat of the Cook tattle-taling on the Manciple engenders the 'jape' of rendering him absolutely incapacitated through more drink. In the Ovidian tale (and Gower's version) the

[104] The vb. and vbl. sb. also refer in ME to the physical beating of someone who is helpless, usually blindfolded. The Cook is blind drunk.

punishment wreaked on the crow is exile and loss of his original whiteness—nothing more. There is no reference to his loss of singing capacity; and beyond that, no reference to the crow's loss of the powers of speech. But this is the whole point of the Manciple's Apollonian punishment:

> And made hym blak, and refte hym al his song,
> *And eek his speche* . . .
>
> (305–6)

In the prologue, Chaucer's imagination turns the Cook into an image of Silenus; the Manciple's 'bourde' turns him into hell-mouth and a playful ape. His 'bobbing' of the Cook at the end of the Ovidian aetiological fable on the origin of the crow, turns the Cook into a kind of speechless crow. There are many points of similarity between the Cook, the crow and the person addressed in the concluding 'sermon': (a) loss of intelligible speech; (b) the hoarse call of the crow and the sounds emitted by the Cook, 'fneseth faste', and having the 'pose', which here probably refers both to nasal catarrh and to continuous coughing;[105] (c) the physical nodding of the Cook ('nodde faste') and the gesture of speechless agreement enjoined in the sermon: 'My sone, spek nat, but with thyn heed thou bekke' (l. 346); (d) the white colour of the crow before transformation and the stark white complexion of the Cook ('full pale', ll. 20, 30; 'sory palled goost', l. 55).

Thus, the helpless, blind-drunk, speechless Cook is satirically cudgelled and verbally whipped lest he think of giving away any of the Manciple's secrets of book keeping. The tale is a comic mixture of the rough, broad, playfulness of common, vulgar humour and the sly workings of a literate mind. The Manciple exclaims several times, 'I am nat textualle'—yet we know from the prologue-portrait that the Manciple is just such a blend of common and uncommon shrewdness:

> Now is nat that of God a ful fair grace
> That swich a lewed mannes wit shal pace
> The wisdom of an heep of lerned men?
>
> (573–5)

'Boystous' though the Manciple calls himself, yet he can aptly and openly quote Aristotle's advice to Alexander. The tale contains many

---

[105] ME 'pose' refers to coughing symptoms as well, cf. the *OED*'s citations earlier and later.

burlesques of poetic style, but the main interest lies in its comic formulation of moral 'bourde' and sermonizing 'bobbing'. It is the verbal equivalent of Molière's dog-Latin ballets and comic initiation rites.[106]

THE PARSON'S TALE

In recognition of the non-aesthetic nature of the Parson's contribution (deliberately offered in a spirit of 'limited co-operation'), most scholarship has either concentrated on the possible source or sources of the work, or argued a complex relationship of the Parson's material with the themes and preoccupations of the pilgrims' arguments and debates: a kind of final religious solution. It is still a matter of some interest as to the 'originality' or not of the placing together of the two kinds of *summae*, one treating penance, the other the Seven Deadly Sins.[107]

[106] Scenes of satirically being rendered helpless, accompanied by mock preaching, are common to comedy. Compare the binding, shaving of the head, and preaching of patience to Dr Pinch in *The Comedy of Errors* (V.i); and the imprisoning of, and preaching of the fool's doctrine (the transmigration of the soul) to Malvolio in *Twelfth Night* (IV.ii). These are 'comic deaths' in Mr Emrys Jones's illuminating phrase. Chaucer and Molière are fond of comic metamorphosis. Laughter often renders one physically helpless, afterwards releasing the mind to new, fresh, impressions.

[107] The 'tract' falls into three main divisions, with the *summa peccatorum* as a central digression in the midst of the two continuous sections dealing with penance. Imagistically, the work presents two antithetical arboreal metaphors, the tree of penance (based on the number three) in 110-25; the tree of the sins (based on the number seven) in 385-90. Friar Lorens, the author of *Somme le Roy*, was fond of arboreal images. The scheme of two opposed trees has a long history. In the pseudo-Hugonian *De fructibus carnis et spiritus* we find two opposed trees of virtues and vices. In the twelfth-century *Liber floridus Lamberti* we have the opposition of *arbor bona* and *arbor mala*. In book IV of Deguilleville's *Pélèrinage de l'âme* there is a dispute between a green tree (the tree of Jesse) and a dry tree (the tree of Adam). This image derives from Luke 23.31. There is a discussion of arboreal images in M. W. Bloomfield, *The Seven Deadly Sins*, Michigan (1952), pp. 84, 125, 367. The monograph by U. Kamber, *Arbor Amoris*, Berlin (1964), pp. 62ff., 129ff., collects some of this material. Cf. also the complex and beautiful 'Tree of Charity' in *Piers Plowman* C.19.1-15. It appears (with variations) as the 'Tree of Patience' in the B-text (passus 16). Seneca (quoted four times by the Parson) uses an arboreal image when speaking of the natural unity between man's reason (*ratio*) and doctrines (*decreta*), *Epistolae Morales* 95.64: '*ergo haec necessaria est, sine qua nec illa sunt. Sed utrumque iungamus. Namque est sine radice inutiles rami sunt et ipsae radices iis, quae genuere, adiuvantur*' (hence reason is necessary; for without it the doctrines cannot exist either. But let us unite the two. For indeed branches are

The English style, frankly, does not suggest a Latin original. I suspect that an old French treatise beginning 'Nostre doulce Seigneur Dieu du ciel, pour quil veult nulle persone perir mais veult que nous arriver tous a la conoissance de lui et a la joyeuse vie perdurable . . .' will turn up one day; and it will contain the two summae placed together after the Parson's way—if not substantially yielding us Chaucer's text. When this point will have been decided there will be little left to talk about in terms of this kind of 'originality'. But we ought to ask ourselves what effect does the Parson's sermon make on us, reading it in this ultimate context, as a part of section XII, accepting as a medieval reader would the integrity of the 'tale' whether invention or translation. When we ask this question, I think we find the Parson's Tale something more than a literary exemplification of a type of narrator and something less than (or at least other than) a complex final answer or type of answer to all the themes and discussions raised since leaving the 'Tabard'.

We have seen how the Parson's prologue prepares us for the last tale in the very last hours, evoking the approach of the 'end-of-day' topos to suggest the literary conclusion and possibly the onset of that 'night . . . when no man can work'. We have seen how carefully the image of the pilgrimage or 'viage' is related to the theme of the 'wey of penaunce'. Thus, lines 47–51 of the prologue are mirrored in section 75–85 of the sermon's exordium,[108] these words anticipated by the introductory Latin text of Jeremiah 6.16 which provides the logical bridge—incidentally giving the author the opportunity to introduce one of his favourite relativistic observations ex persona rectoris: 'Manye been the weyes espirituels that leden folk to oure Lord Jhesu Crist, and to the regne of glorie.' This recalls Astrolabe, prologue, line 40, 'right as diverse pathes leden diverse folk the righte wey to Rome', as well as Troilus II.36–7.[109] This way, then, is but one of the many 'ways'. But as soon as the treatise has established this connection firmly enough, the 'voyage' metaphor ceases to be elaborated or referred to in any way. There is no further attempt to give the sermon any aesthetic organization which would connect it with images or metaphors employed in the rest of the tales. For example, all other uses of

[108] The article by C. O. Chapman, 'The Parson's Tale: a medieval Sermon', MLN 43 (1928), pp. 229–34, remains one of the best pieces written on the tale.
[109] The proverb occurs in the collection attributed to Alan of Lille: 'Mille viae ducunt homines per secula Romam.'

useless without their roots, and the roots themselves are strengthened by the growths which they have produced).

the sb. 'wey' in the sermon fail to glance at any 'path' imagery. The sb. is restricted to phraseological function in formations using the core 'by way of' or in the abstract application 'means'. Beyond the immediate linking device in the *praefatio* and exordium, no attempt whatever has been made to adjust the *summa*-material to the aesthetic context of the *Tales*. It deliberately forces us to take it on its own terms, or to ignore it or to treat it as a merely typological exemplification. If we take it on its own terms, what are we given?

First we are presented with a verbal organization which resembles nothing else in the poem. The medium of discursive prose reminds us naturally of the *Tale of Melibeus*, but the style, cursus and construction of paragraphs are quite unlike. Equally, it is not a self-exposing, satiric type of mock-sermon in the style of Jean de Meun, nor is it a sermon which provides a framework for exemplificating stories—a sermon which is mainly anecdotal and illustrative after the fashion of Robert Mannyng's popular treatise *Handlyng Synne* ('A Discussion of Sin'). It has none of the earnest simplicity, the near-Lollard charm, of Sir John Clanvowe's *Two Ways*,[110] nor has it any of the personal, evangelical warmth of Richard Rolle's scattered and infrequent observations on penance—where he instructs us that our hearts, our intentions, are important to penance, not our outward 'signs', our mere indulgence in the physical discipline. The Parson's drift is single-minded and intense. Whatever the 'ultimate' Latin origins of the two 'parts' in Pennaforte and Peraldus, it recalls Friar Lorens's *Somme le Roy* in spirit, if not in actual points of style. It exhibits the following general discursive characteristics: (1) a prolonged and deliberate methodology, involving categorization, enumeration, subdividing and close internal and external organization of paragraphing; (2) a detailed, logical relation between premises and proofs. The emphasis here would seem to fall on 'realism'. An exact description of reality is most pronounced in the section on *superbia* where contemporary fashions in clothing are illustrated, and satirically characterized in vivid and astonishing detail. It is full, copious, at the level of illustration and related concretely to actual manners and social activity. (3) In addition to an emphasis on

---

[110] Edited from the unique Corpus Christi College, Oxford, MS. 97 (folios 114a–123b) by A. V. Scattergood in *English Philological Studies* (1967), pp. 33–56. A list of mistranscriptions is given by E. Wilson in vol. 11, pp. 55–6, with the recording of a fragment of another manuscript copy in the BM. This part of the Corpus MS. 92, folio 85 to the end, should be dated *c.* 1450 or a little later. Some of the items (indentures, wills, letters), indicate a made-up, commonplace book type of MS. as the exemplar. It had strong connections with Lichfield.

'measure' (there are nearly a dozen references), the work is repetitiously addressed to man's reason, especially to the 'consenting of man's reason'. Throughout, the Parson makes a steady appeal to the 'wey of resoun'. Unlike Rolle and others, there is a strong philosophical connection established through 'reasonableness' between activity ('signs') and intention ('will'). Given its disciplinary ethical basis, it is almost Aristotelian in its insistence on an immediate, practical connection between thought and action, and the necessity of performing social acts in order to acquire and reinforce individual moral validity.

The effect of reading (with attention) the Parson's treatise is to enter into a closely interconnected, logical and analytic account of man's nature which has no connections with the characterization and debate which have been carried on in the 'Canterbury wey' before this moment. The verbal construction, ethical method and religious 'reasoning' combine to give the impression of triumphant autonomousness. Its laws of development and analytical procedure leave the rest of the tales behind. We tend to lose ourselves in the Parson's method until we largely forget what has gone before. His analysis and practical programme have the action of a mental emetic or purge, a *medicina* or *medicamentum* in one of the most common images applied to penance in the Middle Ages. The experience of reading the tale suggests admission into a large hospital where one is obliged to accommodate mentally to the regimen, to the rules of the establishment, and where every mental adjustment raises a growing suspicion that one is never going to come out. There is a certain similarity here to the effect of the view of the Heavenly Jerusalem on the poet-dreamer in the *Pearl*. The exactness of the Spiritual City, its crystalline, non-allegorical quality, is quite unlike the beginning, pre-sleep garden with all its suggestive, metaphoric overtones—those bitter-sweet consolations of the personal imagination. The finite 'thereness' of the visual aspect of the spiritual home of the soul provides a solid, absorbing relief to both the reader and the dreamer after the long toils of the psychological and spiritual struggle embodied in the dialogue between the father and the daughter-image. We, like the dreamer, lose ourselves in the streets of a blissful symmetry, rapt in the ordered clarity of the precious stones and the exactitude of the measurements. All distances are certain here.

The whole method of the Parson, like penance itself, seems aimed at a certain kind of remembering in order to forget properly in obedience to man's reason and our proper spiritual nature. The insistent emphasis on the connection between spiritual and physical discipline in the act of confession connects this tale with Gower's *Confessio Amantis*:[111]

> Like Amans his penitent, he [Genius] is many-faceted; indeed he obliquely reflects the struggle between passion and reason, measure and excess, private interest and public weal, that takes place in all lovers and in all men.

Whereas this intricate process relates to the whole interplay of Amans and Genius, the Parson's concern begins and ends in a more self-contained context, from a more absolute position, coming as it does at the very end of the pilgrims' journey. This end of the journey position, as I have argued earlier, is important in that it represents an exact parallel with the very end of the *Confessio Amantis* VIII. In both Gower and Chaucer, the conclusion of the poems no longer represents a struggle between views of the art of living or loving, but conveys a sterner mood of renunciation leading to the art of taking one's leave in terms of the implied biological metaphor in Chaucer and the life metaphor in Gower. In Chaucer the *licentia authoris*, 'Heere taketh the makere of this book his leve', is written in the very same prose style as that of the Parson. The two styles are as difficult to distinguish as the author's 'voice' and the Host's had been at the conclusion of the *General Prologue*. At the end of the *Confessio*, Amans finally asks of his mentor:

> 'That ye me be som weie teche
> What is my beste, as for an ende.'

Although his Confessor remains silently by his side (l. 2810), it is through the direct meeting with Venus and Cupid that the poet passes into a clear recognition of his old age. After the poet has fully regained his reason and 'was mad sobre and hol ynowh' (l. 2865), Venus asks him 'what love was'. Gower, somewhat confused, answers:

> And natheles I gan to swere
> That by my trouthe I knew him noght;
> So ferr it was out of mi thoght,
> Riht as it hadde nevere be.
>
> (VIII.2874ff.)

Yet before he thinks to go from Venus' court (in reality, the court leaves him), the poet asks for Genius' absolution. His Confessor's answer is significant:

---

[111] J. A. W. Bennett, *op. cit.*, p. xvii.

'. . . Sone, as of this schrifte
Thou has ful pardoun and foryifte;
Foryet it thou, and so wol I.'

(2195–7)

The style and method of the Parson, too, is directed at forgetting. It
would be supremely misguided to try to apply any part of the Parson's
'tale' retrospectively to the rest of the Canterbury adventure for (like
Confessio Amantis VIII.2149ff.) it is a stage, a final stage, in a process,
not a master solution to some vast knot of significances. In terms of a
sequential narrative movement, the reading of the *Parson's Tale* enacts
a transforming experience, an undergoing of a change of heart, and
mind, in order to appreciate the finality of the author's position as
fellow-traveller, pilgrim-poet and human lifespan. It is the rhythmical
equivalent of Gower's recognition of himself as *poeta senex*, that physical sensation—as the dart of love is withdrawn from the heart and the
healing *medicamentum*[112] applied—of the seemingly accelerated process
of ageing. This is Nature's seal on the inappropriateness of the poet's
writing further of love, to prolong the literary adventure beyond this
point:

But now uppon my laste tide
That y this book have maad and write,
My muse doth me forto wite,
And seith it schal be for my beste
Fro this day forth to take reste,
That y nomore of love make . . .

(3738ff.)

Finally, we the reader, like Gower of *Confessio Amantis* VIII and the
Chaucer of the *licentia authoris*, come to forget the trials and tribulations and comedy of the pilgrims' true 'tydinges' and false 'lesinges'—
'So ferr it ben out of oure thoght'. In the *Legend* we saw Chaucer
using the common 'end-of-day' *topos* to conclude the *Prologue*. Here
we have yet another variation, the 'end of a writing life' to conclude
the Canterbury 'viage'. The author seems to vanish, 'New games be-
gun and old ones put away'—and it is a testimony to the quality of the
last section (XII) and the skilful use of the illusion of the 'imperfect
work-of-art' that this concluding literary stratagem seems so close to
our agreed account of the end of Chaucer's literary career as well as
his life.

[112] Cf. *Confessio Amantis* VIII.2816–19.

CHAPTER SIX

The Book of Troilus

The most sustained result of Chaucer's ranging, searching artistic consciousness occupied him during the period *c.* 1385–7. The astro-logical material contained in book III and the death of Randolph Strode provide with some degree of certainty the two termini of the poem. During this time he appears to have lived as a retreating civil servant, using a deputy to perform the function of Controller of the London Custom and Subsidy of Wool while still exercising personal control of the Petty Customs. Both these posts were relinquished by December 1386, and certainly in the autumn of 1385 Chaucer had moved house to Kent in the capacity of a justice of the peace (he was reappointed in June 1386). He served also as a knight of the shire for Kent, being paid for sixty-one days' attendance in Parliament in November 1386. During this time (and afterwards) he may have re-sided in Greenwich—there are certain indications. The same year which saw the death in London of his Oxford friend Strode[1] also witnessed in June the last recorded payment of Philippa Chaucer's exchequer annuity. Like Queen Anne some years later she may have been another sudden summer casualty—or the possible removal out of London to Greenwich after September 1385 may refer to a long period of her ill-health. Whatever the tribulations of those days, the poet completed his *Book of Troilus* before the death of Strode, labouring fairly intensively to absorb the verbal detail of Boccaccio's *Il Filostrato* and to create a totally new and independent poem after May 1385.

However many hours the poet passed at his *pulpitum* shaping his *matere* to his 'boke', modern criticism and scholarship has spent con-siderably longer over both Boccaccio and Boethius in an attempt to find out what Chaucer was up to. The main preoccupation of this travail has been moral and to a lesser extent formal. From the first

[1] For a biography cf. Emden, *A Biographical Register of Oxford Trained Clerks*, Oxford (1959), vol. iii, pp. 1807–8.

critical obsession Chaucer has suffered most from the application of the recent adjective 'Boethian'—one is tempted to imagine that it is a mistake for an earlier formation, 'Boeotian', but that would be uncharitable; from the second concern, design in *Troilus* has suffered more variously by inescapably losing its self-generated shaping capacity, becoming more and more an interpreting mediation between Chaucer's intentions and the text of *Il Filostrato*. The repetitious *Design in Chaucer's Troilus* of Professor Meech lost its way in a proliferation of patterns, analogues, parallelisms and structural correspondences which would never have occurred to an educated reader of the 1380s, much less to Professor Meech, if either had never discovered the identity of Lollius.

A thorough knowledge of Boccaccio's poem is very useful, always fascinating, invariably rewarding, but it was never any part of Chaucer's creative intention that we should repetitiously experience his poem in a comparative mood. None of the extremely numerous variants in the extant manuscripts which point to scrupulous authorial revision suggests a compositional stage at which Chaucer had any hesitation over the larger creative structure of his poem. The long-accepted view that some episodes (the predestination monologue of book IV, the song of Troilus in book III, for example) were the result of later 'insertion' rests partially on our acceptance of Professor Root's identification of two manuscript groups—a theory which becomes less credible the more one examines the manuscripts themselves. The failure of some manuscripts to divide books IV and V may be partly the result of a mechanical omission of a rubric, or partly a misunderstanding of the last words of the invocation to book IV (ll. 26–8):

> This ilke ferthe book me helpeth fyne,
> So that the losse of lyf and love yfeere
> Of Troilus be fully shewed here.

These words refer to the 'heart-rending' conclusion of book IV itself where the departure of Troilus from Criseyde deprives him of his very soul: 'Which that his soule of his herte [breast] rente.' Henceforth, he behaves as a man spiritually dead. That is the strength of 'lyf and love yfeere', and why the verbal priority of 'lyf' before 'love' makes no matter. They mean the same thing for Troilus. That, too, is the strength of 'yfeere', as line 790 later makes plain when Troilus, believing Criseyde dead, makes ready to rejoin her through suicide. But none of the uncontested and genuine 'revisions' may be argued to have had any effect on the shape of the poem or the relation of the parts to the whole.

I have argued earlier (p. 93) that this violent image of conflated parting and spiritual death at the end of book IV is one of the great 'dramatic' images of his work and possibly reflects a reading knowledge of the Roman comedy of Plautus (who was a curriculum author). Conveniently, this characterization of the fused metaphor of spiritual and physical exiting to conclude book IV leads me to the central argument of this chapter—the genuinely 'dramatic' nature of the creative shape of Chaucer's *Troilus*, considered as a whole and as a coherent pattern of episodes, or, as I propose to call them, 'scenes'.

Chaucerian criticism has been reluctant to allow the poet any informed knowledge of what may be termed the 'dramatic',[2] contenting itself with attributing to him its own version of 'medieval notions of tragedy'—that is, the ignorant definition provided by the monk (a reminiscence of part of Isidore's *Etymologiae*[3]), although why one of Chaucer's dullest pilgrims, a man of severely limited imagination and style,[4] should be automatically identified with the poet's creative intelligence is beyond comprehension. Nowhere in Chaucer's writings is there any clear evidence that he had seen a stage representation of a classical play, although there is mention of miracle plays and the 'scaffolds' of such productions. The sources for imagery which relates to vivid presentations of imitated reality spring from other areas of human experience, namely, reflections in mirrors, dreams, literature, wall-painting, portraiture, magicians' shows or formal entertainments designed for *cenae* or 'revels'. Yet medieval sources of knowledge

[2] Typical is F. L. Utley's 'Scene-division in Chaucer's *Troilus and Criseyde*', *Studies in Medieval Literature*, ed. M. Leach, Philadelphia (1961), pp. 109–38. We are told that Aristotle's *Poetics* was not available in Italy until 1498; that Horace's *Ars Poetica* is in no way a 'substitute'; and that 'we are not pressing the dramatic analogies too hard' (p. 111). Not one of these statements is accurate and Dr Utley's scene divisions (pp. 126–30) are mechanical and not in the least dramatic. He even treats the invocations as scenes.

[3] There are other passages close by in the *Etymologiae* which explain the dramatic mode: 'The Theatre' (XVIII.39), 'The Stage' (XVIII.40), 'The Actors' (XVIII.41); and cf. XIX.34 (*De Calciamentis*) under *coturni* ('buskins') for Isidore's knowledge of the acted tragedy.

[4] I have pointed out elsewhere (*Lydgate: Poems*, Oxford (1966), p. 161) Lydgate's assiduous cultivation of the Monk's style, no doubt as being appropriate in the *Troy Book* to his 'estate' as an identifiable author with a knowable biography. It was appropriate in other ways.

of the theatrical and the drama in the classical sense are wider and better informed than the sum of Isidore's or Friar Piers' learning, and some of these accounts passed under Chaucer's eye. Chaucer would have noticed the use of theatrical metaphors in Virgil's *Aeneid* (especially in books I and IV and possibly Servius' interesting notes),[5] and Chaucer actually translated passages in Boethius' *De Consolatione* which refer to the stage, tragedy and acting. In book I prose i, Philosophy satirizes the Muses as *scenicae meretriculae*, 'whores from the theatre'. Chaucer provides a paraphrasing translation which tries to convey the sense of the Latin: 'thise comune strompets of swich a place that men clepen the theatre.' In book III prose vi, *tragicus* (Euripides, the words uttered are a reminiscence of a speech in the *Andromache*) is glossed 'a maker of ditees[6] that highten tragedies'. In the next prose, Euripides himself is mentioned ('*In quo Euripidis mei sententiam probo*', which Chaucer translates without a gloss). More interesting is Chaucer's attempt to give a full and accurate version of Boethius' use of the theatrical metaphor '*scaena vitae*', 'the stage of life' (Ovid was fond of this metaphor, using the phrase '*magna scaena*'), in book II prose iii. The sentence '*An tu in hanc vitae scaenam primum subitus hospesque venisti?*' is rendered:

> Art thou now comen first a sodein gest into
> the shadwe or tabernacle of this lyf?

This is an attempt to capture the theatrical meaning more exactly. Chaucer has consulted at this point Jean de Meun's translation where he found the expanded phrase '*en la cortine et en l'ombre*'. In OF, the sb. *cortine* was extended to refer to 'tents' or other temporary structures. Chaucer then consulted Isidore on 'The Stage' and found that the Hebrews called such buildings *tabernaculae* when they were represented by scene-painting, *skenographía* (*Etymologiae* XVIII.40). Chaucer's decision to incorporate Jean's '*ombre*' is not at first clear but when we consult Nicolas Trivet's commentary to Boethius on this passage we

---

[5] For an account of the medieval use of theatrical metaphors, cf. E. R. Curtius, *European Literature and the Latin Middle Ages*, pp. 138–44. Servius' note to *Aeneid* I.164 explains that *scaena* there means *inumbratio* 'an overshadowing' for '*apud antiquos enim theatralis scaena parietem non habuit, sed de frondibus umbracula quaerebant.*' He gives the etymology of *scaena* as *skia*, '*umbra*'. Servius on *Georgics* III 4ff. is especially valuable on *scaena* as 'scenery'.

[6] In spite of the *MED*'s attempt to define this sb. circularly, Chaucer seems to have intended the meaning 'compositions in verse', just as Horace, *Ars Poetica* 220, uses *carmen* of tragedies: '*carmen tragicum*'.

find not only a reference to Isidore's 'De Scaena' but also the gloss 'umbra' as inherited from Servius and other commentators.[7] He would not have been ignorant of St Paul's famous use of the theatre of life metaphor in I Corinthians 4.9,[8] and his own supremely dramatic and conclusive use of the apotheosis of Troilus' soul at the end of book V whereby it becomes for a moment in the sphere of the moon a spectator of the grief-stricken insubstantial *theatrum mundi* provides eloquent testimony to Chaucer's awareness of the artistic possibilities of the *topos* of 'all the world's a stage'.

More important than these references is the distribution of the actual texts of Plautus, Terence and Seneca,[9] much copied and widely read in the Middle Ages, especially after the thirteenth century. These manuscripts sometimes contained in excerpt *scholia* reflecting Donatus where there is much information on the drama, including the law of five-act divisioning for comedy, reflecting Horace's five-act structure for tragedy as formulated in the *Ars Poetica*—a text much-quoted in *Troilus*. Although none of the fourteenth- and fifteenth-century manuscripts of Plautus I have examined shows act divisions, all the examples show scenic division based on the entrance of a principal character. Thus, all the scenes are paragraphed in the manuscripts by the use of space and at the head of the paragraph all the characters appearing together in the designated scene are entered in a rubric.[10] In this way scenic division would have been apprehended through the function of character-grouping. Of equal importance with the texts of Seneca's tragedies was the widespread distribution of the learned English Dominican friar, the Oxford-trained Nicolas Trivet's detailed commentaries on the tragedies.[11] It was written for Nicholas of Prato,[12]

---

[7] For massive evidence see M. H. Marshall, 'Theatre in the Middle Ages: Evidence from Dictionaries and Glosses', *Symposium* 4 (1950), pp. 1–39. For proof of Chaucer's use of Trivet's *Commentary* on the *De Consolatione* see K. O. Petersen, 'Chaucer and Trivet', *PMLA* 18 (1903), pp. 173ff. She does not cite this passage as an example.

[8] As Curtius pointed out, John of Salisbury devotes a whole chapter to an elaboration of this metaphor as a moment of final judgment in his *Polycraticus*.

[9] Cf. J. R. Dean in *Medium Aevum* 10 (1941), pp. 161–8, for the extent of the popularity of Seneca's tragedies in the Middle Ages.

[10] For a discussion of the scene headings in the early manuscripts of Plautus, cf. W. M. Lindsay, *The Ancient Editions of Plautus*, Oxford (1904), pp. 88ff.

[11] For a biography of Trivet, cf. *DNB* and Emden, *op. cit.*, vol. iii, pp. 1902–3. He also wrote commentaries on other works of Seneca, Livy and Ovid's *Metamorphoses*. He may have written commentaries on Cicero, Juvenal and Virgil's *Aeneid* VI. The text of the introduction and the commentary to the second

dean of the College of Cardinals, *c.* 1315. Trivet's old friend confessed Seneca 'difficult to understand', and having found Nicolas's *Commentary* on the *De Consolatione* 'very helpful', he requested something similar on Seneca. Trivet obliged and the result is an impressive piece of scholarship for the time. The brief introduction gives an eclectic[13] and somewhat 'theoretical' description of the theatre and drama but, however garbled, it conscientiously tries to give a systematic account of the dramatic mode as reflected in the form of the play, and dramatic presentation as made possible by means of the conventions of an actual theatre.

Trivet makes absolutely clear his version of the formal units of tragic drama. He uses the term '*actus*', and of most of the plays[14] he observes '*continet autem hec tragedia quinque actus*'. The act divisions are plainly and accurately reproduced and numbered in the commentary. Scene divisions are not listed under this nomenclature.[15] To mark 'scenes' Trivet uses the sb. *carmen*. The word had been used traditionally to refer to fairly large units of verse, 'strophes', and in a famous passage[16] Livy had used the sb. in a wider, more indeterminate sense

[13] It includes Isidore's *Etymologiae*, St Augustine's *Civitate Dei* VI, Plautus' *Amphitryon*, prologus 50–90, Livy VII.2.4ff., and Servius on Virgil, *Eclogue* III.1ff., among others.

[14] Of the *Hercules Oetaeus* he observes that it has seven acts.

[15] Although scenic divisions date from all the earliest manuscripts of the Roman writers of comedy (fourth century), this technical use of the sb. *scaena* seems not to have circulated outside the commentaries of Donatus on Terence (written in the same century but not recovered until 1433). It perhaps arose out of Aristotle's use of *skené* in the *Poetics* 1455a 25ff.: 'The poet . . . should keep the scene before his eyes. Only thus, by getting the picture as clear as if he were present at the actual event . . .' The medieval Latin translation of William of Moerbeck (*c.* 1278) captures the sense but omits the crucial noun: '*Oportet enim fabulas consistere et locutione cooperari quam maxime pre oculis postitum.*' Elsewhere in William the phrase '*in skene*' means 'on stage'.

[16] VII.2.8. The idea of words sung or narrated to mime also derives from this account; so too the poet as an actual participant in the stage production. It should be remembered that Trivet wrote a commentary to Livy. Cf. J. R. Dean, 'The Earliest Known Commentary on Livy', *Medievalia et Humanistica* 3 (1945), pp.

tragedy, *Thyestes*, was edited by E. Franceschini, *Il Commento di Nicola Trevet al Tieste di Seneca*, Milan (1938). He consulted ten manuscripts widely distributed throughout Europe but there are legions more. One not consulted by him, Bodley MS. 292 (mid-fifteenth century), forms the basis of this discussion.

[12] For a biography of Nicholas of Prato and an account of his relation to Trivet, cf. J. R. Dean, 'Cultural Relations in the Middle Ages', *Studies in Philology* 45 (1948), pp. 541–64.

than 'sung monologue' or 'dramatic song' when he spoke of the early Roman dramatist Livius Andronicus as '*id quod omnes tum errant—suorum carminum actor . . .*', 'like every one else in those days he acted his own pieces'. It is difficult to find the right word for this passage, and perhaps Trivet took over the sb. in this sense of 'some part of the play'. However we choose to render it, the *carmina* of Trivet's commentary correspond to what we now call scene divisions. As in modern usage, Act I includes scene I, but Trivet also designates the appearance of the long formal chorus as a *carmen*. These *carmina* (acts, *carmina* and *chori*) are numbered consecutively from *Actus* I *carmen* I through to the end. Unlike Renaissance and modern usage the scenes are not numbered anew with each act. In almost all cases they correspond exactly with the act, scene and chorus divisions of Renaissance printed texts.[17] Therefore, any reader of Trivet's commentary would have had no problem whatever in recognizing act, scene and chorus divisions of the tragedies. The five-act structure is analysed by Trivet in terms of the broad, continuous plot structure of the whole play. His exposition of the material of the *carmina* mainly is concerned with the more detailed description of event with some comment on psychological predicament. The choruses as lyric or philosophical reflection are analysed into their metrical measures. Here his use of complex metrical terminology reflects an appreciation of scansion which is not much inferior to the learning of the Renaissance.[18] Where the *carmina* are long and complex in structure he subdivides into *partes*. The formal structure of each tragedy is scrupulously, if unimaginatively, described.

In terms of stage presentation Trivet gives a fairly clear account. By choosing to edit only the introduction and the *Thyestes*, Franceschini inadvertently omitted the theatrical information contained in the first speech of Hercules in *Hercules Furens:*[19]

[17] His divisions are entirely accurate for the *Hercules Furens* and the *Thyestes*. Occasionally they do not correspond with Renaissance versions. For example, in the pseudo-Senecan *Octavia* he is accurate until the middle of the third act. Renaissance Act IV sc. i begins at Trivet's Act III, *carmen* x.

[18] Beryl Smalley points out Trivet's shortcomings in her *English Friars and Antiquity in the Early Fourteenth Century*, pp. 59ff.

[19] Bodley MS. 292, folio 1a. MS. reads '*scene*'. The text of the commentary to the *Hercules Furens* has been edited by V. Ussani jun. (*Aedibus Athenaei*, Rome, 1959). His commentary to *Agamemnon* has been edited by P. Meloni (Sassari, 1961); the *Hercules Oetaeus* by Meloni, Rome (1962).

88–98. Marshall quotes part of his commentary on this passage in her article in *Symposium* 4 (1950), p. 27.

Theatrum erat area semicirculans in cuius medio erat parua domuncula
que scen[a] dicebatur, in qua erat pulpitum super quo poete carmina
pronunciabantur. Extra vero erant mimi qui carminum pronuncia-
tionem ad quodlibet ex cuius persona loquebatur.

This account bears a strong family resemblance to Livy and Isidore.
One notices how the stage (*scena*) is identified with a small 'tent'
(*domuncula*), just as Chaucer had rendered Boethius' *scaena vitae* with
the aid of Jean, Isidore and Trivet's *Commentary* to the *De Consola-*
tione.[20]

We are reminded again of the implication of the poet in the actual
stage production. In the matter of production Trivet (following
Servius) distinguishes three modes of dramatic presentation: (1)
dramatic recitation where the poet speaks *solo*; (2) where the poet
narrates and speaks the parts of the personages accompanied by mime;
(3) a mixture of modes where the poet both recites and introduces
the characters who then speak and enact the dialogue, '*ubi et quandoque*
poeta loquitur et persone introducte, sicut Virgilius in Eneidos'. The use of
Virgil as an illustration is very interesting.[21] We can see from Trivet's
exposition that there is no modern absolute distinction between a
tragic form which is purely narrative (as the monk in Chaucer's *Monk's*
Tale would appear to believe) and that which is purely acted (as in the
Renaissance revivals of productions of classical drama).[22] An educated

[20] For a convenient and excellent illustration of a medieval reconstruction of the
Roman theatre, see the miniature from a French manuscript of the early fifteenth
century (Bibliothèque de l'Arsénal, Paris) of *Terence des Ducs* reproduced in
Kindermann's *Theatergeschichte Europas*, Salzburg (1959), vol. ii, plate 3 (facing
p. 17). The classical nature of the theatre is clearly marked: '*populus Romanus*'.
Calliopius (a grammarian and scholiast whose name appears in the codex
Bembinus of Terence) reads a comedy during a performance leaning out from
the *scena* (a covered booth) which stands exactly in the centre of the *theatrum*.
[21] All of this has been adapted from Servius' note to *Eclogue* III.1ff. Isidore also
had this passage in mind. Of *Eclogue* III Servius says: '*unde etiam dramatico charac-*
tere scripta est.'
[22] Greek and mature Roman acting techniques were known to some medieval
scholars, mainly through commentators (John the Scot, for example) who came
in contact with Boethius' definition of *persona* in the *De Duabus Naturis*. Those
who had contact with Chartrain scholars (for example, Gilbert de La Porrée
and John of Salisbury) also knew the unvarnished truth. Boethius' version may
have been preserved in grammatical and theological dictionaries under *persona*
but the method of preservation made the information almost useless. Cf. M. H.
Marshall, 'Boethius's Definition of Persona and Medieval Understanding of the
Roman Theatre', *Speculum* 25 (1950), pp. 471–82. The commentary on Mussato's

medieval reader of Seneca would have imagined the performance of classical drama to have closely resembled Livy's account of early Roman drama before the employment of professional actors (of which Livy strongly disapproved). We get something of this effect in Shake-speare's use of Gower in *Pericles*. If we consider Chaucer's *Troilus* in the light of Trivet's account we can see how naturally close Chaucer's poem is to the 'dramatic mode' in fourteenth-century experience without invoking either Isidore's narrow 'narrative' version or the Renaissance's wholly staged version free from the author's involve-ment in theatrical performance.

Trivet ends his account by dividing the *Hercules Furens* into Aris-totle's four causes: (1) '*causa efficiens fuit Seneca*'; (2) '*causa materialis est furia Herculis*'; (3) '*causa formalis consistit in modo scribendi, qui est dramaticus*'; (4) '*causa finalis est delectio populi audientis . . .*' The most important emphasis in his commentary falls on the formal cause which consists in the mode of composition, the dramatic. Thus, this wide-spread, much read commentary on Seneca's tragedies, easily available in the fourteenth century, puts paid to the notion that Chaucer would only have consulted Isidore on the nature of tragic drama.[23]

Doubtless Chaucer never saw a staged performance of classical drama. The history of the stage production of Roman drama or neo-Latin imitations in Italy in the fourteenth century remains un-documentable. We know how highly Petrarch valued Terence, the tragedies of Seneca (especially the *Octavia* which he regarded as genuine and Seneca at his best), and we know that in his youth he wrote a Terentian comedy in Latin, the *Philologia*[24]—a play with which he

[23] Lydgate consulted this commentary for his description of the Trojan classical theatre and acting in the *Troy Book* II.890ff. Trivet's *Anglo-Norman Chronicle* was not unknown to Chaucer as the *Man of Law's Tale* testifies. Chaucer could also have consulted Vincent of Beauvais's *Speculum Doctrinale* XII.95, 'De Ludis scenicis', where much of this material is repeated in one form or another. There is some material relating to comic acting contained in a commentary on Map's *De Nugis Curialium* 4.3, which in the Cambridge Univ. Lib. MS Ff. 6.12 is attributed to the Oxford Franciscan friar John Ridevall (*fl.* 1330). For a biography, cf. Emden, *op. cit.*, vol. iii, p. 1576, and Smalley, *op. cit.*, pp. 109–32. I am indebted to Keith Bate for calling my attention to this commentary.

[24] Cf. Letter II.7.5. written to Giovanni Colonna in 1331. A single line survives in the author's quotation. It must have been written in prose. The line will not scan, certainly not as a defective hexameter.

Ecerinis written by two Italian scholars no later than 21 December 1317 which draws chiefly on Horace's *Ars Poetica* is aware of the acting nature of tragedy (cf. *Ecerinide Tragedia*, ed. L. Padrin, Bologna (1900), pp. 80–3).

grew disenchanted later in life.[25] The work is lost and it was almost certainly never acted. Boccaccio in his Latin life of Petrarch attributed to him another comedy, the *Philostratus*, but the supposed author never once refers to it. During Chaucer's lifetime (*c.* 1389–90) Vergerio wrote in Bologna a Latin 'university comedy', the *Paulus*—but there is no record of its being produced.[26] Like Petrarch and Boccaccio, there was nothing to prevent Chaucer from reading Roman dramatists or consulting Trivet's commentary to Seneca or Vincent's *Speculum Doctrinale*. The sources for an academic knowledge of the nature of drama and tragedy were obvious, copiously distributed in manuscripts and well represented in libraries. They would have been part of the education of a literary person in the fourteenth century, especially someone of Chaucer's proven Latinity, command of foreign languages, experience of continental travel and interpretative acuity.

We have argued earlier that the shaping of *Troilus* into five books represents Chaucer's intention to give his 'tragedye' (V.1786) a genuinely dramatic structure as based on the five-act principle for tragedy established by Horace and supported by Trivet.[27] The texts of the plays themselves and Trivet's commentary to Seneca would have made Chaucer aware of the basic element in dramatic composition which underlies the act structure: the expressive scene.[28]

[25] Cf. Letter VII.16.6.

[26] There is an account of the revival of the acting of Roman comedies, especially under the influence of Pomponio Leto (remembered by Douglas in *The Palace of Honoure* 911) in G. E. Duckworth's *The Nature of Roman Comedy*, Princeton (1952), p. 399. For a more recent list of productions in the fifteenth century, cf. A. Stäuble, *La Commedia Umanistica del Quattrocento*, Florence (1968), pp. 200–1. He lists the first Roman production as the *Asinaria* (1483–4). The earliest Italian neo-Latin tragedy written in the style of Seneca was the *Ecerinis* by Albertino Mussato (*c.* 1315). There is brief mention of it in M. T. Herrick's *Italian Tragedy in the Renaissance*, Urbana (1965), pp. 1–42. For Mussato's intellectual tendencies, cf. Curtius, *European Literature and the Latin Middle Ages*, pp. 215–21. Mussato also wrote a commentary on Seneca's tragedies. The *argumenta* and excerpts from the commentaries have been edited by A. C. Megas, Thessalonica (1969), pp. 27–77. Mussato has nothing to say on the nature of tragedy.

[27] The notion early appears, briefly mentioned, in Root's edition of *Troilus and Criseyde*, p. xlix. The more recent theory that *Troilus* was modelled on the five books of Boethius' *De Consolatione* (McCall, *Modern Language Quarterly* 23 (1962), pp. 297–308) is a mathematical coincidence. One might as well adduce that it was modelled on the primrose, the cinque-foil or the Pentateuch.

[28] Cf. R. G. Moulton, *Shakespeare as a Dramatic Artist*, Oxford (1906), pp. 322, 329–30; Emrys Jones, *Scenic Form in Shakespeare*, Oxford (1971), pp. 3–8. Classical critics, too, were aware of the importance of 'scene' as an essential element in

While from seeing a performance of English or continental religious 'drama' or even the formal entertainments devised for *cenae*[29] Chaucer could have experienced the vivid impression of a single scenic moment or a conglomerate of several occasions, the poet could not have gathered from such a type of naïve construction any impression of a complex dramatic relationship of scenes contributing to a total intricate plot sequence. The construction of *Troilus* seems to penetrate into the secret of the interrelation of scenes and the overall dramatic sequence for which later critics found terminology: exposition, development, catastrophe, dissolution and denouement—or the earlier classical terms for the developmental characteristics of stages of the plot and action. Trivet in his brief act summaries is aware of this movement although he evolves no terminology; Donatus uses the triadic arrangement of prologue/*prostasis*, catastrophe and *epistasis* in the preface to the *Andria*; William of Moerbeck in his translation of the *Poetics* 1452b took over the Greek terminology: *prologus, episodion, exitus, choricon*.[30] The mystery 'cycle' as a whole form consists of a series of historicized biblical tableaux: enacted illustrations of a too-numerously eventful history of the life of mankind where the moral connection in all of them between plot and character is divine providence. In Aristotelian terms and classical practice it contains too many episodes, too much diversified material, and is far too long for the memory to grasp or relate in any complex fashion. The connection between *ethos* and action is always identical and simple, and resists the generation of individual character at the level of motivation. In my

[29] Most of the English examples of this genre of 'mumming' are later and were composed by Lydgate. For one written during Chaucer's lifetime, cf. the '*Dit des Quatres Offices*' written by Chaucer's friend Deschamps after he had been made one of Louis of Orleans's *maitres d'hotel* in 1392. It was meant to be '*jouer par personnaiges*' and would have made a nice, comic banquet-piece. In it four officers of the royal household, Pantler, Butler, Cook and Sauce-cook, as four old drabs engage in a debate and slanging-match about the relative importance of their services. They are finally made to agree by the Maistre d'Ostel and celebrate their accord by singing a song. There is a certain resemblance to Lydgate's *Mumming at Hertford* written some forty years later. It is not terribly dramatic, though the language used has a certain lively, vulgar, knock-about quality.

[30] Ed. L. Minio-Paluello, *Aristoteles Latinus*, vol. 33, *De Arte Poetica*, Paris (1968).

composition and structure: cf. Aristotle, *Poetics* 1455a 25ff. where he puts the poet into the audience's place during composition and demands a visualization of the 'scene', a 'picture' as vivid as reality. Quintilian, *Institutio Oratoria* X.i.69, in praising the dramatic genius of Menander, says: '*ita omnem vitae imaginem expressit.*'

experience one's attention is only guided into theatrical coherence very late in the performance—in the episode dealing with the life of Christ.[31] The whole pageantry, festival nature of the entertainment with its appeal to a collective mentality tends to diminish classical or neo-classical dramatic interests. The experience of a genuinely dramatic work of art is like taking off one's clothes inside a suitcase. The staging of mystery plays suggests the collection of laundry from a line and its eventual folding away in a capacious hamper. Our attention is arrested or diverted by a simple system of cues. To fully participate in its realization of our *capax ridere* or in our serious concern for moral dignity we need to shed our critical nature and simply to Believe. We are spectators who are gradually being gathered into a recognition of our human nature by the invisible stage management of God and the acting of Christ in a passive capacity. The 'thought' (*dianoia*) of what is represented on the 'scaffold hye' is absolute theologically. But classical drama requires the opposite of passivity; it evokes our active imaginative co-operation and encourages an individual identification of its philosophical causality whether we assent or not. It allows us a variety of impressions and evaluations. Its 'thought' requires us to construct individual processes of mentality and moral decision-making within the personages of the production in addition to inviting us to search out the larger sense of the metaphysical forces operant in a particular play. In the end we must try to imagine comprehensively the artist's conscious formal creation of an aesthetic cosmos, absolute only for the duration of the reality of this theatrical interval. That moment demands interpretation as well as simple realization or identification. Compare the episodes of one 'cycle' with those of another and we are immediately taken up in differences of realization in terms of style (language, stage mechanics, music, employment of realistic colouring). Compare the *Electra* of Sophocles with that of Euripides and we find profound philosophical divergences as well as linguistic and stylistic dissimilarities. Classical drama cannot be equated with a 'somer pleye' or a Corpus Christi excursion in any of its more serious rhetorical or theatrical demands.[32]

[31] There is certain similar structural weakness in Milton's presentation of Adam's vision of universal history in *Paradise Lost*, books XI–XII, although Milton's intricacy of style, arrangement of declining rhythms and visualization of the effects of sin as they expand into the vastness of Time and Space hold one's attention. But the poem is structurally inferior to the *Aeneid*.

[32] These issues are raised by Rosemary Woolf, *The English Mystery Plays*, London (1972), pp. 54–101, but the nature of what constitutes 'the dramatic'

The scenic structure of *Troilus* seems to rely on two basic organizing principles, character-grouping and time-value, the first of which may be traced to an academic or reading knowledge of Roman drama. These areas of scenic delimiting anticipate later Renaissance fascination with one of the two unities which the neo-humanists added to Aristotle's formula of unity of action. Of course, limited and local uses of time factors to give narrative sequences greater emphasis and coherence may be found outside dramatic forms. We should remember Servius' note on Virgil's *Eclogue* III where he cited that *Eclogue* as a work with dramatic properties—mainly in terms of dialogue and characterization —but the *Eclogues* also have a carefully controlled use of the passage of time.[33] Chaucer certainly borrows many devices (turned to dramatic purposes) from narrative poems—Dante's *Commedia*, Virgil's *Aeneid*, Statius' *Thebaid*, and Boccaccio's *Il Filostrato*. But if we consider *Il Filostrato* as a whole and in detail we must be impressed by Boccaccio's lack of interest in *mise-en-scène* or time-values. Further, it is Chaucer's deliberate combination of all these basic elements into the means of producing a type of vivid form which most persuasively argues dramatic formal intentions.[34]

The first principle of scene-marking is that of character-grouping, an organizational element which Chaucer would have apprehended as specifically 'scenic' from a reading of the available manuscripts of Roman comedies and tragedies. Chaucer arranges the sequences of character-grouping far more deliberately than Boccaccio and with a greater sense of organic growth and climactic emphasis.[35] It is entirely

[33] *Eclogues* I, II, VI, VII, IX, X.

[34] This quality in *Troilus* was early appreciated by Sir Philip Sidney. He associates *Troilus* with dramatic context in *An Apologie for Poetrie*. After listing a series of outstanding dramatic characters and their typical emotional essences (Oedipus, Agamemnon, Atreus, Medea), he ends with '. . . the Terentian Gnato, and our Chaucer's Pandar, so exprest, that we now use their names to signifie their trade'. Sir Francis Beaumont also singled out what he took to be Chaucer's greatest literary talent in a letter to Thomas Speght (30 June 1597): '. . . to possesse his Readers with a strong imagination of seeing that done before their eyes, which that they reade, more than any other that euer writ in any tongue.'

[35] Cf. S. K. Langer, *Feeling and Form*, New York (1953), p. 356: 'The tragic rhythm, which is the pattern of a life that grows, flourishes and declines, is

in these 'plays' as theatre remains an unexamined assumption. As dramatic form the 'cycle' is essentially parodistic, an amalgam of substitute presentational modes, not one of which is directly dramatic in the classical or Renaissance sense; a 'speaking picture' will not suffice even if it has been compounded with typology, history, liturgical and processional elements or meditational exercises.

THE BOOK OF TROILUS

distinct in quality from Virgil's narrative patterning where the divine episodes introduce a complicating element,[36] and much of the thematic connecting material and emotional and psychological pointing is conveyed through similes, imagery and symbols: a host of subtle descriptive devices which are not particularly 'dramatic' in nature and in appeal to the reader's literary experience.[37]

Price[38] years ago noticed the percentage distribution of character-grouping into four types: (1) dialogue (64); (2) monologue (18); (3) group-scenes (14); (4) trio-scenes (4). He showed that the monologues were evenly distributed between the two major characters (five to Troilus; four to Criseyde). He was concerned to show the nature of Chaucer's dramatic technique as springing from 'the working of emotion' and to see action largely subordinated to character and psychology (the emphasis derives from Lounsbury and Courthope). Although Chaucer has inextricably connected the growth, maturity and decay of the characters organically with their moral natures and dispositions, yet the real achievement in Chaucerian character-grouping lies in never allowing the rhythm of development of action to disappear under the weight of the observed human detail—or, as often in Boccaccio's narrative handling, to use in a virtuoso way a 'layer' or separate texture method of deliberately shifting from one emphasis or stylistic aspect to another.

Thus, in book II, stanzas 157–86, Chaucer invents a scenic dialogue out of Pandaro's delivery of Troilo's letter. Only a few lines of five stanzas owe anything to Boccaccio's handling of the characters and action. Chaucer first isolates the beginning of the dialogue by making us aware of a new time-value. The scene begins on the morning after the writing of the letter late the night before. Boccaccio's narrative sequence here is continuous and without any temporal expression. The ostensible aim of Pandarus is to deliver the letter and to ensure that Criseyde reads it and writes a favourable reply. The sealed letter is addressed by Troilus in a sentimental farewell: 'My lady shal the see.'

[36] Cf. E. L. Harrison, 'Divine Action in Aeneid Book Two', Phoenix 24 (1970), pp. 320–32.

[37] Cf. V. Pöschl, The Art of Virgil, Ann Arbor (1962).

[38] T. R. Price, 'A Study in Chaucer's Method of Narrative Construction', PMLA 2 (1896), pp. 307–22.

abstracted by being transferred from that natural activity to the sphere of a characteristically human action, where it is exemplified in mental and emotional growth, and the final relinquishment of power.'

Beyond this initial purpose, the next scene ends with the lovers actually seeing each other as spectators. We are treated to a series of ocular unfoldings, moving from privacy and secrecy to a more open and shared appreciation of the situation and the emotions involved. At Criseyde's house in the late morning the letter is thrust on Criseyde, who goes to her bedroom to read it before the dinner hour. After dinner, in the afternoon, Pandarus points out Troilus' palace opposite Criseyde's house. Shortly thereafter she retires and writes a guarded though favourable reply. The dialogue continues between uncle and niece as they sit in the window. Suddenly, Troilus appears in his 'chevauchee' returning to his palace. All three characters are seen together for the first time, and they are obliged, seeing each other, to acknowledge each other's presence; Troilus with the knowledge that Criseyde has read his letter; Criseyde with the knowledge that he will read hers before the day is out. Evening comes and Pandarus takes his leave. The delicious sense of manoeuvring, complex social usage, badinage, humorous evasions and psychological observation is thickly and masterfully invented—but the strong rhythm of visual unfolding (from the sealed letter to the polite bow of Troilus and the blush of Criseyde) is progressively more and more emphatic and irresistible in its accumulating enactment. Further, it is not isolated 'action' but prepares the characters (and the reader) for the actual physical meeting in book III where written words and gestures give way to three-cornered dialogue and finally to the private exchanges of the lovers. The time-values in terms of the duration of Pandarus' visit have been so expressed that the action of the scene seems to have been symmetrically divided into a perfect unit of completion (beginning, middle, end): late morning before taking of dinner, afternoon and evening. All the progressive stages in the action of ocular unfolding and intensification of personal communication are marked by minute activity (entering and leaving rooms, eating a meal) and realistic details of scene-painting (the window which looks directly on to Troilus' palace, the green jasper stool with its cushion of cloth-of-gold).

This framed dialogue in book II is absolutely typical of Chaucer's use of character-grouping to give the 'scene' particularity of form and mimetic coherence. Other connecting and unifying expressive devices, time-value and place, are employed as well. But the use of place to delimit 'scenes' is not pursued by Chaucer although he often employs specific references to place to add to the particularizing quality of a scene. Roman drama did not develop a complex dramaturgical use of scenery although some machinery was available. Roman comedy mainly makes use of generalized out-of-door settings, streets and court-yards, where the stationary representational scene-building provided the atmosphere of particularized space. This is the rule in Terence and Plautus, although Plautus very occasionally experimented with indoor settings. Seneca's tragedies utilize both indoor and outdoor settings but 'place' is not one of the contributing factors of his quality of scenic vividness.[39]

On the whole Chaucer is content to accept Boccaccio's indications of changes of place, and although these *loci* are more carefully and intri-cately exploited, they are not used specifically to indicate changes of scene. In Chaucer, changes of place usually occur within larger scenic structures—with the exception of book V where the Greek and Trojan locations are exploited dramatically as scene-markers since the settings coincide exactly with the split in character-grouping and with the characters' experience of the passing of time. It should be mentioned here that the conciseness and directness of Chaucerian narrative move-ment used extensively as 'bridges' between moments of more direct and vivid presentation also assists in making us aware of the unity of scenes. The poet tends to use a more varied and spacious type of narrative presentation for the important scenes.[40]

The second basic element in the Chaucerian formulation of scene in *Troilus* is that of time-value. Continuity of movement and basic chronology is certainly to be observed in the construction of individual scenes and in the management of the overall plot in Roman drama, but it is not an emphatic formal element in Roman dramatic writing. 'Off-stage' time and 'pauses' are often mentioned but 'on-stage' time seems to have been taken for granted in the comedies. It is certainly not used to relate scenes into larger theatrical rhythms. We can account for the origin in drama of character-grouping as a scenic property, but where did Chaucer derive his complex use of chronology and (more important) the aesthetically significant use of duration of time—that area where the characters and the reader experience moments in

[39] On this quality, cf. L. Herrmann, *Le Théâtre de Sénèque*, Paris (1924), pp. 166ff., 193–232.

[40] Cf. C. Schaar, *Narrative Techniques in Chaucer*, Lund (1955), p. 119: 'The close technique [of narrative], in *Troilus and Criseyde* is noticeable for being used in sections describing the coming and going of the *dramatis personae* and serving as links between more important episodes and dialogues.' Schaar's handling of what he calls 'loose narrative' (pp. 203–14) in *Troilus* is less successful. The terminology itself is misleading.

controlled and peculiarly patterned sequences—where the tensions and emotions of the characters seem to be actively reflected in the passage of time, allowing dramatic expectations to be given visible, formal dimensions? Renaissance drama derived its complex 'on-stage' time from the humanist development of the three unities; thus, the *Comedy of Errors* or *The Tempest* (for example) have a complicated time-metaphor built into the whole structure of the play and in the unfolding of the scenes. Chaucer had no pre-developed area of dramatic theory of this nature to draw on. If one looks at epical forms one finds little which would have supplied his needs. He could barely have developed an intense and vivid time-value from that genre, where immediacy of time has longer origins and contingent historical futurity as well.

However hard we search for the origin of this mimetic function of time among Chaucer's classical authors or his contemporaries in Italy or France, no satisfactory solution comes to light. Here, I think, we are justified in seeing Chaucer borrowing from himself. In chapter 2 (pp. 26ff) it was argued that in many respects the *Complaint of Mars* may be considered a 'miniature *Troilus*'—namely, in its plot structure, characterization, moral interest and philosophical concern with free will and predestination. In the question of the aesthetic use of time-values, the *narratio* in *Mars* was shown to have been meticulously synchronized with an astrologically computed passage of time in a poetic attempt to 'memorialize' tragic human love in a visible arche-type. The poem so conceived develops the continuous use of a poetic 'conceit' possibly only paralleled in its own day by Froissart's *Amorous Clock*. It may be supposed that Chaucer had at his disposal in his close, metaphoric use of the passage of time in *Mars* a suggestive technique for giving his later *Troilus* both general structural coherence (of a kind not found in *Il Filostrato*) and for giving scenic mimesis more individual coherence. This means of organizing *Mars*' plot structure has been applied in *Troilus* to other literary dimensions; it has been distributed beyond plot sequence into the inner lives of the characteriz-ation, into the scenic shape of character-grouping, and into the related, larger tragic rhythm of the whole poem. Little of this technique may be found even in a primitive form in *Il Filostrato*. Let us take book II of *Troilus* again as an illustration.

We have already described the 'second scene' of book II in the dialogue between Pandarus and Criseyde in her house. The 'first scene' (after the poet's invocation) is distinguished not by character-grouping but by time-value. The first major structural unit is carefully divided into a 'single day' duration of time. Again, there is no temporal expression of this episode in *Il Filostrato*. The day is realistically named,[41] the third of May, which has consequences for the overall chronology of the poem (which will be discussed later). The day begins with the unsuccessful-in-love Pandarus 'half in a slomberinge' being aroused to activity by the song of the swallow. Pandarus' initial movements in his amatory embassy are pointed by a *chronographia* (occupying the whole of stanza 10) which has been reworked from Dante's *Purgatorio* IX.13–17.[42] Dante's lines:

> *Nell' ora che comincia i tristi lai*
> *la rondinella presso alla mattina*
> *forse a memoria de' suo' primi guai . . .*

At the hour near morning when the swallow begins her plaintive songs, in remembrance, perhaps, of her ancient woe . . .

have been redirected towards Ovid (*Metamorphoses* VI.668ff.)[43] so as to emphasize the actual mythological content of the myth. Pandarus is physically aroused by the actual mention of Philomela and her rape:

> How Tereux gan forth hire suster take,
> That with the noyse of hire he gan awake.
> (II.69–70)

This *chronographia* with its extensive mythological material is skilfully placed in the reader's mind so that Chaucer can make use of the same myth in an exactly balancing *chronographia* which points the moment at which Criseyde falls asleep (stanza 132, ll. 917–24):

> A nyghtyngale, upon a cedre grene,
> Under the chambre wal ther as she lay,
> Ful loude song ayein the moone shene,
> Paraunter, in his briddes wise, a lay
> Of love, that made hire herte fressh and gay.

---

[41] The use of exact dates in Chaucer's poems is difficult to account for. The date given in the *House of Fame* seems to serve a 'realistic' purpose, following the tradition in OF used by Nicole de Margival. No convincing theories have been yet advanced for any other significance in Chaucer's use of exact dates.

[42] The whole of *Purgatorio* IX had been in Chaucer's mind for the *House of Fame*.

[43] Dante's use of birdsong may recall Virgil's awakening of Evander in *Aeneid* VIII.456ff.

> That herkened she so longe in good entente,
> Til at the laste the dede slepe hire hente.

The dream of Criseyde in which she is converted into a lover follows directly. It structurally recalls the awaking of the unsuccessful lover Pandarus.[44] The direct, authorial presentation of Criseyde's dream of successful conversion to the doctrine of love, the exchange of 'heart for heart', brings to an equally successful end one aspect of the unity of action presented in the first scene: the efforts of Pandarus to prepare Criseyde for loving Troilus. Beyond Pandaro's wholly rational method pursued in *Il Filostrato*, Chaucer's formulation shows how important other influences are in Criseyde's conversion, especially the song of Antigone which has a specific connection with the sources of Criseyde's dream imagery. The whole rhythm of Criseyde's third of May has been given another completed shape; this time by Chaucer's use of episodes. Criseyde's waking day has three main movements: (1) her interview with Pandarus (stanzas 12–85); (2) her monologue (containing a glimpse of Troilus) (86–116); (3) her late afternoon exercise in the garden (containing the song of Antigone) (117–32). Each episode is almost precisely halved in stanza length (73, 30, 15), thereby giving an impression of waning duration in the reader's physical experience. The dream which ends the duration of Criseyde's consciousness is expressed in the smallest complete unit in the poem, one stanza. The other aspect of scene 1 consists in Pandarus' relation with Troilus in his ambassadorial role. To the reader the scene seems to end with Criseyde's dream, but the time-pattern has not yet been completed.

Chaucer prolongs the single day time scheme beyond Criseyde's waking and dreaming experience. In the very next stanza in Chaucer's concise narrative style we are taken back for a moment in time to Troilus' arrival in his palace (after his return at stanza 88ff.). There he sits, barely keeping his patience, until Pandarus is found (having been

---

[44] The connection of the myth with the process of supra-rational experience has probably been suggested by Dante's second use of the Procne legend in *Purgatorio* XVII.19ff. where the spontaneous impression of the myth in the mind of Dante mysteriously initiates him into the mystical imaginative experience of the three visions of destructive anger:

> *Dell' empiezza de lei che mutò forma*
> *nell' uccel ch'a cantar più si diletta*
> *nell' imagine mia apparve l'orma:*

Of her impious deeds who changed her shape into the bird that most delights to sing the impress appeared in my imagination.

summoned by several messengers); the supper hour comes and goes
and finally Troilus is left alone with his friend. The reader's sense of
the author's deliberate prolongation of time is obliquely symbolized
by Troilus' impatience with the slowness of the passage of time until
he is left unattended after retirement so as to be able to talk freely with
Pandarus, and by Pandarus' feigned and amusingly bad-tempered lack
of interest in giving Troilus very much of an account of his conversation with Criseyde (ll. 952–64). He finally relents and the next day's
amorous campaign is planned in detail—including the 'accidental'
viewing of Troilus on his horse and the crucial 'salute'. The scene ends
with his composing an answering letter and its sealing in stanza 156.
Thus, this prolonged time-pattern is concluded by the dramatic and
symbolic sealing of the letter. This action is given a whole stanza
which Chaucer has cleverly adapted from *Il Filostrato* II.107. Unlike
Boccaccio, Chaucer in his stanza makes use of concluding sentence
structures, emphasizing by phonetic and syntactic symbolism the
process of sealing. It has rhythmical finality in place of Boccaccio's
continuous, serial and parallel clausulation which leads up to a single
climax in Troilo's sentimental address to his *'littera pia'*.

> *Scritte adunque tutte queste cose*
> *In una carta, per ordin piegolla,*
> *E'n sulle guance tutte lagrimose*
> *Bagnò la gemma, e quindi suggellolla,*
> *E nelle mani a Pandaro la pose,*
> *Ma mille volte e più prima basciolla:*
> *Littera mia, dicendo, tu serai*
> *Beata, in man di tal donna verrai.*

Having written, then, all of those matters on a single leaf folded
properly for sending, he bathed the stone of the seal with his
thoroughly tearful cheeks, and after having impressed the wax,
he placed it in Pandaro's hands; first he kissed it more than a
thousand times, saying: 'Letter of mine, how blissful thou wilt be,
thou shalt touch the hand of such a lady.'

In Chaucer, the action of folding the letter completes the last line of
the stanza before ('and radde it over, and gan the lettre folde'), so
rhythmically anticipating the repetition of the concluding phrases to
follow:

> And with his salte teris gan he bathe
> The ruby in his signet, and it sette

> Upon the wex deliverliche and rathe;
> Therwith a thousand tymes or he lette,
> He kiste tho the lettre that he shette,
> And seyde: 'lettre, a blisful destine
> The shapen is, my lady shal the see.'

In this poetic form there occur no series of continuous parallel periods leading up to the address to the epistle. The stanza is deliberately divided into halves. The concluding clause of the first half drives home the absolute force of the preterite vb. 'sette' by the emphatic modifying pair of adverbs 'deliverliche and rathe', 'vigorously and quickly'. The closed letter is kissed, but again qualified by the finalizing phrase 'that he shette'. The introductory words of the sentimental address contain no present participle; even the first verb of Troilus' little word of encouragement has no hint of futurity ('*tu serai Beata*'). It is already passive and tinged with the absolutism of Troilus' habitual fatalism: 'a blisful destine/The shapen is.' The implied tactile image has disappeared along with the amorous emphasis in order to accommodate the action of 'seeing'. This provides the visual foundation for the process of ocular unfolding to take place in the next scenic presentation. These illustrations from book II, I hope, will serve to show the two functions, character-grouping and time-value, as helping to create the basic techniques for delimiting scenic forms within the structure of individual books.

Chaucer's imitative use of the dramatic mode as a main shaping device for the narrative form is but one of the many mimetic factors which contribute to the aesthetic force and specificality of *Troilus*. Also dramatic, but not exclusively so, is Chaucer's creation of dialogic intensity with its impression of immediate conversational reality. This quality derives (with modifications) from the 'bourgeois' and 'novelesque' human observation of Boccaccio in *Il Filostrato*. Chaucer also uses essentially rhetorical formulations to give the narrative point and emphasis—following the usual methods for narrative invention—for example, the use of songs. These are shared with Boccaccio, but again the complexity and depth of artistic development has been deepened. Often the crucial narrative use of such material has been suggested to Chaucer from elsewhere. For example, the non-Boccaccian 'Cantus Antigone' (book II. 827–75) which contributes decisively to Criseyde's yielding her love to Troilus and accompanies the unconscious moment when the arguments for and against which had occupied Criseyde's

earlier troubled thoughts are being resolved subliminally—this affilia-
tion of song, moment of conversion to love and the nocturnal time of
total yielding, reflect Chaucer's memory of the moment when Dido,
unaware, falls deeply in love with Aeneas at the end of *Aeneid* I:

> *Dixit et in mensam laticum libravit honorem*
> *Primaque libato summo tenus attigit ore;*
> *Tum Bitiae dedit increpitans; ille impiger hausit*
> *Spumantem pateram et pleno se proluit auro;*
> *Post alii proceres. Cithara crinitus Iopas*   740
> *Personat aurata, docuit quem maximus Atlas.*
> *Hic canit errantem lunam solisque labores,*
> *Unde hominum genus et pecudes, unde imber et ignes,*
> *Arcturum pluviasque Hyadas geminosque Triones;*
> *Quid tantum Oceano properent se tinguere soles*   745
> *Hiberni, vel quae tardis mora noctibus obstet.*
> *Ingeminant plausu Tyrii, Troesque sequuntur.*
> *Nec non et vario noctem sermone trahebat*
> *Infelix Dido longumque bibebat amorem,*
> *Multa super Priamo rogitans, super Hectore multa;*   750
> *Nunc, quibus Aurorae venisset filius armis,*
> *Nunc quales Diomedis equi, nunc quantus Achilles.*
> *'Immo age et a prima dic, hospes, origine nobis*
> *Insidias' inquit, 'Danaum casusque tuorum*
> *Erroresque tuos; nam te iam septima portat*   755
> *Omnibus errentem terris et fluctibus aestas.'*

She spoke, and on the table offered a libation of wine, and after
libation, was the first to touch the cup with her lips. Then she
passed it to Bitias with a challenge. He quickly emptied the
foaming cup and drank deep in the brimming gold; then other
lords drank. Long-haired Iopas, taught by the mighty Atlas, sounds
his golden lyre. He sings of the wandering moon and the sun's
labours; whence sprang human kind and flocks, whence rain and
fire; he sings of Arcturus, the rainy Hyades and the twin Bears;
why wintry suns make such haste to dip themselves in the Ocean;
or what delay stays the slowly passing nights. The Tyrians
applaud again and again with loud cheers and the Trojans follow.
Unhappy Dido, too, with varied talk prolonged the night and
drank deep of love, asking much about Priam and Hector; now
of the fierce steeds of Diomedes; now of the gigantic Achilles.

'Come', she cries, 'and tell us, my dear guest, from the first beginning the treachery of the Greeks, your comrades' misfortunes,
and your own wanderings; for it is now the seventh summer
that carries you a wanderer over all lands and seas.'

The moment of complete capitulation to love is beautifully conveyed
by Virgil in several symbolic formulations which make use of repeated
words and parallelisms. The drink shared by the Carthaginians and
the Trojans after the libation and Dido's first sip (l. 737) is extended
metaphorically and psychologically in the line '*Infelix Dido longumque
bibebat amorem*' (l. 749). The activity which is shared by the Carthaginians and Trojans is Iopas' song. He sings a philosophical composition about Creation: how things came into being. Some of the subjects
are listed (ll. 742–6). This performance is applauded by '*Tyrii, Troesque*'
and then Dido asks about the history of the Trojan conflict. Its subjects are listed (ll. 750–2). The verbal juxtaposition of '*Tyrii, Troesque*',
and the twin lists of subjects of the questioning song and Dido's Trojan
questions invite the reader to see a certain formal parallelism.[45] Other
forms of parallelism accompany: '*vel quae tardis mora noctibus obstet*'
of the song foreshadows '*nec non et vario noctem sermone trahebat . . .
Dido*'. Iopas' song begins with subjects which have been paired syntactically:

(1) *errantem lunam solisque labores*
(2) *unde hominum genus et pecudes*
(3) *unde imber et ignes*

Given the parallel forms of the subjects (natural philosophy/Trojan
matters), the parallel of the audience (Carthaginians/Trojans), the
presence of the chief characters, Dido and Aeneas, it may be seen that
'the wandering moon and the labours of the sun' obliquely represent
Aeneas and Dido. The substantival *errens* occurs in Dido's words to
characterize Aeneas' wanderings in the last lines: '*erroresque tuos;
nam te iam septima portat/omnibus errentem terris et fluctibus aestas.*' In the
uncertain course of his attempts to refound Troy Aeneas is like the
moon. In her nearly completed programme for the building of Carthage, Dido is like the labouring sun. She 'drinks deep of love' while in
the last line of Iopas' song '*Oceano properent se tinguere soles/Hiberni . . .*'[46]

---

[45] Dido, too, wishes to know about the origins of things: '*origine . . . insidias . . .
Danaum.*'
[46] *Aeneid* I.535 and Anna's words in IV.52 indicate that Aeneas has arrived in
Carthage during the winter season.

The closing line of the book recalls the wandering Aeneas' connection
with the sea.[47] The antithetical pair *'imber et ignes'* supports this symbolism and looks forward to future developments in book IV—so, too,
the opposition between the adventurous civilizing design imposed
upon Aeneas by his Fama and the easy epicureanism of Carthage,
'terra dulcis', anticipated cryptically in the antithetical *'hominum genus et
pecudes'*.

By these means the process of Dido's fatal infatuation finds reflection
in Iopas' song. The feast and the song[48] provide the actual moment of
Dido's submission and a symbolic equivalent for the psychological
experience of its taking place; Antigone's song in the garden in Troy
on the third of May performs exactly the same function for Criseyde.
Earlier in the day, on seeing Troilus, she had said 'who yaf me drinke?'
(l. 651), and later her nocturnal memory of the words and images of
Antigone's song creates the symbolic material for her decisive dream.
The complexity and delicacy of the Chaucerian invention, its
imagistic reflections and affiliations, seem to me to have had Virgilian
origins.

The special multidimensional elasticity of narrative, its capacity for
maintaining intensity and continuity of impetus while at the same
time managing to contain digressive, retrospective, introspective and
descriptive elements and excursus requires a different use of the reader's
memory than does the presentation of action in a strictly dramatic
composition. Formally, the narrative mode is polydynamic.[49] The
essence of the successful scene dramaturgically lies in its consistent
coherence of movement and its clear expressive relationship with other
scenes. In an intensified form its rhythm may symbolically 'embody'
or imitate an overall mood, experience or even 'idea' in the whole
drama. Shakespeare is especially fond of this technique. But coherent
development of represented action must always maintain the same
standard of intensity. Scenes may have different 'rhythms' in production, but in the author's mind and on the page all elements which do
not contribute to unified movement and intensity must be eliminated

[47] Pöschl's analysis (*op. cit.*, pp. 150–5) evolves some different identifications but
the basic artistic principles identified are the same.
[48] Cf. Dido's later, deeply sexual longing for the absent Aeneas in IV.77–85 where
she yearns for this very scene, *'eadem convivia'*.
[49] Cf. Aristotle, *Poetics* 1459b 24ff.: 'In a play one cannot represent an action with
a number of parts going on simultaneously; one is limited to the part on the stage
and connected with the actors. Whereas in epic poetry the narrative form makes
it possible to describe a number of simultaneous incidents.'

in the interest of monodynamism.[50] Even the peculiar medieval notion
of dramatic presentation[51] requires that recitation or whatever degree
of mixtures of mime or speaking must progress chronologically and be
irrecoverable in execution. In this sense, *Troilus* is only metaphorically
dramatic and consequently free to utilize all the narrative techniques
which drama cannot accommodate. If we look carefully at the disposition of scenic material in *Troilus* and examine the 'dramatic'
construction of each book, it becomes difficult to escape the conclusion
that book V shows a vast increase in the complexity of scenic structure.
All the previous books seem to contain two to three scenes, if we allow
character-grouping and time-value (as well as narrative continuity)
to decide the number and size of the putative scenes. Book V contains
five scenes with an accompanying pronounced increase in essential
dramatic quality. I think this arises because the balance in the relationship between ordinary narrative accumulative properties and the
mimetic, dramatic and scenic properties is in the process of changing.
Not only is authorial 'distance' being changed,[52] but the degree of
authorial control is being altered. As far as the reader is concerned,
the terrible events of book V must now appear to be slipping from the
author's control. In their concentration and numerousness they are in
the process of achieving the status of history, of impartial fact and re-
grettable evidence—the state from which they were taken by Chaucer
and to which they now return. Actually, authorial control is becoming
more absolute in that all the rhetorical expectations which have been
aroused now must be satisfied in a concentrated, narrow space of lines.
The time draws near when the tragic element in the work must enter
its fullest and most complete state of realization. Book V marks the

[50] It is held by many that Senecan rhetorical decoration is non-dramatic. But
this view overlooks the strong traditional connection between such ornament and
oratory and recitation; such language also had a connection with psychological
and emotional revelation, as in Ovid's *Heroides*. These verbally elaborate passages
are close to the arias in the older Italian *opera seria*.

[51] Cf. Stäuble, *op. cit.*, chapter IV for evidence that the early fifteenth century in
Italy may have attempted the medieval style of mixed presentation in their productions of comedy, probably until the recovery of Donatus on Terence made the
medieval interpretation of Livy obsolete.

[52] M. W. Bloomfield's article, 'Distance and Predestination in *Troilus and
Criseyde*', *PMLA* 72 (1957), pp. 14–26, contains some useful observations, although his concept of 'narrator-character' ignores the role of the participating
author in the medieval version of the dramatic mode. Had he thought of this
active role of the tragic poet in narrative, some of his problems, especially Chaucer's treatment of history, would have had easier solution.

growing curtailment of the hitherto accumulated narrative-dramatic material. The book abounds in images of deprivation, the stripping away of worldly benefits long regarded as belonging inalienably to Troilus or Troy.[53] The mimetic basis of the last book shows the gradual authorial conversion of the balance of narrative and dramatic elements from the dominantly narrative into the basically tragic and dramatic as the scene divisions, characters, situation, morality and metaphysical necessity become more and more obviously and inescapably contingent on each other. The author's position becomes gradually more and more unbearable. As the events themselves become more seemingly immutable and devoted to loss and insubstantiality, reverting to the completed history which had existed at the beginning of book I, so the author becomes increasingly the image of his material, reassuming the lineaments with which he began in his very first invocation, a 'sorwful instrument' bearing 'a sory chere'. The grave countenance of the poet is that assumed by the tragic dramatic poet, as Lydgate knew in his *Troy Book*:

> And after þat with chere and face pale,
> With stile enclyned gan to turne his tale
> And for to singe, after al her loos,
> Ful mortally þe stroke of Antropos . . .
> And whil þat he in þe pulpet stood
> With dedly face al devoide of blood,
> Singinge his dites, with muses al to-rent,[54]

[53] Cf. lines 221–4: the physical loss of Criseyde; 249–59: Troilus' loss of personal security; 299–315: his testament and disposal of his mortal remains; 460–2: the loss of Troilus' capacity for happiness (a musical conceit); 540–53: address to Criseyde's empty palace, embellished by other metaphors: a ring which has lost its stone, a shrine without a saint; 638–44: Troilus' loss of sense of direction (a nautical conceit); 1219–25: Troilus' physical wasting away; 1460–1519: Cassandra's exposition of the tragic dream with its consequences for both Troilus and Troy; 1541–7: the gradual denuding by Fortune of Troy (the violent physical image taken from the *Roman* 11547–8); 1548–55: the death of Hector; 1805–6: the death of Troilus; 1849–55: the author's painful rejection of the values of the pagan world and classical poetics.

[54] Bergen glossed 'muses' as '? a chorus of Muses'. Lydgate is here remembering Boethius' opening elegiac metre of book I of the *De Consolatione*, l. 4: '*Ecce mihi lacerae dictant scribenda camenae*' which Chaucer translated 'For lo, rendynge Muses of poetes enditen to me thynges to be written'. I suspect from the limitations of space in the *scena* ('tent') that Lydgate means by the English equivalent of *camenae* 'the verses themselves as sung', Chaucer's 'vers that wepen as I write'. Cf. P. Courcelle, *La Consolation de philosophie dans la tradition littéraire*, plates 49–61

> Amydde þe theatre schrowdid in a tent,
> Þer cam out men gastful of her cheris,
> Disfigurid her facis with viseris,
> Pleying by signes in þe peples siȝt,
> Þat þe poet songon hath on hiȝt.
>
> (II.867ff.)

So Horace had recommended in the *Ars Poetica* 105–6 in relating the tragic mode of writing to the effect intended on the audience: '*Tristia maestum/Vultum verba decent*' ('pathetic accents suit a melancholy countenance').

If the dramatic and scenic qualities of book V become more complex in detail, the general narrative rhythm becomes more simplified in its effect on the reader. The overall movement is based on a prolonged, falling curve of disappointment, of declining spirits, of failures of promises to be fulfilled. The lovers' insecure compact of reunion within ten days establishes the rhythm which then eddies out into the whole work. Rhythmically it imitates fragmentation and ruin, the consummation of transitoriness.[55] The actions which fulfil their promises lie outside the human and strictly rational or volitional: the Theban historical nemesis revealed through the unconscious mind of Troilus, and the apotheosis of Troilus' soul which becomes a detached spectator of the *theatrum mundi*, looking back for a brief, unpitying moment at the 'shadowe or tabernacle of this lyf' before it takes up a more remote,

---

[55] Cf. Langer, *op. cit.*, p. 351: 'Tragedy is a cadential form. Its crisis is always the turn towards an absolute close. This form reflects the basic structure of personal life [growth, maturity, decline] and therewith of feeling when life is viewed as a whole.' Chaucer's sense of the insufficiency of material life even when lived according to virtue as the basic tragic essence of human endeavour is close philosophically to Seneca's tragic formulation (this will be discussed later). The long, falling rhythm of the book anticipates the structure of Shakespeare's *Henry VIII*, save that each of that play's falls contains an element of supernatural compensation or salvation (Buckingham's religious reconciliation, Wolsey's spiritual illumination, Katharine's celestial vision) which foreshadows the redemption of Henry's fallen and imperfect reign in the prophecy of Cranmer. England will be redeemed after Henry's death through the political age of Elizabeth. The purgatorial nature of Henry's reign is established by the Porter's scene (V. iv: '*Limbo Patrum*') just as the infernal nature of Macbeth's castle is brought to our attention by the Scottish porter.

---

for a selection of medieval illustrations of Boethius surrounded by Muses. Although subdued, none of them is in the least disfigured in lamentation.

virtuous position in some unknowable portion of the vast, indifferent universe.

The author's passionate rejection of the religious and metaphysical values of the pagan world and classical poetics (which nevertheless takes place within the formal pattern of an epical conclusion recalling in part Statius' *Thebaid*) makes up part of the long, declining tragic rhythm, and continues to maintain the mimetic function of the 'dramatic'. Of the formal shapes which we have argued to be imitative of the medieval dramatic mode in *Troilus* (active authorial presence, moral consistency of character, vivid dialogue, intense formal expression of the development of action, scenic formulation, act structure) there remains one dramatic formulation which Chaucer has not imitated—the formal chorus. It is obvious that the narrative aspect of the work, its natural, generating mode, would make the chorus redundant in that the poet's authorial role has the scope and freedom to perform the moralizing and commenting functions of the Senecan chorus: narrative polydynamism can accommodate these choric interventions within the role of the self-conscious poet-figure. But Chaucer's formal, ceremonious use of the authorial *invocatio* seems to me to come very close to the function of the formal chorus in Senecan drama. It might even be argued that the omission of an invocation to book V has been suggested to Chaucer by the number and position of the formal choruses in Senecan tragedy. The five-act structure of the tragedies normally allows four formal choruses, each situated between the acts, the last occurring at the end of Act IV.[56] In addition, two of the plays (*Hercules Oetaeus* and *Octavia*)[57] have a concluding chorus at the end of Act V as well. *Hercules Oetaeus* ends with a philosophical, consoling chorus and prayer after the apotheosis of the soul of the prototype Stoic hero.[58] The *Octavia* ends with the imminent destruction of Rome, already planned by the insane will of Nero and the already arranged murder of the departing, exiled Octavia. The final chorus is emotionally regressive, bitter and fearful—not the least in the mood to be consoled or comforted by wisdom. These two kinds

[56] Cf. Herrmann, *op. cit.*, p. 573.
[57] In the Middle Ages and later the *Octavia* was generally accepted as Seneca's. The balance of belief changes in the late nineteenth century. The problem is far from a solution.
[58] Hercules is identified with God in the *De Beneficiis* IV.8.1. The Stoic god is described by Seneca as being threefold: he is called Bacchus in his creative role; Hercules as the indefatigable hero; Mercury as the aspect of human reason and wisdom.

of final comment typify the main roles of the Senecan formal chorus: (1) the morally alert, offering to the audience and characters advice and philosophical consolation; and (2) the Euripidian, emotionally regressive, fearing all consequences and wishing to be beyond the reach of reason, anxious to be elsewhere. Two good examples of these tendencies are provided by the final chorus in Act IV of the *Troades* (ll. 1009–55) and the final chorus of the *Thyestes* (ll. 789–884). *Troades'* '*Dulce maerenti populus dolentum*' is an utterly calm, rhythmically assured philosophical exhortation to Stoical heroism—the turning of adversity into human dignity through individual and national endurance. The impressive Sapphic measure quietly blends without mannerism of style the extended Stoic image of 'the shipwreck of human life' with the actual, approaching experience of the captive Trojans' voyage into uncharted and irreversible exile. The *Thyestes'* '*Quo terrarum superumque parens*' in emotional and distressed anapaestic dimeters[59] moves from fearful questions to despairing answers. The central section comprises a detailed, horrific imagining of the physical destruction of the whole universe, '*ibit in unum/Congesta sinum turba deorum*'. In bright, hard oratorical word-order the simultaneously feared and wished-for catastrophe takes the form of a vision of the physical collapse of the gigantic Zodiac piece by piece. It creates a brilliant poetic counterpart to Ovid's famous description of the universal deluge in *Metamorphoses* I.293–312.[60]

At the end of *Troilus*, the poet's 'envoi' (ll. 1786–869), although it seems to revert to the dominantly narrative and epical with its close verbal echoing of the *Thebaid* XII.816–17 in stanza 256 and with the closely worked material of *Teseida* XI in stanzas 259–61, yet its overall tone in the ceremonious blending of prayer, emotional exclamation and philosophical consolation combines both separate functions of the Senecan final chorus. But the two dominant moods in the Chaucerian final address do not merely replace each other. There is no orderly progress. The ending seems wave-like, a succession of alternating moods where the final cadence resolves into authorial calm and religious

---

[59] Cf. J. D. Bishop, 'The Meaning of the Choral Meters in Senecan Tragedy', *Rheinisches Museum* (Frankfurt), 3 (1968), pp. 197–219.

[60] Ovid's passage was much admired by Seneca, who quotes it extensively in the *Naturales Quaestiones* III.27.13ff. Seneca believed that the earth was subject to periodic and beneficial deluges and conflagrations confined to the terrestrial sphere. The Stoic philosopher and teacher of Seneca, Papirius Fabianus, believed in the final destruction of the universe, including the fixed stars (cf. *Naturales Quaestiones* III.27.3).

acquiescence by mere repetition and mental exhaustion. Those critics are right, I believe, who see Chaucer escaping from the pagan time-scheme of his *oeuvre*, an emotional and intellectual withdrawal—like the Senecan regressive final chorus: a wish to be removed from the tragic scene in which it has been involved. Through the historical co-consciousness established in the *Troilus* chiefly by the poet's creative activity, the author's removal from the work involves mental distances rather than physical transportation. Even the final prayer suggests a certain fragility of attitude as if the poet were still too close to his 'boke'. It begins majestically and confidently with the closely imitated words and style of Dante's hymn of the prudent (*Paradiso* XIV.28-30) yet ends not on the note of triumphant praise reminiscent of that context but in a personal prayer for peace and mercy, especially for spiritual aid against temporal and spiritual attack. It is closer to the prayer of the wrathful in *Purgatorio* XVI when they repeat the '*Agnus Dei*' than to the song of the already saved in the sphere of the sun.

Thus, the two moods, the regressive emotional and the consolatory philosophical, alternate; they provide both the author and ourselves with a Christian consolation which lies outside the cosmology of the fiction, and with the emotional bitterness of the cursing of the pagan gods and the wholesale rejection of classical poetics. The author's cursing of the gods (ll. 1849-55) has been extended from Troilo's earlier imprecations and reveals Chaucer's oblique identification emotionally with Troilus which parallels Boccaccio's open and deliberate identification of the *autore* with Troilo. With the angry rejection of pagan poetics, 'the forme . . . of poetrie', the two alternating and not wholly successful efforts of authorial dissociation and extrication from the tragic nature of imitated life and life itself seem to subside. In a conventional application of a humility formula Chaucer places the poem under the correction of Gower and Strode. The medieval poet's lack of confidence in his intellectual resources (here concerned with the morality of love relationships and the question of free will and predestination) springs less from a real desire to be emended as it does from the poet's need to name two actual close and living friends whose mere existence and common interests may provide a guarantee of the tangible presence of contemporary experience and domestic comfort. With the naming of John Gower and Randolph Strode the author's enchantment by, and obsession with literary pagan time and his fascination with the manipulation of aspects of historical perspective clarify, simplify and disappear. The inventive spell is broken. The poet-actor leaves his roles in the dressing-room of the here-and-now. The poet is finally alone in his own London environment, the closing prayer for safety and mercy the last trace of a by now wholly un-complicated literary endeavour.[61]

Of all the already noted, similar passages in Boccaccio where the author commits his work to the care of a friend for correction, only the *Ameto* as a work of fiction contains anything like a possible parallel. In section 50 Boccaccio achieves a similar effect of disenchantment by offering the work for supervision to Niccolo di Bartolo de Buono. At the end, the extensive classical fantasies, pastoral versions of reality, antique erudition, allegorical excursus and thinly disguised feelings fall away. As the *Ameto*'s editor (A. Quaglio) observes:[62]

E una voce lamentosa risuona anche nella dedica dell'opera, per la prima volta indirizzata a una persona reale, a un amico; non la mitica Fiametta o le vaghe donne, ma una presenza familiare.

Chaucer has taken leave of his characters on finishing his simple prayer, leaving one unambiguously among the virtuous pagan dead, raised to the stars through the exercise of his martial valour, the other the sadder and wiser lady of Diomedes, conscious of her need for fidelity to her living knight but equally conscious of her faithfulness in memory to her best love, Troilus. Henceforth she will live with her shame—and survive. The 'epilogue's' mental alternations are touched by a profound crossing of views ancient and modern. The pagan view of 'this wretched life' as seen clearly by Troilus from the neighbouring sphere of the moon is not wholly a Christian perspective or Chaucer's. Chaucer's religious universe includes love—Christ's love for mankind (*agape*) is approached in many ways by the virtuous, tender care and affection of Troilus and Criseyde. Their relationship is not all *eros*-centred—just as the Christian Chaucer has understanding and com-passion for his own semi-fictional pagan hero and heroine. They are partially his creation, partially 'Lollius's' and partially the product of

---

[61] The desire for a plain style, a manner perfectly adjusted to the language of simple prayer, explains the Chaucerian revision from the more elegant phrase-ology recorded in BM MS. Harley 3943 and Bodley MS. Rawlinson Poet. 163: 'Trine unite us, from oure cruel foon/Defend'. The collocation *'unica e trina'* occurs in Dante, *Paradiso* XXIV.140 and Boccaccio, *Ameto* 41.

[62] *Tutte le Opere di Giovanni Boccaccio* (ed. V. Branca), Milan (1964), vol. II, pp. 676–7.

historical reality. Certain documents have made them actual persons.[63]
Whatever has contributed to their existence they are in all three aspects
universalizations applicable to all men and women in all ages. 'She is
modern,' exclaims the Jamesian hero who has immersed himself in his
own historical fable in *A Sense of the Past* and is on the point of evolving
a deep attachment for this remote lady. How precisely he has decided
on her temporal status remains mysterious, yet the appeal abides and
develops. Troilus' soul goes to its final resting-place wrapped in the
Roman security of civic and public *virtus* which guarantees neo-
Platonic and Stoic apotheosis. Seneca would have agreed with that
(cf. *Ad Marciam* XXV.1), although elsewhere he shows doubts about
the soul's survival and generously assesses the value of love and friendship. To say he is cold and unfeeling is not to have read him in full.
The Christian universe resembles closely the neo-Platonic in its
mechanics but the value of love, the relationship of man to woman is
one dimension where they do not agree. One must not project
Christianity into Troilus' unfeeling rejection of earthly values or
imagine his world as capable of understanding Chaucer's exhortations
to the young as heirs of Christ's pardon. The critical mistake is to assess
the 'meaning' of the envoi as a simple and summary unity of feeling
and idea—as triumphant Christian apologia, Boethian philosophical
certainty or a despairing humanism clutching at dialectical straws.[64]
The development of the envoi in all its alternating and crossing nuances
should warn us that the head and the heart sometimes find it hard to
agree. The author's position as 'dramaturge', the poet at stage-centre
of his composition, makes him more vulnerable to those passions which
he first must feel before he can induce them in his audience. Horace
has a moving passage on this poetic duty in the *Ars Poetica* 99–105
which the modern critic would do well to read. The Chaucerian tragic
poet is more exposed to the audience's view and so all his techniques
are more visible, more accessible for analysis. Part of the emotional
and formal beauty of the envoi lies in its honesty and sincerity as the
poet in his conclusion discards his fictive resources.[65]

[63] Compare Pope's use of historical truth, fiction and personal relevance in his
Eloisa to Abelard.
[64] Kean's 'Chaucer's Dealings with a Stanza of *Il Filostrato* and the Epilogue of
Troilus and Criseyde' and Dronke's 'The Conclusion of *Troilus and Criseyde*' in
Medium Aevum 33 (1964), pp. 36ff. and 47ff. both make this assumption about
unity of purpose and idea.
[65] The use of an 'epilogue' in Roman comedy is restricted to some plays of
Plautus (who had an interest in the manipulation of illusion and reality), e.g.

If we may grant that Chaucer's poem makes fundamental and extensive use of dramatic-tragic forms as mimetic principles within narrative polydynamism, and delegates to the function of the poet-narrator the dramatic function of the participating medieval tragic poet, then we are entitled to ask what is the 'tragic' nature of the work which Chaucer deliberately calls a 'tragedye'? It cannot simply conform to the vacuous definition provided by Isidore, for Chaucer's knowledge of the genre is arguably wider and more perceptive than this version. It cannot be a 'Boethian tragedy' for there is no such thing in Boethius' account of unhappiness and misfortune in the *De Consolatione*.[66] Boethius' blend of the Stoic and the neo-Platonic leaves no room for a genuine tragic paradox. The lamenting Muses are quickly sent packing and Boethius' tears are hardly tolerated. By book IV we know that wickedness is a form of mental illness. The mistaken and sad are justly rewarded with punishment and they take proper pleasure in that measure of justice whether they are aware of it or not. Boethius' final objections are chiefly metaphysical and are answered in exclusively epistemological terms. The seeming incongruity between suffering, doing and reward, the gap between 'is' and 'ought', is a matter of perspective and time-scale. Tragedy, if it is to exist at all, must involve the emotions as well as the intellect. Pity and fear must play some part. The only wholesome purgation admitted to by Philosophy, *'purgatoria clementia'*, takes place after death (IV prose iv), otherwise Fortune only tests virtue or punishes vice. These are Philosophy's very words.

Although Chaucer creates for both Criseyde and Troilus consistency of moral response which has a close connection with certain peculiarities of temperament, in Criseyde's case a passivity based on feminine fear and timidity,[67] in Troilus' a passivity based on a philosophical disposition to fatalism,[68] yet the poet seems not to give these traits much poetic emphasis in the work. If anything, the poet seeks to neutralize

[66] The defining words *'Quid tragoediarum clamor aliud deflet, nisi indiscreto ictu fortunam felicia regna vertentem?'* are spoken by Philosophy's impersonation of Fortune and represent a double trivialization of the idea of tragedy, ethically, socially and intellectually.
[67] C. S. Lewis in *The Allegory of Love* called attention to this characteristic.
[68] Cf. J. A. W. Bennett, *Medium Aevum* 22, p. 114.

Casina, Rudens, Asinaria, Baccides, Captivi and *Cistellaria*. The *Cistellaria* has a formal epilogue which breaks the illusion of dramatic reality by describing the actors' disrobing in the dressing-room and their behind-the-scene capers even while the theatre is emptying of its audience.

any 'deficiency' in behaviour which the reader might assign to the characters. He anticipates criticism and commends (without irony, I believe) a more compassionate and comprehensive understanding.[69] Chaucer does not seem interested in the more technically-involved Aristotelian ethical definition of tragedy which would spring from either *hybris* or *hamartia*.

Hitherto I have argued that Chaucer's knowledge of the dramatic and tragic mode was influenced by a reading of Seneca's plays and Trivet's *Commentary*. If so, it would follow that Chaucer's view of the nature of tragedy was also influenced by Seneca's plays and philosophical writings.[70] The philosophical works[71] represent practical attempts to evolve principles and 'rules' for facing life. The philosophy which emerges is eclectic and inconsistent. Quintilian long ago complained of Seneca's failure to evolve a consistent method.[72] He even descended to employing research assistants to do his diggings: '. . . *multa rerum cognitio; in qua tamen aliquando ab his, quibus inquirenda quaedam mandabat, deceptus est.*' He is an unsafe author, stylistically and morally; we must be well-trained enough to distinguish between his merits and defects: '. . . *eligere modo curae sit; quod utinam ipse fecisset.*' 'We must be careful in our selection; would he had been as careful himself.' But this very inconsistency, as radical as that of Montaigne, makes him especially valuable as a source for the tragic sense of life. In spite of his Stoical tendencies, he is capable of emotions, if only in his various attempts to suppress them. The 'Nature' and the 'Life' of Seneca are too involved in fleshly interferences. Seneca's images of Life show an awareness of struggle and passion: a journey, a storm, a shipwreck, the arena of gladiatorial combat, a military campaign, a city just captured, a siege[73]—a drama. All of these are agonistic metaphors. Nowhere do we find an artistic form or sequence of thinking which is

[69] We have had Chaucer the Simple, Chaucer the Wise, Chaucer the Ironical and Chaucer the Mischievous, but Chaucer the Malicious is unthinkable even by those twentieth-century standards which have invented Chaucer the Divine.
[70] The Middle Ages assumed that '*philosophus*' and '*tragicus*' were one and the same man. Later times have had their doubts but the older assumption persists and seems, on balance, preferable to other theories.
[71] On the popularity of the *Letters* in the Middle Ages after the twelfth century, cf. L. D. Reynolds, *The Medieval Tradition of Seneca's Letters*, Oxford (1965), pp. 104–24.
[72] *Institutio Oratoria* X.i.125ff.
[73] Cf. Letter 113.27: '*obsidio vitae*', an image not inappropriate to the milieu of Chaucer's *Troilus*.

the equivalent of Boethius' logical dialogue for the promotion and
elevation of other-worldliness—that primacy of the contemplative
activity which ensures that the world of action and pleasure must find
little or no place in our motives for living the ideal life. Although
Seneca defines 'life' as one of the indifferent things:[74]

Vita nec bonum nec malum est; boni ac mali locus est.

Life is neither a Good nor an Evil; it is merely where good and evil
take place.

he cannot manage a consistent philosophical reconcilement to that area
of indifference. Joys, terrors, fears and injuries continue to engage his
attention—and mainly on behalf of others. 'Tranquillity' is one of his
chief aims, but one will find it defined and discussed substantially in
only two works, the *De Vita Beata* and the *De Tranquillitate Animi*. For
the rest of the time his argumentative progress is like that of a country
doctor on his rounds, jolting epigrammatically from mental bedside
to book-lined pharmacy and back again. The intellect and the emotions
are continually at odds, still on speaking terms, and death only ends
their uneasy association. Unlike Boethius' medicine, Seneca's allows
us our memories, joys and sufferings. Stylistically Seneca enjoys surprising us, 'shocking' us. He is full of paradoxes, if only because life
itself provides the model.

The ultimate Stoical *paradoxa vitae* lies in the identical frustration
offered by Nature and Fortune both in external reality and within
ourselves: the continuous clash between our capabilities and our limitations, between what life offers and takes away—nothing permanent,
everything borrowed. The greatest flaw in life is that it is always
imperfect:[75]

We must rid ourselves of this craving for life and learn that it
makes no difference when your suffering comes, because at some
time you are bound to suffer. The point is not how long you live
but how well you live; and often this living well means that you
cannot live long.

The plays of Seneca are imaginary worlds where good and evil
take place; in his theatre of life the spectator sees and experiences how

[74] Letter 99.12.
[75] Letter 101.8. Hamlet would seem to be remembering this passage when he has
yielded to the inevitable tragic rhythm of his life in Act V.ii.212ff.

well or ill we endure the contest. His tragic sense always grows from
the painful lesson set us by Nature and Destiny:[76]

Cuivis potest accidere quod cuiquam potest

Whatever has happened to one man can happen to every man.

It is a simple definition of the tragic but it has complex moral ramifi-
cations and is full of emotional interest. It provides a dramatic paradox,
a tragic struggle, where Boethius yields a perfect explanation. Seneca's
references in his philosophical writings to the drama and especially
to tragedy continuously refer to this flaw in nature, life and destiny.

In addition to the quoting of Publilius Syrus in the *Ad Marciam*
and the *De Tranquillitate Animi*, there are at least four other reminiscences of the theatre in Seneca's *Letters*. There is a curious consistency
in his association of this type of literary experience with the tragic
insubstantiality and inconsistency of fortune, nature and human
existence. The first passage occurs in Letter 8.7:

> *Non attingam tragicos, aut togatas nostras, habent enim hae quoque*
> *aliquid severitatis et sunt inter comoedias et tragoedias mediae—*
> *quantum divertissimum versuum inter mimos iacet! quam multa Publii*
> *non excalcentis, sed cothurnatis dicenda sunt! Unum versum eius, qui*
> *ad philosophiam pertinet, et ad hanc partem quae modo fuit in manibus,*
> *referam, quod negat fortuita in nostris habenda:*
>   *Alienum est omne, quicquid optando venit.*

I am not even speaking about tragedies or our plays on native
subjects where one notes a certain restraint and which steer a

---

[76] This line is quoted by Seneca in the *Ad Marciam* IX.5 and the *De Tranquillitate
Animi* XI.8 in the context of human loss and death. In the first citation he says
that it is too good to have come from the stage; in the last he admits that it comes
from one of the mimes of Publilius Syrus. Shakespeare presents this pity-
creating view of the heroic spectacle of a single mortal and tragic life in *Antony
and Cleopatra* and *Timon of Athens*. The moment comes to Octavius in V.i.31-4
when he sees Antony's sword:

> *Agrippa*: A Rarer spirit neuer
> Did steere humanity: but you Gods will giue vs
> Some faults to make vs men. *Caesar* is touch'd.
> *Maecenas*: When such a spacious Mirror's set before him,
> He needes must see himselfe.

The same effect is made on Alcibides in the final lines of Act V, sc. IV when the
epitaph of Timon brings him to recognize his own humanity. Both plays share
the same source, Plutarch's *Life of Marcus Antonius*. There are other scenic connections, cf. Emrys Jones, *op. cit.*, p. 261n.

middle course between comedy and tragedy—how many striking lines we can find even amongst the mimographers! In the mimes of Publilius Syrus how many verses worthy not of the comic actor but of the tragedian! I will quote you one only which belongs to the philosophic and deals with the subject in hand, namely, that fortune's gifts do not belong to us:

What comes by wishing is never truly ours.

Again, in Letter 76.31, in a passage dealing with the instability of fortune and the certitude of being deprived of what has only been loaned, Seneca returns to a theatrical image connected with tragic acting:

Nemo ex istis, quos purpuratos uides, felix est, non magis quam ex illis, quibus sceptrum et chlamydem in scaena fabulae adsignant: cum presente populo lati incesserunt et coturnati, simul exierunt, excalceantur et ad staturam suam redeunt.

Of all the men whom you see decked out in courtly purple, not one is happy—no more than those stage princelings to whom royal robes and sceptres have been loaned as props for their time on stage. They strut before the audience, posturing on their elevated tragic buskins, then, scarcely having made their exit, they take them off and resume their normal height.

Letter 80.7–8 elaborates the same dramatic and tragic metaphor with a more radical exposure of the element of illusion and reality. Mime (a demotic form) and tragedy are satirically equated:[77]

Saepius hoc exemplo, mihi hic utendum est, nec enim ullo efficacius exprimitur, humanae uitae mimus, qui nobis partes, quas male agimus, adsignat: ille qui in scaena latus incedit et haec resupinus dicit:
        En impero Argis: regna mihi liquit Pelops,
        Qua ponto ab Helles atque ab Ionio mari
        Vrguetur Isthmus,
Seruus est, quinque modios accipit et quinque denarios.

Often that last example returns to my thoughts, the best characterization of the vulgar drama of this life is that which assigns to all

---

[77] Modern editors of Seneca assign the speech to the *Atreus* of Lucius Accius. Klotz (*Scaenicorum Romanorum Fragmenta*, Munich (1953), vol. 1, pp. 190–303) assigns the fragment to an unknown author. Quintilian quotes the first line (IX.iv.140) as an example of the tragic, pompous rhythm.

THE BOOK OF TROILUS

of us a role which each acts badly—that actor who strides across
the stage with head thrown back, arrogantly asserting:

Behold, I rule in Argos, Pelops bequeathed to me these king-
doms, the portion joining the Isthmus which borders the
Hellespont and the Ionian sea,

that same actor a mere slave whose take-home pay is the princely
sum of five pence and five pecks of wheat!

The last example occurs in Letter 115.15–16 where Seneca touches on
the self-defeating desire of wealth and its torment of anticipation and
possession. He quotes six lines of Euripides' lost *Danaë* (fragment 324)
and afterwards comments on this bragging praise of material success:

> *Dabat in illa fabula poenas Bellerophontes,*
> *quas in sua quisque dat.*

Bellerophon in that particular drama was to pay the penalty which
is exacted of all men in their own drama of life.

The dramatic image extracted from tragedy turns radically away from
the deserved ethical satisfaction of greed to the reward which all life
bestows—pain and death, sheer loss. The prose argument logically
takes up the topic of material desire but the theatrical image for a brief
moment goes beyond ethical calculations.[78]

This location of the tragic flaw in the nature of how life must cause
us to experience it, rather than in life itself (one of the Stoic 'indifferent
things') or exclusively in the moral nature of a single character (in
Aristotle's view), provides the central formulation for the Senecan
tragic drama. Seneca's plays (like Euripides') exploit both the universal
tragic limitation of life-experience and how we morally respond to it
individually as the basis for creating pity and fear. Seneca (following
Euripides and Ovid) then varies the basic formulation by inventing a
range of complex psychological responses within an interesting selection of characters who were already tragic types on the Horatian
model. On stage these great types are the equivalent of the *exempla*,

[78] Cf. B. L. Hijmans jun., 'Drama in Seneca's Stoicism', *Transactions and Proceed-
ings of the American Philological Association* 97 (1966), pp. 237ff. This discusses the
use of dramatic similes and techniques in the moral prose. The most striking
passage occurs in the *De Providentia* II.7–12 where the Stoic hero's life is acted
before the gods who are present as spectators and stage-managers. There is extensive use of acting terminology, e.g. *pars* and *exitus*. The universe as *spectaculum*
in the theatrical sense occurs regularly, e.g. *Ad Polybium* 9.3.; *Ad Helviam Matrem*
8.4–6, 20.2.; *De Beneficiis* IV.23.2; *Letters* 89.1–2, 90.42, 92.6.

'the ethical types of history' which Seneca is always urging us to become
in the conduct of our own lives. The worthiest of us, too, should
'labour for eternity'. This invention of character and psychology lends
his plays variety in much the same way that the simple and repetitive
didactic formulations of Brecht are given theatrical interest and variety
by the use of exotic settings (location, scenery, costumes and names)
or by the melodic and orchestral inventiveness of Kurt Weill. In
addition, Seneca also dresses up the simple formulation with rhetorical
and linguistic expressiveness which is not chiefly generated by character
or situation. This has tempted critics sometimes to see nothing else
but rhetorical surface.[79] Unlike Euripides, who usually exploits the
element of pity in his tragic formulation, Seneca habitually increases
the effect of fear on his readers or audience. His is truly a theatre of the
terrible.[80]

This is not the place for an extended critique of Senecan tragedy but
a brief account of the *Hercules Furens* will illustrate my thesis. It is
generally accepted that the sources for the *Hercules Furens* were
Euripides' *The Madness of Heracles* and Accius' *Amphytruo*. So little of
Accius remains that to speculate further would be vain. When we
read Euripides' play it is difficult to see any points of similarity from a
dramatic point of view. Seneca might just as well have acquired his
material from a digest or prose account, so different is the theatrical
treatment. Euripides' play has a dual plot, the first half of the action
dominated by Lycus' tyrannical designs and the audience's expecting and
hoping for the rescue of the family at the hands of Heracles when he has
reappeared from the underworld. This continuous action is interrupted
by the unexpected intervention of Iris and Madness who then, by
instigating the revenge of Hera for Heracles' completion of his labours,
turn the plot in quite a different direction, arousing a totally unfore-
seen set of rhetorical expectations. We change from hope to fear.
Further, the audience's interest is divided equally among the major
characters, and the superhuman aspect of Heracles finds little emphasis.
The sentimental and pathetic elements in Heracles' suffering at the
end of the play are deliberately cultivated. None of this is remotely
like Seneca. How can Euripides have influenced him?

What Seneca has grasped from the dual plot of *The Madness of
Heracles* and the mid-point intervention of Iris and Madness is the

[79] Cf. F. L. Lucas, *Seneca and Elizabethan Drama*, Cambridge (1924). This is one of
the most amusing and one of the worst books written on Seneca. It reminds one
of Aristophanes on Euripides.   [80] Cf. Herrmann, *op. cit.*, p. 389.

enormously unfair, immoral nature of the peripety. It is outrageous, unexpected and undeserved by decent, civilized standards. Hera's revenge is not only offensive morally but in its manner of execution criminally bloody, involving the killing of a whole family during undeserved madness, followed by the recovery of Heracles' sanity and the subsequent, appalling recognition scene. This loathsome sequence recalls the *Bacchae* and Dionysus' 'correction' of Pentheus.[81] It not only appealed to Seneca's sense of the theatre of horror but also to his moral sense of the unjust behaviour of the divine directors of the universe towards those who genuinely 'live well or heroically'. It is not the mere contemplation of the Herculean labours which incenses Juno but the very element of divinity and astonishing human capability of Hercules. She will see to it that he will destroy all that he loves, his reputation and himself, thus helping him to complete the greatest labour of all, his own destruction. It will be war within the self: '*Nemo est, nisi ipse, bella iam secum gerat.*'

The dramatic position of the intervention of this jealousy of the gods for human ability and aspiration is placed in the earliest possible moment. It occupies the whole of Act I and is not announced by a messenger or an allegorical figure. Juno herself, *solo*, speaks it. Seneca is here recalling another Euripidian moment, the opening speech of Aphrodite in the *Hippolytus*. Aphrodite's detailed exposition of her reasons for destroying Hippolytus and how she will bring it about is conducted in passionless, intellectual hatred. It chills the blood in content, inevitability and manner of delivery. Juno in Seneca's portrayal becomes less and less of a divinity as her jealous mind concocts the destructive programme. She becomes progressively more repulsive, embodying the hateful aspects of Roman matron, stepmother and finally mad woman. Juno, in seeking to enter into Hercules to induce insanity, must first become mad herself:

> *Ut possit animo captus Alcides agi,*
> *Magno furore percitus nobis prius*
> *Insaniendum est. Iuno, cur nondum furis?*
> *Me, me, sorores mente deiectam mea*
> *Versate primam, facere si quidquam apparo*
> *Dignum noverca.*
>
> (107ff.)

---

[81] This connection between the two plays was seen by Decharme, *Euripides and the Spirit of his Dramas* (trans. Loeb), New York (1906), p. 171.

So that Hercules, crazed with extreme insanity, shall be subject to
my influence, first I myself must become mad. O Juno, not yet in a
mindless rage? On me, on me first O sister Furies exercise your
powers, transform me that I may be cast out of my sane mind if I
am to prepare anything worthy of a detested stepmother.

She soon imagines herself identified with Hercules in the act of killing
his family. This irrational possession reminds one of Dionysus' impersonation of the soon to be fatally ecstatic Pentheus.[82] We are witnessing
before our eyes the Euripidian process of the psychologization of the
gods as they become transformed into human passions, into the forces
of the *thymos*.[83] As she enlarges her original identity she becomes both
a human passion and the very divinity in Hercules which destroys his
humanity. It can be seen from this brief introduction how the tragic
defect thrives both in the nature of Hercules and in the forces which
shape his life. Human capability and moral conduct no matter how
worthy of cherishing, preservation or honour receive exactly the opposite reward: madness, crime and expiation. The very physical hell which
the chorus had triumphantly announced as having been abolished by
Hercules becomes transformed into Hercules' conscience once he has
recovered his sanity and recognized his victims. Infernal punishment,
too, is internalized and psychologized. All of this should be distressing
to rational, compassionate human nature. Theseus, good friend that he
is, picks up the pieces and conducts Hercules towards expiation.

In *Troilus* the moment of peripety in the plot comes at the very
beginning of book IV. As the hostile events congregate, the reader feels
the unfairness of the destinal pattern and the hatefulness of how we must
experience their lives. The lovers' identification in book III (and earlier)
with the sacred law of Nature, its inevitability and high morality, its
philosophical desirability, the ennobling quality of the lovers' conduct
towards each other and towards others—all this *summum bonum*, this
human felicity, deserves a different reward and resolution. As in Seneca,
the Chaucerian tragic flaw and paradox lie within the experience of life,
nature and destiny. If we are sentient, feeling persons, we are bound to
experience closely the long emotional decline of both Troilus and
Criseyde as they try to keep their honour, love, integrity and will to
live. They are gradually defeated as much by their good qualities as
by the destiny designed for them. Criseyde must go on planning

[82] Cf. Lady Macbeth in I.v.38–48.
[83] Cf. E. R. Dodds, *The Greeks and the Irrational*, Cambridge (1951), p. 186.

solutions—until she can plan no longer. Her last recorded thought is merely another proposed solution. Her final capitulation to Diomedes comes about through her supreme feminine virtue, *pite*, her compassion. Troilus must act rationally and morally: he cannot indulge in private acts of violence and lawlessness against the common good. If he cannot keep Criseyde by force, he must consent to the bill of exchange and go on hoping and believing that she will rejoin him, long after the appointed day has passed. He remains loving even after proven betrayal, just as Criseyde retains in her memory that perfect image of him she had always entertained. She does not devalue or alter him in any way. Neither of the lovers gives way to the bitter hatred and rejection which overtakes Pandarus.

Generally, the rhythm of tragic deline in Seneca is moderately rapid since most of his plays are tragedies of action and motivation rather than of suffering (only the *Troades* and the fragmentary *Phoenissae* are exceptions). Chaucer's rhythm of decline after the catastrophe is slow[84] and imitates gradual deprivation, the stripping away of everything which makes existence endurable. This dominating movement of book V is evolved early in book IV in the person of Troilus himself when he leaves the parliamentary chamber knowing the worst. Boccaccio in *Il Filostrato* (IV.18) characteristically gives the emotionally-dying lover epical status by associating Troilo with a dying warrior simile of *Aeneid* IX.426. Boccaccio's imagery refers to the appearance of Troilo: 'Even as the lily after it has been turned up in the fields by the plough, droops and withers as the result of too much sun and its bright hue alters and fades.' Chaucer's comparison exposes the whole psychological alteration of Troilus. The poet, choosing yet again to orchestrate the emotional line of his poem from Dante's *Commedia*,[85] creates a new simile out of *Inferno* III.112ff.:

> And, as in wynter leves ben biraft,
> Ech after other, til the tree be bare,
> So that ther nys but bark and braunche ilaft,
> Lith Troilus, byraft of eche welfare,
> Ibounden in the blake bark of care,

---

[84] Cf. Chaucer's additions to Boccaccian material when Troilus refers to himself as an *impedimentum mundi*: 'I, combre-world, that may of no thyng serve,/But alwey dye, and neuere fulli sterve' (IV.279–80); Troilus identifies himself with Oedipus (300–1) as a tragic character.

[85] Pain is illustrated by images from *Inferno*; mixed or improving states of mind from *Purgatorio*; resolved or joyful feelings from *Paradiso*.

> Disposed wood out of his wit to breyde,
> So sore hym sat the chaungynge of Criseyde.
>   (225ff.)

Dante's lines which described the souls of the dead being collected for
transport over the Styx have been derived from *Aeneid* VI.309ff. and
emphasize the collecting nature of the concrete imagery:

> *Come d'autunno si levan le foglie*
> *l'una appresso dell'altra, infin che il ramo*
> *vede alla terre tutte le sue spoglie:*

As leaves of autumn fall off one after the other, till the branch
sees all its spoils on the ground:

In Chaucer the force of the comparison has been redirected towards the
figure of Troilus, imagistically the tree itself. The leaves shed are the
joyful and pleasant thoughts ('eche welfare') of Troilus. We have had
earlier, several similes in which the emergence of hopeful thoughts in
Troilus have been compared to the growth, even the recovery after
frost, of plants and leaves. The rhythm of this simile is of progressive
deprivation—gradual loss. Dante's '*l'una appresso dell'altra*' yields 'Ech
after other'. The final image is harsh, 'Ibounden in the blake bark of
care'. The image of the stark winter tree is intensified by the sub-
jectivizing, sensatory shading in the vb. 'Ibounden'. The choice of this
vb. may reflect Chaucer's memory of another Dantean passage, *Inferno*
XIII, in the dolorous wood of the suicides when the poet asks '*come
l'anima si lega/In questi nocchi*' ('how the human soul is bound within
these knotty boles').[86] The syntax of Chaucer's comparison has been so
arranged that the 'as . . . so' construction seems never to take Troilus
out of the comparison.[87] He remains caught up in the arboreal metaphor.
The syntax also includes the observation 'Disposed wood out of his
wit to breyde'. The physical, rapid movement conveyed by 'breyde
out' supports the underlying sense of encircling, constraining, oppres-
sive physical and mental immobility, almost as if Troilus in his progressive deprivation has been transformed, metamorphosed into a tree—like
the souls of the suicides, 'bound' into their thorny forms. I think
Chaucer is remembering the transformation of the weeping sisters of
Phaethon into trees in *Eclogue* VI.62–3:

[86] Dante's arboreal images derive from *Aeneid* III.33ff.
[87] Skeat and Robinson understood the syntax and punctuated correctly. Root
did not.

Tum Phaethontiados musco circumdat amarae
Corticis *atque solo proceras erigit alnos.*

Then he [Proteus] *encircles* Phaethon's sisters *in moss of bitter bark,*
and raises them from the ground as lofty alders.

Moments later Troilus' mental immobility breaks, and in a terrible
'frenesie' erupts into fury and physical violence. This mood then ebbs
away into complaint and self-analysis. The process is described in
detail (a mixture of Boccaccio and new Chaucerian material) but there
is nothing in this close account of psychological reaction which suggests
the peculiarity of modern psychological representation. Troilus' behaviour conforms to a typical pattern. He is in the process of becoming
one of Seneca's dramatic *exempla,* one of the ethical types of tragic
history. Conscious and subconscious realization tend to mirror each
other. Troilus' identification of himself with a tragic figure:

> O Troilus, what may men now the calle
> But wrecche of wrecches, out of honour falle
> Into miserie, in which I wol bewaille
> Criseyde, allas, til that the breth me faille?
> (IV. 270–3)

is later mirrored in his unconscious mind:

> And therwithal he sholde a noyse make,
> And seme as though he sholde falle depe
> From heighe olofte; and thanne he wolde wepe,
> (V. 257–9)

The dream-imagery has been taken from Boccaccio (*Il Filostrato* V.27)
but the earlier conscious, tragic identification is Chaucer's emphatic
addition. The realistic effect of experiencing the psychological worlds
of Troilus and Criseyde is not lessened by the absence of modern
particularity, or rather seeming 'uniqueness' of experience in images and
symbols. Coleridge in a lay sermon once observed that, concerning the
relation of motives and moral action in the past and present, it seemed
to him that in the past people behaved a good deal worse than their
professed principles and that modern persons behaved a good deal
better than their principles. In the conduct of love, the relation of
motive, psychology and moral action may be characterized in a different
way. In the long ages which Richardson's slow, environmental
observations show coming to an end, the relation of lovers exhibits a

considerable amount of external complexity—the moral relationships are made complicated by an already existing code of behaviour, while the psychology of the individual lovers at the level of motivation (and expression of motivation) remains simple and invariably representative. As Lydgate's knight-lover in the *Temple of Glass* observes on the difficulty of obtaining his love's satisfaction because: 'I am so simple and she is so good.' This does not prevent Lydgate from erecting a complex symbolism out of the psychological and moral dilemma, but the imagery and symbolism look more towards Boethius and Chaucer than towards Galen or Macrobius—or the assumptions of modern psychological analysis. Modern love, to borrow Meredith's title, has undergone considerable simplification in its external manifestation (the new code of 'honesty' in the seventeenth century had much to do with this) while the lovers' individual psychology has become progressively more complex, especially in its motivational aspect. At the end of the last century abnormal psychology added another layer of moral implications and set of expressive language to the last refinements of Victorian and Edwardian moral analysis as developed in the novel.

Chaucer's Troilus and Criseyde, Pandarus and Diomede belong to the older world of the complications of honour. They move in a milieu thickly strewn with the occasional tables of signals, signs, messages and observances—a world perfectly intelligible to Choderlos de Laclos. Yet these personages think of themselves as exemplifying kinds of behaviour or moral paradigms of action after ethical configurations, *exempla*, which would have been familiar to Cicero or Seneca. They possess no individual psychology in the modern sense at all. The two dreams, Criseyde's and Troilus', indicate clearly the relationship of individual unconscious mind to waking, external reality. In their ordinary rational conduct, the lovers' motivational field is much more sensitive to the signs and signals of the society before which it enacts its emotional drama, hence the primary need for secrecy and obliqueness—but not arising from the needs of modern 'other-directedness' (if one may be allowed Reisman's convenient terminology). Chaucer's characters are related to a 'tradition-oriented' society where shame is the deepest expression of moral failure, a simpler emotion than guilt. No matter how painful Criseyde's 'guilt' at betraying Troilus, her physical existence would have been impossible if she had lost her honour, her 'shame'.[88] Her society would have seen to that.

[88] Héraucourt's analysis (*Die Wertwelt Chaucers*) of these key words bears out this assumption.

In addition to the implications of fourteenth-century social assumptions, Chaucerian characters in this work also have had their psychological areas considerably adjusted to a pagan world of values. We cannot say at this point in time whether Chaucer considered this representation of antique behaviour as a simplification or a complication of the motivational and social field. It seems to us that the motivation of *Troilus* almost certainly displays a greater degree of self-consciousness in action than almost any other medieval work of art. Yet the penitential complexities (arising out of a sense of religious guilt) of the Parson or the exchanges of Amans and Genius in the *Confessio Amantis* are infinitely more elaborate. But I suspect that they are merely more elaborate, not more complex—if we are thinking of accounts of *moral psychology in action*—as changing forces working together on more than one person's temperament and character. Amans in this respect is more like one of Zola's temperamental diagrams, another version of *la méthode scientifique*. The Parson's world of complex moral analysis and expiation is only an expositional model. Further, Chaucer's characters in this poem have been given an Aristotelian moral consistency according to the Horatian exposition of dramatic character in the *Ars Poetica*. The personages show 'tragic' and 'dramatic' modelling beyond anything which Boccaccio had in mind.

The dreams of the main characters show Chaucer's clear, accurate grasp of the mechanics of classical and medieval psychology dream analysis in detail and in general. Dr A. C. Spearing's recent attempt to see Criseyde's dream in both modern and ancient terms highlights modern difficulties.[89] The sources of her dream-imagery come from wholly rational areas of prior usage and personal experience. The animal 'origins' have nothing to do with modern sexuality or the theory of the primordial. Criseyde's dream belongs to the category of *somnium* which requires 'interpretation' but in Ovid's phrase it is an *equivalent* dream. It is not experienced with either fear or joy. It has nothing to do with anxiety or wish-fulfilment in modern or ancient terminology. Criseyde's dream is a symbolic account of her falling deeply in love with Troilus. Her moral decision is shown here being accomplished at the subliminal level. This can be so accomplished without loss of moral validity for this is a rational dream not an irrational *swevening*. Its imagery has been assimilated from Criseyde's memory of Antigone's song which she had heard earlier in the afternoon during a crucial and wholly unshared moment of emotional activity. Unlike

[89] A. C. Spearing, *Criticism and Medieval Poetry*, London (1964), pp. 141–7.

Troilus' later dream, it is wholly private in reference; it has no general, public, referential area. But its significance is absolutely clear: it requires no interpretation by the poet-figure.

The nightingale singing 'a lay of love' introduces Criseyde to sleep and deposits in her mind the bird-image for her own lover Troilus, who, as a royal suitor, appears in her dream as an eagle. The traditional, poetic nature of this image has been commented on at length by Professor Bennett. In Criseyde's memory of Antigone's 'lay of love', the original power of Amor was expressed in the image of the sun which no person could bear to look upon directly because of its overwhelming brightness (II.862ff.). The eagle in medieval bestiary tradition and lore of natural science can endure to look on the brightness of the sun.[90] He is unique in the animal kingdom in this respect. Thus, the eagle-lover, the royal suitor Troilus, and the very source of the supreme power in love itself are associated in Criseyde's subconscious mind. The eagle exchanges his heart for Criseyde's. This, too, has been remembered from Antigone's song: 'My deare herte, and al myn owen knyght/In which myn herte growen is so faste/And his in me . . .' Even the lack of Criseyde's fear in this exchange reflects Antigone's turn of phrase: 'Now woot I wel, ther is no peril inne.' This answers Criseyde's earlier fears. The colour of the eagle, no doubt generally representing the purity of the lover-figure, owes something to Antigone, who, in assuring Criseyde of the bliss in love, is described as 'fresshe Antigone, the white'. Criseyde has thus moved from being 'somewhat able to converte' (II.903) to a complete state of conversion.

In order to end this 'dramatic' reading version of Chaucer's *Book of Troilus*, it remains to give a brief account of the whole of the work as seen from the dramatic point of view since I have concentrated my argument mainly on the structures of books II and V. To summarize: unlike Boccaccio's segmental, romance structure (compare Boccaccio's use of '*argomenti*'), *Troilus* has a scenic and dramatic plot structure which is altogether more complex. Chaucer manages this by the use of climactic sequences which no longer relate to a mainly lyrical excursus (dependent on the identification of the *autore* with Troilo), but which

[90] Cf. Isidore, *Etymologiae*, XII.7 ('*De Auibus*'). Criseyde's realistic imagining of the eagle's 'longe clawes' has been placed there from Chaucer's memory of *Purgatorio* IX.27, as reflected in *House of Fame* II.37: 'his clawes starke.' From Criseyde's point of view they may reflect her earlier seeing of Troilus in his armour returning from battle: 'For bothe he hadde a body and myght/To don that thing, as well as hardynesse.'

have been formed into a connected, dramatic, deployment of 'scenes' which are differentiated and pointed by character-grouping and a precise sense of time. The passage of time in *Il Filostrato* is vague and for the purpose of lyrical and personal expressiveness ill defined. This vagueness of temporal values is deliberate on Boccaccio's part. It is part of his way of extending lyrical, symbolic autobiography into courtly romance. It is utterly typical of nearly all Boccaccio's experimentation with Dante and with the antique world—with the exception of the *Teseida*. In Chaucer, time-values are carefully exploited in order to give the scenes greater expressive power in their own right. Roughly, there are four main types of formal organization in *Troilus*:

(1) The overall tragic and dramatic orientation into five books corresponding to act division in Seneca's plays, as expounded for Roman tragedy by Horace in the *Ars Poetica* and Nicolas Trivet's *Commentary* to Seneca's tragedies.

(2) The dramatic and triadic organization into a beginning–middle–end sequence of 'wo to wel' and 'after oute of ioie' which produces the pattern: [1–2]+[3]+[4–5].

(3) A closely connected amatory time-pattern which produces another beginning–middle–end sequence:

intense: books 1–3: close time from 30 April to after 12 May.

loose: book 4: short actual duration (cf. 1327, roughly a fortnight) but treated narratively as vague, personal and introspective tragic time.

intense: book 5: close time, from the day of departure+ten days+ six days+one month+all the remaining time until the end of Troilus' life.

This treatment of intensity of time, dividing into three sections, resembles the distribution of mileage in the organization of the sense of duration of time in *Canterbury Tales*, cf. p. 96.

(4) The separate book structures with their complex internal patterns.

The structures of each book are carefully distinguished from each other. Unlike Boccaccio's *Il Filostrato* they have a normative pattern of length as well as regularity in the use of classical invocations. The pattern of book I falls into two main sections which reflects the amalgamation of *Il Filostrato* I and II. The successful fusion is managed by placing the climax of part I in the *cantus Troili* (especially imported from Petrarch) in lines 400–20, and then using the rest of Boccaccio's narrative sequence (to l. 546) as a transition to the second part (made up of 72 stanzas) which is entirely concerned with the *sermocinatio* between Pandarus and Troilus. This section, scene 2, 72 stanzas+*con-clusio* in 5 stanzas (an epitome-history) making 77 stanzas, is almost exactly the length of scene 1 in 79 stanzas. Scene 2, although it makes extensive use of Boccaccio's dialogue, has been given a new climactic pattern through the continual importation of imagery taken from medicine or psychological medicine. None of this is in Boccaccio, e.g. lines 561–74; 572: disese; 707: cure; 727: frenesie; 747–9; 757: cure; 857: helyng, leche, wounde; 886: gan the veyne of Troilus to blede; 916: blanche fevere; 1086–91. This use of recurring imagery turns the whole sequence from a mere dialogue into a psychological investigation, a medical examination, with its own interest and pattern of resolution. This pattern recalls the passages between the poet and the knight-figure in the *Book of the Duchess*. Thus, book I seems to have a simple open structure which recounts the falling in love of Troilus in a progressively tightening, introspective direction and which has its proper dramatic climax in the objectification and neutralization of the mental 'disese', leaving Troilus partially healed.

The structure of book II (after the invocation) falls into two main scenes which recall the pattern of book I but with a more complex use of the reader's consciousness of the passage of time. As I have argued earlier in the chapter, the first scene uses a single day sequence which ends dramatically with the sealing of the letter to Criseyde (stanza 156). The second half of the book (stanzas 157–251) begins scenically, but with the close of the second day (another prolonged night conversation between Troilus and Pandarus) the narrative becomes more varied and rapid in moving between character-groups rather than utilizing time-values. Thus, the second part comprises the various activities of Pandarus in bringing the lovers together in person in a single place. Scene 1 shows Pandarus acting separately on behalf of the pair, and part 2 comprises all the interconnected actions which bring the characters even closer together. Chaucer uses climactic rhythms alien to Boccaccio, especially the scenic arrangement in Criseyde's house where all three characters are seen together for the first time; and this arrangement prepares us for the culmination at Deiphebus' house (ll. 1092–755). Thus, book II is more scenically organized in terms of groupings of the chief personages, localities, and in the careful use of time-consciousness to point the development of the action and the progress of moral awareness in the reader. Book I's two-part division moved from mixed narration to the scenic concentrated dialogue and psychological investigation. Book II's two-part structure moves from the concentrated double single-day scenes to a more various and mixed *narratio* which finally brings the lovers face to face.

The principles for the construction of book III have been suggested by *Il Filostrato*, but with an increased philosophical emphasis imported from Boethius' *De Consolatione*. Book III is basically an enclosed, echoic structure: the invocation of the author and the concluding *cantus Troili* (drawing on the same Boethian themes and images) encloses a three-part narrative sequence. The identification of the *autore* and Troilo was chiefly lyrical and emotional; in Chaucer the identification lies in the philosophical views of the author and his lover. What the author invokes at the beginning of book III is confirmed more fully in Troilus' philosophical hymn. The enclosed three-part narrative traces progressively the physical, emotional and moral development of the lovers: (1) stanzas 8–170, the events leading up to the trysting of the lovers; (2) stanzas 171–218, the first night of the consummation; (3) 219ff., the second encounter and its moral and philosophical significance. Time-values are important here. This three-part narrative movement suggests to Chaucer the basis for the pattern of the next book.

Book IV, after the tragic *invocatio*, falls into three parts:
(1) stanzas 5–136, which is made up of excursions and alarums, and consists of a record of the political events and their effects on the chief characters, first singly, then with Pandarus. This section ends with the lovers' agreement to meet;
(2) stanzas 137–61. This is made up of the wholly Chaucerian temple scene which provides the religious setting for Troilus' long and philosophically confused expression of fatalism. Troilus' tragic determinism is answered (inadequately) by Pandarus' temporizing refutation;
(3) stanzas 162–243. This concluding scene comprises the meeting and dialogue with Criseyde which takes us to the brink of suicide.

Throughout this book character-grouping and time-values have been very important in establishing the rhythmic, scenic movement of the narrative. Although the book closes with a sentimental emphasis, the philosophical monologue lies darkly at the centre of the narrative with its disturbing negativism and tragic passivity. Yet the main sequence of action must lead up to the final trysting of the doomed lovers.

The structure of book V is by far the most complex and interesting of the poem. It is more numerously subdivided into scenes, especially in relation to time-values, physical setting and the climactic moments of recognition of the falling trajectory of the linked fortunes of Troilus and Troy. Book V is divided into five scenes:

(1) stanzas 1–98, which are composed of mixed narrative, complaints and songs which take us rapidly to the advent of the compacted tenth day;

(2) stanzas 99–157; these take us to the Grecian camp and Criseyde. Her decision to attempt to rejoin Troilus is taken exactly on the eve of the tenth day. At once we move from Diomedes' thoughts to the descriptive stanzas of three lovers. So unexpectedly, so prematurely placed, the stanzas have both a prophetic sense and an oddly commemorative finality, as if we are looking at funeral brasses in the future. We finally embark on the tenth day but not in terms of Troy or Troilus. Dramatically, the initiation of the compacting of Diomedes and Criseyde takes place on the tenth day, and is concluded the day after;

(3) stanzas 158–220 bring us back to the tenth day in Troy. The overlapping of the time-scale, so that we have to go back in time to reach Troilus, emphasizes his hopeless passivity. Events have indeed overtaken him. Now Chaucer increases the awareness of the passage of time; the time sequence shows a more minute divisioning: dawn, before noon, thence to afternoon, evening, the closing of the city gates (l. 1183). Now follows the physical and mental decline of Troilus: Troilus' dream, his letter, the morbid persistence of the dream which culminates in Cassandra's exposition of the historical nemesis about to overtake Troy. Personal tragedy and epical history suddenly combine. Individual life is being swallowed up in the sweep of destructive history;

(4) stanzas 221–55 begin with the violent physical image of the plucking alive of the bird Troy, as its feathers of joy are gradually pulled away. The image has been remembered from the *Roman* 11544ff. in a description of the destruction of the unfortunate:

> *Trestuit seur les povres genz cueurent,*
> *N'est nus qui despoillier nes vueille,*
> *Tuit s'afublent de leur despueille,*
> *Trestuit de leur sustance hument,*
> *Senz eschauder tous vis les plument.*

Every one of them falls upon the poor, not one shows the slightest inclination to resist despoiling them. All deck themselves out in the stolen plumage, they suck them dry; scalding them not, they pluck the birds alive.

The very next stanza presents the death of Hector, the signal moment when Troy begins its sharpest descent into final destruction. Troilus' morbidity persists; Criseyde's temporizing letter seems to come from beyond the grave, or rather, seems to be a communication from the living to the dead. The narrative rhythm is now that of disintegration. Troilus discovers the brooch and recognizes the truth of his recurring dream. Troilus now decides to seek his own death honourably in battle. This scene makes up the tragic fragmentation of the life of Troy and Troilus.

(5) The last scene, stanzas 256–67, consist of the envoi, the death of Troilus, the apotheosis of his soul and the author's final address. The effect of this long, falling rhythm is paralleled later in music in Purcell's last scene before the final aria in *Dido and Aeneas*, where Dido's closing recitative addressed to Belinda is punctuated by a series of descending harpsichord arpeggios (descending in note of origin) which at the end of the recitative is taken up by the continuo in a further descending figure before it moves upwards into 'when I am laid in earth'.

This five-scene structure mirrors the overall five-act structure of the poem and has the coherence of a miniature drama: exposition, complication, catastrophe (the 'falsing' of Troilus on the tenth day), dissolution and the final denouement. This miniaturizing of the total poetic structure was probably suggested to Chaucer by book XII of the *Thebaid* (a work very much in the poet's thoughts throughout book V) which is itself an epyllion, a 'Theseid', a miniature epic. But whereas in Statius this repetition of the total structure only contributes to the looseness and episodicism of the narrative construction (Statius squanders a magnificent style on an absurd subject), in Chaucer's tragic-dramatic form repetition creates a more concentrated, doubly dramatic, emphatic experience of the moment of tragic consummation.

We can grasp clearly the main difference between Boccaccio's poem and Chaucer's. The emotion which involves the *autore* within the narrative he is creating arises out of his own experience, it derives from life. Chaucer's gradual entrapment within his own narrative is more progressive and arises out of the act of literary creation. The reader emotionally identifies with Boccaccio through the open use of symbolic biography. He is at the source behind the literary impulse: the reader has become a substitute *autore*. In Chaucer's poem, the reader retains his own identity as audience, for the author's emotions arise on behalf of his own creation. Chaucer and the English audience are not aware of the work symbolizing any other form of activity. Together they seem to be experiencing directly the created reality. Boccaccio's poem has a simple, emotional origin and its aesthetic appeal is to the original, primitive and romantically lyrical. Its narrative form hides another form inside it, the lyric. Chaucer's narrative structure, with all its epical complexity and distance, also hides another form within it—the immediacy of the tragic drama.

CHAPTER SEVEN

The Envoi a Scogan and the Envoi a Bukton

The two extant Chaucerian verse epistles to Scogan and Bukton tell us a great deal about the poet's less public rhetorical voice. These two poems, though slight, are of a high degree of artistic craftsmanship and display a degree and kind of sophistication of tone, a literary elegance and cultivation, which we are more usually asked to associate with the Renaissance, or even with the Augustan temper of social verse of the eighteenth century. Yet this same view of life embodied in cultivated verse is available in the latter part of the 1390s.

If one were to attempt to reconstruct Chaucer's attitude to the verse epistle where would one begin? Most obviously, with the remains of the Ovidian heroic epistle embodied in the *Legend of Good Women* and with the two letters incorporated in book V of *Troilus and Criseyde*. Less obviously, one might begin with the *Envoi a Scogan* or *a Bukton*.

The fragments of the *Heroides* in the *Legend* tell us little or nothing about Chaucer's feeling for the Ovidian heroic epistle. Here the total epistolary format has been abandoned and the heroine's words or quotation of Ovid conform more or less to the narrative lament pattern common to Dido in book I of the *House of Fame* and Criseyde in books II and IV of *Troilus*. Chaucer did not have to rearrange much, for the epistolary texture of the *Heroides* lies mainly in an opening formula approximating to ordinary Roman letter-writing usage: where the writer and the recipient are identified and the primary occasion for writing is mentioned:

> *Hospita, Demophoon, tua te Rhodopeia Phyllis*
> *ultra promissum tempus abesse queror.*
> (*Heroides* II.1–2)

Although Ovid rings many changes on this formula he occasionally omits it. Compare Medea to Jason:

At tibi Colchorum, memini, regina vacavi,
ars mea cum peteres ut tibi ferret opem.
(*Heroides* XII.1–2)

In each case the conclusion of the heroic epistle lacks any stylistic reference to a letter-writing convention of 'signing off'. Thus, the dramatic quality of Ovid's verse is only loosely connected with a letter form. Essentially, the *Heroides* are theatrical *suasoriae*. Chaucer has merely carried the liberation a stage further to suit his own narrative requirements.

In the letters in *Troilus* V, some trouble has been taken to create an epistolary impression. In the case of Troilus' letter (ll. 1317–421) there is an exordium formula where the writer identifies himself (in terms of his function as lover and 'servant' which he imagines, mistakenly, to be unique to him) employing the 'I recommend myself to you' form of opening address.[1] The letter also uses a signing off device common to classical and medieval usage:

> And far now wel, myn owen swete herte.

Apart from these touches, the content of the letter is stylistically indistinct from any of the 'nounal', phraseological verse belonging to the amatory complaint genre.[2] Criseyde's letter (ll. 1590–631) also makes use of an opening formula: 'I send you health', and identifies the recipient (but, significantly, not the writer):

> How myght a wight in torment and in drede
> And heleles, yow sende as yet gladnesse?

The letter ends with the same farewell *topos*. Subscriptions and signatures accompany the letters (Le vostre T and La vostre C) in some MSS. but not in others.[3] Given the normal rhyme-royal pattern of the poem these touches cannot derive from Chaucer *ipse* but must have been incorporated from scribal marginalia.

Chaucer's polite, graceful and conventional style in these letters sets the tone for the vast number of amatory verse epistles which was to be written in England in the fifteenth century.[4] Incidentally, Chaucer's

---

[1] Cf. Norman Davis, *Paston Letters*, Oxford (1958), nos 1–5, 7, 8, 10, 11, etc., for this formula in ordinary use.

[2] Cf. Emrys Jones, *Surrey: Poems*, Oxford (1964), p. xxiii.

[3] MSS. Cp,J,Sl(Le vostre T); H_1, D, S_1, S_2 (La vostre C) include. The rest omit.

[4] Cf. *Index*, p. 753 for a list. The list requires revision, however. Some items are not epistles while other possible items have been missed out.

letter style closely resembles that of two verse epistles written by
Deschamps to ladies of his acquaintance, *Balades* 1244 and 1245.[5]
These letters are formally *balades* in three stanzas with refrain plus envoi
and refrain. They are really '*balades en maniere de lettre*'. Deschamps'
manner in these two *balade* letters does not correspond to his usual
epistolary style reserved for more intimate exchanges.[6] The intimate
verse letters are long rambling affairs poured out in enumerative
octosyllabic couplets. The style is similar in Latin and French. They are
racy, unsophisticated and crammed with detail. Opening, closing and
dating formulae are the rule:[7]

> *Et Dieux qui tous biens fait et donne,*
> *Vous puist telenement ordonner,*
> *Qu'en la fin vous vueille donner*
> *Son saint regne qui pas ne fine,*
> *Si vray que j'eusse en la cuisine*
> *Au jour d'uy voluntiers esté*
> *De mon frere d'umilité,*
> *Delez vous touz pour vous servir,*
> *Si j'en peusse avoir loisir!*
> *Et mauditte soit mon assise*
> *Par qui je pers mon entreprise!*
> *Escript a la Ferté Alès*
> *Ou il n'a que frommaige et lés*
> *Et IIII causes seulement,*
> *Dur vin et mauvais logement,*
> *Ce deuisisme jour de decembre,*
> *En une reumatique chambre.*

Although medieval manuals existed for the writing of actual letters,[8]
the various poetry manuals contain little about verse epistles. Rhetorically, at least, the genre simply did not exist as a distinct formal unit.
In practice, medieval Latin poets cultivated the form after the Ovidian

[5] *Oeuvres complètes* (SATF), VII, pp. 122–5.
[6] Cf. *Lettre* 1358 to Radulphus Vitardus (VII. 128–31); *lettres* 1406–21 (VIII.3–73).
The best example, perhaps, of this kind of verse in English is the first 27 lines of
Dunbar's comic 'Dirige' which are in the Deschampsian epistle style (cf. James
Kinsley, *William Dunbar: Poems*, London (1958), pp. 98–9).
[7] *Lettre* 1419, ll. 94–110 (VIII, p. 66): '*A mes Seigneurs de la Chambre de Comptes,*
disans en l'Ostel de Sire Guillaume Brunel, Tresorier de France.'
[8] Cf. those quoted by C. S. Baldwin, *Medieval Rhetoric and Poetic to 1400*, New
York (1959), pp. 212–27.

distichs of the *Tristia* and the *Ex Ponto*.[9] Although these poets of the
eleventh and twelfth centuries wrote about intimate things, their style
is thoroughly Ovidian: polished, epigrammatic, learned and full of
mythological ornament. There is nothing of the easy, refined Horatian
sermo in their style.

If we bear in mind the Ovidian preoccupations of the French
medieval Latin poets, the '*balade*' and the octosyllabic 'scribbling' style
of Deschamps, it is surprising to see none of this reflected in Chaucer's
two genuine, independent, poetic epistles, the *Envoi a Scogan* and the
Envoi a Bukton.[10] Perhaps equally surprising is that stylistically these
poems bear no resemblance to the letters of Troilus and Criseyde which
so completely came to dominate later exercises in the verse epistle in
England.

Although the two letters (especially the *Envoi a Scógan*) are remarkably independent of poetic models, yet it is valuable to ask if either or
both can be related to any previous poems. The *Envoi a Bukton* has
been compared (unsuccessfully) by Brusendorff and Kittredge to
Deschamps' *Balade* 823.[11] The most striking imagery of the *Envoi a
Scogan* (ll. 38ff.) has been linked by Professor Robinson with Alan of
Lille's prose and verse prefaces to the *Anticlaudianus*; this same imagery
has been associated with Ovid's *Tristia* V.xii.31ff. by Kittredge.[12]
Chaucer's lines (36–40):

> Nay, Scogan, say not so, for I m'excuse—
> God helpe me so—in no rym, dowteles,
> Ne thynke I never of slep to wake my muse
> That rusteth in my shethe stille in pees.
> While I was yong, I put hir forth in prees;

cannot be linked with either Alan or Ovid. The image which is most
pertinent in Alan (prologus 3):

[9] Matthew of Vendôme, Hildebert of Lavardin, Baudry of Bourgueil, Godfrey
of Reims, Radulf of Tartarius. Of these, Radulf is perhaps the most Ovidian.
[10] The title '*L'Envoi*' is normally interpreted to mean 'a poem in balade measure
having an *envoie* as a concluding stanza' (*MED*). The poem to Scogan is cited as
an example of the sb. in this sense. *Scogan* is not in *balade* measure. 'L'Envoi'
here means 'a letter', as the Latin subtitling in the Camb. Univ. Lib. MS. Gg. 4.27
('*Litera de Scogan per G.C.*') indicates. A. C. Baugh, *Chaucer's Major Poetry*,
London (1964), p. 538 correctly identifies the poem as a 'verse epistle'.
[11] Cf. A. Brusendorff, *The Chaucer Tradition*, Copenhagen (1925), p. 487; G. L.
Kittredge, *MLN* 24, pp. 14ff.
[12] Cf. F. N. Robinson, *The Works of Geoffrey Chaucer*, p. 863.

Ne iaceat calamus scabra rubigine torpens

really turns on the notion of the 'reed pen' as 'rusty' in the way that grain neglected or unused lies 'mildewed'. The image is developed in line 6: '*et in tenui lasciuit harundine musa*' ('and the muse sings in the thin reed'). Ovid's lines:

> *adde quod ingenium longa rubigine laesum*
> *torpet et est multi, quam fuit ante, minus.*

Besides, my talent, injured by long neglect, is dull, much inferior to what it was before.

do not properly contain a physical image. '*Rubigo*' in this passage has, in effect, an abstract force. Moreover, the operative element in Chaucer's imagery is not so much 'rust' as the underlying metaphor of the pen=sword. The verbal basis of the image derives partly from the Labin sb. *stylus* which meant either a 'pen' or a 'dagger'.[13] But the complex use of this image reflected in lines 36–40 is derived from Horace, *Satires* II.ll.39–44, a hitherto unsuspected source:[14]

> *Sed hic stylus haud petet ultro*
> *quenquam animantem; et me veluti custodiet ensis*
> *vagina tectus . . .*
> *. . . O pater et rex*
> *Juppiter, ut pereat positum rubigine telum,*
> *Nec quisquam noceat cupido mihi pacis!*

But this pen of mine shall not wilfully attack any man breathing; and shall defend me like a sword that is sheathed in the scabbard; . . . O Jupiter, father and sovereign, may my weapon laid aside wear away with rust, and may no one injure me, who am desirous of peace!

The fundamental force of the image in the Horatian passage (and in most of the examples cited in footnote 13 below) is that a pen is like

[13] Cf. similar uses of this ambiguity in Cicero, *Philippiae* 2.14.34, *Oratio pro Cluentio* 44.123; Pliny, *Epistulae* 7.9.7; Ovid, *Epistulae ex Ponto* IV.XIV.20. Chaucer's use of the image is more compressed in that he uses no concrete sb. to refer to the pen. He allows the physical association of 'shethe' and 'rusteth' with 'muse' to create the traditional sense.

[14] This Horatian passage is not quoted by John of Salisbury in the *Polycraticus* or the *Metalogicon* nor does it seem to have been imitated by medieval Latin poets. It does not occur in any medieval *florilegia* of Horace that I have seen. It is perhaps valuable in proving that Chaucer knew Horace.

a sword when it is employed in writing criticism or satiric verses. Baugh's paraphrase of Chaucer's lines is incomplete:[15]

> As for me, my muse is rusting in its sheath. There was a time when this wasn't so, but all things pass away.

Chaucer has been jestingly exposing and castigating Scogan for his failure to maintain good faith in his recent love affair. He adds that Cupid will have his revenge on the middle-aged. The author then suggests that Scogan is saying to himself 'the old goat is amusing himself in a bit of mocking verse'. Chaucer's reply amounts to a playful, depreciating denial that he is willing or able to write verse—verse of a particular kind, verse that is capable of hurting.[16] After all, the poem humorously chides Scogan for his lack of faith towards his mistress and the envoi makes it clear that Scogan is also neglecting his friend Chaucer. The poem ends with the warning never to 'defy Love again'— or to neglect Chaucer. The reworking of the Horatian passage implies that Chaucer is at once assuring Scogan that he is not really 'getting at him' and suggesting that the aged, neglected Chaucer in this poem has a hit or two left in his sword. Chaucer's ambiguous blend of playfulness and seriousness is typically Horatian. And this brings us to the dominant style of the epistle. It is not 'courtly', nor 'Ovidian' but 'Horatian'. The borrowed Horatian passage and imagery keynote the prevailing artistic mode. One of the most important elements in the Horatian epistle and satire was its easy, urbane, conversational tone.[17] Chaucer has in this poem and in the *Envoi a Bukton* tried to capture the easy, conversational style of the Horatian epistle. It is difficult to prove conclusively that the poem should convey this impression. The following combination of factors probably contributes to an urbane, conversational effect: (1) the large amount of syntactic enjambment combined with a consistent use of inversions and suspensions which suggests intelligence and sophistication. There is a marked absence of implied verse units in terms of single line lengths. At least two stanzas are one, continuous, developing period; (2) the marked absence of final, 'inflexional' syllables (-e, -es) pronounced for metrical value. In forty-nine lines there are only ten possible cases. The balance has been shifted from syllabic consciousness towards a purely accentual tendency without any dis-

---

[15] Baugh, *op. cit.*, p. 538.
[16] For example, the phrase 'putte forth in prees' in this context does not mean 'to compete' (Robinson) but 'to offer battle' (cf. *The Former Age*, line 33).
[17] Cf. E. Fraenkel, *Horace*, Oxford (1959), pp. 309, 399.

ruption of the iambic smoothness of the rhythm. Sense naturally is supported by stress; (3) a complete absence of verse tags or fillers; (4) a complete absence of 'poetic' *fine amour* terms (e.g. 'smerte', 'intent', 'servise', 'pain', 'proof', 'stedfastnes', etc.) in a context where such terms might be expected. In line 44 the nouns *grace* ('power to bestow favours'), *honour* and *worthyness* refer to the values of *philotimía* not to the courtly values of *philhedonía*. While the syntax, imagery and tone of the poem imitate Horace's satires and epistles, the structure is not typical of these Horatian genres. The poem's structure is indirect and disproportionate.[18] The whole poem, with the exception of the envoi, rebukes Scogan elaborately for his cowardly behaviour towards a woman. It is only in the envoi that the 'real' subject emerges: Chaucer, in unrewarded obscurity in Greenwich, reminds Scogan, at court at Windsor, that Cicero in the *De Amicitia* recommends true friends to share possessions should adversity overtake one or the other.[19] The love affair of Scogan is turned into a poetic equation for Scogan's friendship with Chaucer. Hence the half-concealed force of the concluding warning 'never eft Love defye'.[20] It may be suggested that the structure of the letter to Scogan perhaps derives not from Horace's epistles or satires but from his odes.[21]

Chaucer's achievement in the letter genre is stylistically distinct from that of his medieval forerunners and of his fifteenth- and sixteenth-century imitators. Only one English verse epistle[22] of Charles of Orleans aims at a conversational style. It is only moderately effective for it fails to achieve easy intimacy. Charles has not yet shed the time-worn amatory phraseology of the *fine amour* mentality—or at least has not put them to sufficiently fresh use:[23]

> Offence? nay, þe offence hit is in me!
> For what, as loo, y ought me welle content
> In what ye say—so hit yowre plesere be:
> The which þe amverse took in myn entent.

---

[18] Cf. W. H. French, 'The Meaning of Chaucer's *Envoy to Scogan*', *PMLA* 48 (1913), pp. 289–92.
[19] Cf. Jean de Meun's paraphrase of Cicero in the English version, *Romaunt* 5513.
[20] Cf. Cicero, *De Amicitia* VIII.26ff. where he links Love and Friendship etymologically: '*Amor enim, ex quo amicitia nominatur est . . .*' and XVII.100 *passim*.
[21] Cf. *Odes*, II.5; IV.12 for good examples of indirection as a structural device.
[22] R. R. Steele, *The English Poems of Charles of Orleans*, EETS (1941), pp. 206–7.
[23] Cf. Wyatt's more original handling in 'Greting to you bothe yn hertye wyse' (K. Muir, *Collected Poems of Sir Thomas Wyatt*, London (1949), pp. 139–40).

> I, crewelle, lo, and ye to pacient
> Me to rebewke as of my gret outrage
> And squaring of my ruggid fowle langage!

In the *Envoi a Scogan* the command of urbane conversational syntax and style, of sly and playful use of mythology, of structural indirection, together with the Horatian borrowing, marks Chaucer out as the first English poet to master the essentials of the Augustan verse epistle.

While the letter to Scogan would seem, then, to grow out of a direct Horatian reminiscence, the letter to Bukton has no such ostensible origin. Yet it, too, is a carefully contrived Horatian answer to a question which had already had another sort of answer from a Roman satirist. That satire is the sixth of Juvenal, addressed in part to Postumus who is about to marry. The personal addressee and cause of the poem is only an artistic excuse for a very long and very savage diatribe against women. It ends in universal *femme fatalité*, the streets choked with Danaides and Eriphylae:

> *Mane Clytaemnestram nullus non vicus habebit.*

Not a street but will possess its Clytaemnestra.

But the account against which Chaucer's poem is addressed is not the Juvenalian original but Jean de Meun's summary of *Satire* VI in the *Roman* 8735ff.:

> Juvenaus meismes escrie
> A Postumous qui se marie:
> 'Postumous, veauz tu fame prendre?
> Ne peuz tu pas trouver a vendre
> Ou harz, ou cordes, ou chevestres,
> Ou saillir hors pars les fenestres,
> Don l'en peur haut e loing voeir,
> Ou laisser tei dou pont choeir?
> Quel Forsenerie te meine
> A cet torment, a cete peine?'

For Juvenal likewise wrote to his friend Postumus who intended to get married: 'Postumus, you're going to marry? Can't you find for sale a rope or halter or any kind of cord? Can't you jump from a high open window, or fall into the river from some bridge? Which of the Furies forces you to embrace such torment, such pain?'

This summary represents *Satire* VI.28–32:

> *Certe sanus eras! Uxorem, Postume, ducis?*
> *Dic, qua Tisiphone, quibus exagitare colubris?*
> *Ferre potes dominam, salvis tot restibus, ullam?*
> *Quum pateant altae caligantesque fenestrae?*
> *Quum tibi vicinum se praebeat Aemilius pons?*

Well, you used to be sane! You, Postumus, going to marry? What Tisiphone, what snakes are driving you mad? Can you submit to be the slave of any woman whilst so many halters are available? so long as high and dizzy windows are open and the Aemilian bridge presents itself so conveniently?

The Old French suppresses some of the local classical detail (e.g. *Aemilius pons*) and expands on the image of binding with ropes, halters and cords. It also gives *Satire* VI a poetic register which it never had; that is, Jean states that it was conceived as a letter to a friend: '*Juvenaus . . . escrie a Postumous.*'

Chaucer's letter to Bukton is just such a verse epistle, couched not in Juvenalian indignation and violent, repulsive images, but in the quiet, calm, gently jesting style of Horace—a style abounding in indirection, subtle parallelism, double negatives, modifications, self-accusations and ironic reproaches rather than the Juvenalian attack frontal. The formal structure (three stanzas and an envoi) is evenly divided into balanced units in pairs: the first stanza balances Holy Writ (John 18: 38) against personal experience; the second balances what he is not going to say (yet does say) against personal statement; the third balances St Paul against a more incisive personal injunction; the envoi balances personal exhortation against the advice of the poet's own creation, the Wife of Bath. Here (presumably) the types of contrasted statement, written authority and experience, will exactly reinforce each other:[24]

> My maister Bukton, whan of Criste our kyng
> Was axed what ys trouthe or sothefastnesse,
> He nat a worde answerde to that axinge
> As who saith 'noo man is al trew', I gesse.
> And therfore, though I hight to expresse
> The sorwe and woo that is in mariage,

[24] The only MS. authority is that of Fairfax 16 (folio 193b). I quote from this version. Its readings are ignored by Robinson and are not noted in the textual apparatus.

I dar not writen of hyt noo wikkednesse
Lest y my-self falle eft in swich dotage.

I wol nat seyn how that hyt is the cheyne
Of Sathanas on which he gnaweth euere—
But I dar seyn, were he oute of his peyne,
As by his wille, he wolde be bounde nevere.
But thilke doted foole that [e]fte hath leuere
Y-cheyned be than out of prisoun crepe,
God lete him neuer fro his woo disseuere
Ne noo man him bewayle, though he wepe!

But yet, lest thow doo worse, 'take a wyfe,
Bet ys to wedde than brenne in worse wise.
But thow shalt have sorwe on thy flessh thy lyfe
And ben thy wifes thral, as seyn these wise.
And yf that hooly writte may nat suffyse,
Experience shal the teche: so may happe
That the were lever to be take in Frise
Than eft falle of weddynge in the trappe.

[Envoi]

This lytel writte, prouerbes, or figure
I sende yow. Take kepe of hyt I rede:
Vnwise is he that kan noo wele endure.
Yf thow be siker put the nat in drede.
The wyfe of Bathe I pray yow that ye rede
Of this matere that we haue on honde.
God graunte yow your lyfe frely to lede
In fredam—for ful harde it is to be bonde.

A cautious and a quiet life is what Chaucer suggests. The poem's moral is deliberately isolatable in the Horatian double negative:

Vnwise is he that kan noo wele endure.

Like Jean, Chaucer dwells on images of binding, of the loss of liberty: the chain of Satan, the fettered prisoner, and finally 'ful harde it is to be bonde'. The whole plot of the poem consists in a piece of social and psychological tact. Chaucer, having been asked by Bukton to write a letter confirming his decision not to marry (proving 'the payne and woo that ben in mariage'), dares not to do so too openly, lest by taking up an extreme position against marriage, he should thereby fall into the opposite extreme and succumb to marrying himself. The poem is a moderate rejection of entering the state of matrimony not out of any judicious consideration of the alternatives but out of deadly fear of marriage itself!

The addressee is more difficult to identify, but Sir Peter Bukton of Holderness in East Yorkshire would seem to be the most reasonable candidate. What has not been noticed is the appropriateness of quoting that Canterburian paragon, the Wife of Bath, to Sir Peter. Bukton was one of the spellings (an earlier one) of the place name Boughton. And as we all know from the *Canterbury Tales* G 556, Boughton was in the 'Canterbury wey'. These two very private poems show Chaucer's close attention to, and intimate appreciation of, the mood and verse style which we now call 'Horatian'.

If we cast our minds back over the varied Chaucerian production of poems, from the early *Book of the Duchess* to the last Horatian epistles written during his ultimate retirement from public life, we can see one great consistency: the mimetic process is minutely concerned with artistic means and ends. All his form-bearing qualities exhibit an extremely close articulation of intention, form and content. Chaucer's abiding fascination with dream-poems stems from a philosophic concern with modifying a received idea of reality by means of a new, seemingly not wholly appreciated, experience of the original situation. On the other hand, the *Tales* are concerned with multiple views and versions of reality (and our ideas of reality) by means of a certain naturalism—by a realization of the commonplace image of the whole of human life as a journey or pilgrimage. Theseus in the *Knight's Tale* is concerned with the universe's parts and whole coherence in terms of Boethian perfection. Chaucer is interested in life's imperfection, its incompleteness and the comic vitality of its determination to prolong itself: 'at the worste it may yit shorte oure weye'—'entente', form and content have been perfectly adjusted. The *Legend* is a sophisticated, less public, forerunner of the unfinished, serial and penitential *oeuvre*. It arises out of private and court experience. It, too, has its appropriate style and form, delicately combining sincerity, irony and elegant pathos. *Troilus* gives us an authoritative version of the tragic contest of all our lives, interpreted through past fact, present fiction, and future hope, in so far as we can bear the painful limitations which we recognize in ourselves through the appreciation of the events of 'sondry londes' and 'sondry ages'. Through Chaucer's minute realization of what he understood as tragic form and the mode of the dramatic, the poetic, the historical and the tragic are genuinely identified:[25]

> The scene where Ulysses listens to the story of his own life is paradigmatic for both history and poetry; the 'reconciliation with reality', the catharsis which, according to Aristotle, was the essence of tragedy, and, according to Hegel, was the ultimate purpose of history, came about through the tears of remembrance.

In Shakespeare's later plays reconciliation through remembrance returns us, spectators or actors, no matter how altered (by theatrical experience, suffering, ageing or growing up) to a prosperous and optimistic sensation of existence. In Chaucer's tragic formulation we must be satisfied with loss itself[26] or with unrelated garlands of stars, or with compassionate but not quite satisfying promises of Eternity. The architectonics of *Troilus* are sustained and completed through the whole range of fused narrative-dramatic techniques. Critical attempts to see the poetry of Chaucer as 'inorganic form', just another example of medieval additive, loose patterning,[27] seem to me wholly misguided. I commented some time ago on the weakness of medieval aesthetics— that it is too often only a culture of style. Chaucer basically belongs to an order of creativeness which is interested in form as well as style. His mind and his intentions (in so far as we can reasonably imagine them) are as far from Lydgate's deliberate, flatfooted, honest confections as they are from Gower's charming, encyclopedic compilings—or Hoccleve's garrulous, touching obsessions with the bruises of his own life, in spite of the literary task at hand. He had long practice at the official desk, the hand going one way, the mind another. Langland's accumulative, multiplicative sense of verbal organization bears no resemblance to Chaucer's opulent fastidiousness. The only thing which links these figures together is the accident of time and the fact that some of them were aware of each other's existence. The educational shape of their literary culture ensured that they tended to read the same authors, to learn the same extracts, to have been trained to write from the same rhetorical system; but their relative successes in performing these activities would surely indicate the individual artist's ability to understand, assimilate, reproduce and, finally, to create anew.

[25] H. Arendt, *Between Past and Future*, p. 45.   [26] Cf. Seneca, Letter 98.10–11.
[27] Some of the arguments are openly *simpliste*, others such as Jordan's *Chaucer and the Shape of Creation* are more complicated, not to say grandiose, but the basic aesthetic assumptions remain simplifying and resistive to literary expansion.

In Chaucer we meet a mind we cannot patronize (in spite of some criticism)—a mind with immense technical resources in the arts of rhetoric and poetry, but with even greater resources in the art of reading literature at an excellent linguistic standard in at least four languages. A mind must be brought which attempts to be equal but not superior to the book. Chaucerian criticism on the whole seems happiest when relating Chaucer to the limitations of his contemporary writers, to tame conventions, to a range of ideas, complicated only in their being accommodated to the various academic arguments, otherwise narrow and largely unconsciously dismissive of the intellectual activity of the poet, his best-informed friends or the poetic fascinations of a great classical and late antique literature. Deschamps' contemporary praise and assessment of the living Chaucer always was nearer the truth.[28]

[28] Chaucer's literary aspects are characterized serially, first by *exampla*, then by images (the gardening image is central): Socrates, Seneca, Anglus, Ovid; an eagle of theoretical inquiry (a possible reference to the *House of Fame*), a gardener who has transplated a rosebush in England (a reference to the translation of the *Roman*), an 'earthly God of Love' (a possible reference to the *Legend of Good Women*), the lord of the manor of Helicon, a 'lofty poet' in whose garden Deschamps would figure as a lowly nettle. The best text and translation is that given by Paget Toynbee in the *Academy* for 14 November 1891, pp. 432–3. There is a later (and infinitely worse) text and translation by Jenkins (*MLN* 33 (1918), pp. 268–87). Some words and phrases are very obscure and much more remains to be done for the text and the allusions.

Moderatio, Moderation and Measure

The purpose of this appendix is to examine the concept of moderation in medieval Latin and vernacular authors strictly in terms of the writers which Chaucer is known to have read and may have known about first-hand or from quotation. I have deliberately refrained from trying to provide a more comprehensive account of the history of the concept in the philosophers and writers of classical antiquity. Professor Helen North's *Sophrosyne: Self-Knowledge and Self-Restraint in Greek Literature*, Cornell University Press (1966), collects nearly all the relevant material for a very wide study, including a chapter on Roman usage which contains a valuable section on Cicero. Professor North's short-comings (lack of appreciation of the subtlety of linguistic usage and neglect of the whole and intricate nature of the literary expression and formulation of the notion in certain authors, notably Sophocles) illus-trate some of the dangers of a compendious and lexicographical treat-ment.

The notion of 'moderation' in medieval Latin authors comes to be expressed in many overlapping lexical formulations: *moderatio, moderan-tia, moderamen, modestia, temperantia, mediocritas, modus, medium*. In Chaucer, the sbs. 'mesure', 'mene', 'attemperaunce', 'suffisaunce' corre-spond roughly to the Latin terminology and semantic areas. Concep-tually, the idea takes in the strict axiomatic sense of 'self-restraint' and extends as far as the more complex notion of 'moderation' as a 'mean' in the proportional relation between the 'extremes' in a neo-Aristo-telian system. Literary authors often seem to be blending several shades of meaning so as to exploit different philosophical aspects or even whole systems.

Briefly, one might say that the general history of the development of the ethical notion in medieval authors exhibits a division into three main schools of thought: (1) the patristic-based schemes of virtues and vices which had been developed by a Christian codification of the older pagan Four Virtues into principal or cardinal virtues. These Greek, Latin and Stoic constellations of virtues were utterly transformed by the theological emphasis of Christianity. The patristic treatment would seem to be chiefly concerned with absolute imperatives which in the case of the Cardinal Virtue of *temperantia* stresses the self-restraining, Ciceronian side of moderation, and consequently corresponds to the appropriate sense of the Greek sb. *sophrosyne*. This application is invariably preceptive, proscriptive and rigid. In some patristic writers Temperance as a principal virtue establishes a direct and subjective link with divine approval or even assimilation with God. (2) The neo-Platonic view of moderation which has two separate applications: (a) the cosmological which may be traced directly back through Boethius and Cicero to Plato's *Timaeus*, and (b) the ethical which is wholly separate and unrelated to the cosmological usage. The moral aspect is related to the popular Greek and Latin axiomatic application and shares the main features of the Christian and Ciceronian systems in that it tends to stress the 'self-controlling' side of moderation. It is often openly opposed to a peripatetic 'relational' value-system. (3) The Aristotelian doctrine of moderation emphasizing a proportional ethical system concerned analytically with *mediocritas* and the notion of the 'mean' as enunciated in the *Nicomachean Ethics* II and III. Outside the ethical works of Aristotle there is a tendency in him to relate the concept of the mean to wider contexts, including the social, literary, psychological and biological. One would have expected Plato with his penchant for analogy to have developed a connection between the ethical application and the cosmological. At one point in the *Timaeus* he comes close to beginning this process but the connection is never fully established or developed.

In actual practice, the individual systems are capable of further lexical and notional refinement, and the terminology becomes more discrete and extensive. For example, the various systems elaborate in Latin[1] all

---

[1] The view expressed by Professor North (*op. cit.*, p. 310) that the unified Greek concept of *sophrosyne* underwent a 'fragmentation' conceptually in Roman culture ('Rome's failure to grasp the totality of the Greek concept') was somehow symbolized by the 'fragmentation of sophrosyne into clementia, moderatio, temperantia and pudicitia' seems to me based on a linguistic misconception. Lexical multiplication or polyonymy in the case of certain words may be the expressive means by which a writer and a literature specify preciseness of application without arousing wider philosophical implications. After all, the Latin sb. *innocentia* tends to remain mononymic—it retains its formal simplicity while performing a wide range of specific semantic functions. On the other hand, Greek

the corresponding senses of the Greek sb. *sophrosyne*, e.g. *prudentia*=
sensibleness; *modestia*=purity. Creative authors also seem prone to
blend various parts of different systems. This tendency is most pronounced in the poetry of Alan of Lille and Jean de Meun, authors whom
Chaucer knew intimately and who clearly encouraged his complex
sense of the concept of moderation. Manifestly Christian authors with
theological training are least likely to evolve terminology which embraces more than one value-system. Alan when writing with his
doctoral hat on stays very close to the Cardinal Virtues system. The
ethical composition of human nature as elaborated in the *Anticlaudianus*
finds not the slightest echo in his *De Virtutibus et de vitiis et de donis
Spiritus Sancti*.[2] Although St Thomas is sympathetic to Aristotle's
argument in his commentary to the *Ethics* and shows himself a patient
expositor, he nowhere shows the least enthusiasm for his author, nor
has Aristotle's 'mean' had much effect on St Thomas's ethical thinking.
On the other hand, St Augustine (who normally discusses 'temperance'
and 'moderation' from the Ciceronian and Stoical point of view, and
in the *De Moribus Ecclesiae Catholicae* takes up a more Ambrosian doctrine linking the moral virtues to purification and love) in the *De Beata
Vita* discusses *temperantia* in relation to *modus*, 'measure'. His argument
in this work shows distant peripatetic linguistic colouring (II.32–4).
In his late *Retractationes* (I.i.4) he regrets having written the too philosophical *De Beata Vita*. But it would be misleading to say that St
Augustine shows any genuine appreciation of the Aristotelian formulation. The method of his argument is to 'identify' a series of terms.
Through etymologizing, *modus* and *temperantia* are identified rapidly
with *plenitudo* (the opposite of *abundantia*). *Plenitudo* has already been
proved a primary quality of divinity. *Modus* is then identified with 'the
measure of the soul' and *sapientia* identified with plenitude. This
'wisdom' ('true wisdom') and plenitude are together identified with
divine status and origin. The argument consists of a series of conceptual
substitutions accompanied by multiplication of the value and the
ultimate status of the ideas being identified. It shows a certain facility in
assimilating a philosophically based set of ethical terminology to an
absolute theological resolution. But the argument (no matter how
unconvincing at the logical and ethical level) is historically important

[2] For a text see Dom Odon Lottin, *Psychologie et morale aux XIIe et XIIIe siècles*,
Gembloux (1960), vol. 6, pp. 25–92.

---

literature generates many sbs. for the corresponding shades of meaning. No one
has suggested serious philosophic consequences in this case.

for establishing a connection between divine plenitude, created nature and the concept of moderation seen as an expression of perfectly just divine intention towards creation: '*Sed etiam summus modus necesse est ut verus modus sit.*' Alan of Lille invokes this argument in book VII of the *Anticlaudianus* in explaining how the perfect physical nature of the human being came to be evolved:[3]

> *Nil imperfectum, quia perfectissimus actor,*
> *Nec maius uoluit quam quod satis omnibus esset,*
> *Nec decuit fecisse minus qui plus potuisset.*

Nothing in man is imperfect since the most perfect steward [Nature] has not intended more than would be enough for all, nor has it been proper for one to have done less who could have done more.

It would be reasonable to assume that Chaucer acquired his knowledge of the concept of moderation from the authors he seems most to have been drawn to: namely, Boethius, Macrobius, Alan of Lille and Jean de Meun. In their turn, these authors obviously have drawn on classical or curriculum authors whom Chaucer must have read either extensively or in extract. But I shall begin by concentrating on this matrix group.

Recently, Dr Brewer in an interesting paper for the Oxford Medieval Society outlined a moral system for Chaucer based on a 'code of honour'. It would seem to have been elaborated from a mainly lexicographical collection of various isolated usages in Chaucer without sufficient regard for the complexity or density of context or the 'identity' of the speaker. Why, for example, should we attribute Pandarus' view on 'purity' to Chaucer? On the other hand, an earlier more systematic writer on Chaucer's values, Héraucourt, presents us with other problems. In the case of moderation, Héraucourt's method avoids rather than mistakes the issue (*Die Wertwelt Chaucers*). His division of Chaucer's total world of values into a conventional classical and Christian formulation of four Cardinal Virtues, *prudentia, justitia, fortitudo* and *temperantia*, has caused him to overlook the occurrence of the sb. 'mene' in Chaucer and the specialized sense of 'mesure' signifying 'the mean'. Thus, he is unaware of the existence of any reference to Aristotelian *mediocritas* in Chaucer. The *Book of the Duchess*, line 871, where the

---

[3] Although these lines (VII.50–2) do not occur in the large MS. group FGHIN, there is no reason to doubt their genuineness. They occur in the group AEL and are accepted by Bossuat in his text.

immediate context indicates that 'mesure', '*moderatio*', signifies an activity which 'moderates' between the poles of elleipsis and hyperbole, is simply treated as the axiomatic equivalent of *sophrosyne* or temperance (pp. 294ff.). So, too, is the adjective 'attempre' (l. 341) although it, too, in context proves to be a metaphorical introduction to Aristotelian proportional relationships.[4] Consequently, Héraucourt subdivides his Cardinal Virtue into the conventional Stoic range: moderation, abstinence, modesty and chastity. This is valuable but basically incomplete and ultimately misleading. His splendidly clear account of the 'static' value-system of the Middle Ages merging into the 'dynamic' 'new ideas' of the fourteenth century (pp. 14–31) is too schematic, too dependent on the textbooks, too disregarding of the authors which Chaucer read and paid the compliment of imitating or quoting. In literature it is not 'centuries' or even 'dominant ideas' of a given time which come into conflict or show alteration, but the thoughts of an individual man whose experience (drawing on many persons and many times) usually ignores chronological arrangements in the overriding interest of creating a coherent and cohesive philosophical position. In view of Chaucer's close translation of the whole of Boethius' *De Consolatione Philosophiae* (with the extensive help of Jean de Meun's prose translation), what would Chaucer have gathered of the concept of moderation from Boethius' famous work?

Boethius' views on moderation belong unambiguously to the neo-Platonic school of thought. The ethical and the cosmological expressions of moderation are entirely separate and unconnected. At one point (IV pr. vi) he obliquely refers to the physiological composition of the human body in terms of the proportioning of the elements into a 'temper' ('*modum temperamentumque . . . sanitatis . . . atque aegritudinis*') but this usage remains strictly medical and technical. It is never connected, for example, with the cosmological arrangements of the elements in the universe, where in an isolated phrase '*elementa in se invicem temperat*' (IV pr. vi) Boethius suggests the proportional, mean-ratio theory of Plato. Chaucer translates 'atempreth the elements togider amonges hem-self'. The vb. 'atempre' and the sb. 'attemperaunce' are

---

[4] The moderating climate of the dream landscape not only supplies a ratio between the extremes of hot and cold but also provides the personal, individual relationship of the representational expression of moderateness to the poet's temperament, his psychological health. Like Aristotle's 'mean', Chaucer's use of 'mesure' in the poem shows a dual aspect, one having general reference, the other an individual, personal application.

used several times by Chaucer to translate Boethius' *tempero* and *tem-peries*. In the verbal application it should be noticed at once that Boethius habitually uses *tempero* in the sense 'to rule, regulate, govern'. Chaucer uses 'atempre' in exactly this sense. 'Attemperaunce' has much the same semantic colouring.

The cosmological context of moderation is touched on briefly and mysteriously in the great panegyrical metre '*O quam perpetua*' (III.m.9. 25–30). The passage is obscure (so intended by Boethius) and what Chaucer made of it is not clear. The Latin reads:

> *Tu triplicis mediam naturae cuncta moventem*
> *Connectens animam per consona membra resolvis.*

Chaucer translates:

> Thou knittest togider the mene sowle of treble kinde, moeving
> alle thinges, and devydest it by membres accordinge;

The lines which follow, describing the *membra* as two circular move-ments, one moving round on itself generating pure contemplative energy, the other moving outwards turning the physical universe 'by semblable image' would seem to suggest that Boethius had Plato's *Timaeus* 36e in mind:[5]

> He fabricated within it [the Soul] all the corporeal, and uniting them
> centre to centre he made them fit together. And the Soul, being
> woven throughout the heaven every way from the centre to the
> extremity . . . is a compound, blended of the nature of the Same
> and the Other and Being.

In this reading, the 'triple nature' of the soul refers to the Same, the Other and Being (not the Aristotelian division into rational, sensitive and vegetable), and the expression '*media anima*' refers to the middle point where the two circular souls are joined together, '. . . *kaí méson mései xunagagón prosérmotten*'. The sovereign soul moves about on its own mid-point, itself unmoving. This image occurs again in IV prose vi in a comparison:

> *Nam ut orbium circum eundem cardinem sese vertentium, qui est intimus,*
> *ad simplicitatem medietatis accedit, ceterorumque extra locatorum*
> *veluti cardo quidam, circa quem versentur, existit: extimus vero majore*
> *ambitu rotatus, quanto a puncti media individuitate discedit, tanto*

[5] Cf. F. Klingner, *De Boethii Consolatione Philosophiae*, Zurich (1966), p. 45.

amplioribus spatiis explicatur: si quid vero illi se medio connectat et societ, *in simplicitatem cogitur, diffundique, ac diffluere cessat.*

For right as of cercles that tornen about a same centre or about a poynt, thilke cercle that is innerest, or most withinne joyneth to the simplesse of the middel, and is, as it were, a centre or a poynt to that other cercles that tornen abouten him; and thilke that is outterest, compassed by larger envyroninge, is unfolden by larger spaces, in so moche as it is forthest fro the middel simplicitee of the poynt; and yif ther be anything that knitteth and felawshippeth himself to thilke middel poynt, it is constreined into simplicitee, that is to seyn, into unmoevabletee, and it ceseth to be shad and to fleten dyversely.

Chaucer uses the adj. and sb. 'mene' four times in his translation of Boethius. The first use, in this passage to render the collocation *media anima*, is purely cosmological and in the true Platonic spirit remains wholly metaphysical. It is not connected in any way with ethical moderation. Chaucer's three other uses occur in one passage dealing with moderation in terms of human behaviour.

Boethius' soul-oriented philosophy is not much concerned with practical virtue, the art of managing one's own life in relation to other lives. Philosophy's emphasis always falls on single man and on his relationship with the metaphysical universe. Hence, the ethical aspect of moderation enters Boethius' system at one point only—and that in a very limited context. In IV pr. vii Philosophy urges practical adoption of 'virtue' in that it accepts the necessity of whatever we are given in the way of 'fortune', neither requiring us to rejoice too much in prosperity, nor to complain overmuch in adversity. This is the old popular maxim 'nothing too much' given a minor role within Boethius' more sophisticated arguments and overall design. Philosophy says:

Firmis medium viribus occupate. Quidquid autem infra subsistit, aut ultra progeditur, habet contemtum felicitatis, non habet praemium laboris.

The compact sentence of Boethius is given more emphatic treatment by Chaucer:

Occupye the mene by stedefast strengthes. For al that ever is under the mene, or elles al that overpasseth the mene, despyseth wele- fulnesse . . . and ne hath no mede of his travaile.

The last phrase 'non habet praemium laboris' indicates the pragmatic nature of Boethius' concern. There is no genuine ethical system here, only the old practical wisdom which would have appealed equally to the author of the *Distichs of Cato* (see II.6) or the Anglo-Saxons, whose *gemetgung* and *gemetfaestnes* had severely practical reference. Boethius would have made Chaucer aware of the Platonic dichotomization of the notion of moderation into two unrelated spheres, the metaphysical and the ethical, but a reading of the *De Consolatione* would have given Chaucer little insight into either a complex ethical usage or a fully elaborated metaphysical justification or explanation.

When we come to Macrobius' *Commentum* to *Somnium Scipionis* (probably written towards the end of the fourth century) we find a situation not unlike that presented by the *De Consolatione*. This work, too, belongs to the neo-Platonic school, certainly as far as moderation is concerned. Although not as thoroughly neo-Platonic as Macrobius, the Platonizing tendency is present, too, in Cicero. The civic and moral side of Cicero, his intricate Roman interest in *temperantia*, although well represented in the *Res Publica*, is not present in the excerpted text of the *Somnium Scipionis*. The rest of the text of the *Res Publica* was available to the Middle Ages only in fragments preserved in other authors. Chaucer would have had to read the *De Finibus*, the *Tusculanarum Disputationum* or the *De Officiis* to have gathered something of Cicero's ethical concern with moderation. The *Tusculanarum Disputationum* III.x.22 makes it abundantly clear that Cicero has no intention of understanding the Aristotelian view of moderation. His failure to be convinced is based on a wilful misunderstanding of Aristotle and supported by the Stoical use of a health metaphor. The soul, on the analogy of the body, may suffer from disease, i.e. immorality:

> . . . *nam Peripatetici, familiares nostri, quibus nihil est uberius, nihil eruditus, nihil gravius, mediocritates vel perturbationum vel morborum animi non sane probant. Omne enim malum, etiam mediocre malum est.*

> for the Peripatetics, friends of ours as they are unequalled in resourcefulness, in learning and in earnestness, do not quite succeed in convincing me of their 'mean' or moderate states either of disturbances or of diseases of the soul. For every evil even a moderate one is an evil.

III.xvii.36 indicates the proscriptive form of moderation which compels Cicero's admiration:

Aderit temperantia, quae est eadem moderatio, a me quidem paullo ante appellata frugalitas—quae te turpiter et nequitur facere nihil patientum.

Next will come Temperance, who is also self-control, and called by me a little while ago, 'frugality', and will not suffer you to do anything disgraceful and vile.

All of Cicero's many uses of the various aspects of moderation lead us to see this virtue as essentially public (beneficial to others) and beneficial to ourselves only when considered as a means to mental health. In the *Verrines* we find Cicero employing descriptions of exemplary figures as models of virtues and vices. In this collection, Scipio Africanus Major appears as the chief model of *continentia* and *temperantia*. The organization of the topic may be rhetorical but Cicero's habitual method of commending self-control always conveys a hint of the exemplary as well as the preceptive. In the more philosophical *De Officiis*, he makes an interesting connection between moderation and *humanitas* by defining virtue as a controlling relationship between reason and impulses. In his view wisdom and moderation cannot be rationalized as extensions of animal characteristics (justice and courage are so attributable). Man is the only 'animal' which has an instinctive inclination for order, propriety and moderation (I.4.14). In the *Res Publica* Cicero evinces a unique social application of moderation in constructing a theory of the ideal ruler who has a unique public reason for possessing *moderatio* since he must balance and concordize all the differing elements and interests in the state (he is not only *rector* but *moderator*). The use of a Platonic musical metaphor (II.42.69) perhaps betrays one of the origins of this notion.[6] The constitution which receives the moderator's rule is *moderatum et permixtum* (II.29.45). But none of this occurs in *Somnium Scipionis*. Chaucer could have read some of this unique argument in St Augustine's *De Civitate Dei* II.21, where this passage of the *Res Publica* (II.42.69) is quoted with minor variations:[7]

ex dissimillimarum vocum moderatione concors tamen efficitur et congruens, sic ex summis et infimis et mediis interiectis ordinibus ut sonis moderata ratione civitas consensu dissimillimorum concinat.

But the *Somnium* is little more than an excuse for Macrobius to

[6] Probably a conflation of Plato, *Timaeus* 32a–c with 35d and then extended to a social context.
[7] Chaucer's Nature in the *Parliament* is just such a moderator. But this social application of *moderatio* need not be traced to Cicero. The social application is everywhere explicit in Alan of Lille.

indulge his extensive encyclopedist's taste for natural philosophy—the metaphysical mechanics of the cosmos after the style of Plato and Porphyry. Chaucer would have found in Macrobius the old Platonic dualism between metaphysical and ethical moderation—and the same lack of attention to the ethical—but the 'scientific' side of Macrobius is fascinated by proportions and ratios. Whereas Boethius shows little interest in the structure of the cosmos which involves *moderatio*, Macrobius would have provided Chaucer with a detailed and intricate picture of the cosmological aspect of moderation.

All of Macrobius' 'scientific' descriptions of the physical construction of the universe in connection with moderation are reflections of similar passages in Plato's *Timaeus*. They are digests and simplifications. The first and most extensive passage describing cosmological moderation concerns the composition of the chain of the elements (a subject which Boethius was to touch on later in the *De Consolatione*). In I.6.22, Macrobius sets out the arithmetical ratio which gives unity to the basic physical coherence of the universe while providing for its otherness and diversity. This is essentially a digest of *Timaeus* 32a–b:

> *Item scimus secundum Platonem . . . illa forti inter se vinculo conligari, quibus interiecta medietas praestat vinculi firmitatem. Cum vero medietas ipsa geminatur, ea quae extima sunt non tenaciter tantum, sed etiam insolubiliter vinciuntur. Primo ergo ternario contigit numero, ut inter duo summa medium quo vinciretur acciperet, quaternarius vero duas medietates primus omnium nactus est. Quas ab hoc numero deus mundanae molis artifex conditorque mutuatus, insolubili inter se vinculo elementa devinxit, sicut in* Timaeo Platonis *advertum est, non aliter tam controversa sibi ac repugnantia et naturae communionem abnuentia permisceri—terram dico et ignem—potuisse et per tam iugabilem conpetentiam foederari, nisi duobus mediis aeris et aquae nexibus vincirentur. Ita enim elementa inter se diversissima opifex tamen deus ordinis opportunitate conexuit, ut facile iugerentur . . . Haec tamen varietas vinculorum, si elementa duo forent, nihil inter ipsa firmitatis habuisset; si tria, minus quidem valido aliquo tamen nexu vincienda nodaret, inter quattuor vero insolubilis conligatio est cum duae summitates duabus interiectionibus vinciuntur . . .*

Moreover, we know, according to Plato . . . that those bodies alone are closely held together which have a mean interposed between extremes to create a strong bond. When that mean is doubled the extremes are bound not only firmly but even indissolubly. Now the number three is the first to have a mean between two extremes to bind it together, and the number four is the first of all numbers to have two means. Borrowing the means from this number the Creator of the universe bound the elements together with an unbreakable chain, as who affirms in Plato's *Timaeus* (32c) in no other way could the elements earth and fire, so opposed and repugnant to each other and spurning any communion of their natures, be mingled together and joined in so binding a union unless they were held together by the two means of air and water. For thus, in spite of the utter diversity of these elements, the Creator harmonized them so skilfully that they could be readily united ... These different bonds would have no tenacity, however, if there were only two elements; if there were three the union would be but a weak one; but as there are four elements, the bonds are unbreakable, since the two extremes are held together by the two means.

This exposition is supported by a short passage in I.6.29 and paralleled by a musical ratio which ensures the cohesion of the *Anima Mundi* in II.2.15. This is a quotation summarizing Plato's *Timaeus* 35b–36a:

> *post hoc spatia quae inter duplos et triplos numeros hiabant insertis partibus adimplebat, ut binae medietas singula spatia colligarent, ex quibus vinculis hemiolii et epitriti et epodoi nascebantur.*

> After that he [the Creator] filled up the intervals between the numbers of both series [odd and even] by inserting further positions so that there might be two means in each interval. From these means came the sequialiter, sesquitertian and the superoctave.

This 'mean' becomes the principle of harmony in the world-soul through the union of equal and unequal numbers.

Macrobius' brief interest in ethical moderation occurs in a single passage, I.8.7. Whatever author Macrobius had in mind (he thought himself to be citing Plotinus' *On the Virtues*), he classifies the Four Virtues into four types, the political, the purifying, virtues of the purified mind and the exemplary virtues. *Temperantia* figures in the political category and shows heavy borrowing from various passages in Cicero's *De Finibus*. This passage in Macrobius achieved wide popularity since it was to be quoted extensively by Vincent of Beauvais in the *Speculum Doctrinale* IV.9ff.

> *Temperantiae nihil adpetere praenitendum, in nullo legem moderationis excedere, sub iugum rationis cupiditatem domare.*

To have [political] temperance, one must strive after nothing that is base, in no instance overstepping the bounds of moderation but subduing all immodest desires beneath the yoke of reason.

Macrobius, following Cicero, goes on to say: 'Temperance is accompanied by modesty, humility, self-restraint, chastity, integrity, moderation, frugality, sobriety, and purity.' This last collection of 'family' qualities represents the essence of Cicero's preceptual, self-controlling view of moderation: the complex notional and verbal subdivision of *temperantia* into related forms of self-abnegation. For Cicero it has a kind of puritanical aestheticism,[8] a humane severity which anticipates Aubrey's early and veracious partial portrait of John Milton.

In the matrix group of four authors, it is the poets, Alan and Jean, who show a really complex appreciation of the concept of moderation in its ethical application and at the same time exhibit no neo-Platonic dissociation of the ethical and cosmological aspects of the notion. External reality and the composition of the human being reflect mutually a unified notion of the moderating principle. Significantly, Alan, though Paris-trained, was the poetic heir of Chartrain philosophical concerns and Jean poetically was his spiritual son. But it must not be assumed that poetic sensitivity to post-Chartrain moderation is chronologically or doctrinally automatic. Bernardus Silvestris who 'perhaps rose to be Chancellor' of Chartres (*c.* 1156)[9] and who wrote his poem *De Mundi Universitate* perhaps a quarter of a century before Alan began the *De Planctu*, manifests little interest in the doctrine of moderation. The structure of his poem (two books, one dealing with the macrocosm, the other the microcosm) encourages separate and unrelated ethical and cosmological interests in moderation. Moderation in geographical and atmospheric arrangements are stressed (I.ii.31ff. and 113ff.) and the disposition of the zones of the earth shows a tripartite division which reflects a moderate climate enclosed by two extremes (I.iii.61ff.). The last arrangement depends upon Plato and Macrobius. In book II, when Nature is bidden to look about she sees (II.viii.5–6):

> Quid mediis extrema liget, quid foedera iugat,
> Quid caelum moveat quidve movetur humum.

but here the visual lesson ends. The long prose description of the composition of the human being, apart from the usual moderate mixture of

[8] Cf. *De Officiis* I 4.14.
[9] Cf. F. J. E. Raby, *A History of Secular Latin Poetry*, 2nd ed., Oxford (1957), vol ii, p. 8.

the corporeal elements, shows no especial philosophical concern with moderation (II.xii). Lastly, the physiological position of the faculty of reason occupies a mid-position in the cranium (II.xiv.7ff.) but nothing further develops from this commonplace 'anatomical' observation. If Alan knew Bernardus' poem (some have so argued), a preoccupation with the concept of moderation did not emanate from there.

John of Hanville's *Architrenius*,[10] written after 1184 and therefore roughly contemporary with Alan's *De Planctu*, is more concerned with moderation, but the notion is distinctly Ciceronian in origin and develops no further than the sphere of self-restraint. It is a disappointing poem, tiresomely obscure in style and language. In spite of the wanderings, places visited, curiosities enumerated,[11] in an unsubtle and mechanical fashion, the poem deals with human defects serially, generating a string of critical observations which calls forth a catalogue of set speeches from a parade of ancient moralists. Predictably, *moderatio* enters with the appearance of Cicero in book VI. He comments in his oration:

> *Dando tamen praefige modum, substringe solutos*
> *Muneris excursus, justo moderantia fine*
> *Temperet expensas, cedatque improvida caeci*
> *Ebrietas luxus, moderandi limite dandi*
> *Luxuriem praecinge, pati largito fraenum*
> *Noverit, et quantum permittit copia funde.*

Although faithful generally to the spirit of Cicero, it shows no poetic subtlety or originality of treatment or formulation. The resolution of the poem is brought about by the marriage of our Arch-mourner to Moderation on the advice and sponsorship of Dame Nature (book IX). Here, surely, we shall find something interesting. Alas, serialism infects even the climax of the poem: we get a description of the scene, bridesmaids, patrons of the various alliances, and the actual parts of the ceremony. Under the 'wedding-dishes' we receive our final view of moderation, predictably as a principle devoted to regulation of the diet—another Ciceronian set of restraining advice. Lady Moderamen, although a bride present at the feast with her shy husband-poet, never really enters the poem. The poem develops no complex view of human

[10] There is a text in T. Wright, *The Anglo-Latin Satirical Poets of the Twelfth Century*, Rolls Series, London (1872), vol. i, pp. 240ff.
[11] Cf. the compendious account of pears growing on the Mount of Ambition (ii.294) which is nothing more than a versification of Macrobius' discussion on pears in the *Saturnalia* (II.19).

character as activity. It is all tiresome description, worthy of scholarly neglect.[12]

Alan's *De Planctu Naturae*, written some time before *c*. 1184 and which would seem stylistically to predate the *Anticlaudianus*,[13] makes a much fuller contribution to an original and creative discussion of moderation. What is missing in Bernardus' poem is here supplied. Alan links together the metaphysical and ethical aspects of the concept by a persistent use of personification, principally in the description of Nature and to a lesser extent in the depiction of Genius. The emphasis on personification ensures the constant humanizing of attributes which traditionally belonged to enormous physical and cosmic forces. The ethical aspect is provided by a parallel *ethopoeia* of Temperantia in prose viii. But even here the essential self-controlling aspect of Temperantia is by various poetic devices extended towards reminiscences of Aristotelian proportional modification. Alan uses a syntactical device in prose and verse whereby he evolves a period with two almost equal clauses balanced on a single adversative adverb or conjunction. There is repetition of phraseology with the verbs providing the sense antithesis. In the case of Temperantia, the following sentence is typical of this kind of construction:

> *Aetas vero meridianam vitae tendebat ad horam, vitae tamen meridies in nullo pulchritudinis obviabat aurorae.*

Here the twin clauses balance on *tamen* and in each clause certain lexical items or arrangements of items are repeated with reversed sense, the verbs (with accentuated movement and activity especially in the repeated imperfect tenses) forcing the phrases *meridianam vitae . . . horam* and *vitae meridies* into a suspended mutual modification:

> Truly, her age tended to approach the noon hour of life, yet the noon of life in no way hindered the dawn of beauty.

---

[12] A sympathetic account of the poem is given in W. Wetherbee's *Platonism and Poetry in the Twelfth Century*, Princeton (1972), pp. 242–55, which appeared too late for consideration in this book. He admits to the poem's 'fundamental defects' (p. 242) but then goes on to allow it more philosophical acuity and poetic vitality than it is entitled to. Less pretentious philosophically but more accurate as regards literary merit is M.-R. Jung's account in his *Études sur le poème allégorique en France au Moyen Âge*, Berne (1971), pp. 113–21. He dates the poem after Alan's works, '*composé vers 1284*' (p. 113), which must be a misprint for 1184 for he asserts correctly in footnote 11 on p. 121: '*Le succès du poème dut être immediat: des vingt-sept manuscrits peuvent être datés autour de 1200 . . .*'

[13] Cf. G. R. de Lage, *Alain de Lille, poëte du XIIe siècle*, Montreal (1951), pp. 23–5.

This aspect of Temperantia goes beyond self-restraint. The middle years of life, an Aristotelian image of *mediocritas*,[14] becomes a mutual proportion identifiable with a tempering of qualities belonging to two ages—a tempering immediately modified in the next sentence by a further relation to old age. All this produces a proportional tension between the three terms of the Aristotelian division of the human lifespan.

> *Pruina, etiam senectutis crinem suis nivibus tentabat aspergere . . .*

Even now the frosty winter of old age was attempting to sprinkle her hair with its whiteness . . .

The temporal force of *etiam* and the imperfect tense contribute to a situation which makes it no longer important to imagine a mathematically designatable age. Conceptually we are meant to see the symbolic middle age as harmonizing all three stages of human life, and the modifying, proportional artistic expression of this relation enacts the essential quality of its existence. Alan, who is capable of a wider variety of styles than has been imagined,[15] repeats this modifying, 'processive' arrangement of syntax and vocabulary over and over again. It is not a mere rhetorical mannerism—a mental stammer—but an aesthetic means of conveying Alan's sense of the harmonious changefulness and ordered variety of the natural world. This verbal schematization is as much an essential part of his poetic mentality as the habitual use of a heavily hyperbolic verb placed immediately after a pronounced caesural pause embodies the innermost impudence of Marlowe's verse:

> And make whole cities caper in the air.

This sense in nicely conveyed in a cosmological description in prose iv:

> *Sicque res generum oppositione contrarias, inter quas locus ab oppositis locum posuit, cujusdam reciprocae habitudinis, relativis osculis foederando in amicitiae pacem lites repugnantiae commutavit. Subtilibus igitur invisibilis juncturae catenis concordantibus universis, ad unitatem pluralitas, ad identitatem diversitas, ad consonantiam dissonantia, ad concordiam discordia, unione pacifica remeavit.*

[14] Cf. Aristotle, *De Rhetorica* 1389b ff.
[15] In the *Anticlaudianus*, for example, the invocations are written in an Augustan, classical style wholly unlike the Sidonian rhetorical colouring of the rest of the narrative.

Accordingly, things inimical from their opposed natures, between whom space appointed a fixed place by reason of contradiction, he united with mutual and fraternal embraces, changing the strife of hatred into the peace of amity. Thus, all being agreed through subtle and invisible bonds of union, plurality changing to unity, diversity to identity, dissonance to harmony, discord to concord, he returned home with peace-offerings from unity.

Each sentence possesses a resolving rhythm, interlocked sentence structure gradually simplifies, the climax kept back to the ultimate clause, the unifying verb (governed by *'artifex universalis'*) in the ultimate position (*commutavit, remeavit*). A few lines further he obliquely refers to the neo-Platonic moderating ratio in the phrase:

> ... *omniaque sibi invicem legitimis proportionum connubiis maritavit.*

> ... and he married all of them in binding wedlock with proportions mutually acceptable to each one.

But whereas Macrobius sees in this elemental diversity and unity an opportunity for explaining mathematical ratios based on 'means', Alan, stressing the social and human implications through the Boethian metaphor of marriage, immediately passes on to the equally Boethian preoccupation (II.m.8) with the necessity of maintaining the stability and order of human civilization through a legitimate reproductive cycle *'rerumque series seriata reciprocatione nascendi jugitur texeretur ...'*. Even in this context the 'cycle of birth and death' (*'circuitu ... nascendi occidendique'*) is viewed as *'mutuae relationis'*, 'the cycle of *mutual relation* of birth and death'.

The *ethopoeia* of Temperantia in prose viii presents an interesting exposition of *sophrosyne* which relates several aspects of all of the three main value-systems in a fascinating creative amalgam. Given Chaucer's close knowledge of the work, he would not have failed to have been attracted by it. The whole passage is as follows:

> *Cumque eidem Natura festivitate collocutionis applauderet, ecce matrona regulari modestia disciplinans incessum ad nos videbatur sui itineris tramitem lineare. Hujus statura mediocritatis erat circumscripta limitibus. Aetas vero meridianam vitae tendebat ad horam, vitae tamen meridies in nullo pulchritudinis obviabat aurorae. Pruina etiam senectutis crinem suis nivibus tentabat aspergere, quem ipsa virgo humerorum spatio inordinata fluctuatione non permiserat juvenari, sed sub disciplinatione*

ejus cogebat excessum. Vestes vero nec nobilis materiae gloria superbire,
nec ejusdem vilitatis jacturam videbantur deflere, sed mediocritatis
obedientes canonibus, nec nimiae brevitatis decurtatione truncatae, a
terrae superficie peregrinantes evaserant, nec portionibus superfluis terrae
faciem tunicabant, sed eam brevi degustatione osculi libabant. Zona
namque tunicae moderando decursum, enormitatem revocabat in regulam.
Monile autem sinus excubando vestibulis, manui negabat ingressum.
In vestibus vero, pictura suarum litterarum fidelitate docebat, quae in
hominum verbis debeat esse circumcisio, quae in factis circumspectio,
quae in habitu mediocritas, quae in gestu serenitas, quae in cibo refrenatio
oris, quae in potu castigatio gutturis. Praefatam igitur virginem, pedis-
sequarum paucitate vallatam, festinae obviationis applausu Natura
suscipiens, multiplici osculorum epilogo, specificatae salutationis auspicio,
suae dilectionis cumulum figuravit; expressaque sui nominis proprii
expressio, Temperantiae favorabilem expressit adventum.

Now whilst Nature was making Chastity welcome with humorous conversation, lo and behold a mature lady with moderate and
measured pace could be observed making her way towards us.
Her height was confined within the limits of the mean. Truly, her
age tended to approach the noon hour of life, yet the noon of life
in no way hindered the dawn of beauty. Even now the frosty winter of old age was attempting to sprinkle her hair with its whiteness—which hair the maiden herself did not permit to play in
wanton waves over her shoulders but restricted its aberrations
under an artful discipline. Indeed, her clothing did not appear to be
magnificent in the glory of superior material, nor to deplore its
omission in cheapness, but obedient to the rules of moderation they
neither escaped wandering from the surface of the ground (cur-
tailed by excessive briefness), nor did they coat the surface of the
earth with superfluous length, but brushed it with the savour of a
brief kiss. For indeed, a belt regulated the fall of her tunic and
checked irregularity in a patterned rule. Moreover a collar keeping watch over the entrances to her bosom denied admission to the
hand. Throughout her dress an embroidery instructed with faithful
lines in her own fair hand, what restraint ought to be in human
discourse, what caution in man's actions, what moderation in
dress, what calmness in gestures, what curbing of the mouth in eating, what tempering of the throat in drinking. Consequently, Nature recognized the aforesaid maiden though she was accompanied

by few servants, and she hastened to welcome her, showing the full measure of her love by her initial warmth of greeting and concluding multiplicity of kisses; the plain expression of her own name announced the gracious arrival of Temperance.

This *ethopoeia* stylistically divides into two modes: plainness of word-order and preciousness of expression in verbal arrangement and circumlocution. This stylistic emphasis is supported by the division of Temperantia into those qualities which belong to her person and those precepts embroidered on her clothing. The arrangement tends to underline two aspects, the Aristotelian and proportional (*mediocritas*) and the preceptual and self-restraining (*temperantia*). Alan extends the function of moderation by interweaving elements of 'the mean' into the attributes of the other Virtues and powers who attend Nature in this scene. In the case of Hymen his varying size is regulated '*aequilibratae mediocritatis libramen*' ('according to the scale of an equally balanced mean'). Hymen's face '*nec fletus imbribus compluta, nec risus erat lasciviis serenata, sed ab utroque servata modestia, magis aspirabat in lacrimas*' ('was neither drenched in floods of tears, nor glowed with the frolics of laughter, but watched over by both in moderation rather favoured giving way to tears'). Each of the other Virtues (Chastity, Generosity, Humility) partake of moderation. Chastity's eyes '*simplicitatis disciplinati modestia, nullius petulantiae lasciviebant excursibus*' ('were governed by a simple modesty and did not wanton with any impudent sallies'). Generosity, otherwise given to magnitude, wears a diadem which shows a certain tempering of its absolute dominance of wealth and excellence through a paradox:

> *Diadema vero, non operis insignitate materiae redimens paupertatem, nec ejusdem nobilitate materiae vilitatem recuperans, sed in utroque singularem praeferens monarchiam, sine morsu peremptoriae proprietatis ardebat in capite.*

A diadem which did not redeem poorness of material by excellence of craftsmanship nor atone for shoddiness of workmanship by richness of material but which revealed in both a unique and absolute monarchy (without pain of that final, uncontradictable state) glowed on her head.

The snail's pace approach of Humility also does not sin against moderateness: '*ad nos divertere suam testudinei gressus modestiam hortabatur*' ('she urged herself, almost overcome by reticence, to turn towards us her measured yet exceedingly slow pace'). Similarly, Genius partakes of moderation in his physical size in prose ix:[16]

> *Cujus statura mediocritatis canone modificata decenter, nec de diminutione conquerebatur aphaeresis, nec de superfluitatis prothesi tristabatur.*

> His stature, properly measured by the canon of the mean, neither complained of diminution by abbreviation nor sorrowed over superabundance of addition.

If the Virtues show a family resemblance through shared characteristics of moderation, the Vices show related lack of the mean. The figure of Bacchilatria in prose vi illustrates the rule of excess where immoderateness accompanies ' the darkness of brutish sensuality'. In metre 9 the music of the wedding procession enacts the concord of moderation on the analogy of the unifying of the elements in prose iv:

> *Cum strepitu dulci ructabant organa ventum,/Dividitur juncta, divisaque jungitur, horum/Dispar comparitas cantus, discordia concors,/Unio dissimilis, similis dissentio vocum.*

> The stringed instruments gave forth airy commotion with sweet sound, joined then divided, divided then joined was the uneven equality of the song, harmonious discord, dissimilar unity, concordant disagreement of the voices.

But it is in the description of Nature herself in prose i (especially in connection with parts of the body) that Alan places his main emphasis on moderation. The following selection gives a fair picture of the attribution of moderation to Nature:

> *quam duplex tricatura diffibulans, superna non deserens, terrae non dedignabatur osculo arridere.*

> her tresses unbuckling twice as much hair, not forsaking the region high over her head, yet did not disdain to smile at the earth with a kiss.

> *Supercilia vero, aureo stellata fulgore, non in pilorum evagantia silvam, nec in nimiam demissa pauperiem, inter utrumque medium obtinebant.*

> Truly her gold-starred eyebrows, neither a spreading out into a

---

[16] The use of *prothesis* and *aphaeresis* illustrate Alan's penchant for sbs. of Greek origin, fondness for grammatical and rhetorical metaphors and fascination with precious phrases. It is a very pedantic way of saying 'by the tiniest amount'.

forest of hairs nor a retiring into excessive poverty, between both
preserved the mean.

*Naris utraque odore imbalsamata mellito, nec citra modum humilis nec
injuste prominens vultui, quiddam praesentabat insigne.*

Both nostrils honied with balsamed odour, neither out of measure
low nor excessively prominent, exhibited a certain distinction.

*Laterum aequata convallatio, justae moderationis impressa signillo,
totius corporis speciem ad cumulum perfectionis eduxit.*

Her flanks equal in concavity, impressed by the seal of lawful
moderation, brought her whole bodily appearance to the height of
perfection.

Nature's diadem contains references to the mean, for example, the
stone in her crown which represents the constellation Virgo:

*Secundus, non superfluo splendore luxurians, nec penuriosi splendoris
mendicans scintillulas, flamma moderata gaudebat.*

The second [stone] neither luxuriating in excessive brilliance, nor
begging the sparklets of a meagre brightness, rejoiced in a modest
blazing.

Finally, in prose iii, the body of man in its temperament, its combination of the humours, resembles the universe in being formed by
Nature into a unity by a moderating ratio:

*Sicut enim quatuor elementorum concors discordia, unica pluralitas,
consonantia dissonans, consensus dissentiens, mundialis regiae structuras
conciliat, sic quatuor complexionum compar disparitas, inaequalis
aequalitas, deformis conformitas, diversa identitas, aedificium corporis
humani compaginat. Et quae qualitates inter elementa mediatrices con-
veniunt, hae eadem inter quatuor humores pacis sanciunt firmitatem.*

For just as of the four elements, the concordant discord, the single
plurality, the dissonant consonance, the disagreeing agreement,
bring together and produce the structures of the earthly Court,
so, of four complexions, the similar dissimularity, the unequal
equality, the misshapen symmetry, diverse identity, joins together
the building of the human body. And those qualities which come
together as mediators between the elements, these in the same way
ordain a firm peace among the four humours.

The aspect of moderation in the long *ethopoeia* of Nature and the complex account of Temperantia contain something of the moral beauty which goes beyond obedience to a single virtue considered as a moral imperative—which moves towards a pervasive proportion or ratio operating in conjunction with all the other attributes of Nature: unity, multiplicity, fulness, contradiction, order and coherence. As always with Alan, the poetic detail has a certain Ovidian exuberance but the philosophical implications remain static and basically pictorial. But the poetic suggestiveness is never entirely nullified by the philosophical limitations.

The more mature *Anticlaudianus* in its exposition of Nature shows the same concentration on the complexity of a compositional (rather than a compensational) ethical system of *mediocritas*. But there is a distinct increase in the number of references and images used to convey the concept's whole compositional existence. Finally, as in the *De Planctu*, there is a direct description of Modestia in book VII, lines 117ff. This *ethopoeia* concentrates less on the Aristotelian elements and more on the preceptual and self-controlling; yet the axiomatic is extended to include the whole composition of man, '*totum componit hominem*' (l. 121) where 'acts' and 'passions' are included with manners and ethical behaviour generally.

Alan begins by introducing the concept in a series of conventional phrases, e.g. in the opening collection of the council of the Virtues (I.37–8): '*et certo contentia Modestia fine/Et Racio mensura boni . . .*' The imperfect part of the house of Nature in book I refers obliquely to a proportional ethical system by isolating failures to observe 'the mean' in lines 175–9:

> *Illic diues eget, sitit aurum totus in auro*
> *Midas, nec metas animo concedit habendi.*
> *Militis excedat legem plus milite miles*
> *Aiax milicieque modus decurrit in iram.*

The rich man is poor, Midas covets gold totally encased in gold, nor permits any limits to his passion for possessing. Ajax exceeds any discipline of the serving officer, outsoldiering the soldier and skirmishes far beyond the conventions of war in his rage.

The most eloquent image of moderation is that enunciated by Nature herself in the definition of the ideal and potential human being (I.240–5):

Sic homo sicque deus fiet, sic factus uterque,
Quod neuter mediaque via tutissimus ibit,
In quo nostra manus et munera nostra loquantur.
Sic speculum nobis, ut nos speculemur in illo
Que sit nostra fides, que nostra potencia, virtus
Que sit in quantum melius procedere possit.

Thus a man, thus a god will be created, and thus made both and neither, he will walk most securely by the middle path, in whom our workmanship and our function speak unmistakably. Let him be a mirror for us, so that we may reflect ourselves in him in order that we may embody whatever faith, power or virtue there is in us, in so far as he can proceed the better.

The simple notion expressed in Bernardus' *De Mundi Universitate* II.x.19: '*Diuus erit, terrenus erit, curabit utrumque*' ('He will be a divinity, he will be mortal, he will be concerned with each') here has been given a more complex, compositional aspect by being fused with the doctrine of the mean, and in fusing the essential composition of being with ethical proportions it provides a radical basis for the as yet potential neo-Platonic forms to become visible and actual in a specific morally-based model.

Some of the seven Liberal Arts reflect qualities of moderation (as the family of Virtues did in the *De Planctu Naturae*). Compare the dress of Grammar (II.412–14):

> . . . *forme non detrahit illa nec illi*
> *Forma nocet. Cultus forme connubia grata*
> *Nectunt et sese proprio uenerantur honore.*

The papyrus does not detract from the form, nor does the form harm the papyrus, but the formal elegances contract successful marriages with it, and they venerate each other with due honour.

The function of 'diction' in composition enacts the doctrine of the mean (although Alan's style here may not to our ears exactly embody it) (II.467–9):

> *Cur partem capiens ab utroque, rependat utrinque*
> *Dictio quod debetur ei, sic reddit utrumque*
> *Quod neutrum, mediumque tenens mediatur utrinque;*

Why, taking a part from each, diction repays to each what it owes, and so renders to each something which neither has, and holding the middle course, is shared equally on both sides.

The physical appearance of Logic, too, obeys the mean (III.31–2):

> *Non sordis scalore iacens, non luce superba*
> *Vestis erat mediumque tenens, utrinque redacta.*

Not basely descending to the cheap, she was not dressed in supreme brilliance, but holding the mean, withdrawn from either extreme.

In book III, Arithmetic's principal task is to proclaim a science which is concerned with cohesion: 'in what manner number binds all things in the embrace of concord, combines separate things, rules the world.' She finally proclaims (III.331ff.).

> *Que numerum numero concordia nectit et unde*
> *Prouenit ut uicibus mediis extrema ligentur;*
> *Cur duo quadrati medio nectantur in uno*
> *Vel solidos nectat mediis iunctura duobus.*

What harmony joins number to number and whence it happens that extremes are tied to middle positions. Why two squares are tied in the middle in one, or why joining together connects solid bodies in two central points.

This mean ratio is faithfully reflected in the poet's prayer to God in book V, the emotional centre of the whole poem (V.291–3):

> *Qui ueterem massam de uultus sorde querentem*
> *Inuestis meliore toga, formeque sigillo*
> *Signans, excludis nexu mediante tumultum.*

Who robes the primeval material mass (complaining ever of its ugly appearance) with a better peaceful garment, and stamping it with the seal of form, removed the disquietude by means of a mediating bond.

Nature's creation of man in book VII ushers in a long serial description of the predominant intellectual and moral virtues (they are not distinguished by Alan) and Modestia holds second place after Concord, Modestia is followed by Reason, Honesty, Understanding, the Liberal Arts, Piety, Faith and Moral Goodness. This is an unconventional and extremely numerous grouping. Some of the more traditional virtues show curious emphasis. For example, Faith (VII.344ff.) soon abandons its religious application for the secular. By line 357 it has moved on to the topic of Love (*amor*), love which is concerned with unselfish and all-confiding friendship. Of this love Alan says (368ff.):

> *Sicque relatiua dilectio, mutuus adsit*
> *Nexus amicicie, quam nec Fortuna nouercans*
> *Soluat, nec casus agitet, nec gloria frangat.*

Hence love is relative, and there exists a mutual bond of friendship which neither hostile Fortune breaks, misfortune disquiets nor ambition shatters.

We have here Alan's habitual emphasis on relation, mutuality, concord—and *concordia* is the first of the divine gifts. But before any of these life-giving donations appears, Nature first fashions the physical man in abundant beauty. Here, too, moderation plays an important role (VII.45–9):

> *Hoc magis in signum speciei donaque forme*
> *Cedit, quod nulla corpus pinguedine surgit,*
> *Sed magis in maciem tendit, sic omnia iuste*
> *Possidet et nullo decor eius claudicat, immo*
> *Nil maius conferre potest Natura uel ultra.*

It is transformed into this sign of beauty as well as gift of form because the body swells into no fatness but rather tends towards leanness, thus it possesses all things in due proportion, and in nothing is its beauty incomplete—on the contrary, Nature can confer nothing more or add anything beyond.

The beauty of the body lies in its physical appearance which defines 'due proportion'. This arrangement is then identified with perfection in terms of Nature's purpose.

This selection from the *Anticlaudianus* by no means exhausts the references to moderation. It clearly shows that between the writing of the *De Planctu* and this poem (a space of no more than ten years), Alan had not lost his affection for the concept but has developed its interconnectedness ethically and metaphysically in greater detail. He has become interested in the correlation of the elements and humours and the arithmetic mean ratio of concordance between them in man and the universe. He has also introduced the Augustinian notion of the identity of just divine intention, Creation, *plenitudo* and moderation (VII.50ff.). He has taken the trouble to define man essentially as a behavioural mean between pure mortality and pure divinity. This tendency to compound ideas in Alan produces a full-vigorous and attractive view of human capacity, his *aptus*, his innate ability for cultivation of moral beauty in its due proportion. This is especially stressed by distributing moderation among some of the Liberal Arts, and by the inclusion of the Artes as a necessary vehicle for Nature's education for the creation of man within the epical motif of the 'journey beyond'. Chaucer could not have failed to have noticed this emphasis, even if he had not read Alan's *Regulae* where the social and creative side of man's natural composition is copiously explained.

In the *Roman*, Guillaume de Lorris's interests are more psychological (heavily influenced by Ovidian reminiscence) than philosophical. Nevertheless, the figure of Reason has been given characteristics borrowed from Moderation:

> *El ne fu juene ne chenue*
> *Ne fu trop haute ne trop basse,*
> *Ne fu trop graille ne trop grasse,*
> *Li ueil qui en son chief estoient*
> *Con deus estoiles reluisoient.*
>
> (2978–82)

She was neither too young nor too old, nor too tall, nor too short, nor too fat nor too thin. Her eyes shone like two stars.

Here Guillaume's interest in moderation ceases. Jean de Meun's continuation is characterized by two related interests: a penchant for philosophical excursus and an affection for Alan's poetry. Although Jean does not share Alan's deep concern for the social and ethical functions of 'the mean', he twice refers to moderation in a cosmological function and once in an interesting biological application. A coherent philosophical system of moderation (such as that proposed by Alan) does not emerge from Jean's poetry. A certain quality of disconnection is not unfamiliar in Jean's many and varied philosophical divagations. Perhaps the satirist is too active in his poem as well.

Jean's first use is in connection with the Creation (16747ff.). The sources here (according to Langlois) seem to have been the *De Planctu* and the *De Consolatione*—and perhaps we should add the Creation passage in *Anticlaudianus* V:

> *E le fist au comencement*
> *Une masse tant seulement*

Qui toute iert en confusion,
Senz ordre e senz distinccion,
Puis le devisa par parties
Qui puis ne furent departies,
E tout par nombres assoma,
E set combien en la some a;
E par raisonables mesures
Termina toutes leur figures,
Et les fist en rondece estendre
Pour meauz mouveir pour plus comprendre . . .

In the beginning he brought into being a mere confused mass lacking order and without any distinguishing qualities. He then divided it into elements never to be disconnected, and numbered all of them and knew how many made up their sum. And he set limits to every figure in reasonable measures and decreed that in order to move better and include more they should be round . . .

The sbs. *figures* and *mesures* are probably deliberately ambiguous, containing in the first instance a mathematical sense and a geometrical extension into 'shape'. *Mesure* probably contains the sense of 'a unit of measure' and 'a mean measurement'. The collocating with *raisonable* suggests the sense of 'just proportion'. The second cosmological passage occurs in Nature's description of the position and function of the sun. This passage draws on Macrobius' quotation of Cicero's *Somnium Scipionis* in the *Commentum* I.17.3:

Li beaus solauz qui le jour cause,
Qu'il est de toute clarté cause,
Se tient ou mileu come reis,
Trestouz reflambeianx de rais.
Ou mileu d'eus a sa maison;
Ne ce n'est mie senz raison
Que Deus li beaus, li forz, li sages,
Vost que fust ileuc ses estages;
Car, s'il plus bassement courust,
N'est riens qui de chant ne mourust;
E s'il courust plus hautement,
Freiz meist tout a dannement.

(16911–22)

The beautiful sun which is the cause of day and cause of all light and illumination, sits in the very middle like a king crowned with flaming beams. It is most reasonable that he should take his residence in the very middle, since God, so fair, so wise and so powerful, has written that he should have his place. For if he were nearer and lower the whole earth would die with heat, and if he moved higher and further away, frost would be the common doom.

The third use of moderation occurs in lines 20797–804 in a description of the 'shrine of shame' situated *'entre deus pilerez'*. This *templum Pudicitiae* is a combined religious, anthropomorphic and moderative adaptation of images to describe the perfect physical adaptability of the female sexual organ.[17] As a biological description it seems to have no identifiable source. Bernardus Silvestris uses no such image in the *De Mundi Universitate* XIV.153ff. There is a hint of a similar metaphoric treatment in the *Timaeus* 91d when Plato says of the uterus that it is a *'zôn epithumetikòn enòn tês paidopoiías'*, 'an indwelling creature desirous of child-bearing':

> Cil pileret d'argent estaient
> Mout gent, e d'argent soutenaient
> Une image en leu de chaasse,
> Qui n'iert trop haute ne trop basse,
> Trop grosse ou trop graille; non pas
> Mais toute tailliee a compas
> De braz, d'espaules e de mains
> Qu'il n'i faillait ne plus ne mains.

These pillars were of finest silver, and supported an image in the form of a shrine—an image which was not too tall, nor too short, not too fat, nor too thin, but perfect in proportion of arms, shoulders and hands which lacked in nothing.

From the evidence provided by this matrix group of authors, it can be seen that the poets' uses of moderation (pre-eminently Alan of Lille) would have been instrumental in providing Chaucer with an interesting and complex view of the concept. Perhaps more interesting is Chaucer's interest in neo-Aristotelian *mediocritas* exemplified in the passage in the *Legend of Good Women* (F text 160ff.) already discussed on p. 65:

[17] The image may be more conventionally understood as a reference to the maiden's body as a whole, but Jean's language in this section seems satiric, playful and full of sexual nuance.

Al founde they Daunger for a tyme a lord,
Yet Pitee, through his stronge gentil might,
Forgaf, and made Mercy passen Right,
Through innocence and ruled Curtesye.
But I ne clepe nat innocence folye,
Ne fals pitee, for 'vertu is the mene,'
As Etik saith, in swich maner I mene.

This combined linguistic and ethical discussion of 'innocence' in the *Legend of Good Women* 163ff. closely resembles the philosophical-linguistic method pursued in *Ethics* II.7 (1107b–1108a 29), save that the sb. *innocence* (Latin *innocentia*; Greek *anaítion, akakía, euétheia*) does not there form one of Aristotle's examples. Aristotle deals with *akakía* (rendered *innocentia* in the standard early thirteenth-century Latin translation known as the *Ethica Vetus*[18]) and its connection with

---

[18] Aristotle's *Ethics* would have been available to Chaucer in at least five versions in Latin, several Latin and vernacular adaptations and one good complete translation in Old French. The Latin translations were: (1) *Ethica Vetus* (books I and II) before 1215; (2) *Ethica Nova* (book I) *c.* 1215; (3) *Translatio Arabica* (ten books) translated by Hermannus Allemanus in 1240 from a paraphrase of the *Ethics* contained in the *Intermediate Commentary* of Averrhoes; (4) *Summa Alexandrina* (an abbreviated compendium of ten books) translated from an Arabic original in 1243–4 by Hermannus Allemanus; (5) *Vetus translatio*, the first Latin translation of all ten books from a Greek original in *c.* 1245 by Robert Grosseteste, bishop of Lincoln. Cf. *Nicole Oresme, Le Livre de Ethiques d'Aristote*, ed. Menut, New York (1940), where the adaptations and translations are clearly identified and described. There were many commentaries besides that of St Thomas. The most modern commentary which Chaucer could have consulted would have been the *Commentary* of Walter Burley, a long, patient and clear exposition, written between 1340 and 1345 and dedicated to the University of Paris. Chaucer would have been too young to have known Walter (sometime Fellow of Merton College, Oxford), but the poet knew and was a close associate of Walter's two famous kinsmen, John and Simon (cf. *Chaucer Life-Records*). In addition to the accurate scholarly versions and commentaries, the *Ethics* had passed into the great encyclopedia of Vincent of Beauvais. Vincent in the *Speculum Doctrinale* summarizes and quotes verbatim from the *Ethica Vetus* translation in book IV, chapters X, XVI and XVII. X represents a digest of the whole of *N Ethics* II.6 and XVI and XVII contain lengthy quotations, including an example of the Aristotelian linguistic method in direct quotation from II.6 and II.7. The Latin text of the *Ethica Vetus* is very close to the sense and the style of the Greek, actually reproducing the highly condensed syntax and elaborately connected style characteristic of Aristotle in this work. The English copies of the Latin text are remarkably free from mechanical error or verbal variation from the received text. An English copy made in the late thirteenth century (Bodley MS. Auct. F5.29, folios 159a ff.), although heavily abbreviated, is a very sound text. I have

pity (*miseriordia*) within the linguistic formula of excess-mean-defect in a famous passage in the *Rhetorica* II (1389a–1390b 11) where the life of man as a biological unit is divided into youth, manhood, old age.[19] The schematization depends on two interacting factors: (1) amount of experience; (2) the natural supply of emotional energy. Youth and old age are then seen as forms of extremes: youth representing a combination of excess of emotions and defect of experience; old age embodies the opposite extreme: excess of experience accompanying defect in emotions. The mature man in middle age represents a perfect functioning proportion of both experience and emotion. The passages which touch on credulous innocence, excessive and misplaced pity, just judgment (Chaucer's 'folie', 'fals pity', 'innocence') are the following:

(1) *Youth* (1389b): He is ready to pity others because he thinks every one honest, or anyhow better than he is. He judges his neighbour by his own harmless nature (*gàr autôn akakía toùs pélas metroûsin*) and so cannot think he deserves to be treated in that way.

Renaissance Latin translations: *et misericordes sunt, quia omnes bonos et meliores existimant: sua enim ipsorum innocentia ceteros metiuntur;*

William of Moerbeck's translation (*c.* 1270): *et miserativi quod omnes bonos et meliores arbitrantur. sua enim innocentia promixos mensurant.*

(2) *Old age* (1390a): old men may feel pity, as well as young men, but not for the same reason. Young men feel it out of kindness, old men out of weakness, imagining that anything which befalls anyone else might easily happen to them, which, as we saw, is a thought which excites pity.

Renaissance Latin translation: *misericordes vero etiam senes sunt, sed non eadem de causa ac iuvenes: illi etiam, quia humani, hi vero, quia debiles: omnia enim existimant proxima esse sibi, quae patiantur; hoc autem erat misericordia.*

William of Moerbeck's translation: *hi quidem enim propter amicitiam humanam, hi autem propter imbecillitatem. Omnes enim putant esse prope ipsis in pati. hoc autem erat miserabile.*

[19] Aristotle's division is uniquely based on a threefold philosophical formulation. The longer and gloomier divisions into six or more ages are reflected in Isidore and Vincent. Horace in his *Ars Poetica* 160ff. divides life into a dramatic and satiric 'characterization' based on four ages (but not connected with the four seasons as in the *Secreta Secretorum*).

noticed on average only about five minor verbal substitutions per page and only rarely a minor mechanical error. The received text was edited by C. Marchesi, *L'Ethica Nicomachea nella tradizione latina Medievale*, Messina (1904).

(3) *Manhood* (1390b): they neither trust everybody nor distrust everybody, but judge people correctly.

Renaissance Latin translation: *neque omnibus credunt, neque omnibus non credunt, sed ex veritate iudicant magis.*

William of Moerbeck's translation: *neque omnibus concredentes, neque omnibus discredentes, sed secundum veritatem iudicantes magis.*

Although Vincent is familiar with the *Ethica Nova* and *Vetus* texts of the *Nicomachean Ethics*, I cannot find this particular passage of the *Rhetorica* quoted or cited in any of his *Specula*. The *Rhetorica* seems only to have been translated twice in the Middle Ages: (1) the *translatio Vetus*; (2) the translation of William of Moerbeck (*translatio Guillelmi*) done from an Arabic version about 1270.[20] Verbally and stylistically his text differs from Aristotle radically but the sense of the passages just quoted is not seriously affected. The importance of the Chaucerian passage in the *Legend of Good Women* is that the linguistic and moral analysis resembles nothing else in Middle English literature. It concretely shows Chaucer's grasp of Aristotelian procedure:

elleipsis	*mesotes*	*hyperbole*
folie	innocence	fals pitee

Chaucer may have been influenced as well by Aristotle's exposition of mean and excess in the *Ethica Eudemia* II.3 (1220b ff.) where Aristotle lists a series of sbs. in triplets to illustrate the relation of mediety to excess and defect in the series excess–defect–mean. His last example is *panourgía (versutia)* 'cunning'–*euétheia (stultitia)* 'simpleness'–*phrónesis (prudentia)* 'prudence'. The Latin texts of the *Ethica Eudemia* are difficult to trace.[21] Chaucer may have seen this passage quoted in one of the many commentaries. It would have been a natural passage to illustrate the Aristotelian method. Walter Burley deals with the relationship of want of knowledge (*ignorantia*) to pity and forbearance (*venia*) in his

[20] The Latin text of William was edited by L. Spengel, Leipzig (1867). For a life and brief account of his translations cf. M. Grabmann, 'Le Tradizioni di Guglielmo di Moerbeke' in *Miscellanea Historiae Pontificae*, XI, Rome (1946).

[21] Cf. Grabmann, *op. cit.*, p. 104. The Loeb editor states that there was a thirteenth-century Latin translation 'attributed to William of Moerbeke'. He says it follows the Greek closely and includes it in his textual apparatus under the *siglum* 'Guil.' There is not a single reference to it thereafter. A. Pelzer, '*versions latines d'Aristote*', *Revue neo-scolastique de philosophie*, 23 (1921), pp. 317–18, was sceptical of medieval knowledge of the *Ethica Eudemia*. What they knew and quoted was books IV–VI which are identical with books V–VII of the *Nicomachean Ethics*. They also knew of a fragment of book VII of the *Ethica Eudemia* preserved in the *Liber de bona fortuna*.

commentary to *Ethics* III (1110a–1113a), but I cannot find an exact parallel.

It is not within the scope of this appendix to give an account of Aristotle's doctrine of 'the mean'. But in view of the many and often difficult accounts provided by philosophers, I shall conclude with a short interpretation of Aristotle's *mediocritas*. Professor North[22] (following Jaeger and others) notices the growth of the concept 'out of medical parallels', yet it may well prove to be the case that Aristotle's ethical concept of the mean originates in, and derives its philosophical validity from the biological sciences.[23] Monan recently thought that the original 'quantitative' meaning (derived from the measurement of nutriment or addition or subtraction of elements from works of art) lost its quantitative force, becoming 'qualitative' by nature of its simple contextual application in the *Nicomachean Ethics*.[24] But in many of the various applications and extensions of 'the mean' (biological, social, political, rhetorical, artistic), Aristotle thinks of the mean as both a quantitative measurement and a qualitative state of being[25]—not only the best and to be identified with virtue, but the natural mode of an organism or object in its biological or existential functioning—the necessary adaptation of the individual and the class to which it belongs to its position or environment. In terms of its healthy or proper functioning it develops a general set of 'laws' about behaviour and at the same time develops an individual, relativistic set dependent on both local external conditions and the particular structure of the individual. The ethical doctrine of the mean has this same dual aspect. Aristotle's concept in the *Nicomachean Ethics* shows a further complication in its connection, analogically, with pleasure and pain (1105b 15ff.). Virtuousness which relates to 'states of character' stands in a certain relation to passions in being 'felt' through the phrase 'we stand badly if we feel too violently or too weakly' (of anger). This state of character, this experience of being virtuous, is partly sensation and partly how we view it as affecting us. Our feeling includes the fact of sensation and the

---

[22] *Op. cit.*, pp. 197–211. It is a very clear and convincing account.

[23] J. H. Randall (*Aristotle*, London, 1960) stresses Aristotle's biological training as as important element in his development as a philosopher (cf. pp. 220ff.). Unfortunately he only sees the *Ethics* as about 'means' (see p. 248).

[24] J. D. Monan, *Moral Knowledge and its Methodology in Aristotle*, Oxford (1968), p. 100.

[25] The clearest statement of the deliberate fusion of quantitative and qualitative in the theory of the mean is given in H. House and C. G. Hardie's *Aristotle's Poetics*, London (1956), p. 109 where it is traced to musical origins.

act of judging, the subjective and the objective. The linked function of
feeling and how we imagine we should be judged by others corresponds
in biology to the function of the organ, part or organism and its physical
appearance or position. Compare in the *De Partibus Animalium* the
description of the physical construction of the hand considered in its
primary function of grasping (687b 18):

> The finger which stands at the other end of the row is small, while
> the central one of all is long, like a centre oar in a ship. This is
> rightly so, for it is mainly by the central part of the encircling
> grasp that a tool must be held when put to use.

We can see here how anatomical shape and function are combined:
the physical size of the middle finger corresponds to its importance in
function and its relational location in the 'row' of fingers. It rightly
occupies the middle position and is at once compared to a mechanical
work of human construction. The middle oars were the longest in
ancient ships and in Apollonius Rhodius (*Argonautica* I.395) were
reserved for Hercules and Ancaeus since they were the strongest of the
heroes.

We find the same relationship expressed at 702b 18 where Aristotle
is concerned with the physical position of the 'soul' in the body:[26]

> Now since the left and right sides are symmetrical, and these
> opposites are moved simultaneously, it cannot be that the left is
> moved by the right remaining stationary, nor vice versa; the
> original must always be in what lies above both. Therefore, the
> original seat of the moving soul must be in that which lies in the
> middle, for of both extremes the middle is the limiting point.

This central physical position and primary initiating function is compared with the governing of a state:

> The individuals each play their assigned part as it is ordered, and
> one thing follows another in its accustomed order. So in animals
> there is the same orderliness—nature taking the place of custom—
> and each part naturally doing its own work as nature has com-
> posed them. There is no need of a soul in each part, but she
> resides in a kind of central governing place of the body, and the

[26] Cf. *De Incessu Animalium* 707a 7ff. and compare the *De Generatione Animalium*
76719ff. for the same principle in the balancing of male and female elements in
reproduction.

remaining parts live by a continuity of natural structure, and play the parts Nature would have them play.

This same political analogy is pursued later in the *Nicomachean Ethics* 1113a 8ff. where the image used is that of a Homeric monarchy. In anatomy we find that the physical composition of the brain and its position in the body is essentially connected with its function (652b 18ff.):

> But as all influences require to be counter-balanced so that they may be reduced to moderation and brought to the mean (for in the mean and not in either extreme lies the true and rational position), nature has contrived the brain as counterpoise to the region of the heart with its contained heat, and has given it to animals to moderate the latter, combining in it the properties of earth and water . . . The brain, then, tempers the heat and seething of the heart. In order, however, that it may not itself be absolutely without heat, but may have a moderate amount, branches run from both blood vessels.

As Aristotle argues in the *De Generatione Animalium* (767a 19ff.):

> . . . for all things which come into being as products of art or of nature exist in virtue of a certain ratio. Now if the hot preponderates too much, it dries up the liquid; if it is very deficient it does not solidify it; for the artist or natural product we need the due mean between the extremes.

This selection from among the many biological passages which indicate the mean position, ratio or relationship as being necessary to existence, the most naturally suitable, the best and also the most powerful, illustrates Aristotle's preoccupation with this idea. Application outside biology and ethics shows the same emphasis: for example, in the *Poetics* when discussing the beginning-middle-end sequence in tragic plots, Aristotle resorts to a biological analogy, a beautiful living creature (1450b 31ff.).[27] The creature's natural function and its beauty are dependent on two factors: (1) order and arrangement of its parts (qualitative), and (2) being 'of a certain definite magnitude. Beauty is a matter of size and order.' It is both qualitative and quantitative. The examples which fail to satisfy our sense of proportion are either too small or too large. Although Aristotle does not say so, we are left

[27] For a discussion of this image and its origin in Plato's *Phaedrus* (264c) cf. House and Hardie, *Aristotle's Poetics*, pp. 48–51.

to imagine the mean as the most satisfying and the beautiful. Thus, perfect proportion in terms of parts and whole is both in the object and in its perceivableness. It must exist in scale with the faculty which is perceiving it. The unit of measurement for plot is memory.

Similarly, in political or social application, in the *Politics* 1295b–1296a, Aristotle sees the mean as a method of constitutional functioning whereby the different sections and interests of the state remain mixed and have balanced representation:

> For as it has been rightly said in the *Ethics* that the happy life is the life which is lived without impediment in accordance with virtue, and that virtue is a middle course, it necessarily follows that the middle course of life is the best—such a middle course as it is possible for each class of men to attain. And these same criteria must also necessarily apply to the goodness and badness of a state, and of a constitution—for a constitution is a certain mode of life of a state.

Here we find three applications of the mean deliberately used together, the social, the ethical and the biological. The constitution is referred to by a biological analogy: 'a certain mode of life.' Its best condition for functioning lies in a proportioning ratio where the mean itself occupies the ruling or predominating position.

Thus in Aristotle theories of moral training and behaviour are always relational; they habitually reflect an interest in reconciling the individual will with the larger corporate behaviour of the community (cf. *Rhetorica* 1366b 13–15 where laws which enforce *sophrosyne* effect a balance between individual virtue and public welfare). In Plato's *Republic*, *sophrosyne* takes its conventional place in the training of a political *élite* but it does not become a combinative element in the physical functioning life of the state. Plato's ideal state develops the means to resist change, Aristotle's develops the capacity to adapt and survive.

In the last resort, although nourished by different sources (apart from Plato), philosophical method and qualities of mind, both Alan of Lille and Aristotle share a certain common ground concerning the concept of moderation. Both men show an appreciation of

(1) the complex functioning of being based on the interplay of parts and whole made possible by the existence of a mean ratio or moderating forces;

(2) the harmonious co-operation of the individual entity in both its natural existence and within the life of the community;

(3) the tendency to see 'moderation' as a principal form of physiological and natural adaptability and as an integral part of a wider, socially important design. Aristotle's wider context is the state, Alan's the Christian cosmos.

Alan arrives at his cohesive account eclectically in the usual synthetic medieval way, grafting parts of this on to parts of that: *Timaeus*, Cicero, Boethius, modified by traditional accounts of the biological elemental composition of the human body, and possibly by certain passages of Aristotle deriving from Arabic digests or filtered through Boethius. Aristotle seems to have developed his sense of moderation from the specific and analytic application of a biological model to various related spheres of natural activity. Alan's concept of Nature has a well-developed social aspect and, like Aristotle, he has a strong 'compositional' sense. So, too, has Alan's great admirer, Chaucer.[28] Neither Alan nor Chaucer—whatever their susceptibility to Aristotelian doctrines—had the relevant texts in a wide enough range. But as the passage in the *Legend of Good Women* shows, Chaucer had probably read the *Ethica Vetus* text of the *Ethics*. It remains for someone else to show Alan's knowledge of that work.[29]

---

[28] Cf. J. A. W. Bennett, *The Parlement of Foules, passim*. Gower's sense of *mesure* is compensational and always used in strict ethical application, cf. *Confessio Amantis* I.18ff.; V.7641ff.; VII.2151ff., 4559ff.; *Mirour de l'Omme* 16213ff.; *Traité* 1–4, 15–16.

[29] It is generally taken that Alan knew Aristotle through whatever of Boethius' works on him survived in his day (cf. de Lage, *op. cit.*, p. 70). Aristotle is chided by Alan for his obscurity in two places in the *De Planctu* and the *Anticlaudianus* but in the house of Nature (*Anticlaudianus* I.132) Aristotle is praised for his contribution to logic and in book V when Phronesis penetrates beyond natural laws, he is found in good company: 'wisdom falters, Cicero is tongue-tied, Aristotle becomes dull, Ptolemy's understanding clouds over' (V.371ff.).

SELECT BIBLIOGRAPHY

The critical literature on Chaucer has become large. Three Chaucer biblio-graphies will take the reader from *c*. 1908 to 1968: (1) D. D. Griffith, *Biblio-graphy of Chaucer 1908–1953*, Washington (1955); (2) W. R. Crawford, *Bibliography of Chaucer 1954–1963*, Washington (1967); (3) A. C. Baugh, *Chaucer*, New York (1968). After 1968 the reader should consult *The Year's Work in English Studies* and *The Annual Bibliography of English Language and Literature*. The Modern Language Association of America publishes an annual bibliography which includes books and articles. The *Social Sciences and Humani-ties Index* (New York) includes only periodicals but has the advantage of appear-ing more frequently during any most recent tract of time. Volume I of the *New Cambridge Bibliography of English Literature* should appear during 1974. This Select Bibliography contains only what the author at the present time regards as essential reading.

GENERAL

Arendt, H., *The Human Condition*, Chicago (1954).
Arendt, H., *Between Past and Future*, London (1961).
Auerbach, E., *Literary Language and its Public in Late Latin Antiquity and in the Middle Ages*, London (1965).
Bennett, J. A. W., *The Parlement of Foules: an Interpretation*, Oxford (1957).
Brusendorff, A., *The Chaucer Tradition*, Copenhagen (1925).
Clemen, W., translated C. A. M. Sym, *Chaucer's Early Poetry*, London (1963).
Coghill, N., *The Poet Chaucer*, Oxford (1949).
Courcelle, P., *La Consolation de philosophie dans la tradition littéraire*, Paris (1967).
Curtius, E. R., *European Literature and the Latin Middle Ages*, London (1953).
de Lage, R. G., *Alain de Lille; poète du XIIe siècle*, Montreal (1951).
Gradon, P., *Form and Style in Early English Literature*, London (1971).
Héraucourt, W., *Die Wertwelt Chaucers*, Heidelberg (1939).
Lewis, C. S., *The Allegory of Love*, Oxford (1936).
Lewis, C. S., *The Discarded Image*, Cambridge (1964).
Lowes, J. Livingston, *Geoffrey Chaucer*, London (1934).

Mathew, G., *The Court of Richard II*, London (1968).

Morris, C., *The Discovery of the Individual, 1050–1200*, London (1972).

Paré, G., *Les idées et les lettres au XIIIᵉ siècle*, Montreal (1947).

Patch, H., *The Tradition of Boethius*, Oxford (1935).

Preston, R., *Chaucer*, London (1952).

Raby, F. J. E., *A History of Secular Latin Poetry in the Middle Ages*, 2 vols, 2nd ed., Oxford (1957).

Seznec, J., *The Survival of the Pagan Gods*, New York (1953).

Stahl, W. H., *Macrobius's Commentary on the Dream of Scipio*, New York (1952) (Introduction).

Stahl, W. H., *Roman Science: Origins, Development and Influence to the Middle Ages*, Madison (1962).

Stahl, W. H., and Johnson, R., *Martianus Cappella and the Seven Liberal Arts*, vol. 1, New York (1971).

Tuve, R., *Allegorical Imagery*, Princeton (1966).

Ullman, W., *The Individual and Society in the Middle Ages*, London (1967).

LANGUAGE AND STYLE

Atkins, J. W. H., *English Literary Criticism: the Medieval Phase*, Cambridge (1943).

Faral, E., *Les ars poètiques du XIIe et du XIIIe siècle*, Paris (1924).

Geoffrey of Vinsauf, translated M. F. Nims, *Poetria Nova*, Toronto (1967).

Kerkhof, J., *Studies in the Language of Geoffrey Chaucer*, Leiden (1966).

Mackenzie, B. A., *The Early London Dialect*, Oxford (1928).

McKeon, R., 'Rhetoric in the Middle Ages', *Speculum* 17 (1942), pp. 1–32.

Mersand, J., *Chaucer's Romance Vocabulary*, New York (1937).

Mustanoija, T., *A Middle English Syntax*, vol. I, Helsinki (1960).

Naunin, T., *Der Einfluss der mittelalterlichen Rhetorik auf Chaucers Dictung*, Bonn (1929).

Payne, R. O., *The Key of Remembrance: a study of Chaucer's Poetics*, New Haven (1963).

Skeat, W. W., *The Complete Works of Geoffrey Chaucer*, 6 vols, vol. 6 (Glossary).

Tatlock, J. S. P., and Kennedy, A. G. (eds), *Concordance to the Works of Geoffrey Chaucer*, Washington (1927).

ten Brink, B. (translated from the 2nd ed. by M. B. Smith), *The Language and Metre of Chaucer*, London (1901).

LIFE

Armitage-Smith, S., *John of Gaunt*, 2 vols, London (1904).

Brewer, D., *Chaucer in his Time*, London (1963).

Crowe, M. M., and Olson, C. C., *Chaucer Life-Records*, Oxford (1966).
Howard, D. R., 'Chaucer the Man', *PMLA* 80 (1965).

MANUALS, GUIDES AND LIBRI SPECIOSI

French, R. D., *A Chaucer Handbook*, 2nd ed., New York (1947).
Hammond, E. P., *Chaucer, a Bibliographical Manual*, New York (1908).
Hussey, M., *Chaucer's World*, Cambridge (1967).
Loomis, R. S., *A Mirror of Chaucer's World*, Princeton (1965).
Rowland, B., *Companion to Chaucer Studies*, New York (1968).

MANUSCRIPTS AND PALAEOGRAPHY

Brown, C., 'Author's Revision in the Canterbury Tales', *PMLA* 57 (1942).
Chaucer Society Publications: Parallel- and Six- and Eight-Texts editions from 1871 onwards.
Dempster, G., 'The Fifteenth-Century Editors of the Tales and the Problem of Tale Order', *PMLA* 64 (1949).
Denholm-Young, N., *Handwriting in England and Wales*, Cardiff (1964).
Hammond, E. P., *Chaucer, a Bibliographical Manual*, New York (1908).
Ker, N., *Facsimile Edition of The Owl and the Nightingale, BM MS. Cotton Caligula A*, EETS, O.S. 251 (1963) (Introduction).
Lieftinck, G. I., and Batelli, G., *Nomenclature des écritures livresques du IXe au XVIe siècle*, Paris (1954).
Manly, J. M., and Rickert, E., *The Canterbury Tales*, 9 vols, Chicago (1940) (vols I and II).
Owen, C. A., 'The Canterbury Tales: Early Manuscripts and Relative Popularity', *JEGP* 54 (1955).
Parkes, M. B., *English Cursive Book Hands 1250–1500*, Oxford (1969).
Root, R. K., *The Manuscripts of Chaucer's Troilus*, Chaucer Society, Oxford (1914).
Severs, J. B., 'Author's Revision in Block V of the Canterbury Tales', *Speculum* 29 (1954).
Wright, C. E., *English Vernacular Hands from the Twelfth to the Fifteenth Centuries*, Oxford (1960).

WORKS

Complete Works
Skeat, W. W., *The Complete Works of Geoffrey Chaucer*, 6 vols, Oxford (1894).
Robinson, F. N., *The Complete Works of Geoffrey Chaucer*, 2nd ed., Cambridge, Mass. (1959).

Separate Works
Book of the Duchess
Harrison, B. J., 'Medieval Rhetoric in the *Book of the Duchess*', *PMLA* 49 (1934).
Lewis, C. S., *The Allegory of Love*, Oxford (1936), pp. 167–70.
Lawlor, J., 'The Pattern of Consolation in *The Book of the Duchess*', *Speculum* 31 (1956).
Clemen, W., *Chaucer's Early Poetry*, London (1963), pp. 23–66.

Complaint of Mars
Brewer, D. S., 'Chaucer's *Complaint of Mars*', *N & Q*, November 1954.
Stillwell, G., 'Convention and Individuality in Chaucer's *Complaint of Mars*', *Philological Quarterly* 35 (1956).
Clemen, W., *Chaucer's Early Poetry*, London (1963), pp. 188–97.

Parliament of Fowls
McDonald, C. O., 'An Interpretation of Chaucer's *Parliament of Fowles*', *Speculum* 30 (1955).
Bennett, J. A. W., *The Parlement of Foules*, Oxford (1957).
Clemen, W., *Chaucer's Early Poetry*, London (1963), pp. 122–69.

House of Fame
Sypherd, O., *Studies in Chaucer's Hous of Fame*, Chaucer Society, 1907.
Ruggiers, P. G., 'The Unity of Chaucer's *House of Fame*', *Studies in Philology* 50 (1953).
Manzalaoui, M. A., 'Three notes on Chaucer's *Hous of Fame*', *N & Q* 9 (1962).
Clemen, W., *Chaucer's Early Poetry*, London (1963), pp. 66–121.
Bennett, J. A. W., *Chaucer's Book of Fame*, Oxford (1969).

Legend of Good Women
Moore, S., 'The prologue to Chaucer's *Legend of Good Women* in Relation to Queen Anne and Richard', *Modern Language Review* 7 (1912).
Amy, E. F., *The Text of the Legend of Good Women*, Princeton (1918).
Meech, S. B., 'Chaucer and an Italian Translation of the *Heroides*', *PMLA* 45 (1930).
Tatlock, J. S. P., 'Chaucer and the *Legenda Aurea*', *MLN* (1930).
Young, K. L., 'Chaucer's Appeal to the Platonic Deity', *Speculum* 19 (1944).
Rowland, B., 'Chaucer's Daisy', *N & Q* 10 (1963).
Frank, F. W., 'The Legend of the *Legend of Good Women*', *Chaucer Review* 1 (1966).

Book of Troilus
Root. R. K., (ed.) *Chaucer's Troilus and Criseyde*, Princeton (1926).

Griffin, N. E. and Myrick, A. B., *The Filostrato of Giovanni Boccaccio*, Philadelphia (1929). (The text is not that used by Chaucer. Cf. the edition of V.
Branca, Milan (1965).)

Lewis, C. S., 'What Chaucer Really did to *Il Filostrato*', *Essays and Studies* 17
(1932).

Lewis, C. S., *The Allegory of Love*, Oxford (1936), pp. 176–97.

Bennett, J. A. W., 'Chaucer, Dante and Boccaccio', *Medium Aevum* 22 (1954).

Joseph, B., '*Troilus and Criseyde;* "A Most Admirable and Inimitable Epicke
Poeme" ', *Essays and Studies* 7 (1954).

Bloomfield, M. W., 'Distance, Predestination and the Narrator in *Troilus and
Criseyde*', *PMLA* 72 (1957).

Jordan, R. M., 'The Narrator in Chaucer's *Troilus*', *ELH* 25 (1958).

Meech, S. B., *Design in Chaucer's Troilus*, Syracuse (1959).

Bayley, J., 'Love and the Code: *Troilus and Criseyde*' in *The Characters of Love*,
London (1960), pp. 49–123.

Longo, J. A., 'The Double Time Scheme in Book II of Chaucer's *Troilus and
Criseyde*', *Modern Language Quarterly* 22 (1961).

Donaldson, E. T., 'The Ending of Chaucer's *Troilus*' in *Early English and Norse
Studies*, London (1963), pp. 26–45.

Davis, N., 'The *Litera Troili* and English Letters', *Review of English Studies* 16
(1965).

Durling, R. M., *The Figure of the Poet in Renaissance Epic*, Harvard (1965),
pp. 44–66.

Salter, E., '*Troilus and Criseyde*: a Reconsideration', in *Patterns of Love and
Courtesy*, London (1966), pp. 86–106.

Shepherd, G. J., '*Troilus and Criseyde*' in *Chaucer and Chaucerians*, London
(1966), pp. 65–87.

Jordan, R. M., *Chaucer and the Shape of Creation*, Harvard (1967), pp. 61–110.

Owen, C. A., 'Mimetic Form in the Central Love Scene of *Troilus and Criseyde*',
MP 67 (1969).

Gordon, I. L., *The Double Sorrow of Troilus*, Oxford (1970); and cf. the review
by C. A. Owen in *MP* 69 (1971), pp. 63–5.

Canterbury Tales

Manly, J. M., and Rickert, E., *The Text of the Canterbury Tales*, 8 vols, Chicago
(1940).

Bryan, W. F., and Dempster, G., *Sources and Analogues of Chaucer's Canterbury
Tales*, London (1941).

Lawrence, W. W., *Chaucer and the Canterbury Tales*, New York (1951).

Bennett, J. A. W. (ed.), *The Knight's Tale*, London (1954).

Muscatine, C., *Chaucer and the French Tradition*, Berkeley (1957), pp. 166–243.

Craik, T. W., *The Comic Tales of Chaucer*, London (1963).

Ruggiers, P. G., *The Art of the Canterbury Tales*, Madison (1965).

Schultz, H. C., *The Ellesmere Manuscript of Chaucer's Canterbury Tales*, Huntington Library Publications (1966).

Jordan, R. M., *Chaucer and the Shape of Creation*, Harvard (1967), pp. 111–241.

Bishop, I., 'The Narrative Art of the *Pardoner's Tale*', *Medium Aevum* 36, 1967.

Whittock, T., *A Reading of the Canterbury Tales*, Cambridge (1968).

The shorter poems

Shannon, E. F., 'The Source of Chaucer's *Anelida and Arcite*', *PMLA* 27 (1912).

Tatlock, J. S. P., 'Notes on Chaucer: Earlier or Minor Poems', *MLN* 29 (1914).

Koch, J., *Geoffrey Chaucers kleinere Dictungen*, Heidelberg (1928) (Introduction).

Kokeritz, H., 'Chaucer's *Rosemounde*', *MLN* 63 (1948).

Pace, G. B., 'The True Text of the *Former Age*', *Medieval Studies* 23 (1961).

Norton-Smith, J., 'Chaucer's *Etas Prima*', *Medium Aevum* 32 (1963).

Cross, J. E., 'The Old Swedish *Trohetsvisan* and Chaucer's *Lak of Stedfastnesse*, a Study in a Medieval Genre', *The Saga Book* 16 (pt 4, 1965).

MISCELLANEOUS

Bloomfield, M. W., 'Authenticating Realism and the Realism of Chaucer', *Thought* 39 (1964).

Burrow, J. A., *Ricardian Poetry*, London (1971).

Coulton, G. G., *Chaucer and his England*, 8th ed., London (1963).

Evans, J., *English Art 1307–1461*, Oxford (1949).

Friedländer, P., *Johannes von Gaza und Paulus Silentiarius: Kunstbeschreibungen Justinianischer Zeit*, Leipzig (1912) (Introduction).

Harvey, J., *The Medieval Architect*, London (1971).

Holzknecht, K. J., *Literary Patronage in the Middle Ages* (1923); reprinted London (1966).

McFarlane, K. B., *John Wycliffe and the Beginnings of English Nonconformity*, London (1952).

McKisack, M., *The Fourteenth Century 1307–1399*, Oxford (1959).

Pickering, F. P., *Literature and Art in the Middle Ages*, London (1970).

Rickert, E., *Chaucer's World*, London (1948).

Rickert, M., *Painting in Britain, the Middle Ages*, London (1954).

Salzman, L. F., *Building in England down to 1540*, Oxford (1952).

Smalley, B., *English Friars and Antiquity in the Early Fourteenth Century*, Oxford (1960).

Stone, L., *Sculpture in Britain; the Middle Ages*, London (1955).

Trigona, F. P., *Chaucer Imitatore del Boccaccio*, Catania (1923).

Waugh, W. T., 'The Lollard Knights', *Scottish Historical Review* 11 (1914), pp. 55–92.

Webb, G., *English Wall Painting of the Fourteenth Century*, London (1955).

INDEX

Clanvowe, Sir John, 63n, 66n, 71n, 84n, 156
Claudian, Claudius Claudianus, 39
Clemen, W., 6, 7, 11, 27
De Clericis et Rustico, 77
Clerk, N. W., *see* Lewis, C. S.
Coleridge, Samuel Taylor, 120, 134, 203
Colin Clout, 82n
Colonna, Giovanni, 168n
Columella, Junius Moderatus, 26n
The Comedy of Errors, 154n, 176
Commentary to Seneca, 90n, 164–9
Complaincte en Songe, 16
A Complaint to his Lady, 20n
Complaint to my Mortal Foe, 20
Complainte Ageyne Hope, 21
Complainte Amoureuse, 21
Complainte de Saint Valentin, 17, 25
Concordia, 63n, 67n, 69ff, 71n, 79
Confessio Amantis, 64n, 65n, 69ff, 71n, 72, 87n, 88ff, 94, 113n, 151n, 152, 158ff, 205, 260n
De Consolatione Philosophiae, 42, 44, 51, 60–1, 68, 70n, 86, 102, 128ff, 132n, 141ff, 163ff, 169n, 185n, 192, 209, 230–3, 235
Corinthians, 164
Courcelle, P., 185n
Crabbe, George, 113
A Cristemasse game, 135n
Crump, M. M., 32n
The Cuckoo and the Nightingale, see *The Boke of Cupide*
Cunningham, J. V., 112n
Curtius, E. R., 4, 37n, 163n, 169n

Danaë, 197
Dante Alighieri, 8, 42, 54, 55, 57ff, 105, 117, 172, 177–8, 189, 190n, 201–2, 206n, 207
Davis, N., 214n
Dean, J. R., 164n, 165n
Debussy, Claude, 30

Decameron, 78n, 96–7
Decharme, P., 199n
Deguilleville, Guillaume de, 154n
de Lage, G. R., 239n
Deschamps, Eustache, 17, 55–6, 63n, 67, 69, 170n, 215ff, 225
Dido and Aeneas, 211
Disciplina Clericalis, 77
The Distichs of Cato, 233
Dit des Quatres Offices, 170n
Le Dit dou Lyon, 115n
Divina Commedia, 8, 42, 54, 55, 57ff, 117–18, 172, 177–8, 189, 190n, 201–202, 206n
Dodds, E. R., 200n
Donatus, Aelius, 123, 164, 165n, 170, 184n
Donner, M., 149n
Douglas, Gavin, 126n, 169n
Dryden, John, 110, 134n
De Duabus Naturis, 167n
Duckworth, G. E., 169n
Duino Elegies, 1
Dunbar, William, 25, 215n
Durling, R. M., 103

Ecerinis, 168n, 169n
Les Echeques Amoureux, 57–8
Ecloga Theoduli, 40
The Eclogues, 77, 102n, 165n, 167n, 172, 202–3
Edgeworth, Maria, 3
Edward, 2nd Duke of York, 111
Electra, 171
Emden, A. B., 160n, 168n
Epistle of Eloisa to Abelard, 191n
Epistulae Petrarchi, 26n, 117n
Epistulae Plinii, 42, 217n
Epistulae Senecae, 42, 97n, 147n, 154n, 193n, 194ff, 224n
L'Espinette Amoureuse, 16–17
Ethica Eudemia, 255
Ethica Vetus, 253ff, 260
Ethics see *Nicomachean Ethics*